Foundation Dreamweaver UltraDev 4

Rob Paddock
Spencer Steel

Foundation Dreamweaver UltraDev 4

© 2001 friends of ED

All rights reserved. No part of this book may be reproduced, stored in a retrieval system or transmitted in any form or by any means, without the prior written permission of the publisher, except in the case of brief quotations embodied in critical articles or reviews.

The authors and publisher have made every effort in the preparation of this book to ensure the accuracy of the information. However, the information contained in this book is sold without warranty, either express or implied. Neither the authors, friends of ED nor its dealers or distributors will be held liable for any damages caused or alleged to be caused either directly or indirectly by this book.

First printed March 2001

Trademark Acknowledgements

friends of ED has endeavored to provide trademark information about all the companies and products mentioned in this book by the appropriate use of capitals. However, friends of ED cannot guarantee the accuracy of this information.

Published by friends of ED

30 Lincoln Road, Olton, Birmingham.
B27 6PA. UK.
Printed in USA

ISBN 1-903450-34-9

Foundation Dreamweaver UltraDev 4

Credits

Authors	Rob Paddock, Spencer Steel
Additional Material	Paul Doyle
Content Architect	Andrew Tracey
Editors	Andrew Tracey, Matthew Knight, Alan McCann, Mel Orgee
Graphic Editors	Deborah Murray, William Fallon, Katy Freer
Author Agent	Gaynor Riopedre
Project Administrator	Fionnuala Meacher
Technical Reviewers	Paul Doyle, Hesan Yousif, Simon Guerney, Garrett Carr, Mel Jehs, Dan Bevan, James Penberthy, Steve Silvester
Index	Andrew Criddle, Michael Brinkman
Cover Design	Katy Freer
Proof Readers	Joel Rushton, Fionnuala Meacher

About the Authors

Rob Paddock is a Freelance Web Developer who is responsible for one of the major IT Recruitment Companies in the UK (ResourceMatters.com), along with numerous other e-commerce clients. He and Spencer met on the Drumbeat (precursor to UltraDev) discussion boards and found that they had a lot in common, both working in the same dynamic industry and both having to deal with the same "sticky-fingered users".

Thanks

Firstly, I would like to thank my partner Sally for keeping Cassie, Ashley 'Kevin The Teenager', Meg and the numerous cats at bay while this project was taking place, especially with Meg wanting hourly feeds and Ashley needing bail money. She also made a good temporary secretary, answering the phone every fifteen minutes from Spencer or hassling technical editors.

Speaking of the man himself, I would like to thank Spencer who managed to teach me more about the English Language than I ever learnt in school - it certainly made writing this book a lot easier. I would also like to mention the support I got from my Web Hosting Company (Totalweb.co.uk) who allowed us to demo all our pages on their servers. A gratuitous plug for a deserving company.

As Spencer mentions the other people who helped out technically with this book, I would just like to thank Julie Thompson of Macromedia who has been a constant help in all our Ultradev Projects. Hopefully this pathetic crawling should ensure our places on the next beta.

Incidentally, both of us are available for web contracts, consultancy and pantomine.

About the Authors

Spencer Steel was born of a jackal on the 6th June 1966, although strangely he is now only 29. He can currently be found building cutting-edge recruitment software at Informatiq Consulting Ltd – the UK's most innovative and dynamic recruitment company.

When not listening to Nine Inch Nails or other such noise – Spencer can either be found at live gigs around the London area – or desperately trying to find a pub in Watford that doesn't play tedious house music. Either way, a couple of pints are always on the agenda.

Thanks

I would like to say extra special thanks to John Scott for letting me work on the book when I should have been doing my job and the Chicken for not going out anywhere interesting for 3 months while I wrote the damn thing.

I would also like to say 'gwaaargh' to Tickle & Pickle, Pete & Mel, Jim, Bianca & Simone, Fraser & Frost, the people of Informatiq, Gary & Carol and... God, this is really tedious... does anyone actually read this bit? No thought not – anyone fancy a pint?

Contributors & very nice people

Thanks to the following people who helped us in times of stress. Which, let's face it, was most of the time.

George & Waldo of UDzone.com
JAG of Magicbeat
Tom Muck

Finally – thanks to Gaynor Riopedre and all her little elves at friends of ED.

Table of Contents

Introduction   1

Welcome 1
The aim of this book 2
No Macs - sorry 3
What you'll need to know 3
Your UltraDev Set-up 4
    Making sure that you don't lose things in UltraDev 5
    What to do when you lose things in UltraDev 6
Conventions 7
Download Files 8
Support: we're your bestest friends 9

1 Getting Started with UltraDev   11

Setting up the UltraDev Authoring Environment 12
    Getting Started 14
    What do I need to Start? 15
Setting up a Server 15
Setting up your KoolKards Site 16
    The Data Source Name (DSN) Entry 20
    Opening a Page and Viewing the Code 27
Summary 31

2 Client/Server Concepts   33

In the Beginning 34
    Dumb Terminals Get Smarter 35
    Many Hands Make Light Work 35
    Millions of Hands Make for Something Special 36
ASP in Action 37
Writing Web Pages for Client/Server Models 39
Client-side Scripting 39
Server-side Scripting 41
    ASP Servers 41
    JSP Servers 42
    ColdFusion Servers 42
    Server Choices 42
Inside the Code 44
Extensions and Behaviors 47
Summary 51

Table of Contents

3 Objects — 55

Objects 62
    The Response and Request Objects 63
Homemade Cookies 68
Summary 80

4 Moving Data between Pages — 83

Sending Data between Pages with POST 84
Sending Data with GET 88
Session Variables 93
Request.ServerVariables 96
Summary 98

5 Displaying your Database — 101

The Database 102
Recordsets 106
Displaying the Recordset 111
Introducing Live Data View 113
The Code 117
Recordset Navigation 119
Our Navigation Controls in Detail 121
Summary 125

6 Amending your Database — 127

Detail Pages 128
    Filtering your Records 130
Linking Results to Detail 135
    Into the Code 138
    Shortcut to the Detail Page 138
    Go to Detail Live Object 139
Administration Pages 144
Update Pages 145
    How the Update Behavior Works 152
Deleting Your Records 156
    How It All Works 158
Summary 160

Table of Contents

7 Searching your Database — 163
- What is SQL? 165
  - Creating Parameterized Queries 169
  - Time for a Database Change 176
  - Editable and Non-editable Regions of Templates 183
  - Searching for all with numerical values 191
- Summary 194

8 User Login and Registration — 197
- Breaking down the Problem 198
- The Login Table 199
  - Levels of User Rights 202
  - Duplicate Usernames 204
  - Form Validation and Password Protection 206
  - Passing Back the QueryString 208
  - Code Time 214
- Improving our Login Page 216
- Remember Me? 218
  - More Tweaking 220
- Going to Pages Depending on Rights 222
- Further Discussion 223
  - Securing All your Pages 224
- Summary 225

9 Creating a Shopping Cart — 227
- What Exactly is a Shopping Cart? 228
  - Commercial Shopping Cart Solutions 228
    - Shopping Carts Purchased through Resellers 229
    - Off-the-shelf Shopping Carts 229
- The UltraDev Shopping Cart 230
  - Installing the Shopping Cart 230
  - A Sneak Preview 231
  - Payment Options 233
- Creating the Number of Items and Total Cookies 240
  - The Cart Code 244
    - Recap & Refresh 245
- Updating the Cart 246
  - The Empty Cart Code 252

Redirect if Empty 252
Summary 254

10 Adding Cart Functionality — 257

Additions to our Cart 263
    The Check Box Remove Code 265
    Creating a Pop-up Reminder Picture 265
Adding Tax Calculations 270
Writing the Shopping Cart to a Database 272
Databases 273
    Get_ID table 275
    Get Order ID 276
    The Customers Details Order Page 276
    The GetID Code 278
    Recap 284
Summary 289

11 E-mail in UltraDev — 291

Using CDO Mail 294
Creating a Contact Form 299
Sending the Shopping Cart via E-mail 302
Creating a Simple Newsletter 308
Sending Files from the Browser to the Server 312
    Pure ASP File Send 313
    Upload Code 315
SAFileUp 321
Summary 323

12 Server Behaviors — 325

User Interfaces 327
    Creating your own Server Behaviors 328
    Packing up Server Behaviors 339
Summary 349

13 Stored Procedures — 351

Introducing SQL Server 352
Why Use Stored Procedures? 353
What are Stored Procedures? 354
Setting up an SQL Database 354

Table of Contents

Generating a Random Record 365
Creating Stored Procedures with Parameters 367
    Passing a Parameter to a Stored Procedure 368
Creating Procedures with Output Parameters 371
Checking the Parameter Values 377
Failure Message 377
    Further Discussions 378
Summary 379

14 A Step Further   381

Taking Web Applications Further 382
    Shopping Cart Applications 382
    News Updates and Web Diaries 382
UltraDev Extensions 383
    WAP / WML Extensions 383
    Web Learning Applications 383
Using UltraDev with Macromedia Flash 384
Alternative Server Models 390
    Java Server Pages (JSP) 390
ColdFusion 392
Summary 394

A Preferences   397

General 398
Code Colors 400
Code Format 401
Code Rewriting 401
CSS Styles 402
File Types / Editors 403
Fonts / Encoding 404
Highlighting 405
Invisible Elements 406
Layers 406
Layout View 407
Panels 408
Preview in Browser 409
Quick Tag Editor 409
Site 410
Status Bar 411

B Access Primer — 413

- Overview of Relational Databases 413
- Our Database Example 415
- Starting MS Access 416
- Creating the Tables 418
- Entering Some Data into your Table 421
- Creating the Purchase and the Artists tables 423
  - Purchase Table 423
  - Items Tables 424
  - Populate the New Tables with Some Data 425
- Creating a Query 426
- Running your Query 429
  - Sorting 429
- SQL 430
- Another Query 431
- Conclusion 432

C OLE DB Connections — 435

- Creating a DSN-less Connection for Microsoft Access 439

D Resources — 443

- Foundation UltraDev Links 443
- Authors Home Pages 443
- Official Links 443
- Top UltraDev Resources 443
- Other Sites 444

Index — 447

Introduction

Welcome

The web is a continually evolving arena, making ever-increasing demands on those who work in and with it. These demands come quick and fast – attractive looking sites, functionality and ease of use, the ability to be dynamic and pull changing data out of a database to react to daily changes in content and the personal preferences of the user.

How can any one person become master of these varied trades? Is the day when one person could conceivably design a web site on their own receding fast into history in the face of increasingly specialist technology in all these areas?

One answer to this question is Macromedia's Dreamweaver UltraDev. Macromedia's Dreamweaver has been a leading visual web design tool for many years, allowing thousands to exchange the murky world of plain text code for easy drag-and-drop interfaces. UltraDev takes Dreamweaver as a base and goes further by adding some substantial features for creating web sites that work with database components.

This has made the newly released Dreamweaver UltraDev 4 the premier visual solution package for designers who want to create true dynamic web applications – web sites that interact with users and return continually changing information from a database. This is an emerging and exciting new world. As a result of Macromedia bringing UltraDev versioning into line with Dreamweaver, UltraDev 4 follows UltraDev 1 and the new edition can only cement UltraDev's already substantial industry reputation.

We aim to give you a solid foundation in the skills you'll need to run with the crowd. We'll start by putting your UltraDev site on a firm foundation, and we'll then continue to follow our real-world example through the steps needed to take it out of its cocoon and onto the cutting-edge of dynamic e-commerce sites. We end by showing you a few of the possible paths to take once you've got a solid grounding in UltraDev.

We're going to be dealing with some code at some stages in the book but don't worry – we'll be taking you through it step by step. Learning UltraDev won't stop you from being a designer, it will open up new and fantastic ways for you to create the web sites that you want to. This book is about taking another step towards being able to realize your ideas.

The aim of this book

This book concentrates on the UltraDev part of the Dreamweaver UltraDev package, which will teach you how to make dynamic, interactive and engaging sites. Admittedly, we can't cover every possible use and application of UltraDev in 470 pages, but we're going to give you a secure foundation that will let you harness the incredible power of UltraDev with confidence by the end of the book.

We don't believe in books that show principles using theoretical examples that would just never hack it in the real world, so we are using a genuine real-world commercial project (featured on the Macromedia UltraDev showcase) as our case study. With the emphasis on practicality rather than theory, each chapter will follow the Foundation model and introduce a new topic, backed up with step-by-step examples that combine into a working web site by the end of the book.

Take a look at KoolKards.co.uk to see what you'll be doing by the end of this book:

Introduction

We'll be:

- Moving information between web pages
- Displaying information from our database on our web pages
- Creating a web page from which our admin team can easily amend the database
- Creating a search capability for your page
- Building a shopping cart
- Using automated e-mail to alert us to orders and contact customers

Obviously, our case study is taken from the world of e-commerce, an area where UltraDev's abilities are often used. This is by no means the full extent of what you will learn from this book – what you'll learn will have possible applications in any dynamic web application, commercial or otherwise.

No Macs - sorry

The most common server model used for UltraDev is ASP with VBScript (don't worry, we'll explain what this actually means in chapter 1). This is probably the easiest model to use and we've used it for the majority of the exercises in this book, although we have taken a look at the other models towards the end. ASP is a Microsoft product, which means that the book is based around a PC/Windows user. The Foundation series is based on a fully detailed practical tutorial basis and to ensure that this continues, we've concentrated on the PC user.

What you'll need to know

Not a great deal! This is a beginner's book for people with a little experience of creating web sites and an interest in taking that further. Perhaps you have already created your own page or site on the web and been frustrated at the limitations of what you can do with so-called 'static' HTML. Maybe you are looking to add a small database to your site, or have signed a guest book on another site and thought 'I wish I could do that'. Whatever your situation, if it's a dynamic site you're after, Dreamweaver UltraDev 4 has the power to make it happen, and this book is your fast-track to getting great results.

We expect you to know your way around Windows and be comfortable with creating folders, renaming files and so on. We also recommend that you get a little experience

Foundation Dreamweaver UltraDev 4

using Dreamweaver's visual editing tools before we start, although we will be giving you full instructions throughout. If you've never used Dreamweaver before, we suggest that you follow one of the Dreamweaver tutorials included in UltraDev by selecting Help > Using Dreamweaver. This book is for you whatever your previous experience – picking up how to use these tools is extremely simple.

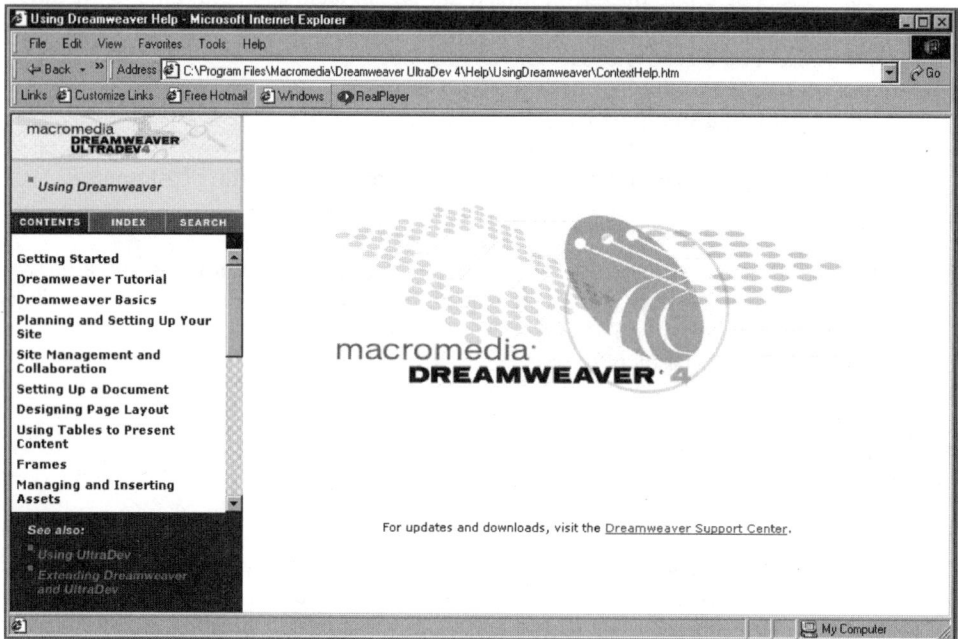

Your UltraDev Set-up

You can mould the look and feel of the UltraDev environment to suit your preferences, so if you've done anything at all with UltraDev, you've probably changed a few settings. This book has been written using the default preferences so you might notice that a few screenshots don't match if you've altered yours.

If you've just installed UltraDev, we'd recommend that you keep the default preferences. We'd also recommend that you spend some time getting to know what preferences you can change and what they do – we've provided a fairly comprehensive preference breakdown as an Appendix.

Before we go any further, we need to dispense with a potential hurdle if you're going to run through the exercises using your machine as a server and usually access web pages via a proxy server: the proxy for local host settings on your browser. If you're an Internet

Explorer user, open up an browser window and select Tools > Internet Options. Go to the Connections tab and click the LAN Settings... button. In the LAN Settings window, make sure that the Bypass proxy server for local addresses box is checked, as pictured. If you're a Netscape user, then ensuring Preferences > Advanced > Proxies is set to Direct Connection to the Internet achieves the same goal.

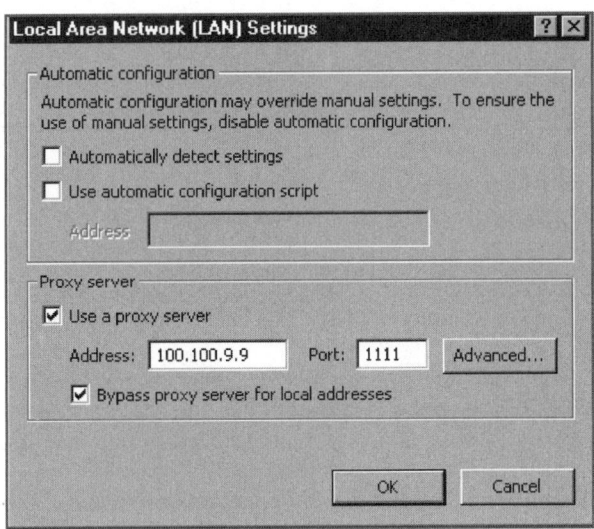

Making sure that you don't lose things in UltraDev

It's probably worth us talking a little about naming conventions – the black art of making sure you use meaningful and acceptable names – before we start. If you start to get into good habits now, it's much easier than trying to break bad ones later...

It's good practice to use lower case for single word names and replace any spaces with an underscore. Spaces in names can cause particular problems in UltraDev, so please use those underscores. It's not such a bad idea to prefix certain object names with a three letter prefix, so frm for form and txt for text and so on.

When creating names with more than one word, it can be useful to use proper noun case, My_Results_Page.asp for example. You'll see that we do this at various points throughout the book but it's really down to personal choice when you move onto your own projects – consistency is far more important than the initial choice.

Each of the many parts of a standard UltraDev form is given a name and you'll make things far easier on yourselves if you give them meaningful names. If you look at the screenshot for example, you'll see that we've created a box for users to type in their name. The screen shot also shows the Properties panel for the TextField. Don't worry too much about what this does, but do notice that we've renamed the text field firstname so we can refer to it later without any problems.

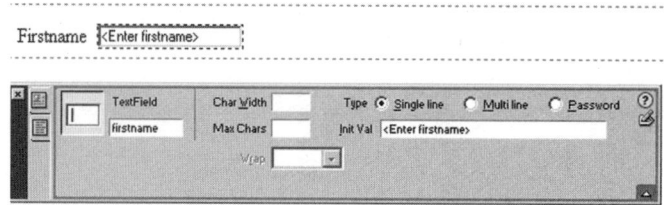

What to do when you lose things in UltraDev

Losing things is very frustrating, so we thought that we'd better tell you at the outset how to find those pages and lines of code that go for a wander just when you need them most.

If you have problems finding your web pages or linking to another web page then it's likely to be one of two things – you've either not linked to the page correctly, or you've been misusing relative links. A relative link is a link that presumes that you're going to stay in the current directory, so doesn't give the full path of the file. This can confuse UltraDev when you do change directories. Either way, your solution is to run the link checker, which will tell you if either of these scenarios is the case. The link checker is accessed through Site > Check Links Sitewide, as shown.

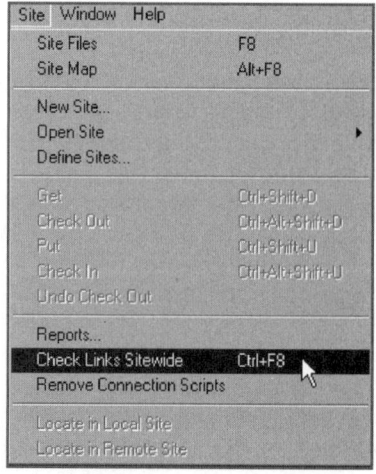

Having problems finding a particular line of code in the code view window is even more likely to happen – it can blur together all too easily. However, simply right-click anywhere in the Code View, and you can do a text search. Much easier.

Introduction

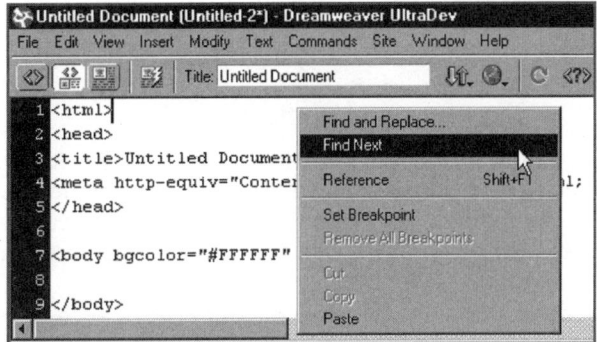

Conventions

We've tried to keep this book as clear and easy to follow as possible, so we've only used a few layout styles:

- When you come across an important word or phrase, it will be in **bold** type.

- We'll use a different font to emphasize phrases that appear on the screen, code and filenames.

- Menu commands are written in the form Menu > Sub-menu > Sub-menu.

- When there's some information we think is really important, we'll highlight it like this:

> *This is very important stuff – don't skip it!*

- Worked exercises are laid out like this:

    1. Open up UltraDev
    2. Save your file as spencer.asp
    3. and so on.

- When the code we're showing you is too long to fit onto one line, we've used a code continuation character like this ➥ to show you that the code is still on the same line in UltraDev. If you see an ➥, don't go hitting that enter key.

Foundation Dreamweaver UltraDev 4

Download Files

We've included all source files and the fully completed files for every exercise for you to download from www.friendsofed.com along with a copy of the finished KoolKards site. Do whatever you like to them, but when things go wrong with your version, take advantage of the ability to compare your file with the finished file before giving up – it often helps.

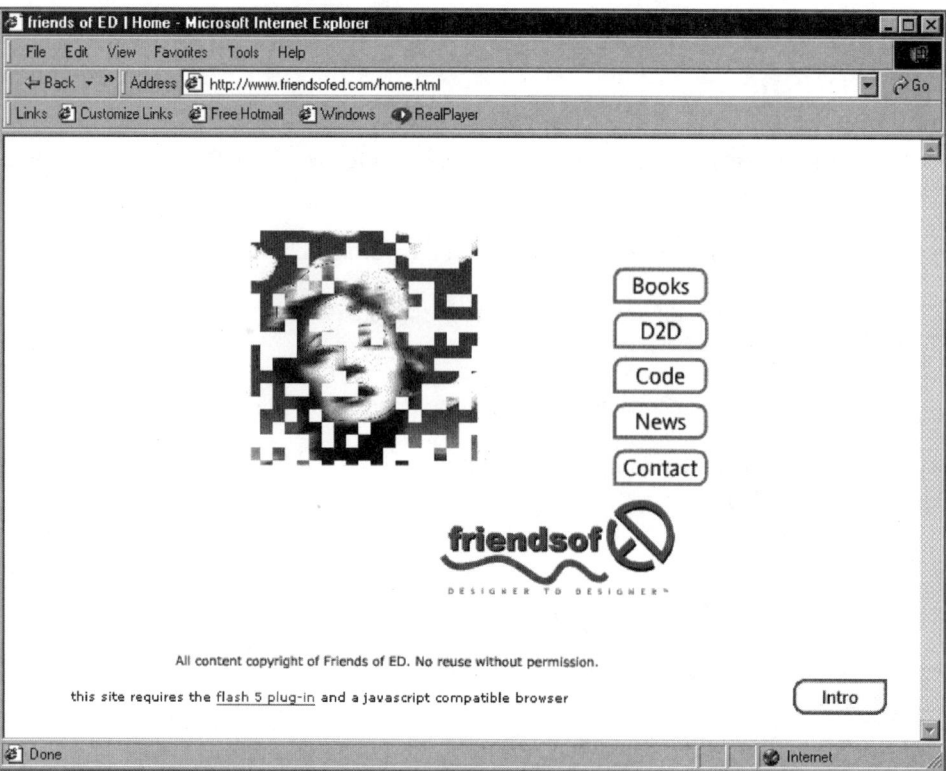

MDAC (Microsoft Data Access Components) contains all of Microsoft's software components for database access; it's a collection of little programs that tell your computer how to connect to all kinds of databases. As long as you have the latest release they'll look after themselves, so it's worth downloading the current version from: www.microsoft.com/data/download.

Introduction

Support: we're your bestest friends

If you have any questions about the book or about friends of ED, check out our web site www.friendsofed.com. There's a range of contact addresses there, or you can just use feedback@friendsofed.com.

There's a host of other features on the site: interviews with top designers, samples from our other books, and a message board where you can post your own questions, discussions and answers, or just take a back seat and look at what other designers are talking about. If you have any comments or problems, please write to us – we'd love to hear from you.

1 Getting Started with UltraDev

What we'll cover in this chapter:

- ***Defining*** *your site: letting UltraDev know the details of your web site, and downloading the files to use throughout the book*

- ***Data Binding****: connecting your site to a database*

- *Using one of UltraDev's **Live Objects** to create your first dynamic web page*

1 Foundation Dreamweaver UltraDev 4

As you read this you might be feeling a little daunted by the prospect of getting to grips with UltraDev, but there's no need to worry – we're here to guide you.

We'll start by taking you through the UltraDev interface and setting up your system so you can work through the rest of the examples in the book.

Setting up the UltraDev Authoring Environment

When you open UltraDev for the first time, the myriad of options can be a little overwhelming. However, what you'll find is that once you've set up an environment that is comfortable *for you*, UltraDev provides a great way to build sites, whether you're a graphic designer or a hardened coder.

The key to getting the environment right is to not open too many pop up windows at once – take a look at this screen shot, from a standard 17-inch monitor running at a resolution of 1024x768. See how confusing things can get, leaving you little room to create your page, or see your code:

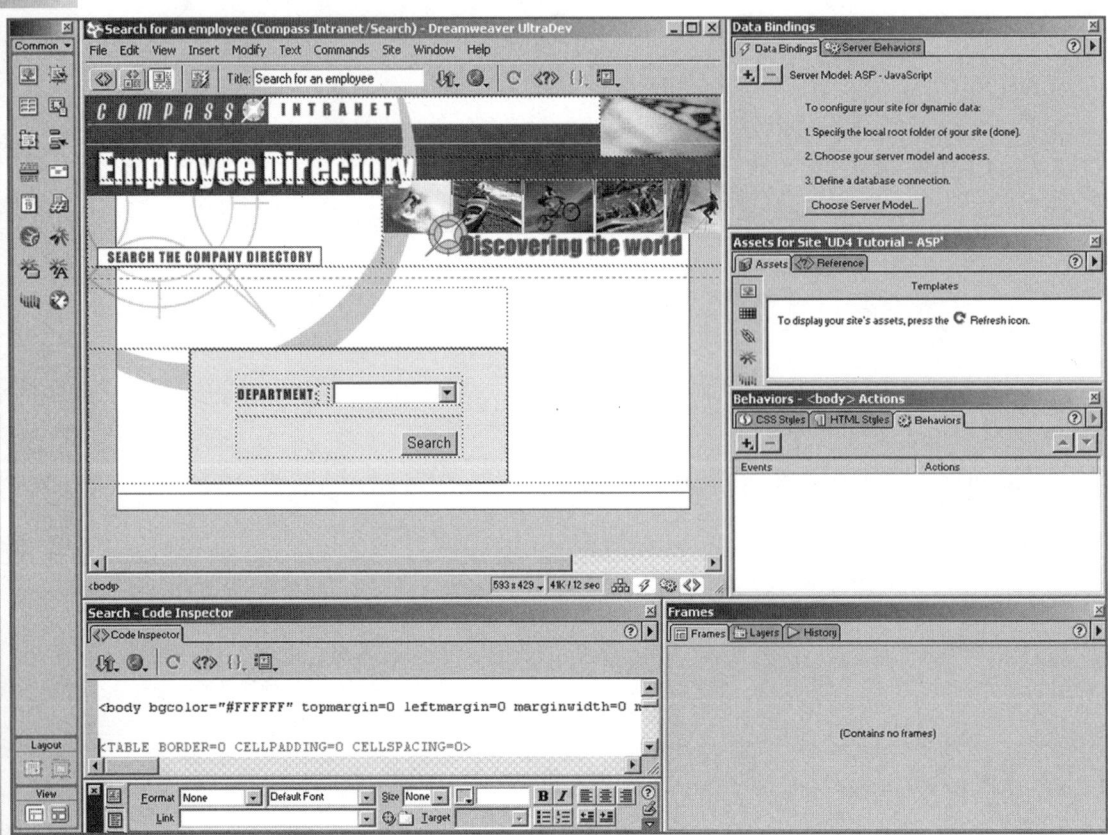

Getting Started with UltraDev 1

It may impress your friends, but working like this soon becomes a nightmare.

The best way to build an environment that suits you (apart from buying two 25-inch monitors) is to strip UltraDev to nothing more than what you absolutely need. Only as you start to find yourself using the same window again and again have it displayed constantly.

Try making yourself one panel with your most commonly used functions on it. Also, UltraDev is a piece of software that really gets moving if you can learn some of those keyboard shortcuts.

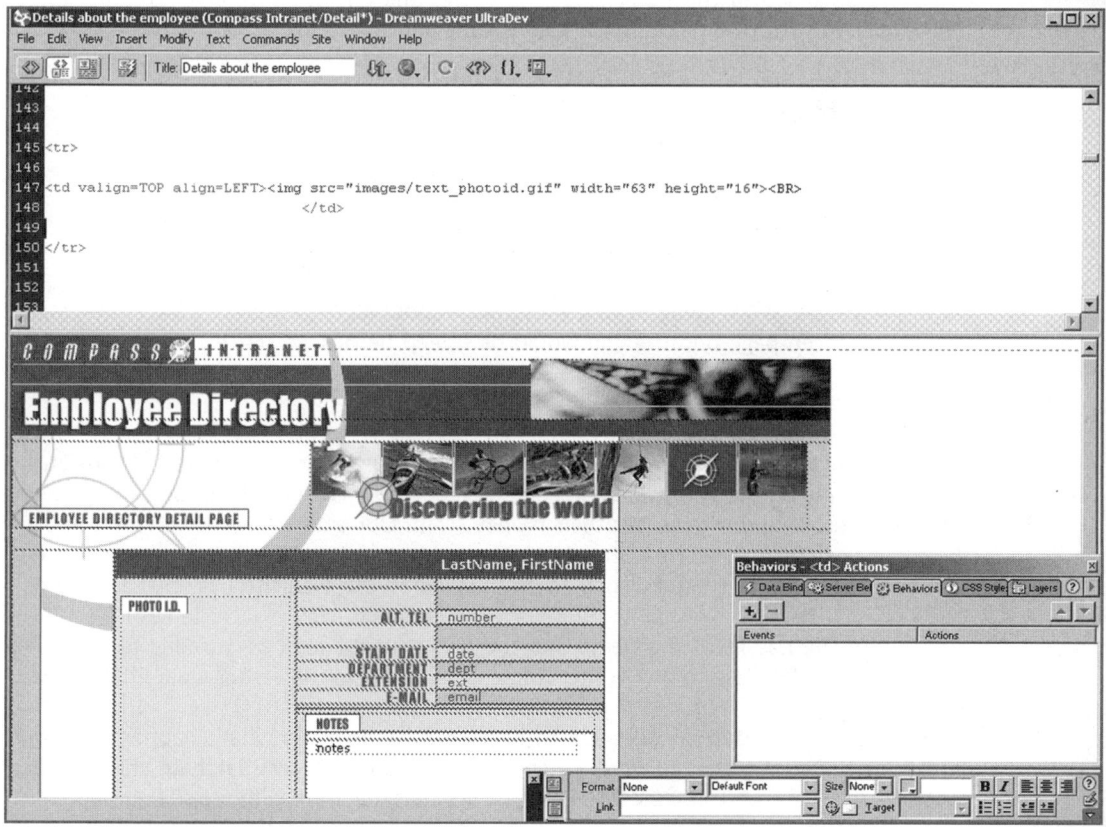

As you can see in the screenshot, by combining some of my frequently used options we've created a more manageable working environment. To begin with, what you'll need is a clear view of the Objects, Properties and Server Behaviors panels. The good news is that once you become familiar with UltraDev's keyboard shortcuts, you'll be able to toggle the main panels on and off as you need them.

1   Foundation Dreamweaver UltraDev 4

Another good thing about the UltraDev environment is that it ties in with Macromedia's other products, like Fireworks for example (their graphics editor), which makes switching from web-building to graphic-editing a breeze – you can simply edit your graphics in Fireworks, switch back to UltraDev and they are already updated in your site. Flash 5 is another example of how the suite of development and design tools integrate seamlessly into your UltraDev environment. Take a look at chapter 14 for some more information.

As this book progresses, we want to be constantly looking at the code that UltraDev generates. We won't expect you to understand it all at first but the sooner you get into the habit of watching our code build in the Code View, the quicker you'll understand the concepts discussed in the book and in turn the quicker you'll be able to apply these techniques to your own pages, once you're done with the book.

Getting Started

We could spend the next four chapters getting to know every nuance of the UltraDev interface – there's so much to learn. We've already discussed how UltraDev provides an environment not just for the developer but also for the designer.

At this stage, we're not going to worry too much about all the different aspects that make up a data-driven page because you would be asleep before we started! Just put on your water wings as we're going to get our feet wet and venture out into the pool with a simple example.

In our **KoolKards** site, we keep a record of all our customers in a database. Obviously, every company on the Web will be keeping track of their customers, so they know where to deliver goods and who to get their money from. Our site will be no different and so over the next few pages we'll show you how easy it is to add a new customer to the customer database table and display the results within our web site.

Because of the nature of the demo and the environment we'll be working in, if you've never linked a database to a web site before, you may find the setting up a little tricky.

Take it slowly – we don't expect you to necessarily understand what's happening in our first tutorial. Basically though, you're going to download an Access database and link your web site to it – so we can view the records from that database within our web pages.

If you do get stuck on making the connection, you can find even more help within the UltraDev help files, under Setting up a DSN. (DSNs will be explained shortly.)

You can download all the templates, files, and databases that you'll need from the friends of ED web site at www.friendsofed.com.

Getting Started with UltraDev

Once you've downloaded the files we need to go about setting up the basic UltraDev environment for this project. We have made some technical choices for you, specifically the 'server model' we'll use (the ASP/VBScript Server model), but we'll fully discuss this and other options later on.

What do I need to Start?

There are a number of things you'll need before you can start creating data driven pages.

- A Web Server (FTP or otherwise)
- A Database
- A DSN (Data Source Name)

When you were installing UltraDev you may have been warned that you need a set of components called **MDAC** version 2.1 or above. MDAC stands for Microsoft Data Access Components and is effectively a set of database drivers that allow UltraDev and other programs to talk to a variety of databases. Your system won't run correctly without this version, so if you need to, download the latest version from http://www.microsoft.com/data/download.htm. It's a good idea to keep your MDAC drivers up to date by visiting the site regularly.

Setting up a Server

The following steps explain what you need to do to be able to test your dynamic web sites locally using Windows. This first section explains how to set up a web server. Although these instructions are specific for Microsoft's **Personal Web Server (PWS)** and **Internet Information Server (IIS)**, you can actually use any web server.

Windows NT Server ships with IIS. NT Workstation users can download IIS as a part of the NT 4.0 Option Pack. Windows 98 comes with the PWS. Be sure you're using Microsoft Internet Explorer 4.01 or higher. If you're using Windows 95, you can download PWS from Microsoft's Web site as we'll explain in a moment.

Windows 2000 Professional & Server comes with IIS (version5) on the CD. If it hasn't been installed, go to Settings > Control Panel > Add/Remove Programs in the Start menu, and then select Add/Remove Windows Components. Check the IIS box and follow the installation instructions.

Foundation Dreamweaver UltraDev 4

Do one of the following:

- If you're using Windows 98, run the PWS `setup.exe` program from the Windows 98 CD. The PWS is stored in the `add-ons\pws` folder on the Windows 98 CD.

- If you're using Windows 95, you can download PWS from:

    http://www.microsoft.com/msdownload/ntoptionpack/askwiz.asp

    You'll have to fill out an online profile form to download the option pack. Choose Option 1 if you're running Windows and select Windows NT Option Pack Download Wizard for Windows 95. Click on the `download.exe` link that's stored at the location closest to you. Save the file to your hard drive and then run the `download.exe` program. Choose the Typical installation and accept the default settings. This downloads the installation files on your computer. Run the `setup.exe` program. The `setup.exe` file is stored in the PWSetupFiles folder.

- If you're using Windows NT, Service Pack 6 or higher must be installed on the target system before you install the Windows NT 4.0 Option Pack. You can download Service Pack 6 from the same page as PWS. You'll have to fill out an online profile form to download the option pack. To get Service Pack 4, go to the following URL:

    http://www.microsoft.com/ntserver/nts/downloads/default.asp

    Be aware that the Service Packs and NT 4.0 Option Pack are quite large.

- Choose the Typical installation and accept the default settings. The Personal Web Server (WWW service) is set up in a folder named Inetpub\wwwroot. The System Settings Change message box appears, informing you that you must restart your computer before the new settings will take effect.

- Choose Yes to restart your computer.

Apart from the Microsoft servers there is a product available for Unix & Linux users called Chili!Soft. You can find information on Chili!Soft at www.chilisoft.com.

Setting up your KoolKards Site

You now need to download the web files necessary for this chapter from the friends of ED web site.

Getting Started with UltraDev

You should ensure these files are placed in C:\Inetpub\wwwroot\KoolKards\ – if this directory doesn't exist already, create it.

After downloading the zip and extracting the files you should have a directory structure similar to the one shown here:

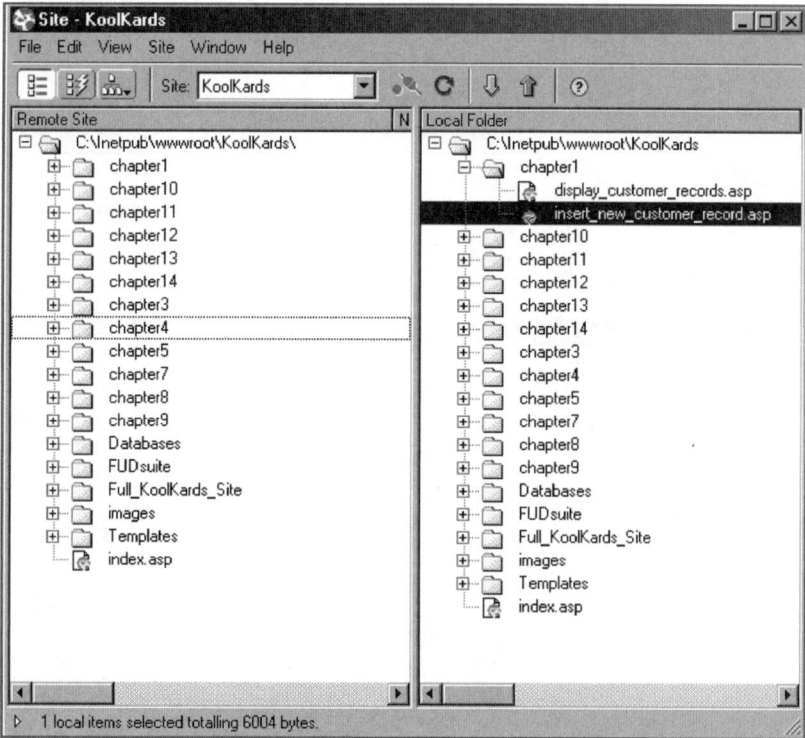

Remember, at this point UltraDev doesn't know anything about the type of server code or database type you wish to use, so the next stage is to set up your local site.

Setting up a site in UltraDev is much the same as setting up a site in Dreamweaver. Click on the Site menu and select Define Sites...

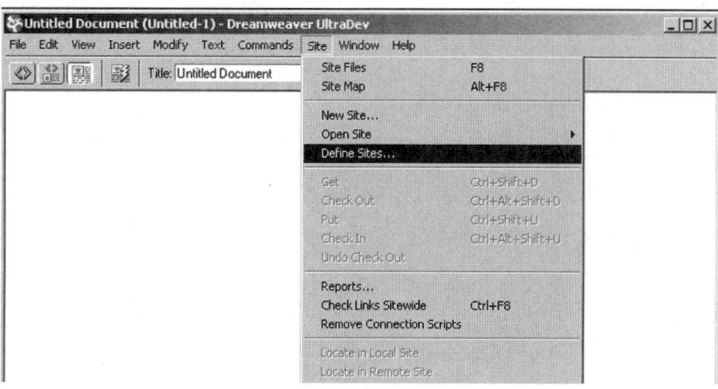

Foundation Dreamweaver UltraDev 4

This will bring up the panel you see here, which displays your currently set-up sites:

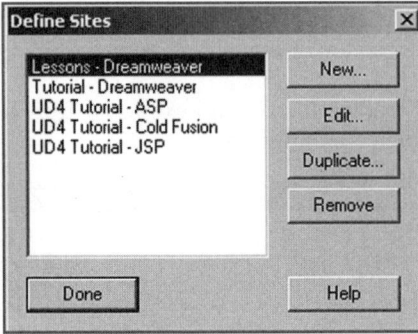

Unless you've deleted them you will have a few tutorial sites already set up.

Click New...

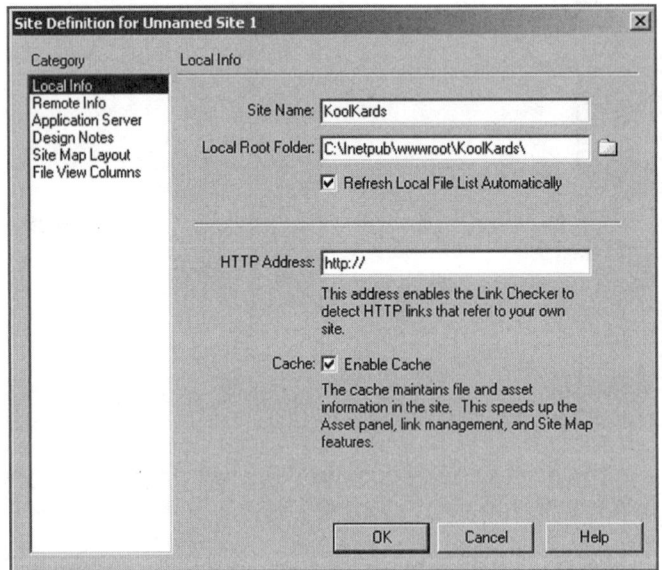

Make sure that you have the Local Info category selected. You'll need to enter the following information into the different sections:

- In Site name: enter KoolKards

- In Local Root Folder: enter C:\Inetpub\wwwroot\KoolKards\

The HTTP Address: isn't needed at this stage as we're only setting up a local site.

Getting Started with UltraDev

Now select Remote Info in the left-hand pane:

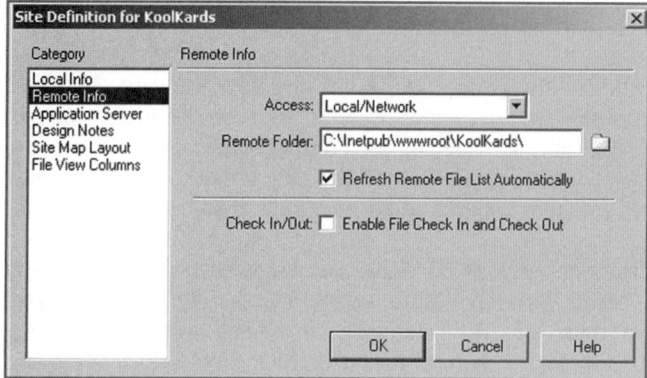

Remote Info sets up where your web server lives.

- Access: Select the Local/Network option from the drop down box

- Remote Folder: Enter your path to your web server folder; if it's PWS or IIS then it should be C:\Inetpub\wwwroot\KoolKards\

- Refresh Remote File List Automatically: this needs to be checked

- Check In/Out: please leave this unchecked for now

Now select Application Server from the left-hand pane:

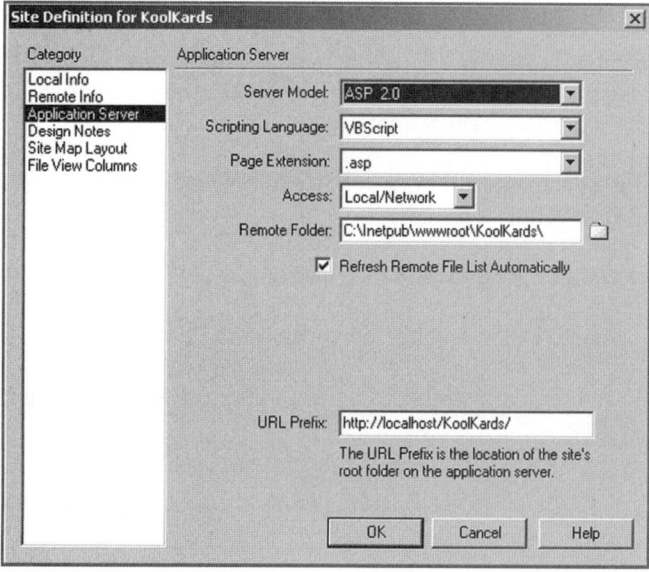

Foundation Dreamweaver UltraDev 4

The Application Server screen allows you to tell UltraDev which server model you're going to use. We've chosen ASP 2.0 using Visual Basic Script for the scripting language. Make sure your screen matches our example.

For the URL Prefix, you should enter http://localhost/KoolKards/ if you are using your machine as the web server as well as your development machine (as we are in this example). Basically, we're telling the computer that if we want to look at a page called, for example, MyDetails.htm – to add the URL prefix to the front, thus creating the full URL path. Your computer will automatically know that 'localhost' means 'this machine'.

It's important to get this bit right, as later we'll be looking at a rather nifty feature of UltraDev called **View Live Data**, which enables you to look at your web page, with full database results, *within* the design environment rather than having to keep switching to your web browsers. This time-saving feature relies on this entry being correct. More on this feature later in the book, but for now, if you're following our example, just type the entry as above if it hasn't been filled automatically.

Once you've entered these details you're pretty much done for now. You can have a quick look over the other site options later, but for now we won't need to enter any more details.

Click OK to close the Site Definitions window. UltraDev will created the 'cache' for your site which will take a few seconds. Let it do its work, then hit Done on the Define Sites window, to return to your main environment.

We're now in a position to move on to setting up your database connections.

The Data Source Name (DSN) Entry

Since a database can contain personal and sensitive information it has to be *very* secure. Understandably then, quite a lot of information is needed before a database will give up its secrets – especially over the Internet.

In order for a database to allow a web site to view information, it requires answers to some important questions:

- Who is asking for this information?

- Should I allow this person access to the data?

- Do I require a password before I give out this information?

Getting Started with UltraDev

So, whenever we want some data from a database, we're expected to provide security information – pretty much like logging into Windows. Our system needs to know if we're to be trusted before it can go any further. But for a developer, having to manually provide this security information every time we want to query a database can become very tedious.

By creating and using a **Data Source Name** (**DSN**) entry (as we shall shortly) we can provide a trusted connection between the application and the database, which, once saved, the application can use over and over again.

There are two main connections that we can use between UltraDev and our database of choice, Access. OLE DB is a newer, more powerful set of interfaces for data access than ODBC, providing a flexible and efficient database architecture that offers good access to Microsoft and third-party databases.

The benefits of using OLE DB as opposed to ODBC are two-fold. When you use OLE DB, you are actually 'closer' to the data source than when you use ODBC and this means that, as your code does not have to pass through as many layers, you get much better performance. OLE DB also lets you interrogate a wider variety of data sources, such as Microsoft Exchange, Microsoft Index Server, and ADSI (Active Directory Service Interfaces).

OLE DB might sound pretty good but it comes with certain configuration issues. We aren't going to bombard you with technical issues but each OLE DB connection is specific to your own set up, so it's going to be more difficult to make sure that we're all starting at the same place.

This means that, for the sake of simplicity and user friendliness, we're going to use ODBC (Open Database Connectivity Interface), which is a standard for communicating with different types of databases.

Connecting your Web Site to a Database

We already have a server set up, our files have been downloaded and our site defined, and UltraDev is ready and waiting to help us create dynamic pages. The missing link is the one that joins our web site to our database and gets them talking.

1. Switch to any web page – or create a new one if one isn't open.

2. If you look closely at the bottom of the document (main) window, at the far right of the status bar, you can see some handy shortcut icons. By clicking on the lightning icon, you can launch the Data Bindings window (if it's not open). Even easier, use the keyboard shortcut CTRL+F10.

This Data Binding window should appear (note – if it doesn't, repeat the previous, as all windows work on a turn on/off basis).

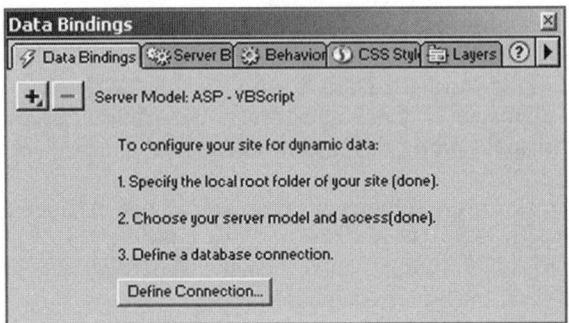

We're now going to define our connection with our database.

3. The first step is to click on the Define Connection... button, which will bring up the Connection for Site 'KoolKards' box:

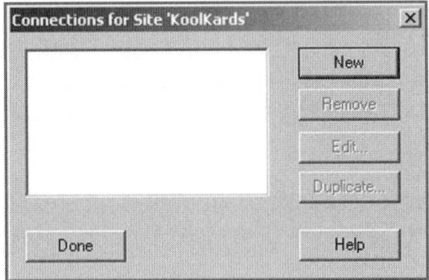

4. Now select New and choose Data Source Name (DSN).

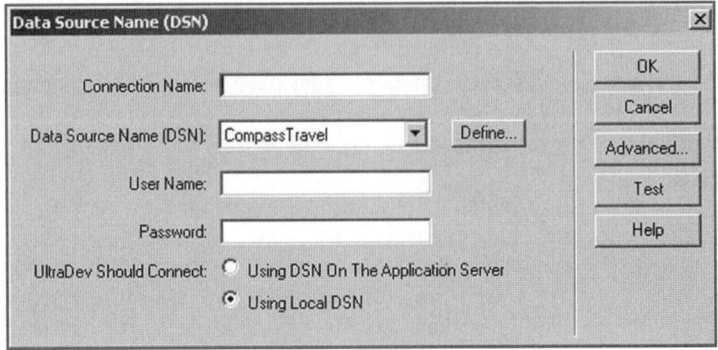

Don't let the entry in the DSN: field confuse you. This is just your current computer's default.

Getting Started with UltraDev

5. At this stage you won't have a DSN set up so click the Define button, which will open up your computer's ODBC Administrator:

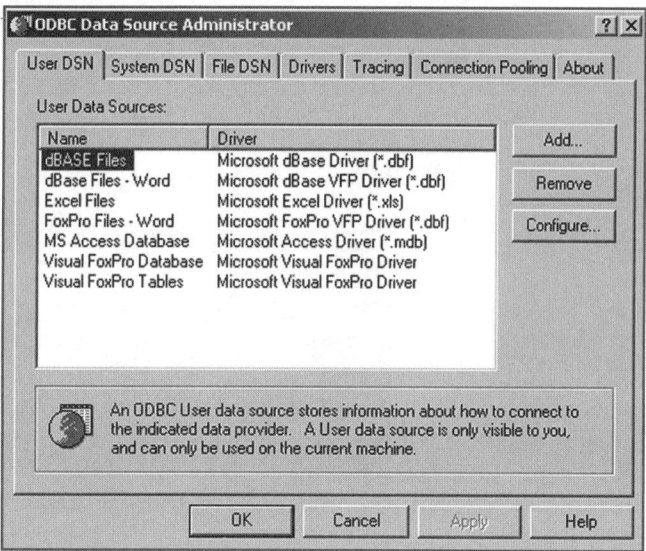

6. Now select the System DSN tab. The difference between a User DSN and a System DSN is that a User DSN can only be used by connections on this machine. This is fine for our purposes – but if another machine wants to use the connection to connect to our database, they won't be able to – which is completely inappropriate for our web applications. Therefore, whenever we create a DSN for web applications we always use a System DSN.

7. Click Add to bring up the Create New Data Source window and you'll see a list of sources similar to those here:

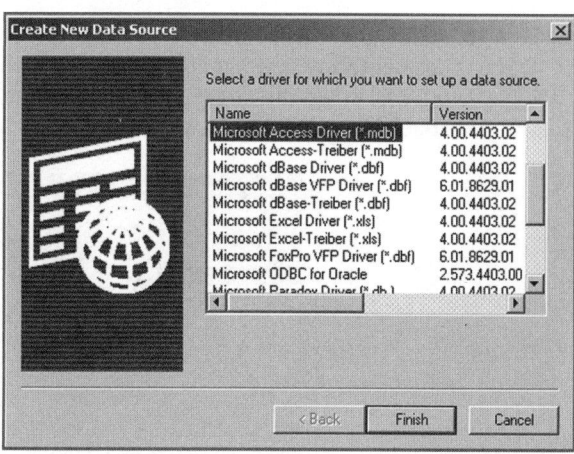

Foundation Dreamweaver UltraDev 4

There are many different types of databases and each type requires its own special driver, which allows the application to talk to the database, finding and extracting the information it needs. In our example, we'll be using Microsoft Access so we need to select the special Microsoft Access Driver.

8. From the list within the Create New Data Source window select a Microsoft Access (*.mdb) Driver. Then click on Finish and you'll see the ODBC Microsoft Access Setup window:

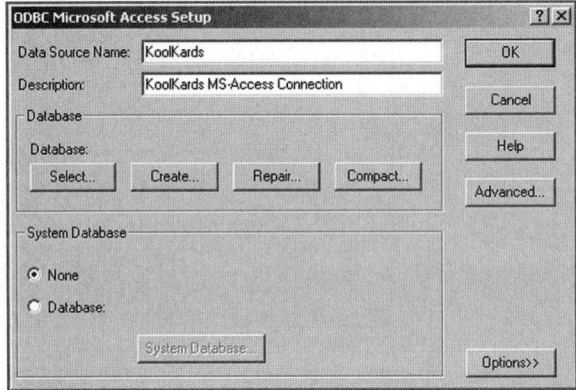

We'll use this to point the DSN to our database and enter some basic naming properties.

9. Enter KoolKards in the Data Source Name text box and KoolKards MS-Access Connection as a description.

Now, to complete the connection, we are going to tell our DSN connection where the database actually resides on our hard drive.

10. Click the Select button located under Database: and you will be presented with a familiar looking directory browsing screen. You need to drill down the directories to locate the actual location of your Access database (C:\Inetpub\wwwroot\KoolKards\database).

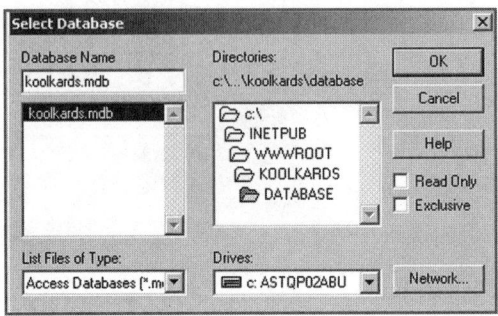

Getting Started with UltraDev

11. Select it and OK all of this.

12. The last step is to type in KoolKards as the Connection Name: and select the DSN that you've just created from the drop-down box.

    - PWS users – make sure you have checked the Using Local DSN radio button:

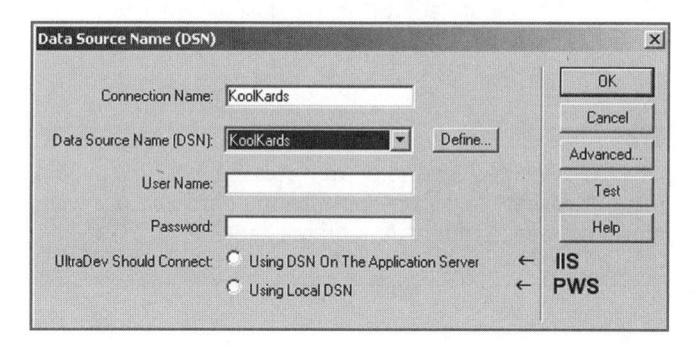

    - IIS users need to select Using DSN on the Application Server, the Define button will now read DSN and when you click it, another window will pop up:

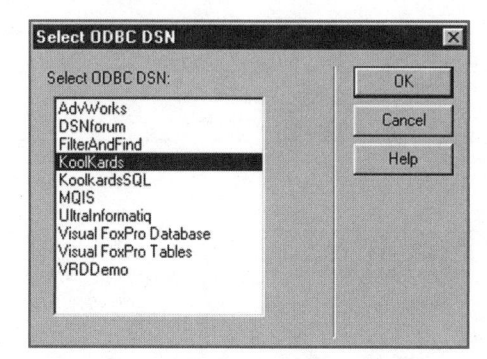

    Choose your KoolKards connection.

13. To make sure that you've set your DSN up correctly, quickly click on the Test button. You'll be pleased if this box appears:

Foundation Dreamweaver UltraDev 4

14. Click OK twice and you'll be returned to the Define Sites dialog box, which should now be displaying KoolKards as a defined site.

15. Click Done and the KoolKards Site Management Screen will appear. If it doesn't (and for future reference) you can get to this screen by going to Site > Open Sites > KoolKards.

    Congratulations! You've just created your first site connected to a database!

> This is the first and most important step in creating a dynamic page. Now that we have a connection between the data and our web page we can place our ever-changing data on the page!

Phew – that was a lot of clicking around. Effectively though, we've created our DSN, created our database and imported some of our ready to go files. If it's any consolation, once you've done this a few times, it becomes second nature.

```
±─ chapter8
±─ chapter9
±─ Connections
±─ Databases
```

> You'll see that UltraDev has created a folder called Connections for you, and inside there is a tiny connection file which your pages can call upon.

Now we can finally get down to doing something with our web site, and even this early on in the game, we'll be adding some dynamic features.

Getting Started with UltraDev 1

Opening a Page and Viewing the Code

Providing your chapter download has been completed you should see a folder called chapter1. Select this folder and open `insert_new_customer_record.asp`.

Before we go any further, let's briefly discuss one of the key aims of this book – to make you look, read and appreciate the code that is generated by UltraDev. By watching the code take shape as you use the tools within UltraDev, you will become more familiar with code as it happens. Although this is very early days and we won't expect you to understand much yet – now is still an excellent time to open up the Code View window, so you can see the code and your graphics on the page.

Open the Code View by clicking the Show Code and Design Views icon, which you'll find below the File menu on any web page. (You may like to click all three icons to see how they affect the views if this is new to you);

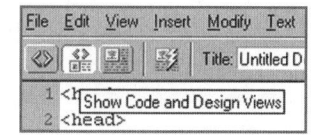

If you have everything set up correctly you should see something like this:

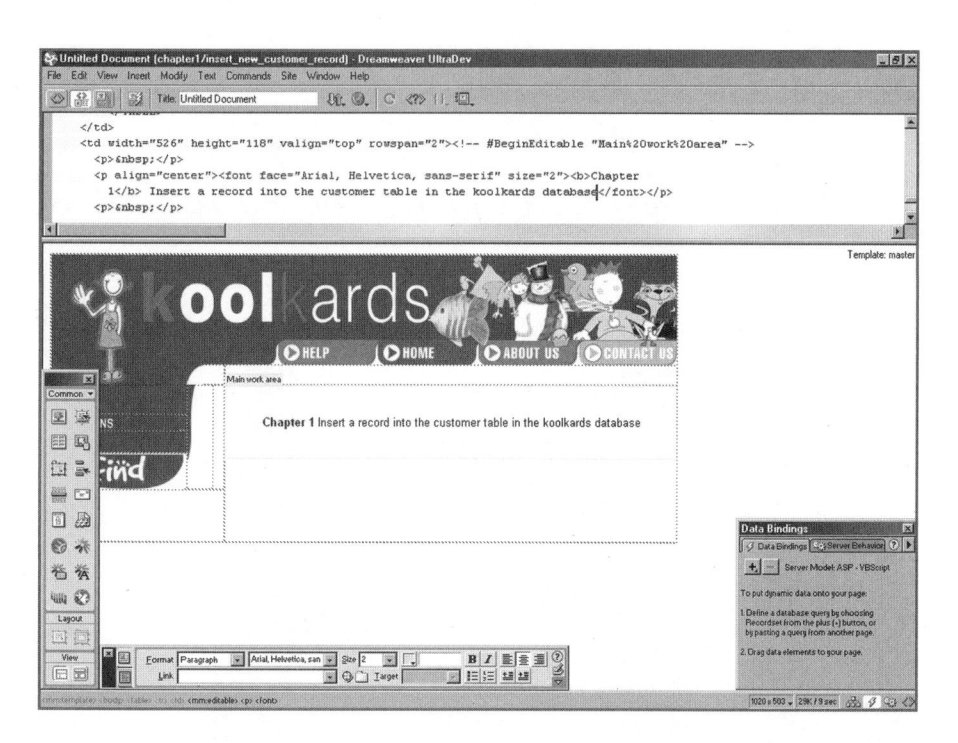

Foundation Dreamweaver UltraDev 4

Over the next few pages we're going to develop this page to allow a new customer record to be created. Once the customer has entered their details we'll redirect them to a page that immediately displays a list of all customers currently held in the customer table. Possibly not the most impressive 'real world' example, but it's one that will show us that we're entering a record into our database via the web page, and on the second page, confirming the record is there.

> *Both of the authors of this book come from a small community of Drumbeat users and we were massively aided by Drumbeat and in particular its wizard called the DataForm Wizard. This was a great little tool for the beginner that would create your update, insert, search and results pages in a few clicks. The good news is that Macromedia have taken the idea and incorporated it into UltraDev 4 as Live Objects...*

UltraDev's Live Objects will now help us create a dynamic web page.

Your first dynamic page

In this exercise we are going to use one of UltraDev's Live Objects to quickly place a record insertion form on our page. Live Objects are a very useful and powerful collection of tools, as you will soon see...

1. Find the Live Objects as shown by clicking the little arrow on the Objects panel and selecting Live.

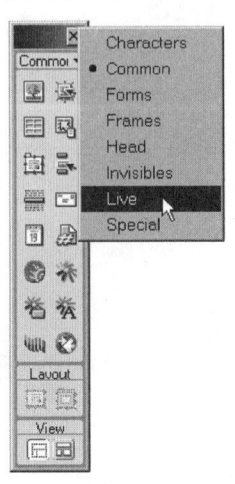

Getting Started with UltraDev

2. You should now see the Live Objects panel – with the collection of objects showing.

3. The first thing we are going to need is an insert page, so select the Insert Record Insertion Form live object.

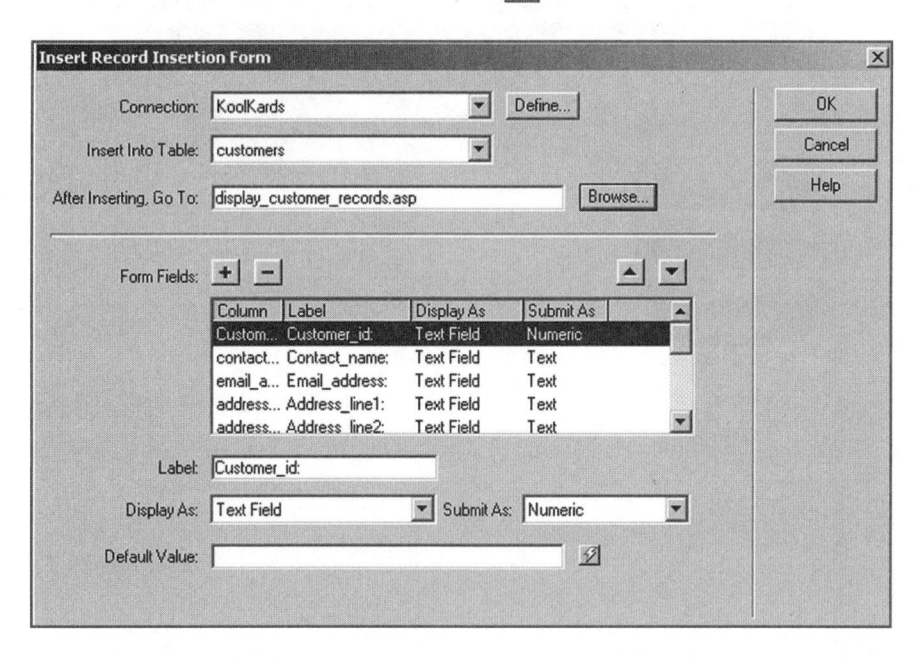

```
Insert Record Insertion Form
    Connection:        KoolKards          ▼   Define...         OK
    Insert Into Table: customers          ▼                     Cancel
    After Inserting, Go To: display_customer_records.asp   Browse...   Help

    Form Fields:  [+] [-]                                   [▲] [▼]
                  Column    Label           Display As    Submit As
                  Custom... Customer_id:    Text Field    Numeric
                  contact... Contact_name:  Text Field    Text
                  email_a... Email_address: Text Field    Text
                  address... Address_line1: Text Field    Text
                  address... Address_line2: Text Field    Text

    Label:         Customer_id:
    Display As:    Text Field         ▼   Submit As: Numeric   ▼
    Default Value:
```

4. The Insert Record Insertion Form should now be displayed. We just need to enter the necessary information so the wizard can add the necessary code to our page.

   - Connection: Select KoolKards from the drop-down box.

   - Insert Into Table: We want our new record to go into the customers table.

   - After Inserting, Go To: Browse to display_customer_records.asp because we want to jump to this page to display our records, including our new one.

   Everything else can be left as default for now.

5. Click OK and watch the magic happen.

Foundation Dreamweaver UltraDev 4

The page should look something like the one shown here:

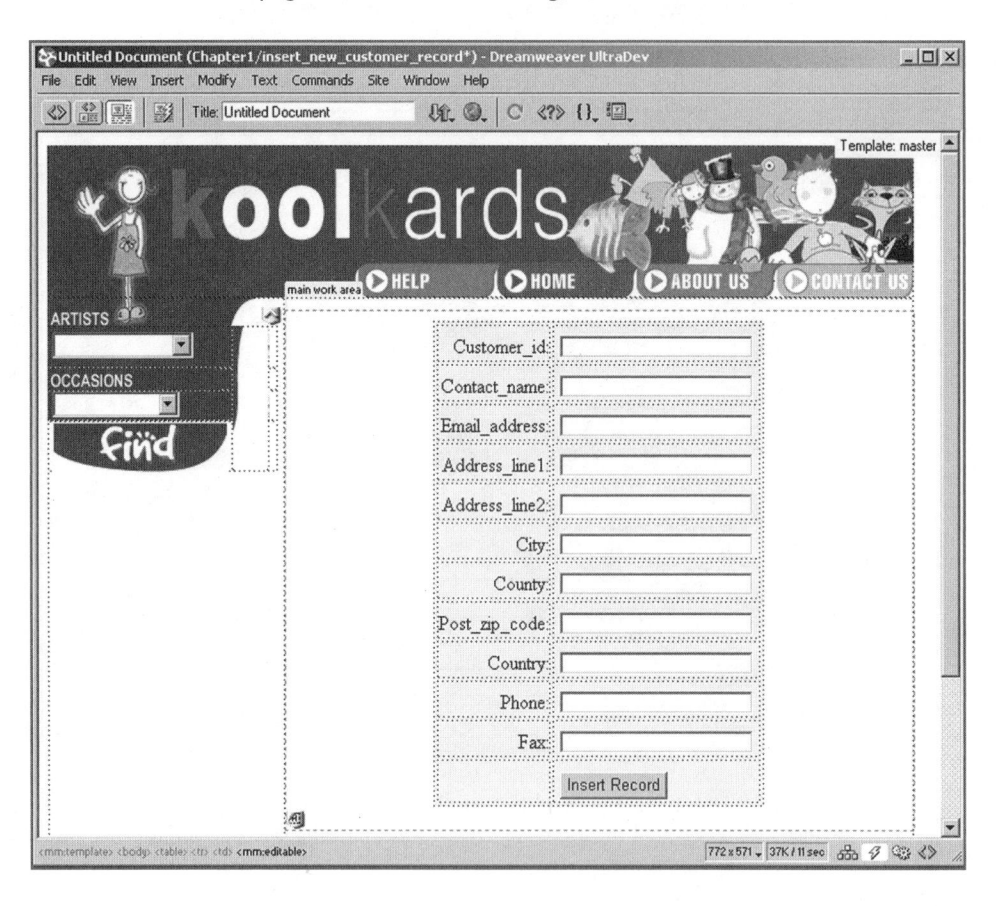

6. It's now time to save your page (CTRL+S) and test it in your browser. Launch your web browser and type in your local web site address:

   http://localhost/koolkards/chapter1/insert_new_customer_record.asp

   This will display the page you've just created.

7. Enter a sample set of details, and click the Insert Record button. You will be immediately redirected to a page that will display all the customer records plus the new one you just inserted.

Getting Started with UltraDev

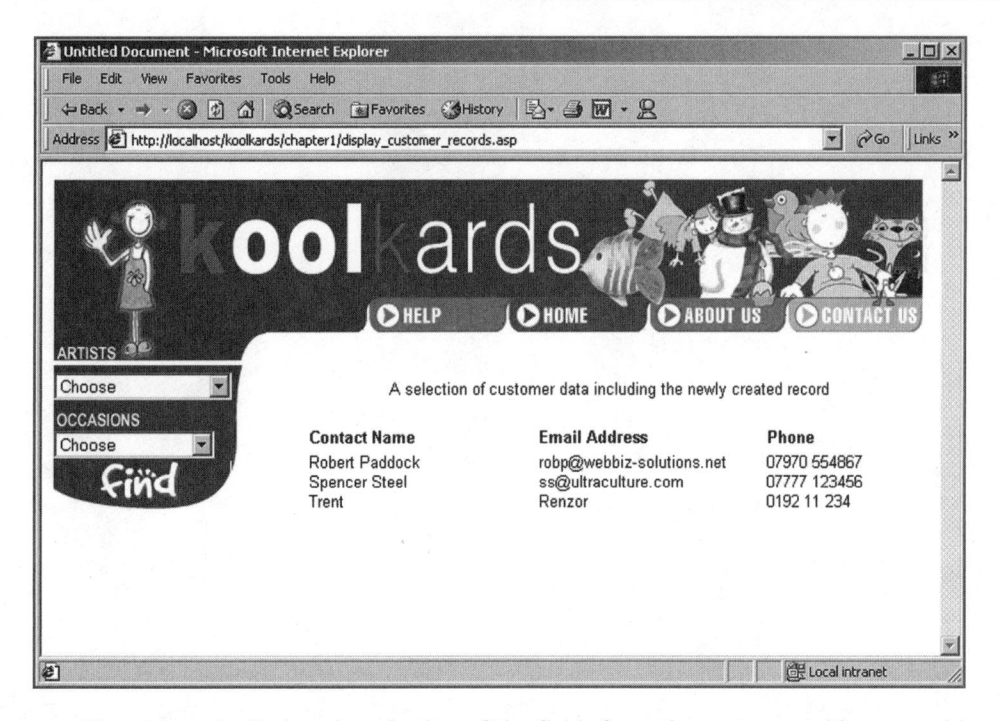

As you'll see we only displayed a selection of the fields from the customer table, we could display any combination of fields with many different criteria to select them. How to achieve this will be introduced as we continue through the book.

Summary

You may not think you've done a huge amount but you've just created your first truly dynamic web pages. Well done!

- We've taken a brief look at the UltraDev environment

- We've set up our local site on UltraDev, and defined a connection to our database using the Data Bindings panel

- Using the tools within UltraDev we've created a record insert page that would take an expert ASP coder quite a while to write

With this backbone connection between our database and our web site, we are in a position to start learning why we do things the way we do, and that's what Chapter 2 is all about. By the end of Chapter 2 you should feel comfortable with why we are doing what we are doing, what part of our setup is doing what and how we are going to expand on this in the coming chapters.

koolkards

2 Client/Server Concepts

What we'll cover in this chapter:

- *The early development of computers and the advent of the **server***

- *An introduction to **client/server** relationships*

- ***Scripting** on the client side and on the server side – with brief descriptions of the programming languages and options available*

- *The basics of **Active Server Pages** and how they work*

- *Using UltraDev's **server behaviors** and downloading more from Macromedia Exchange; introducing extensibility*

Foundation Dreamweaver UltraDev 4

Well, if you've just finished Chapter 1, you're probably feeling pretty pleased with yourself – and rightly so. In a few short pages, you've made your first database connection, created a *dynamic* web page and seen it working!

In this chapter, however, we must put down our web site for a while and go back to the theory behind it...

When we sat down to draft this book, one of our prime goals was to make sure that we showed you *how* and *why* things work like they do. For example, in Chapter 1 we built a rather clever insert page from an UltraDev wizard – but although it works well, we have no real understanding of *how* it works, and if I now asked you to go away and manually build me an Update page, you'd probably get unstuck pretty quick.

The purpose of this chapter is to introduce some fundamental **client/server** techniques. By the end you should understand which part of our model is doing what, how they interact with each other and what languages each part is using, as well as looking at some raw code and trying to fathom out how all these wonderful wizards work!

One of the first things we're going to do is break down what we really mean by client/server techniques, because it's important that you fully understand the subjects and the terms we'll discuss in this chapter. If you've used some basic client/server techniques, you may find some of this familiar, but it doesn't hurt to refresh your memory.

Before we take a look at a typical client/server set-up, let's take a short (if not 100% thorough) overview of the history of computing, to see how we have arrived at today's 'web-based' model.

In the Beginning

...there was the **mainframe**.

You've probably all heard the legends of these huge mythical beasts that took up whole rooms in special temperature-controlled buildings – the kind of computers that needed men in white coats tending to them 24 hours a day!

The model of the mainframe was simple – one very large computer with each user logging in via 'dumb' terminals. The dumb terminals were really just a keyboard and a monitor linked into the mainframe, which effectively did all the processing work. The user queried the mainframe from his terminal, the mainframe worked out the results and the results were then displayed on the monitor.

Client/Server Concepts | 2

In our diagram below, we can see the topology (organization and interconnection) of the network, where the mainframe is the **server** and the terminal is the **client**.

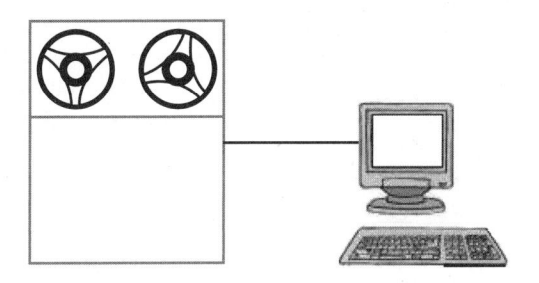

Right now you're probably thinking "What has this got to do with UltraDev?" Well, keep reading because you'll discover how history has this uncanny knack of repeating itself...

Dumb Terminals Get Smarter

We come to the next step in our brief history of computing – the advent of **smart terminals**, or PCs as we know them. By giving the terminals ever-increasing processing power of their own, the desktop PC was born.

The massive advantage was that the PC could work as a standalone machine, with each PC becoming the client *and* the server (like the Personal Web Server we set up in Chapter 1). The first PCs were never networked together as such, but sharing data with other machines was made possible by swapping large floppy diskettes.

Many Hands Make Light Work

Things really started to get interesting when someone thought of linking (or **networking**) those standalone PCs together. With file- and print-sharing, linking up our PCs gave us distributed processing power – one PC could be a network **document server**, another could be a **print server**. In this topology, no single machine was the client or the server:

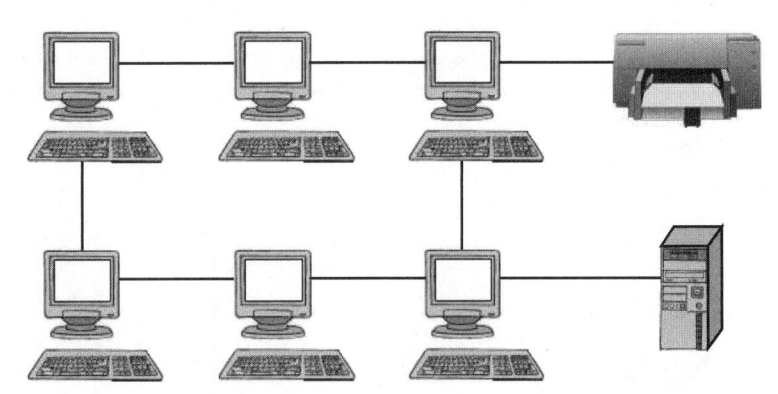

2 Foundation Dreamweaver UltraDev 4

Millions of Hands Make for Something Special

While all these different office-based topologies were mutating over the years, in the Universities and Government buildings in America the Internet was being born. The history of the Internet is well documented and we can honestly say that without a doubt it is here to stay. Nowadays the World Wide Web is not so much a haven for 'techies' but more like a utility that is piped into our homes in the same way as water or electricity.

The topology for the Internet is fairly basic considering how vast it is. In its simplest form the Internet consists of various servers that are available for your web-browser (the client) to read from.

Let's take a look at how a web server handles a request from your browser to view some static (non-dynamic) HTML pages:

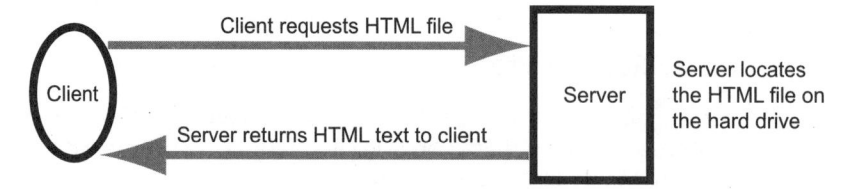

```
Client ──Client requests HTML file──▶ Server    Server locates
       ◀──Server returns HTML text to client    the HTML file on
                                                the hard drive
```

As you can see, the client is your computer/browser:

- It asks for a web page, say www.foundationultradev.com/index.htm.

- The correct server (which hosts that domain/site) is located on the Internet.

- The server then finds the HTML file in its directory and returns it to your browser.

- Finally, your browser converts the HTML into pretty pictures and text, and it displays the page and all its components on your screen.

As you can see, in this topology the server is doing nothing special – it's doing no real 'working out' as such, merely acting as a file server, returning the HTML document to the browser.

Now let's look what happens in our dynamic web application scenario:

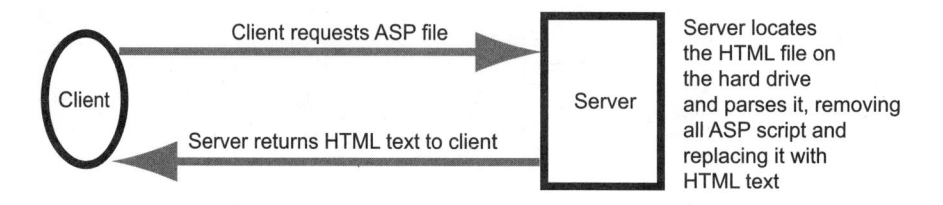

```
Client ──Client requests ASP file──▶ Server    Server locates
       ◀──Server returns HTML text to client   the HTML file on
                                               the hard drive
                                               and parses it, removing
                                               all ASP script and
                                               replacing it with
                                               HTML text
```

Client/Server Concepts

As you can see the model is effectively identical, with one small but rather important change. In the above example the server looks up an **ASP** file. ASP stands for **Active Server Page**, which as you can tell from the name, requires much more action from the server than a plain HTML file does.

The server first determines which part of the code is ASP code and which part is HTML code. It then acts on the requirements of the ASP instructions and constructs a totally HTML code page and passes it back. This HTML page could be different each time, depending on what the ASP part of the page asks for. Remember – this is what we mean by *dynamic*.

To clarify this, let's look at a simple dynamic page in action on the Web and see how the server has changed the HTML.

ASP in Action

Go to our site on the web www.koolkards.co.uk and from the homepage, use the Occasions drop-down box to select Christmas, then click Find – the page returned will contain all the Christmas cards in the collection! This special page was generated based on the ASP instruction to 'find all the Christmas cards'.

Let's look at the HTML created. If you right-click on a part of the page (not a picture), and click View Source on the context menu, the raw HTML code will pop up in a new Notepad window:

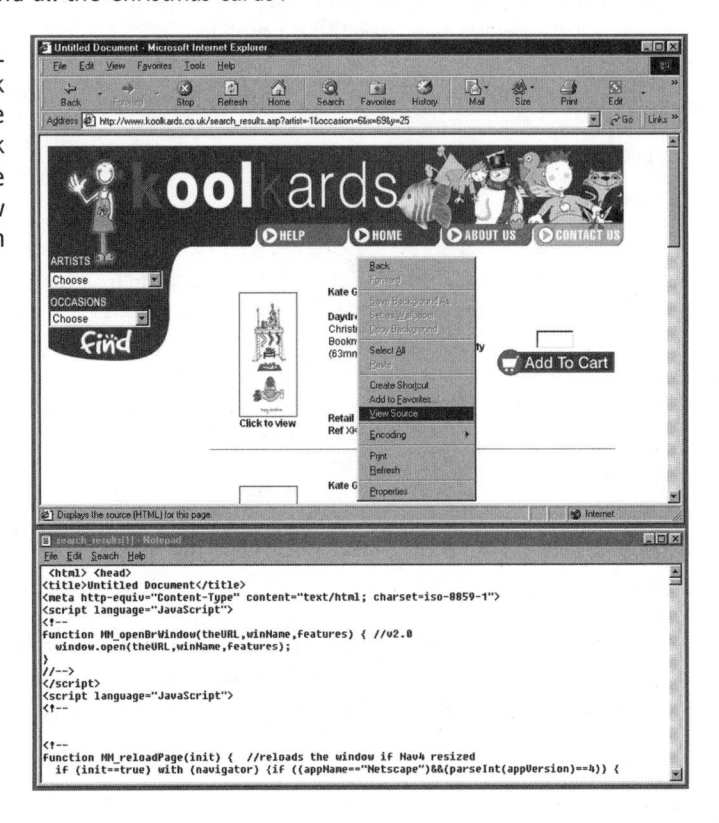

Skimming through the code we can locate the part relating to the search we just performed. It's about halfway down and should look like this:

```
              <div align=center><a href="#"
➡ onClick="MM_openBrWindow
➡ ('full_image.asp?image=XKG001_full.gif','display',
➡ 'width=400height=475')"><img
➡ src="images/XKG001_thumb.gif"border="1"></a><br>
          <b>Click to view</b></div>
       </td>
       <td height=135 valign=middle width="134">
         <p><b>Kate Gardner<br>
          <br>
          </b><b>Daydreams<br>
          </b>Christmas<br>
          Bookmark Range (63mm * 178mm)
         </p>
```

With a basic understanding of HTML and a little common sense we can tell that the images referred to are the images of the cards displayed on our screen. The image called XKG001_thumb.gif is the thumbnail we see and XKG001_full.gif will be opened in a new window when you click the thumbnail.

OK – now choose Birthday from the drop-down search menu and click Find again.

Let's look at the resulting page's HTML code...

```
              <div align=center><a href="#"
➡ onClick="MM_openBrWindow('full_image.asp?image=KG001
➡ _full.gif','display','width=400,height=475')"><imgsrc=
➡ "images/KG001_thumb.gif" border="1"></a><br>
          <b>Click to view</b></div>
       </td>
       <td height=135 valign=middle width="134">
         <p><b>Kate Gardner<br>
          <br>
          </b><b>Daydreams<br>
          </b>Birthday<br>
          Bookmark Range (63mm * 178mm)
         </p>
```

As we can see, the images have changed, as has the code, but here's the important bit – *both results pages are effectively the same basic page*. Whatever we select as our search criteria, the server *dynamically* changes the parts of the HTML code on that page to show us our results.

Client/Server Concepts

Now, look closely at the HTML. Can you see the code that actually changes the images depending on what was selected? No!

> You can't see the server code from your browser. You only see the end result! So, unlike 'static' HTML, you can't view (or steal) server code. Why? Because it's on the server – another computer – and not on the client (your computer). This means if you want to create dynamic code, you'll have to learn how to write it!

To recap, we've now learned what is meant by client/server and seen how an intelligent server can dynamically build an HTML page. We've also discovered which part of the client/server model does what.

Now we have a better understanding of the client/server model, we need to ask ourselves "How do we write the code?"

Writing Web Pages for Client/Server Models

Basically, there are two types of code, or **scripts**:

- The client-side scripts
- The server-side scripts

This is possibly the hardest thing for the beginner to get their head around. In one long page, we're going to incorporate code that's to run *on the server* and code that's to run *on the client* (that is, the viewer's computer and browser).

To confuse matters even more, we're going to include code that is **JavaScript** and also code that is **VBScript** (**V**isual **B**asic **Script**)! You may now be a bit confused, but I promise that it will all make sense as we take you through this little by little.

So, we have client-side scripts and server-side scripts, but what do they do and what's the difference?

Client-side Scripting

As you might already be aware, there are two main giants amongst internet browsers: Netscape's Navigator and Microsoft's Internet Explorer. Historically, it's been very difficult to develop software for both platforms.

When browsers started out, there really only was client-side scripting; that is to say everything that happened in your browser window was performed by the browser 'on the fly'. Therefore, the interpretation of the code was strictly down to the browser. This can lead to all kinds of problems. Namely, something that looked fantastic when designed and run on Internet Explorer would look dreadful or not run at all on Netscape. We still have this problem to a lesser degree today, but more on that later.

The other real problem with having everything client-side is that as time progressed we came to need ever more powerful browsers to make the most of the Web. This became impractical. The main ethos behind HTML was that pages could be viewed by anyone, anywhere, regardless of monitor size, modem, user preferences, etc. With the advent of laptops and mobile phones this universality became more important than ever. Therefore, the power moved away from the browser and back onto the server.

If you've used Dreamweaver or FrontPage before, you've probably seen client-side scripts. Basically, these are small routines (tasks) that are executed by your browser. For example, a routine that changes an image when you move your mouse over it (a rollover effect) – that's run client-side by your browser. It is completely browser-specific; if your browser doesn't understand the script, it will ignore it, report a script error, or probably just try and make do without it.

There are a couple of points to note about client-side scripting.

Firstly, people can easily see your code (like we did earlier with the View Source command). Because code is executed on the browser, it's not secure; you can't hide the code because the user's computer has to receive it and read it to be able to display the page at all. This isn't a huge problem, though, because most client-side scripts are public domain anyhow, and the sharing of these scripts is part of the fun.

More importantly, JavaScript is the only language supported on the client-side by all browsers. Internet Explorer can understand JavaScript and VBScript, but Navigator can only read JavaScript (without a plugin). Therefore, while it's perfectly acceptable to purely develop in VBScript for a corporate intranet that only uses Internet Explorer, it would be foolish to use VBScript client-side scripts for web applications, since about 15-20% of your users will be using Netscape.

You'll probably have had experience of building web pages using static HTML. You might also have used DHTML (Dynamic HTML) for whizzy effects; you may even have used a little JavaScript for things like rollover buttons, sound effects and reveal/hide effects. All of these are great, and as you've been using Dreamweaver you should be familiar with these techniques, whether you coded them or they were coded for you with 'wizards' like Dreamweaver's behaviors.

Client/Server Concepts

Like we said, these client-side scripts are all acted on by your browser. However, in the same sense that we need to write in HTML and Javascript for our browsers, we need a language to program our server.

And just to confuse the issue, we have a choice.

Server-side Scripting

> *This next section will introduce you to a mind-numbing array of new buzzwords and technologies – don't panic, we'll end the section with the best choices for our requirements and for the rest of the book. However, we feel it's important to make you aware of your other choices.*

UltraDev supports three different application server models. Each server computer will run its specific operating system, plus the additional software that makes it a *web server* (that is, an NT computer only becomes a web server with the additional IIS software). This software will allow it to understand a specific language and serve out the pages accordingly (that is, an NT web server-enabled box will understand ASP but not WebSphere).

Let's take a look at the three application servers and how they are built.

ASP Servers

ASP (**Active Server Pages**) is the Microsoft solution for hosting dynamic web pages. ASP servers run Windows NT or 2000 Servers and in addition **Internet Information Server** (**IIS**) – which controls the directory structure of the web pages, including who has access to what, in a very similar way to your Windows Explorer. If you have access to a Windows NT Server, you'll find IIS in the Options pack, as a free add-on. You can, of course, download it too from the Microsoft web site.

One alternative is **Personal Web Server** (**PWS**) – which you may already be running – which is essentially a scaled down version of IIS. Effectively, your computer is now acting as the client and the server. It can be confusing, but just think of PWS as a totally separate computer – the server. Try to imagine it in another room, or another country! There's no difference between uploading your web pages to your PWS and uploading to your ISP over your telephone or any other web server on the Internet. When you then look at your work via a browser on your computer, you are passing the same information in the same way as you do when you look at any other page or site on the Internet.

Although the page itself is an ASP page, we can choose to code these pages in VBScript or JavaScript or even both! More about this later, but for now, don't worry too much about it, because we're going to use VBScript on the server as it's generally more user-friendly.

JSP Servers

JSP stands for **JavaServer Pages** and effectively does the same thing as ASP. The only difference is that, instead of IIS, the hardware and operating system must be able to run a server such as IBM's WebSphere, Jrun (from Allaire, which Macromedia has just acquired) or any application that supports JSP.

JSP pages use **XML** (e**X**tensible **M**ark up **L**anguage) tags and scriptlets written in the Java programming language to create the server-side logic that generates the content for the page, in much the same way as ASP pages use VBScript.

ColdFusion Servers

These are any servers that run Allaire's **ColdFusion** 4.0 or later. Again, the theory is similar; the language itself is different. ColdFusion uses a tag-based, server scripting language designed for programming web applications. It's a compiled language, which makes it faster than other languages in theory (however a 33k dial-up modem will soon kill that off!) ColdFusion's Mark up Language (CFML), allows coders who are familiar with HTML to learn quickly how to build dynamic database-driven web sites. ColdFusion supports tags for accessing databases, manipulating files, managing e-mail, transferring XML, and much more. Finally, ColdFusion is a great tool for development teams – programmers can create custom tags that designers can easily use to extend their development skills.

Server Choices

Before we look at the particular server that we chose to use, let's have a recap of all these options:

- **ASP (Active Server Pages)**: a dynamically created web page – usually written in VBScript (can be JavaScript).

- **Internet Information Server**: runs on NT platforms (including 2000) – turns the NT platform into a web server.

- **Personal Web Server**: cut down version of IIS – will run on Windows 95/98/ME – fine for testing but not scalable.

- **VBScript**: based on the Visual Basic programming language, but much simpler.

- **JSP (JavaServer Pages)**: platform-independent alternative to ASP, but using the Java language.

- **JavaScript**: a scripting language developed by Netscape – can be used on the client or the server.

Client/Server Concepts 2

- **ColdFusion**: originally created by Allaire, but Macromedia now own this development toolset designed to integrate databases and web pages.

- **CMFL**: ColdFusion Mark up Language (CFML) – the tag based language of Cold Fusion.

The Choice is Made

We stated at the start of this section that there was a lot of technologies and choices to take in. Well, relax ... We're going to make all those choices for you, because at this stage there really is only one logical choice for you. For better or worse, and maybe unsurprisingly, we're opting for the Microsoft model.

We're going to be looking at:

- An ASP Server

- Running IIS or PWS

- Using VBScript on the server

VBScript is very user friendly and easy to read, so the novice can understand it a lot more easily than JavaScript. More importantly though for us, it's *not* case-sensitive, so it thankfully offers far more forgiving error-handling!

Due to the nature and popularity of the Visual Basic suite, there's a myriad of information available on the subject of VBScript – books, web sites, discussion forums, etc.. The pool of resources available is massive, but a good place to start is www.asptoday.com.

Currently one of the most popular models to use is:

- **Server Model**: NT/2000 running IIS

- **Server Script**: VBScript

- **Client Script**: Javascript

We're sure you're going to meet many passionate Cold Fusion developers, as well as JSP lovers, but for the sake of clarity, we'll continue the rest of the book with the most popular choice. Just because it's more popular doesn't necessarily make our ASP/Windows option the best choice, but, due to the differences in code syntax, it would just be impossible to include all server models in this book. The choice we've made is a good one, though, and should you wish to change at a later stage, the theory remains fundamentally the same.

Foundation Dreamweaver UltraDev 4

Just remember, it's beyond the scope of this book to teach you how to become a proficient ASP coder – but we should familiarise ourselves with what an ASP page looks like. In the next chapter, we'll be looking at some basic hand-coding techniques. Later, we'll study ways to change the code generated by UltraDev to get even better results for our specific needs.

> *The good news is that UltraDev will create lean, fast code that's in the right place, in the right language and without speling misdakes!*

Let's have a look a page of UltraDev-generated ASP code and see if we can work out what is doing what.

Inside the Code

Go back to the insert page we've created within UltraDev and look at the code it generated for us. Switch to Code View (by pressing the button in the top left hand corner) and you'll see something similar to the screenshot below:

Take a few minutes to scroll up and down the code, and see if there is anything familiar to you there. Note how, further down the page, the HTML code comes into play.

Client/Server Concepts

As we said earlier, it's not the aim of this book to make you into an ASP guru, but let's look at some of the basics of our ASP page.

Go to View>Code View Options>Line Numbers to turn on the line numbering, and scroll back up to line 1 to take a look ...

```
<%@LANGUAGE="VBSCRIPT"%>
```

Well, not particularly difficult to fathom out, but this is telling the server that the language we're about to use is VBScript (you can actually mix and match any supported language during the page, as long as you always tell the server what's coming next).

More interesting, perhaps, are the tags around the statement.

Just like in HTML, we need an opening and closing tag. In this case, we use:

```
<%
```

This tells the server "This is now ASP Code". The @ is simply a way of specifying the language, whilst the %> at the end of the line closes the ASP coded part of our script.

You'lll become very familiar with this line of code as you make your way through the world of ASP coding. It's actually the shortened way of writing the following:

```
<SCRIPT LANGUAGE = VBSCRIPT RUNAT = SERVER>
```

... Asp script here ...

```
</SCRIPT>
```

This does exactly the same as our one-line version. There's no need to specify where to run the code, as the default is SERVER. Also, using <% instead of </SCRIPT> has become more popular due to it being easier to read and quicker to type!

So far so good...

The next line should read:

```
<!–#include file="../Connections/KoolKards.asp"–>
```

As we've closed off the previous ASP code section, the server will know this is basic HTML and pass it to the client accordingly. As a point of interest, this include file is how UltraDev stores our connection to the database we made in Chapter 1. Rather than repeating the complex connection string we made with the wizard on each page, UltraDev stores it away in a separate ASP page, which it calls as and when it needs it.

Foundation Dreamweaver UltraDev 4

You can find the file that contains the connection string in the Connections folder under the KoolKards directory. With this method UltraDev is potentially saving you hours of coding, because if your Database Administrator made some changes to where your database lives, you would otherwise have to go and alter every page in your site that used the database.

On the next line, we can see the little ASP opening tag again...

```
<%
```

...the difference being that, this time, it doesn't close again straight away. Therefore, the server now expects a chunk of VBScript code until it meets the closing `%>` sign.

The next line begins with a **comment**, or **remark**:

```
' *** Edit Operations: declare variables
```

A comment is a note placed in the text that maybe describes what a particular string does or makes a personal remark about it. Comments are completely bypassed by the browser so you can make them say anything you want. To place a comment into your code you need to prefix your note with a simple `'`. The asterisks are there just to make it stand out more ... they are totally optional.

The following line starts with an example of something you'll see an awful lot:

```
MM_somename
```

The MM stands for Macromedia – and that's a pretty good way of telling what special code routines have been automatically generated for you by UltraDev.

Now, don't panic we're not going to go through each line – we would be here all day. But slowly scroll down again, looking in particular for the opening and closing of the server-side code. This is all the code you don't see when you View Source from your browser.

When you've finished browsing the code, look at what's generated for the `display_customer_records.asp` page. Scroll down towards the very end of the page. Look at how towards the end of the HTML code we reintroduce some more server-side VBScript:

```
<%
While ((Repeat1__numRows <> 0) AND (NOT rs.EOF))
%>
   <tr>
   <td width="159"><font face="Arial, Helvetica, sans-serif"
➥  size="2"><%=(rs.Fields.Item("contact_name").Value)%>
```

Client/Server Concepts

```
    </font></td>
    <td width="158"><font face="Arial, Helvetica, sans-
    serif"size="2"><%=(rs.Fields.Item("email_address").Value)%>
    </font></td>
    <td width="99"><font face="Arial, Helvetica, sans-
    serif"size="2">
<%=(rs.Fields.Item("phone").Value)%></font></td>
    </tr>
    <%
    Repeat1__index=Repeat1__index+1
    Repeat1__numRows=Repeat1__numRows-1
    rs.MoveNext()
Wend
%>
```

This routine displays the details of each user in the database, using a hybrid of a VBScript WHILE ... WEND loop and HTML code. A WHILE ... WEND loop is basically one way of saying "Repeat this section of code WHILE a condition is true and WHEN it's not true, END."

This is how we can mix our VBScript with our HTML to produce dynamic web pages.

> *Remember: all this code was automatically generated by UltraDev – don't panic – you're not expected to learn all this now!*

Extensions and Behaviors

Thankfully, as we've already seen, UltraDev is capable of writing an awful lot of code for us. Those clever people at Macromedia have created many reusable, inbuilt code routines intended to save us an awful lot of time – which is the whole point of buying UltraDev in the first place.

The little pieces of pre-written code are called **behaviors**, which were first seen in Dreamweaver and remain here in UltraDev. If you're from a Dreamweaver background, you'll be more than familiar with the concept, but in case you're not, here's a quick overview.

Behaviors are pre-written by Macromedia or a third party and they perform a certain function on your web page. In most circumstances, you'll be expected to provide a couple of properties for the behavior to work properly, but no coding knowledge will be required.

A simple example would be a behavior that makes one image visible when your mouse hovers over another image. If you wanted this function, you would select the behavior from the list, apply it and type in the names of the two images on your page. That would be all you need to do – the code would be written to your page, and we could even edit that code directly.

In the simple example above, we've talked about a client-side behavior. These types of 'visual' routines were very common in Dreamweaver, and UltraDev maintains them for all your design needs.

However, for our purposes, we'll be more interested in the server-side behaviors, which in UltraDev are simply known as **server behaviors**. The principle is exactly the same except the routines will affect something happening on the server rather than the client (hopefully, you're beginning to see why we needed to learn the difference!).

Examples of server behaviors would be "Move to last record in my database when I click button x." or "Delete current record when I click y.".

Open the insert page that we created in Chapter 1. If it's not already open, press CTRL+F9 to open the Server Behavior panel. You can see that UltraDev has inserted a server behavior for us:

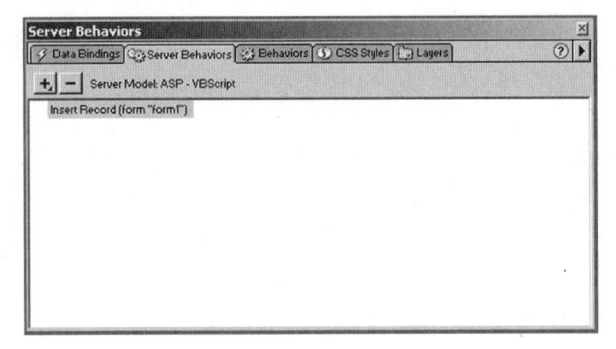

If you now double-click the server behaviour called Insert Record, we can change the properties and attributes easily. So, for example, if we want to change the page the form redirects to, we can do it quickly and easily here:

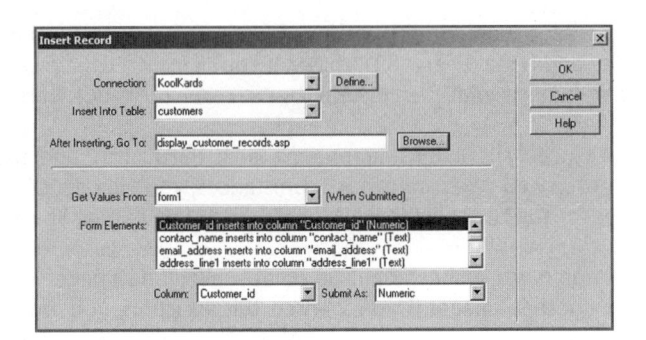

Client/Server Concepts

As you'll find out later, we can have multiple behaviors on a page, and start to build some really powerful ASP pages without in-depth coding knowledge.

Perhaps the most impressive feature of UltraDev is the ability to turn your own code into behaviors to reuse again and again. Behaviors can be packaged into **extensions**, which can be downloaded and installed using the **Extension Manager**. There is an ever-expanding wealth of behaviors for you to download and use, with one of the largest resources on the Macromedia Exchange site:

http://www.macromedia.com/exchange/ultradev

You may wish to take a look at just how many behaviors are currently available. Some of them may seem a bit baffling at first, but you can feel good about the fact that if you find yourself stuck in the future, trying to do a particular task in UltraDev for which you don't have the right coding knowledge, there's a very good chance someone has written a behavior that will do the job for you.

This idea of sharing behaviors is one of the key selling points of UltraDev. It's known as **extensibility** – the power to keep adding new bits to your software. As we'll see later on, the UltraDev Shopping Cart (written by the multi-talented Rick Crawford) is nothing more than a series of very well written and powerful server behaviors. Of course, sooner or later you'll want to do something that someone else hasn't already done and that's why we're learning to hand code! And once you've created your own pet routines, you can turn them into your own behaviors!

After a while, expect to find your copy of UltraDev has many more 'add-ons' than when you first loaded it up. For this reason, Macromedia has provided a plug-in called the Extension Manager – a handy way of keeping track of what extensions/behaviors you have on your system. You need to install this on your system before you can use downloaded extensions. The Extension Mananger is part of the Ultradev 4 installation and can be accessed by choosing Manage Extensions from the Commands menu. From the Extension Manager you can add, remove, copy and generally manage your individual extensions.

Towards the end of this book, we'll be looking at how to write your own server behaviors. It's not the easiest thing in the world to start with, but, as your coding techniques grow, you may find that you write a behavior that the rest of the world needs to know about. And although most behaviors are on a free-for-all basis, you can even think about selling some of the more complex behaviors if they're really good!

But to bring us crashing back down to earth we are going to look at importing an extension from the Internet and then installing it using our Extension Manager. We'll then use our new, custom behaviors in Chapter 3.

Open your Internet browser and point it at: http://www.friendsofed.com/code.html

Find the extension file and download to your hard drive and save it somewhere safe.

Foundation Dreamweaver UltraDev 4

> Now might be a good time to create a separate folder on your hard drive called UltraDev Downloads. It's pretty good practice to download all your files into the folder, then extract and import them into UltraDev. This way you can make a backup of all your critical UltraDev files quite easily. It's a very good idea to make regular backups of your downloads once you start using UltraDev heavily. It can be heartbreaking to lose your collection of extensions and behaviors and, due to the nature of the 'shareware' of a lot of the extensions, it can become really difficult to track them all down again. A reinstall of UltraDev is easy – but a reinstall of a year or so's extensions is a tough job. You have been warned!

Once downloaded, just open the file as you would any other (double-click), click Accept at the disclaimer and you should be presented with the following message:

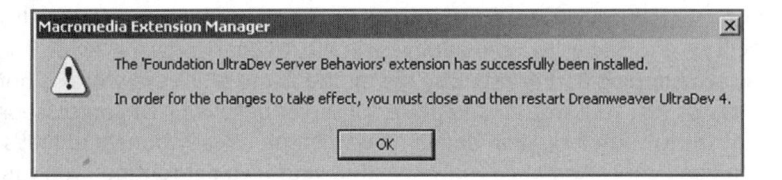

Macromedia Extension Manager

The 'Foundation UltraDev Server Behaviors' extension has successfully been installed.

In order for the changes to take effect, you must close and then restart Dreamweaver UltraDev 4.

OK

You'll have to restart UltraDev before you can access your new extension. For the moment, click OK and the new extension will appear in your Extension Manager list (Commands > Manage Extensions):

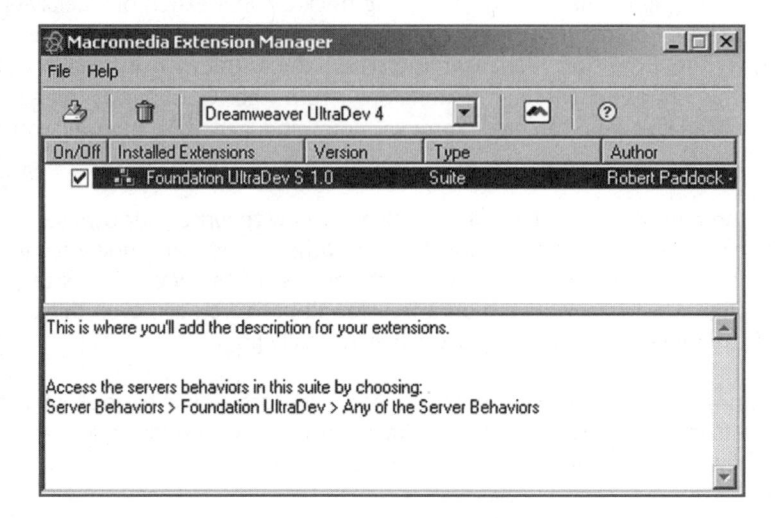

Macromedia Extension Manager

On/Off	Installed Extensions	Version	Type	Author
✓	Foundation UltraDev S	1.0	Suite	Robert Paddock

This is where you'll add the description for your extensions.

Access the servers behaviors in this suite by choosing:
Server Behaviors > Foundation UltraDev > Any of the Server Behaviors

Client/Server Concepts 2

Now close and restart UltraDev, and open any page.

We can check that our new server behavior is registered with UltraDev by bringing up the Server Behavior panel (CTRL+F9) and clicking the + button to drop down the list of behaviors.

You'll find a list entry Foundation UltraDev, which will in turn open not one, but five new server behaviors for us to use in the next chapter. Don't select any of the behaviors yet, close your page and prepare for our next session.

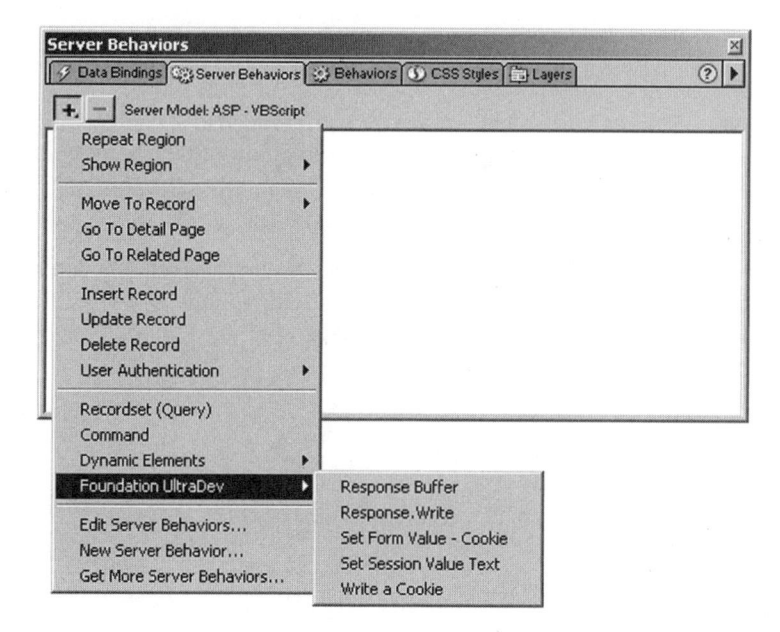

As you can see, being able to extend UltraDev like this is just great. There are many very talented developers currently working on all manner of powerful, reusable extensions for us all to deploy in our web pages. Hopefully, by the end of this book, you'll be ready to add your name to the list!

Summary

So, what have we learned? Lots. I expect you'll be relieved to move on from this chapter. However, as we said at the start, an understanding of client/server interactions – where the code executes and what takes place – is massively important. We've looked at:

- Writing scripts (code routines) on the client side and the server side.

- Client-side scripts can be seen using the View Source command, are usually written in JavaScript, and include rollover images and text effects.

- Server-side scripting offers greater choice – including ASP, JSP, and CFML, but we chose to write our server-side scripts using ASP servers and the user-friendlier VBScript.

- In ASP pages, the server constructs the HTML code depending on instructions from the ASP code, and returns it for display on the client.

- We had a glimpse of some ASP code and saw how it is distinguishable from HTML, and also learned how to spot Macromedia's pre-written behaviors in the code.

- Server behaviors are pre-written codes which can perform functions such as inserting a record or redirecting a page, and they also save us a lot of time!

- UltraDev is extensible – meaning it can be added to and extended by downloading new behaviors from http://www.macromedia.com/exchange/ultradev and other third-party sites.

In the next chapter we'll be looking at some common server ASP commands, and – with a lot more 'hands-on' examples – we should complete our understanding of the fundamentals of creating basic dynamic pages.

Client/Server Concepts 2

kool kards

3 Objects

What we'll cover in this chapter:

- How to use **HTML** forms
- What an **object** is
- Our first sight of the **Response** and **Request** objects
- **Cookies** – what they are and what we can do with them

Foundation Dreamweaver UltraDev 4

Throughout this chapter, we'll be working with HTML forms. HTML forms are just like the form that you might fill in with a pen to apply for a bank account or answer a questionnaire. From a user's point of view, you'll spend time filling in forms in just about any dynamic web application. Registering with an online store? Booking a flight? – first name, surname, date of birth, credit card, yawn...

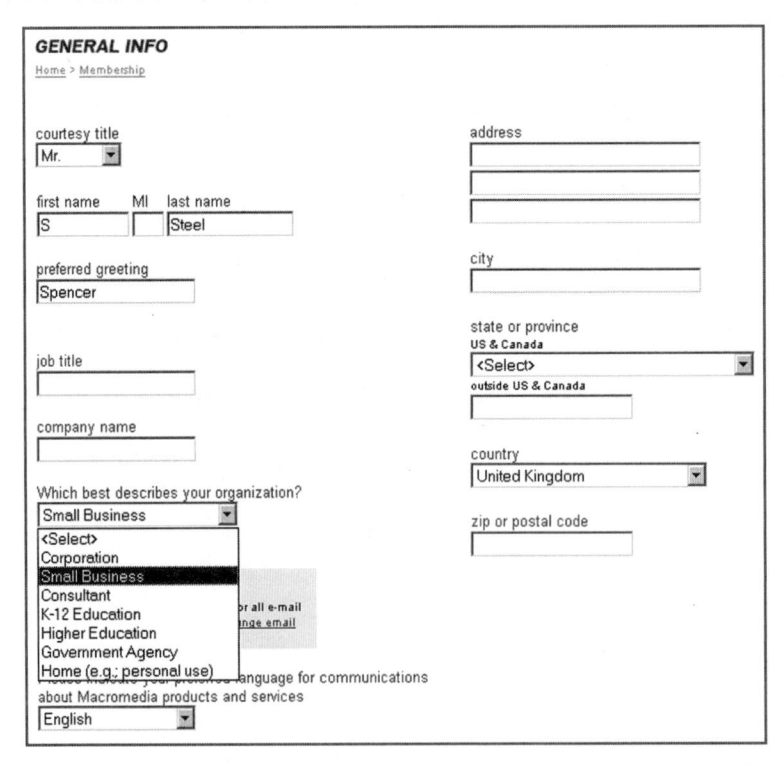

Each form in UltraDev can consist of any amount of edit boxes, radio buttons, drop-down boxes, check boxes or any of the other common form elements. The form elements in UltraDev are located on the Objects toolbar – that's the one on the left of your screen by default, and you can use CTRL+F2 to toggle it on or off. You'll need to select Forms from the little drop-down menu at the top of it:

Objects 3

You can build forms from this toolbar simply by dragging the form elements onto your page in the same way that you create graphics on your web page in UltraDev. Let's make sure that we've got the hang of this before we move on. We'll create a simple form that allows the user to enter their name and click a submit button. We'll use the form later on in the chapter to print this information out in another page.

Creating an HTML Form

1. Create a new UltraDev file (File > New). Save it as `login.asp`.

2. Make sure that you can see the Form Object panel we showed you a moment ago, and that you have the Show Code and Design Views button selected so we can see everything that's going on:

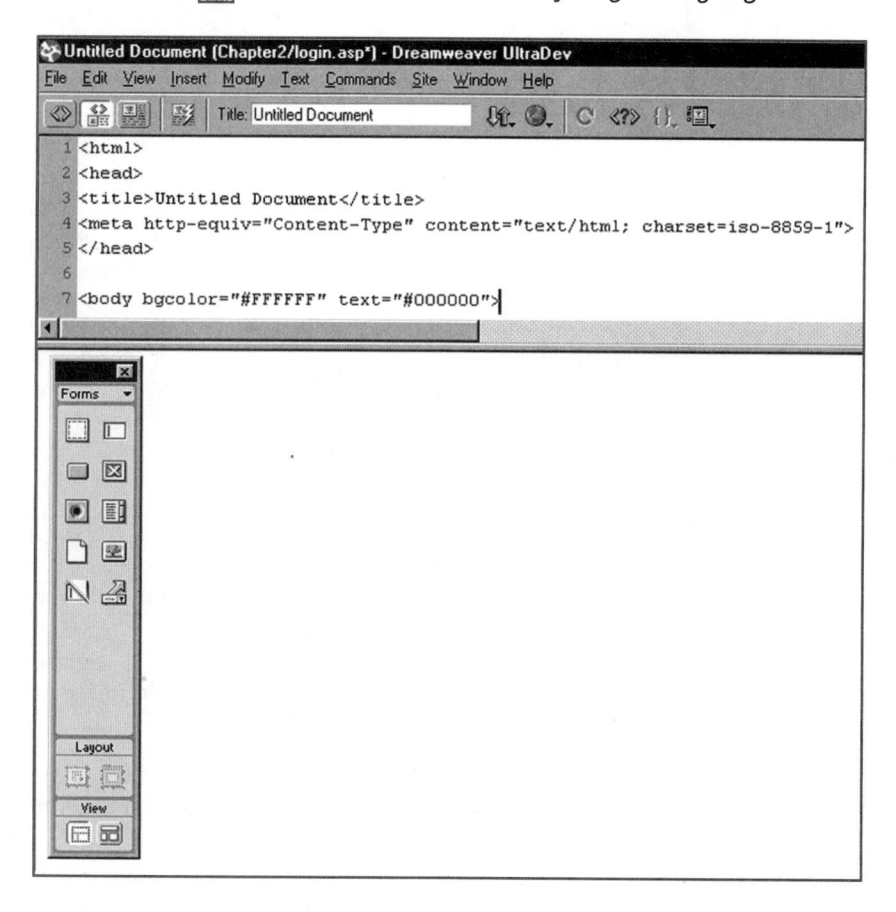

3. Click on the Insert Form button on the Objects panel. You'll get two red lines that define the form border:

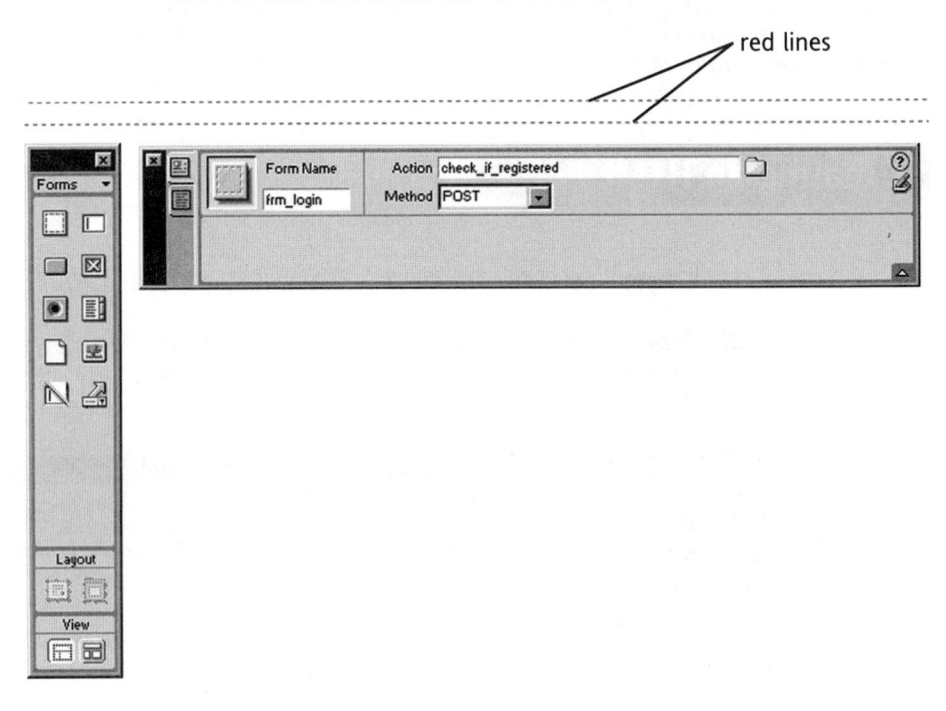

   red lines

4. Click once inside the two red lines and, if it's not already there, bring up the Properties Inspector (use CTRL+F3, or Windows > Properties). Enter frm_login under Form Name.

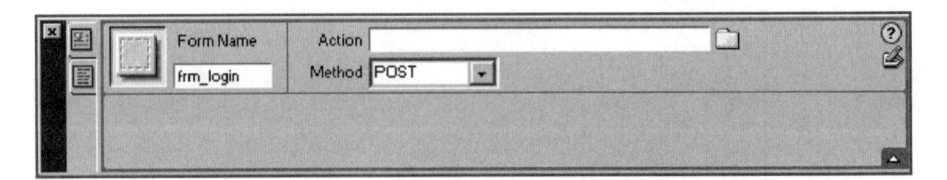

5. In the Action box to the right, enter check_if_registered.asp. This is the page that UltraDev will go to after the form has been submitted, which we'll create later in the chapter.

6. Make sure that your cursor is between the red lines. Click on the Insert Text Field button under the Forms section of the Objects Panel to insert a text field into your form.

| Objects | 3 |

7. Using the Properties Panel, rename the text field name. Enter an initial value, or in UltraDev's abbreviation, an Init Val of enter name here.

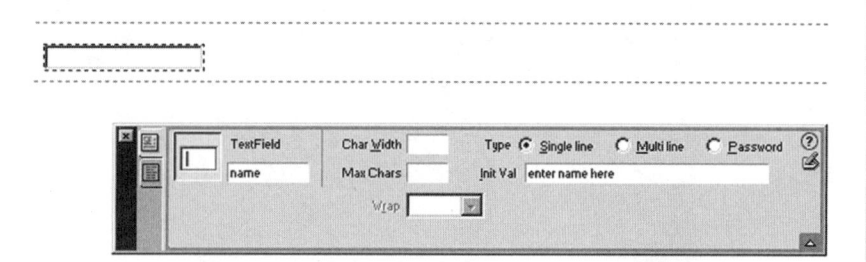

8. Make sure your cursor is just after the edit box you've just inserted and click on the Insert Button option in the Objects window's Forms section:

9. Enter login_submit under Button Name. Leave the Label as Submit, as most people will be familiar with a Submit button. Make sure that the Submit Form option is checked:

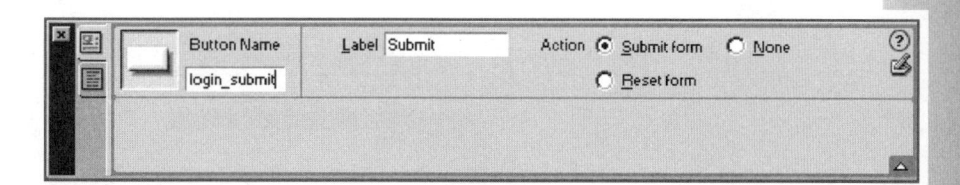

Foundation Dreamweaver UltraDev 4

10. We're going to use a template to apply the standard KoolKards look to our page. From the main Menu on your page, select Modify > Templates > Apply Template to Page:

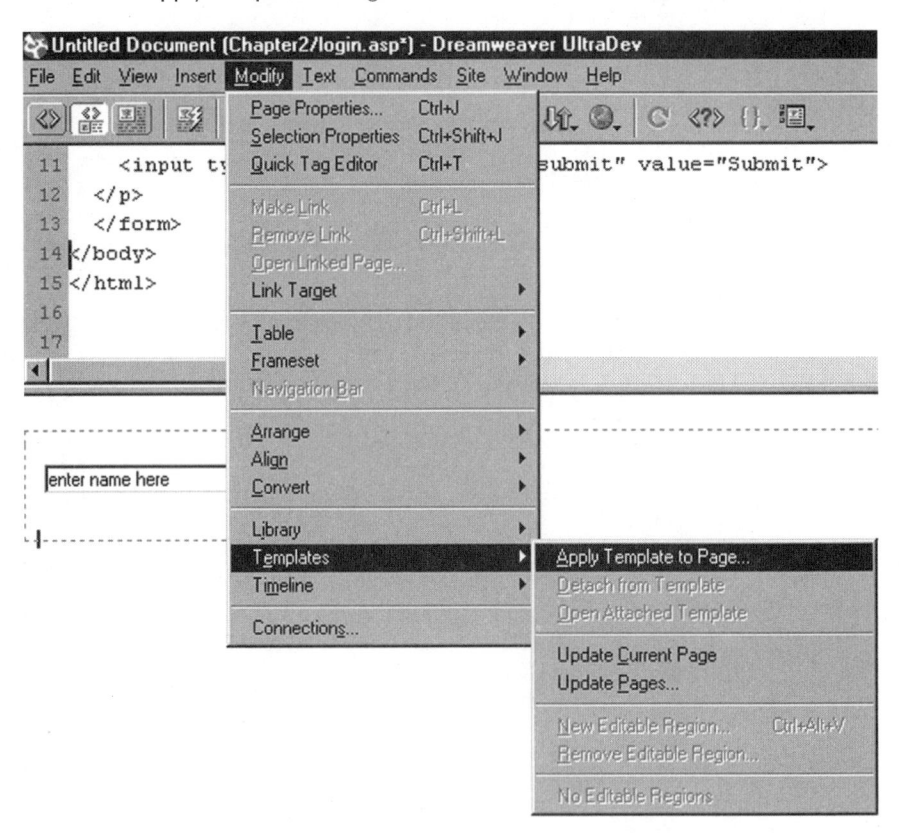

11. You should see the files listed in the Select Template window as they are below. If you don't, then you need to go away and check that the two template files you have (`master.dwt` and `admin.dwt`) are in the same directory as your other KoolKards files:

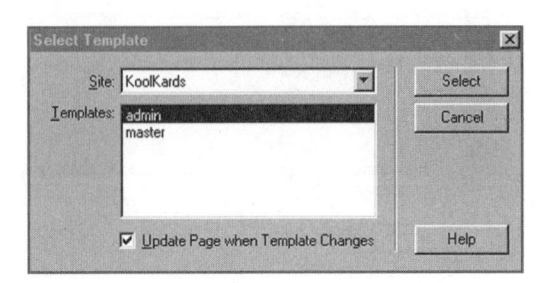

Objects 3

12. Select the master template. You'll probably be asked to choose where you want to place your page within the template. If this happens, choose main work area and you're away:

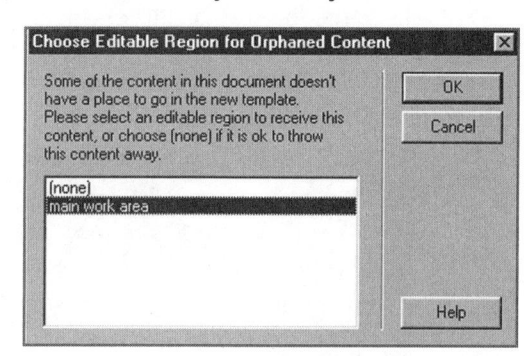

You've just created your first UltraDev form. We'll be covering templates later, but you can see how using the template applied the nice KoolKards look to your form. If you've already used Dreamweaver before coming to UltraDev, this is where you have a bit of an advantage. If you don't feel quite confident with all of this, try doing something else – put a table in using the Common menu in the Objects panel and move the Submit button below it for example.

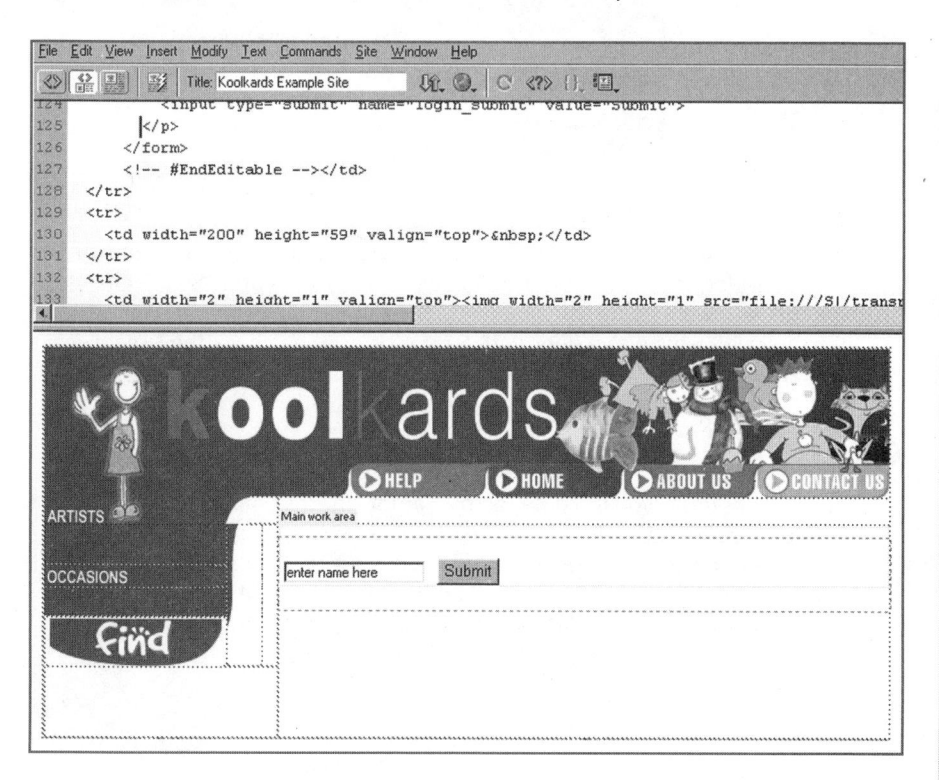

13. Test your page by pressing F12 and previewing it in your browser. Enter your name and click OK. You will be taken to another page we have created for you which returns your name. If this doesn't happen, then check the location of the `check_if_registered.asp` file that you referred to when setting up your form earlier. It should be in the same directory as your `login.asp` file. As always, there are completed versions of these files in the download file for this chapter.

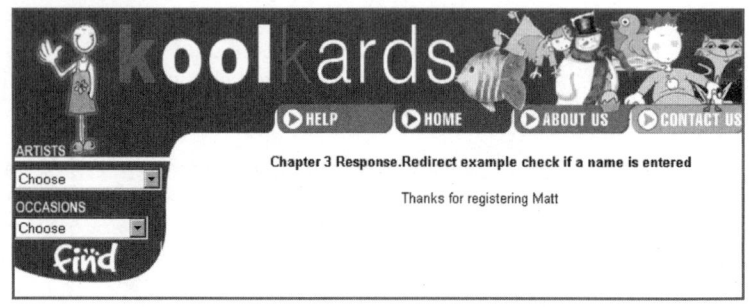

Next, we'll look at the way that the second page 'calls' your name out of the first page. We've provided most of the forms needed for this chapter as downloads, as we didn't think that you were going to enjoy doing the same thing over and over again. If you're still not happy with what we've done with HTML forms, then check the Dreamweaver Help files in UltraDev for more and come back – we'll be waiting.

Objects

Object is a term you'll come across a lot in the modern computing world. Let's take a brief look at what an object is. Let's compare an object to a normal, everyday object – say, any given shiny CD. The object is a CD and it could be used in several ways – it could be a rewritable CD that contains data, it could be a music CD, it could be a DVD.

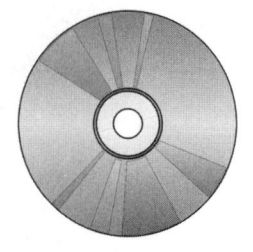

Objects 3

The Object has **properties**, which might look like:

```
CD.Type = "Music"
CD.Artist = "Papa Roach"
```

Or even:

```
CD.Type = "CD-RWR"
CD.Contents="image files"
```

How does this translate into computing terms? Even if you do own a CD-writer, the chances are that you're lazy like me and you're far more likely to go down to the shops and buy "New Fantastic Tunes vol. 147" than create your own compilation from scratch. It's just like this in the computer world, where most computer languages have resusable objects for us to put to use, each of which have their own properties.

For example, if you used the inbuilt scripting ability in Access (called Access VBA), then this would be a form with an **object** called MyButton, (which is a clickable button), with the backcolor **property** set to vbgreen:

MyButton.backcolor=vbgreen

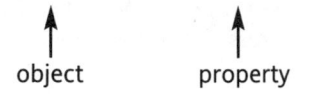

   ↑   ↑
object   property

We didn't have to create .backcolor, it was already there as part of Access VBA. This is a simple example of how we use objects and their properties, and there are a variety of objects available to you depending on what script or language you use in UltraDev. Active Server Pages, which we're using, includes several built in objects that allow you to extend your coding and we're going to be introducing the most common objects over the next couple of chapters.

The Response and Request Objects

First, let's look at one of the most commonly used server commands, the **Response** and **Request Objects**.

They have a number of uses, depending on what **properties** you give them, but they are two of the most powerful server commands you will come across. **Request** lets you request information from the server ('show the user some data') and **Response** lets you tell the server to do something ('go to a different page'). These commands sit at the heart of all ASP coding and we'll soon be using them, so let's take a look at a few examples of the Response object.

3   Foundation Dreamweaver UltraDev 4

For example, `Response.Write` in its simplest form means 'write something on the screen for me'. This could be worked out by the server, as would happen with the results from a database search. `Response.Redirect` would tell the server to 'take the user to another page' and `Response.End` would just say 'stop running the code here'.

You should be able to see the server behaviors created for this chapter by looking in the same place as we did in the last chapter. We've provided these server behaviors so that you'll see how powerful extending UltraDev can be and so we can explore these Response and Request objects without having to know the exact code syntax, but still gain a full understanding of how they work.

Using a Server Behavior

Let's start with a simple example of how we can make the server do something for us.

1. The first thing we need to do is create a blank web page to work with, so create a new page and call it `Foundation_Examples1.asp`.

2. In our Server Behaviors window, select the Response.Write behaviors from the Foundation UltraDev menu (press CTRL+F9 to toggle the window on and off):

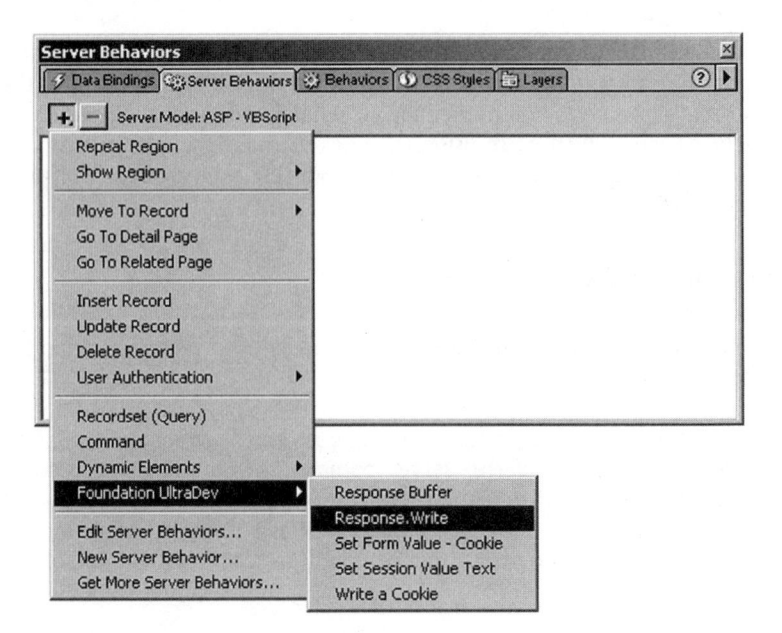

Objects   3

3. You will be presented with a dialogue box. As you've probably guessed, we're just going to tell our server to print, or 'write', a message on the screen, so enter Hello World! and then click OK.

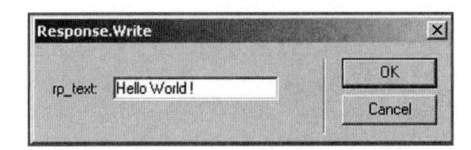

Take a look at your Code Inspector, and the code that the server behavior has generated. You'll see from the very first line – LANGUAGE="VBSCRIPT" – that this code has been written in VBScript. This is because the Response.Write behavior was written in VBScript.

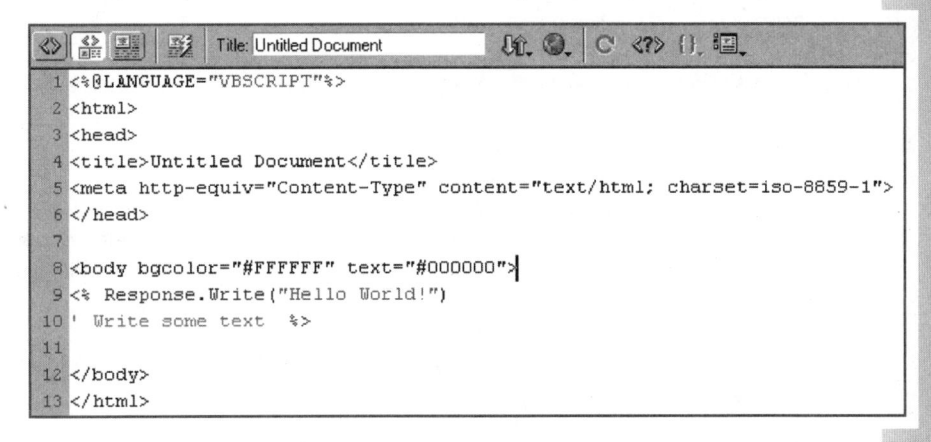

```
1 <%@LANGUAGE="VBSCRIPT"%>
2 <html>
3 <head>
4 <title>Untitled Document</title>
5 <meta http-equiv="Content-Type" content="text/html; charset=iso-8859-1">
6 </head>
7
8 <body bgcolor="#FFFFFF" text="#000000">
9 <% Response.Write("Hello World!")
10 ' Write some text %>
11
12 </body>
13 </html>
```

We could have typed this straight in without using a behavior at all, but this way we don't have to worry about the syntax.

4. Save your page in your chapter folder and preview it from your web site by pressing F12.

Here's our screen – not very exciting, but don't write it off just yet. We'll use the Response.Write object a lot for testing and debugging as we move onwards on our UltraDev journey.

We've used one of our server behaviors, looked at the code, tested it in a browser and noted the results. Now we'll look at some of the other functions in the same way.

Response.Redirect

`Response.Redirect` does exactly what you would expect it to – it redirects the user to another web page. You've already seen an example of this in Chapter 1 when we were creating our Insert Record page. There, you were asked which page you would like the browser to take you to afterwards. In a typical web application you are constantly being redirected around automatically.

A common example of redirection is the 'Log In' application. We'll be looking at this in depth in a later chapter but the redirect is very important, since it is this function that moves you either into your account or to a 'Log In Failed' page if your password is incorrect.

The way that we use `Response.Redirect` is like this:

```
<% Response.Redirect ("AnyPage.asp") %>
```

In order to avoid potential problems, `Response.Redirect` can only be used before any text is sent to the browser. Place some graphics or text above your `Response.Redirect` command and you'd get the following error when viewing the page in your browser:

```
Response object error 'ASP 0156 : 80004005'
Header Error
<full path of file>, line #

The HTTP headers are already written to the client browser.
Any HTTP header modifications must be made before writing
page content.
```

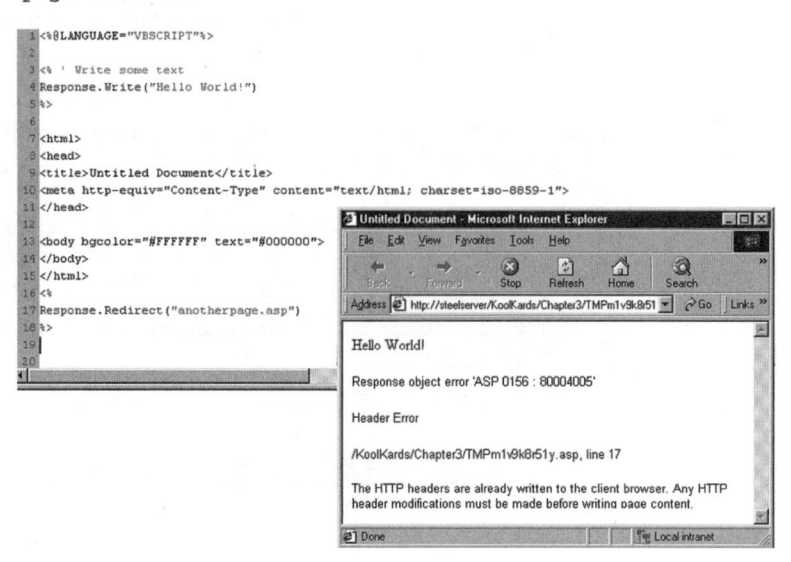

Objects 3

It's worth taking a mental note of the error message, as most people experience it at some point in their lives.

Using the Response.Redirect Behavior

1. Open `login.asp` again and re-test it in your browser (with F12) but this time, don't enter a name. It will still work.

   This isn't great – we don't want people who don't give a name to progress any further. What we are going to create in our small example is a trap that redirects the user back to the login page if no value was entered. There are other ways of doing this, but this way will demonstrate our Redirect code nicely.

2. We need to add the 'trap' that assesses whether or not someone has entered their name in the second page, the `check_if_registered.asp` page. We're going to go to the second page, check for a name and go back to the first page if there isn't one. This will all happen so quickly that the user will never know they've switched pages if they do go back to the first page.

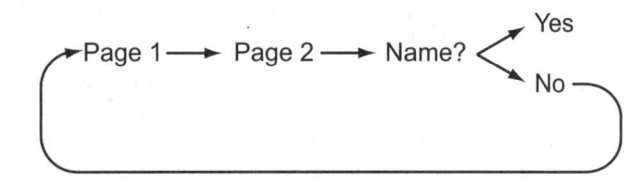

   ```
   ┌─ Page 1 ──→ Page 2 ──→ Name? ──→ Yes
   │                                └─→ No ─┐
   └─────────────────────────────────────────┘
   ```

   So, go to your Chapter 3 folder and open it up.

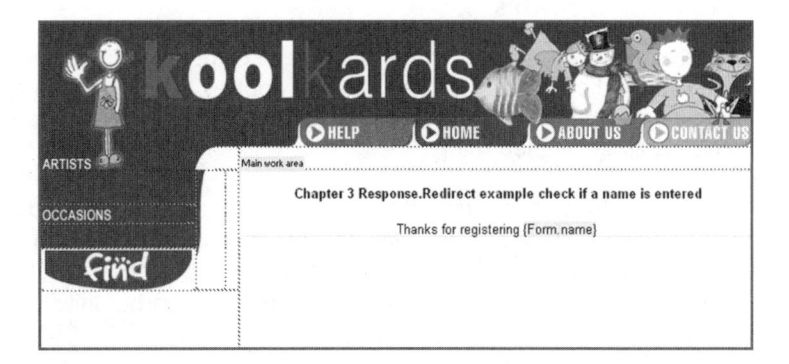

   ```
   koolkards
         ● HELP   ● HOME   ● ABOUT US   ● CONTACT US
   ARTISTS     Main work area
               Chapter 3 Response.Redirect example check if a name is entered
   OCCASIONS
                       Thanks for registering {Form.name}
      find
   ```

   Let's look at that blue {Form.name} block – the part that calls back your name. If you remember back to when we where designing our form, we called the text box from which the user enters their name – `name`.

3. Click on the blue {Form.name} to select it and look in your code view. You should see this:

```
<%= Request.Form("name") %>
```

What does this mean? `<%=` is a quick way of saying `Response.Write`. We're requesting information from the form on the previous page, and the content of the form element is our text box, called name. So, we're saying 'write the content of the form element name to the screen'.

4. We're going to add some ASP code to check if the user typed in their name in login.asp. If the user hasn't entered their name, we'll direct them back to the login page. We haven't created a redirect behavior for you here, so we're going to have to do this one from the beginning. Enter this code above the `<HTML>` tag at the top of the page.

```
<%
If (Request.Form("name")="") Then Response.Redirect
➥ ("login.asp")
%>
```

This says that if the value of the edit box called name on the form on the page called login is equal to nothing –""– then go back to the login page.

5. Now preview your page in your browser with F12. This time if you enter nothing, you should get redirected back to the login page. This won't be the last time you'll see `Response.Redirect` in the book, so make friends with it now.

Homemade Cookies

Cookies are small text files written to a user's computer by your web site, which can then be read by the server at a later date. As cookies are written on the client's computer, specific information can be saved for each user. This reduces the load on your web server, which is always a good thing.

For cookies to work properly the user must have cookies enabled on their browser, and most browsers have cookies switched on as a default value. If you're using Internet Explorer, you can go to Tools > Internet Options > General > Settings > View Files and look for the .txt files with Cookie: in them. This can be quite telling as to where your browser has been over the last few months.

Objects 3

Who uses cookies? Many e-commerce sites make extensive use of cookies to keep track of what a customer is ordering; or, as with Amazon, to save you logging in if you are a regular customer. Amazon also uses cookies to track a user's particular browsing habits. Their 'recommendations' use the cookie from your last visit to come up with similar titles.

Many non e-commerce sites use cookies to personalize their sites in the same way. Visit www.resourcematters.com and enter a search for ASP, view the results, close your browser and then reopen it. The jobs now listed will all be jobs related to ASP.

Cookies can be created, read and modified using client-side JavaScript code. The problem with doing things on the client-side is that, if we want to make decisions based upon the values in the cookies, it's very difficult. The cookies stay with the client, and this means that you can't use a database with the cookie. ASP, however, can create, read and modify cookies on the server side.

UltraDev provides all sorts of ways to read and use cookies but someone forgot to create a server behavior to create them. You'll find a number of cookie behaviors scattered around the Macromedia Exchange but before you go and search, we've come to the rescue and created the server behaviors you need to create simple cookies. Let's put on our oven gloves and make a cookie.

Making a Cookie

1. Open up the `Foundation_Examples1.asp` page we created earlier.

2. Open up the Server Behavior dialog box and look under the Foundation UltraDev menu for Write a Cookie. Select it.

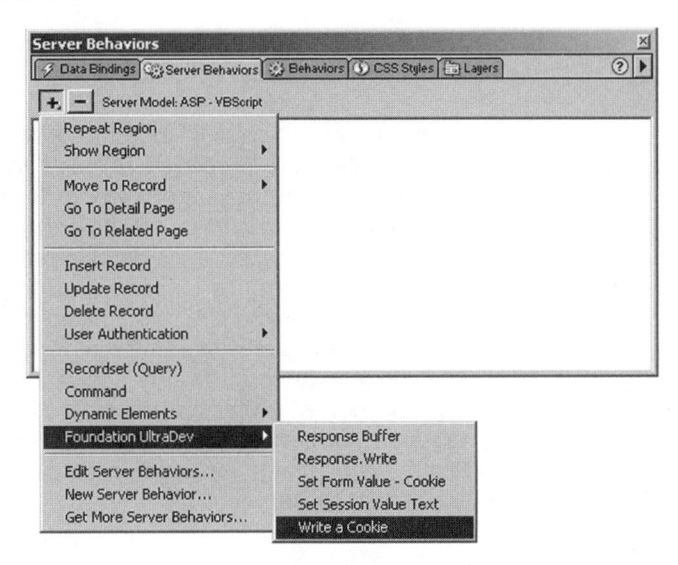

3. You should now see the Write a Cookie box. In the Cookie Name field, enter the name of the cookie as name, and under Cookie Value, type your own name:

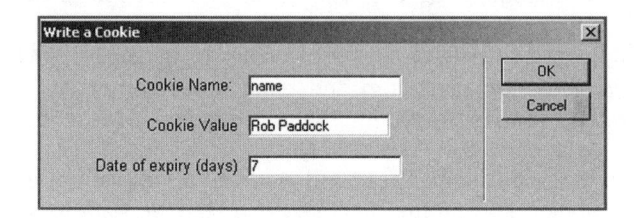

```
Write a Cookie
    Cookie Name:    name
    Cookie Value    Rob Paddock
    Date of expiry (days)   7
                                        OK
                                        Cancel
```

4. In the Date of Expiry field, enter 7. There are a few reasons why you want a cookie to expire. You may want to time them to expire along with special offers that last for say, 28 days from the user's first visit. You may want the cookie to expire after three months in order to take customers who haven't been back for a while through the login procedure again. Generally, it's good practice to keep your customer's cookie list clean if they don't come back to your site, so we've gone for 7 days.

5. Let's have a look at the code the behavior has written by looking at the code view:

```
<%@LANGUAGE="VBSCRIPT"%>
<%' Write a Cookie Robert Paddock (17/02/2001)
    Response.Cookies("Name") = "Rob Paddock"
    Response.Cookies("Name").Expires = Date + 7
%>
```

You can see very easily where the details we just entered in our dialog box have been placed in the code.

6. Save your file – we're going to come back to it in a moment. It's possible to add more properties to our cookie than the name and expiry value we've just given it. We have to do this manually, as our behavior only asks us about the properties we've just set. As an example, the default value of the **domain** property of a cookie is set to the domain that created it – in other words the only site that is allowed to read the cookie is the one that created it. You might want to alter this so that a sister site with a different domain name could read the cookie, and you could do this by adding the highlighted line below. Testing out whether a sister site accepts the cookie or not probably has to wait until you've finished this book and designed a whole string of successful sites – what's important is that you can see how you would add a property to your cookie.

Objects 3

```
<%@LANGUAGE="VBSCRIPT"%>
<%' Write a Cookie ver 1.0 robp
    Response.Cookies("name") = "Rob Paddock"
    Response.Cookies("name").Expires = Date + 7
    Response.Cookies("name").Domain =
    ➥ "www.friendsofed.com"
%>
```

So far, our cookie has only held a name. What if we want our cookie to hold other information as well? Let's say we want to hold the first *and* last name of a user separately. This would let us be more informal in our greeting and say Hi Spencer instead of Hi Spencer Steel, for example. From what you've seen so far you could do this:

```
<% Response.Cookies("firstname") = "Spencer"
   Response.Cookies("lastname") = "Steel"    %>
```

This would work fine, but amounts to two cookies. There are limits on cookie use – most browsers only allow you to use twenty cookies per domain with a maximum size of 4k each. If we carried on using this method, we could soon run out of space in the cookie jar.

The solution to this is to use a **dictionary cookie**, which is capable of holding several values in one cookie. Take a look at the code below:

```
<% Response.Cookies("name")("first") = "Spencer"
   Response.Cookies("name")("last") = "Steel" %>
```

We've placed both pieces of information into our name cookie. Let's create a monster cookie called MyDetails.

7. Type the following code in place of our previously limited information, substituting the question marks with your details:

```
<% Response.Cookies("MyDetails")("firstname") = "???"
   Response.Cookies("MyDetails")("lastname") = "???"
   Response.Cookies("MyDetails")("age") = "???"
   Response.Cookies("MyDetails")("postcode") = "???"
   Response.Cookies("MyDetails")("interests") = "???"
Response.Cookies("MyDetails").Expires = Date + 7
%>
```

8. After you've entered the code above, view it in your web browser. You won't see anything happen, but your cookie will have been created.

9. Let's see if there is a cookie anywhere on your system. If you're using Internet Explorer, open your cookie list by going through Options as

described earlier and look for a cookie that has just been dumped by administrator@localhost, or if you're specified as an administrator under Windows NT/2000, loginname@localhost. If you're using Netscape rather than Internet Explorer, I'm afraid you'll have to go for the old fashioned Search > For Files or Folders option in your Start menu, specify your local hard disk > Program Files > Netscape > Users and sort the files by date created to find it.

10. Open and view this cookie from Notepad or whatever text viewer you are using. You'll see something like this:

```
MyDetails
➡ postcode=WD25LX&age=28&lastname=Steel&interests=
➡ Live+Gigs&firstname=Spencer
```

You might see it in one long line, along with some odd looking characters that are used as delimiters to separate out the text, but you'll still be able to see that the cookie contains all the information we provided using one cookie name, or a **Key** as it is known. In our example the Key is MyDetails.

Keys are very useful as they allow you to create some powerful ways of storing temporary data on a user's machine. If you think about a shopping cart scenario, you browse items in the 'shop', add them to your cart, remove items and proceed to the checkout. All of this information can be kept in a cookie, each item adding to the Key list until the final transaction happens. Only then will the server think 'OK – let's get all the items from the user's cart cookie and ask for the payment'. We've put the information in the cookie, so it's time to learn how the server gets hold of this information.

Reading from Cookies

One of the uses of cookies that we talked about earlier was to personalize a site and here, we're going to make use of what we've learnt to create a Hello. Welcome back [your name]! page. We need to create two pages for this – one for the user to enter his name and one for the Hello screen.

1. As you've already made one form in this chapter, we've created the form page for you to save time, so open the page called create_a_cookie.asp in Chapter 3:

Objects 3

2. In Server Behaviors > Foundation UltraDev select Set Form Value – Cookie.

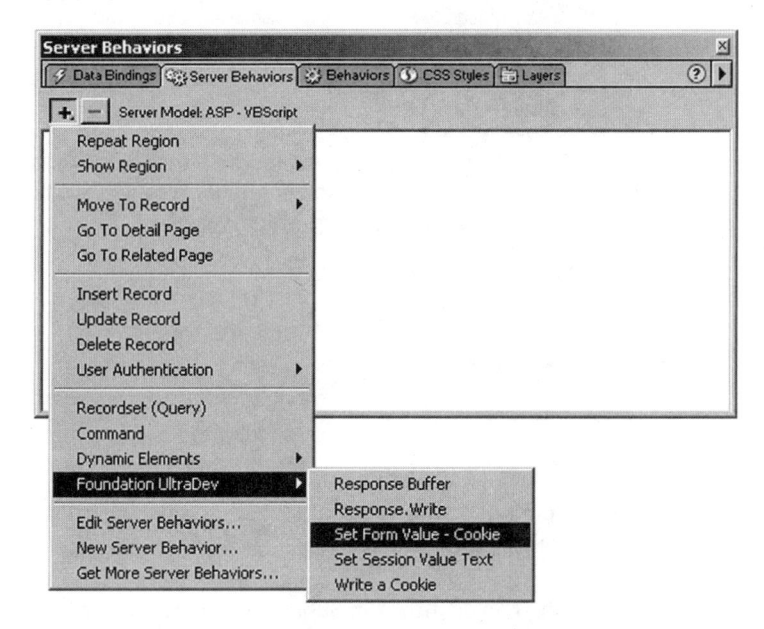

3. This is very similar to our previous example, except that we've introduced a new object: **Request.Form**. We'll be coming back to this, but it represents the name of the Edit Box where the user will type their name on the previous page.

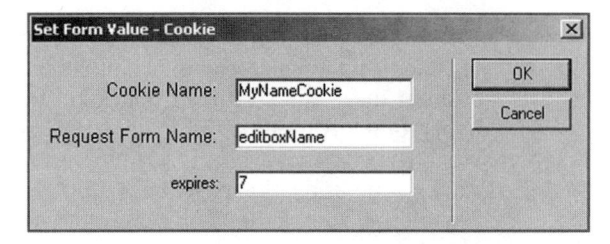

4. Enter MyNameCookie under Cookie Name, editboxName under Request Form Name and 7 under expires.

5. Click OK and take a look at the code generated at the top of our page:

   ```
   <%@LANGUAGE="VBSCRIPT"%>

   <% ' Set Form Value to a Cookie Robert Paddock
        ➥ (17/02/2001)
   ```

```
Response.Cookies("MyNameCookie")=
    Request.Form("myname")
Response.Cookies("MyNameCookie").Expires date + 7 %>
```

Notice where the values we entered in our server behavior have appeared.

6. Now the cookie is created, we should be ready to move the user straight to the Hello screen, right? Wrong. Let's take a look at our code again – can you see a problem here?

```
<%@LANGUAGE="VBSCRIPT"%>

<% Response.Cookies("MyNameCookie")=
    Request.Form("myname")
Response.Cookies("MyNameCookie").Expires date + 7 %>

<html>
```

If you read the code, you'll see that the cookie is created straight away when the page first loads, before the user has had a chance to enter any information. The cookie won't work like this, so we need to create the cookie after the Submit button is pressed. You might think that we could move the code so that it is run when someone clicks the Submit button, but we can't do this because the OnClick event that we would use to activate our code when the button is clicked is a client-side operation. As we said earlier, the server must create the cookie if we want to use it in combination with a database.

This scenario is very, very common in client/server development and it is important that you understand these concepts. Unfortunately, we cannot make the server do things 'on the fly' like we can with client operations. For the server to perform another transaction, we must send the information back up to the server. The only way of doing this is by submitting the page back to the Server. In our example, our solution is one of the two following methods.

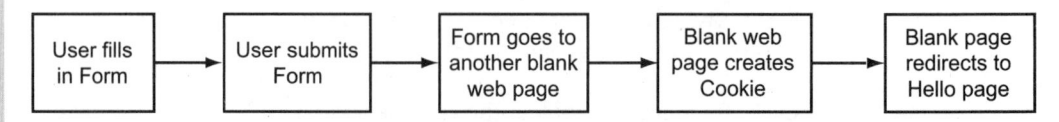

| User fills in Form | → | User submits Form | → | Form goes to another blank web page | → | Blank web page creates Cookie | → | Blank page redirects to Hello page |

The first option creates a blank page that sits between our form and Hello page and creates the cookie from the information on the form. Though there will be occasions when you will want to create these 'blank' server pages in complex environments, creating blank pages can be confusing and messy, and it isn't good practice to start using them now.

Objects 3

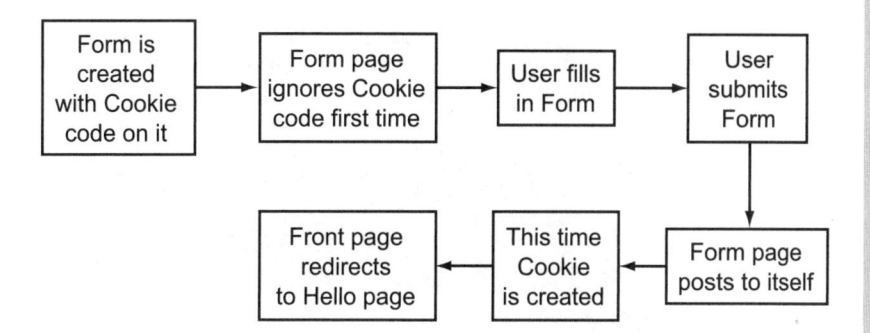

```
┌─────────────┐   ┌─────────────┐   ┌─────────┐   ┌─────────┐
│  Form is    │   │  Form page  │   │User fills│  │  User   │
│  created    │──▶│ignores Cookie│──▶│ in Form │──▶│ submits │
│with Cookie  │   │code first time│ │         │   │  Form   │
│  code on it │   │             │   │         │   │         │
└─────────────┘   └─────────────┘   └─────────┘   └─────────┘
                                                        │
      ┌─────────────┐   ┌─────────┐   ┌─────────────┐  │
      │ Front page  │   │This time│   │  Form page  │  │
      │  redirects  │◀──│ Cookie  │◀──│ posts to itself│◀┘
      │to Hello page│   │is created│  │             │
      └─────────────┘   └─────────┘   └─────────────┘
```

The second option uses the common technique of Submitting Form to Self. The trick is to present the user with a form, and get the form to submit back to the same page. You then get the page to do any additional processes with the form data and redirect automatically, leaving the user unaware that they have very briefly returned to the same page before moving on.

This isn't as hard as it sounds. If we think about it, what we need is some sort of **counter** or **flag** that we can check against, to see if the form has already been used. This would be a Boolean value, which is to say that it could be either true or false. This way we can submit the form back to itself and if our **flag** is **true**, we can get the server to process the additional commands and move the user on to the final page. Let's look at how we can achieve this:

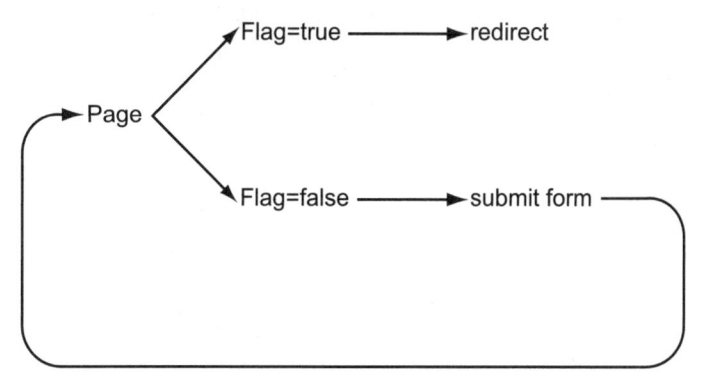

```
                    ╱ Flag=true  ──────▶ redirect
        ▶ Page ◀
        │           ╲ Flag=false ──────▶ submit form ─┐
        │                                              │
        └──────────────────────────────────────────────┘
```

7. Bring up the Objects > Forms panel, select a Hidden Field 🆖 and drag it onto our page. A Hidden Field is basically an invisible text field, so we can use it to hold a value without the user seeing it in their browser. This is ideal for our flag, which we want to set once the form has been filled in and the Submit button is pressed.

Foundation Dreamweaver UltraDev 4

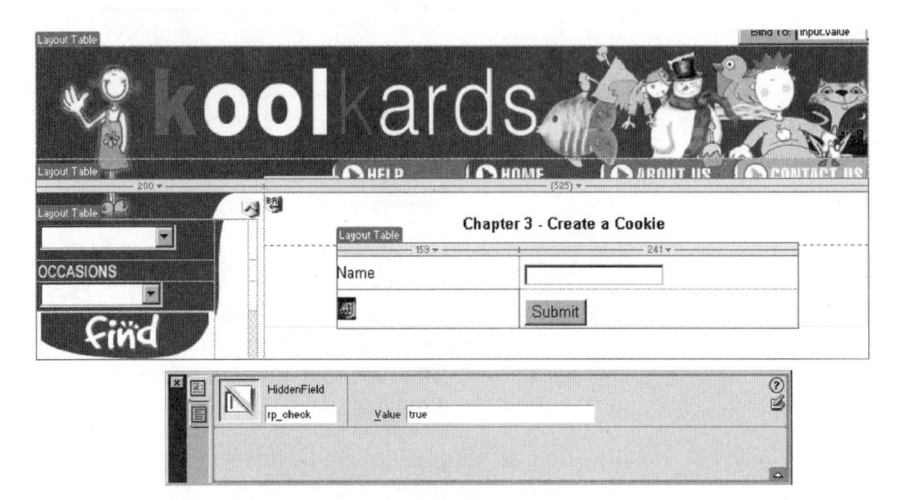

8. In the Design window, the Hidden Field shows up as a small, gold icon. Double-click on it to bring up the attributes on the Property Inspector toolbar.

9. Give the hidden field the name rp_check and a value of true. You can set the initial value and name by making sure your hidden box is highlighted with your cursor and then bringing up the properties panel with CTRL+F3.

    You may well be wondering whether setting rp_check to true as an initial value is a bit daft, given that we've just said this will perform the redirect action. Logically, it seems like setting it to `false` initially and then setting it to `true` once the Submit button is clicked is better. Let's have a look at our code and find out why this is the best way to do things.

10. Bring up your code view (it should be open) and amend the code at the top of the page so it reads like this:

    ```
    <%@LANGUAGE="VBSCRIPT"%>
    <% ' check to see if form has been posted
    If Request.Form("rp_check") = "true" then %>

    <% Response.Cookies("MyNameCookie")=
        ➥   Request.Form("MyName")
       Response.Cookies("MyNameCookie").Expires date + 7 %>

    <% Response.Redirect("read_cookie_value.asp")
       End If %>
    <html>
    ```

Objects 3

The first time our server code runs, there is no such thing as `rp_check` because it hasn't yet been created by the HTML which is further down in the code. Therefore the `If` statement is `false` and the cookie code which comes next is ignored.

Then the form is created by the HTML code, including our hidden field with a value of `true`. Because the `If` statement is at the top of the code and has already been processed, the server won't realise that the value of `rp_check` has changed until the server code runs again.

The server code doesn't run again until the Form **submits to self** after being filled in and the server code runs again. This time, `rp_check` is `true`, forcing the code to run the cookie code that follows the `If` statement. Then, the `Response.Redirect` code moves us out of the page before the HTML form is redrawn. This all takes a few milliseconds and the user is totally unaware that they have returned to the same screen.

This is what happens:

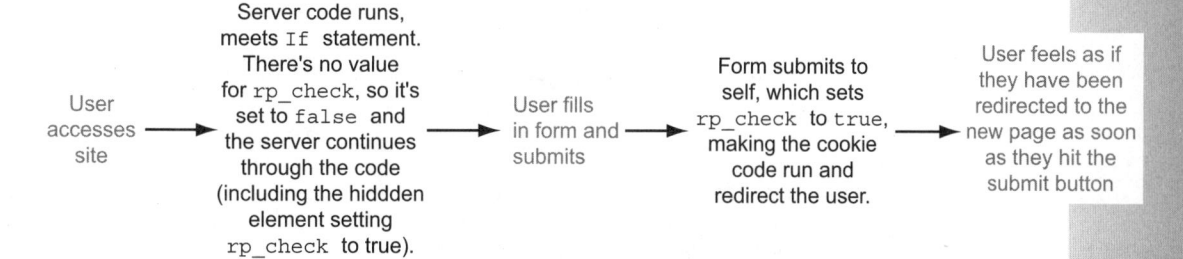

User accesses site → Server code runs, meets `If` statement. There's no value for `rp_check`, so it's set to `false` and the server continues through the code (including the hiddden element setting `rp_check` to true). → User fills in form and submits → Form submits to self, which sets `rp_check` to `true`, making the cookie code run and redirect the user. → User feels as if they have been redirected to the new page as soon as they hit the submit button

11. Save your work.

We've completed the steps to create the cookie value, so now all we need to do is read that value and display it on our page.

12. Open up the page `read_cookie.value.asp`.

It's time to introduce you to a new dialog box – the Data Bindings box. Every page that features information that can change will have at least one data binding which 'binds' or creates the link between the data and the page, so we'll be using the data bindings a lot. Here we specify our data source, whether this is a recordset, a cookie or another server-side component. Let's look at a cookie data binding.

Foundation Dreamweaver UltraDev 4

13. The Data Bindings panel can be found next to the Server Behavior tab, or can easily be launched by clicking this symbol [⚡] (keyboard shortcut CTRL+F10).

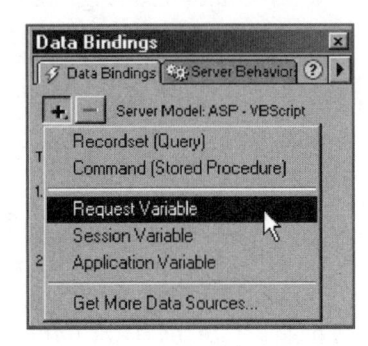

14. Once you can see this box, click the + symbol and select Request.Variable. This will launch the Request Variable box. If the panel is grayed out, then you need to click once inside your form to select it.

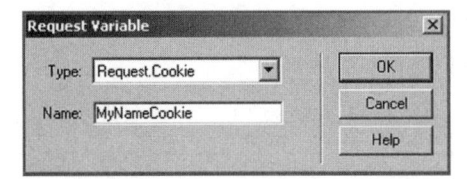

15. Here, specify Request.Cookie from the drop-down Type menu and MyNameCookie in the Name field. The cookie name will now be displayed in the Data Bindings box.

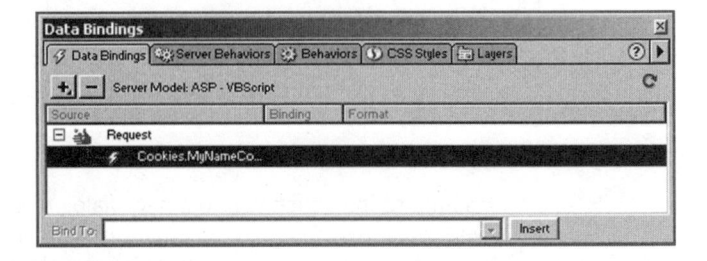

This allows you to use your cookie data binding on your page by dragging and dropping it whenever you want. This drag and drop functionality is the real point of using Data Bindings and setting things up like this saves a lot of time in the long run. We're going to use this to put the value of our cookie onto our page.

16. Click the cookie or the lightning icon in the Data Bindings toolbar and drag it into the page, placing it over the existing Cookie. {Cookies.MyNameCookie} will automatically appear on the page. Use your mouse to position your cursor, and type Hi to the left of it, and and welcome to KoolKards on the right of it. Give the text an appropriate size – say 3 – using the Properties panel.

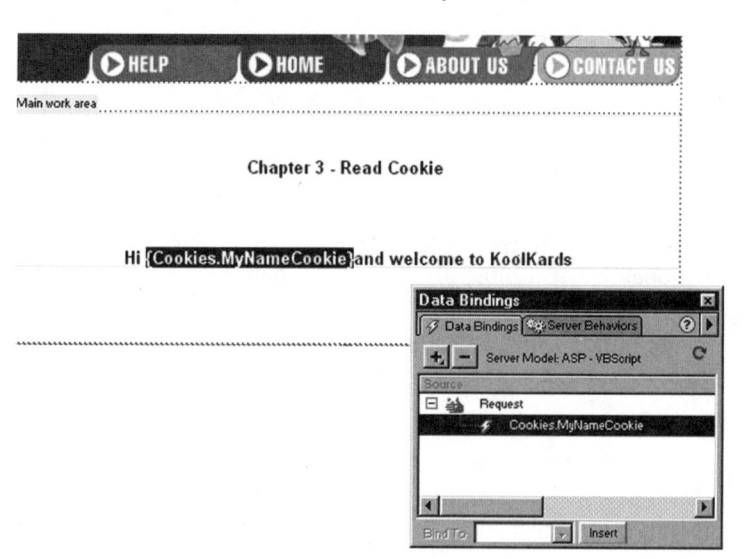

Let's just take a moment to look at the actual code that has been written. Click on {Cookies.MyNameCookie} and this code should be highlighted in the code inspector:

```
Hi <%= Request.Cookies("MyNameCookie") %> and welcome
➥ to KoolKards</font>
```

If we look at the ASP code inside the HTML code, we can see what's happening. Remember that `<%=` is a quick way of saying `Response.Write`.

17. Save the page and try it out in your browser. You need to start off on the `create_a_cookie.asp` page.

You should now see your name on the welcome screen of Koolkards. As we set the expiry time of the cookie for seven days, you can close down your browser, switch off and go for a well-earned drink. Come back, fire up the page again and you will notice that your name still appears.

18. Set the number of days to 0 and see what happens. The page should now display no name at all because setting the expiry time to 0 has immediately deleted the value set in the cookie.

Foundation Dreamweaver UltraDev 4

Summary

This chapter has covered a lot of ground. We're going to carry on looking at UltraDev objects in the next chapter, but now's the time to have a well earned break and reflect on what you've learnt about:

- HTML forms in UltraDev.
- Objects – what they are and how we use them.
- How to bake UltraDev flavor cookies.

As we journey further into UltraDev, we're beginning to find out the incredible functionality that it offers us. Things can only get better as we continue further towards the heart of UltraDev, so stick around.

Objects 3

kool kards

4 Moving Data between Pages

What we'll cover in this chapter:

- The **POST** and **GET** methods of moving data between web pages
- **Session variables** and when to use them
- The **ServerVariables** collection of the **Request object**

Passing information between pages will be a major part of your web application. In our shopping cart, this data will be the items that the user has put in it on previous pages, but the data could be anything from the category in which the user is interested to general preferences. As we've seen in the last chapter, we can use cookies to store information, which can then be called back on demand. Cookies tend to be used for specialist information that we will need to return to again and again, like your name. We need a different solution for passing temporary information between pages and that's what we're going to look at here.

As usual, there's more than one possible solution. We're going to work through practical examples of the two major ways of doing this. It's very important that you see these two methods in action, as we'll be using the tools that we're showing you in these first four chapters to create some fantastic dynamic web applications in the rest of the book.

Let's start by looking at how we can pass information in a form from one page to another and then display the information on the second page. We won't be using a database to permanently 'store' the information, nor will we be using cookies to 'write' the information. Instead we'll look at the `Request.Form` object.

We introduced you to some objects in the last chapter, and you saw then how easy it was to use them in UltraDev. We're going to be using them a lot more in this chapter, so this is the place to explain a little further. In object-oriented programming, a **variable** is simply a container that can hold some data, which might change. So you could have a `weather` variable that holds the state of the current weather, for example.

An **object** is simply a collection of pre-defined variables, so we could have a weather object that consisted of the variables `todayweather`, `tomorrowweather` and `yesterdayweather` for example. When we're hard coding, it becomes quite important to know all about these, but in UltraDev we can simply access variables and objects through menus, which is part of why UltraDev can save us so much time. We'll be seeing this in action when we look at the `ServerVariables` collection of the `Request.object` in a little while.

First, we want to look at how we send information between web pages. When information is sent from the client to the server in a form, we call it **posting** – think of it as posting a letter, but a little bit quicker. There are two methods of posting: POST and GET. We'll look at them both in turn here.

Sending Data between Pages with POST

We're going to create two pages in UltraDev, one with a form to enter some information on, and one to report the data entered on the first page back to us. We'll use a model that you may have seen quite often: asking for a name and a telephone number (though it could just as easily be an e-mail address or other information) and then checking with the

Moving Data between Pages 4

user that they've typed their details in correctly. Starting with an example using POST to send the information to the second page. We'll then change our pages to use GET so that we can see the practical differences between the two.

Using POST

1. Create a new UltraDev document. Select Forms > Insert Form from the Objects panel.

2. Make sure that your cursor is inside the red lines which denote your new form and click Insert Text Field to insert two text boxes into your form. Use the Property inspector to call them name and telephone. You'll notice that we've given ours an Init Val (Initial Value) of not specified as well.

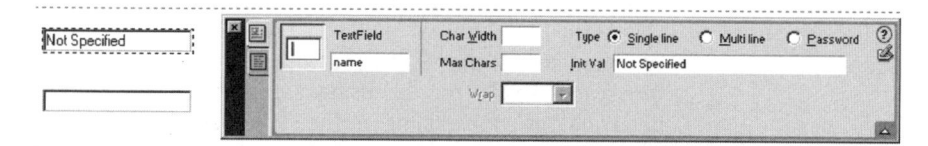

3. Add some text next to the boxes to make users aware that they should enter their name and telephone number in them:

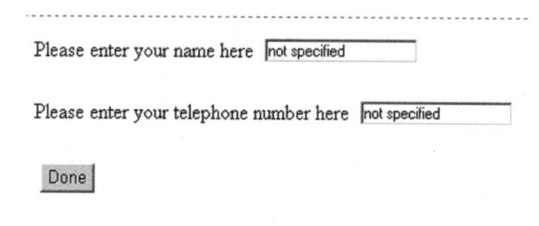

4. Add a Submit button, just like we did to our form at the beginning of the last chapter. Change the label from Submit to Done.

5. Click on one of the red dotted lines to make sure that the whole form is selected, rather than one individual text box, and bring up the Property inspector. Select POST from the drop-down list in the Method field:

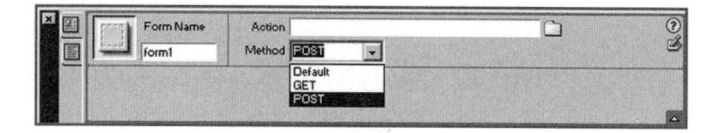

Foundation Dreamweaver UltraDev 4

6. Still in the Property inspector, set the Action to `read_form.asp`. This will be the page that reads back our input, which we'll create in a moment.

7. Save your page as `create_form.asp`.

8. We need to create the page that will extract the form information and display it on the new page. Open a new page and call it `read_form.asp`. Here we'll confirm to the user that they have entered their name and telephone number.

9. Insert a form into the new file and then add this text to it:

    The following information was sent from the form you just submitted.

    Your name is:

    Your telephone number is:

    We need to tell UltraDev about the values we wish to display beside these and we do this by using a technique very similar to that of declaring our cookie name on the Hello page. This time, we're going to use `Request.Form` rather than `Request.Cookie`.

10. Open up the Data Bindings window, click on the + button and select Request Variable. In the Type: field select Request.Form from the drop-down menu and enter the name of the form element you wish to use, which in our example is name. Select OK.

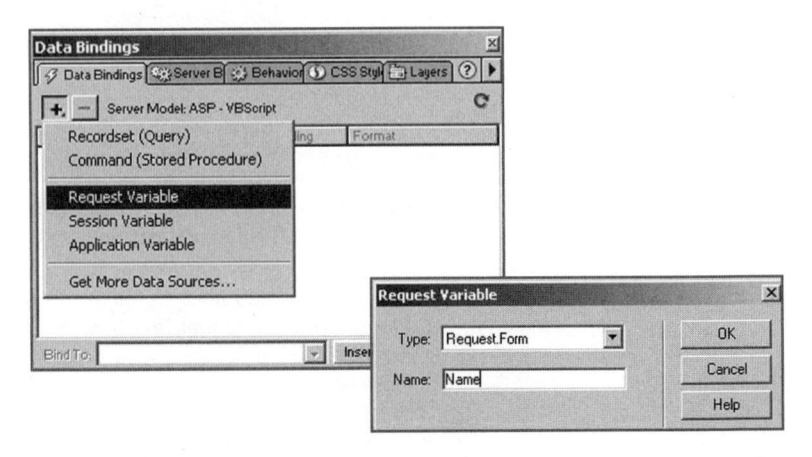

11. We need to do this for each element that we want to access, so repeat the process for telephone. Your Data Bindings box should look

Moving Data between Pages   4

something similar to the one pictured, with a data binding for Form.Name and Form.telephone showing:

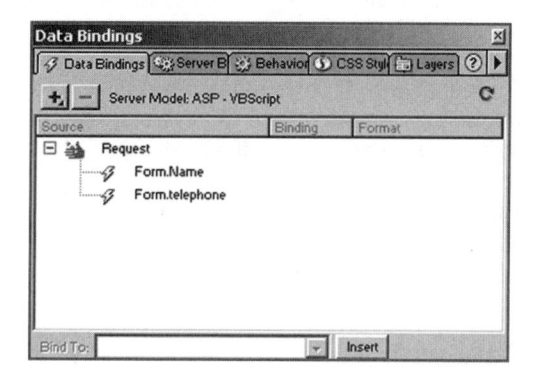

12. Drag the two Request.Form elements we've just created so that they're just after the relevant text in the form:

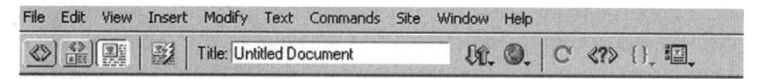

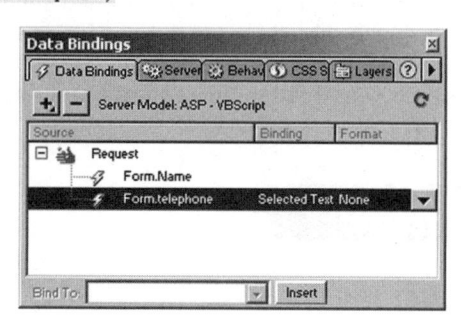

13. Have a look at the code. You'll notice that it's just a series of Response.Write statements shortened to <%=

```
<p>The following information was sent from the form
↪ you just X submitted </p>
<p>Your name is : <%= Request.Form("Name") %></p>
<p>Your telephone number is :<%= Request.Form
↪ ("telephone") %></p>
```

14. Open your browser and try the two pages out by going to http://localhost/koolkards/chapter4/create_form.asp. You should see the details you entered into the form appearing on the next page after you hit the Done button.

This is an excellent way of passing data from page *a* to page *b* but there is a catch. As the information isn't stored anywhere, you can only use this method once. Like a baton, it can only be passed from one page to the next page – it can't skip pages.

We'll look at a method that can hold data for longer than one page change when we learn about session variables in a moment. First, we're going to move on to look at the GET method of sending data across pages.

Sending Data with GET

You've probably been to web pages, tried to copy the URL and found out that it goes on forever and has the same type of delimiting characters as our cookies had when we looked at them in a text file. You've probably not thought of it in this way before, but the URL box in your browser can store data so that you can pass information between pages as well as taking the user to a new destination. This is what happens when you use the GET method.

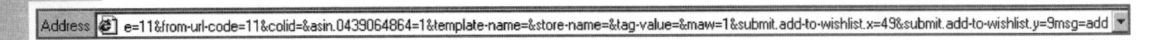

Address | e=11&from-url-code=11&colid=&asin.0439064864=1&template-name=&store-name=&tag-value=&maw=1&submit.add-to-wishlist.x=49&submit.add-to-wishlist.y=9msg=add

This method of passing data around sends all the variables and form data to the URL, which can then be extracted out for use by the server. We are going to see what affect this has on our site by changing our posting method to GET. If you use POST, the form data is sent through the request header and is not visible in the URL.

Using GET

Let's try this out and see GET in action.

1. Open our create_form.asp page from the last exercise and in the Property inspector change the posting method to GET:

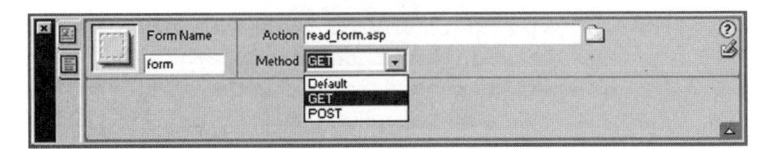

Moving Data between Pages   4

2. Save create_form.asp, go to your browser and test the file again. Enter some information into the text boxes and hit the Done button.

3. No information will be displayed in your actual browser, but if you look in the URL window in your browser, you should see something like the text below. Look more carefully and the information you entered should be contained with in the text:

   http://localhost/koolkards/chapter4/read_form.asp?Name=Robert&telephone=01352+123456&Submit=Submit

4. If we want to display the information on the page using GET, we need to change the way in which we ask for that information so that we extract the information from the URL. This means altering our request object to Request.QueryString instead of Request.Form.

5. Go back to read_form.asp from the last exercise and open the Data Bindings window. We need to make two new Request.QueryString variables to replace the two old ones.

6. Follow the same method as our previous example, but select Request.Querystring from the drop-down Request Variable menu:

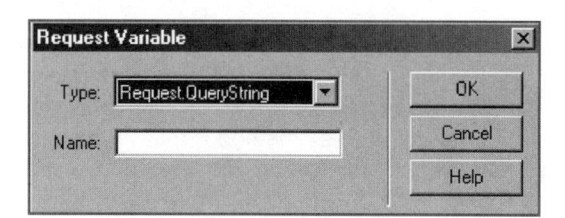

7. In the Data Bindings window highlight the old {Form.Name} and {Form.telephone} on your form and delete them. Drag and drop your QueryString objects onto your page:

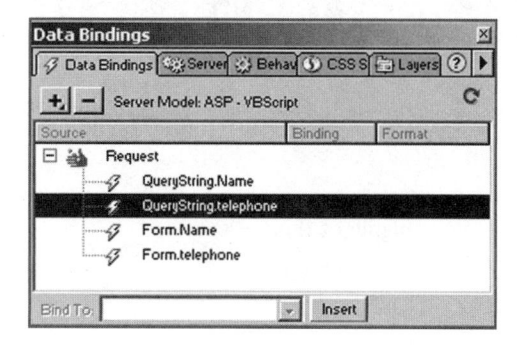

Foundation Dreamweaver UltraDev 4

8. Try out your pages again and you should see your information being displayed in the URL and repeated back to you on the `read_form.asp` page:

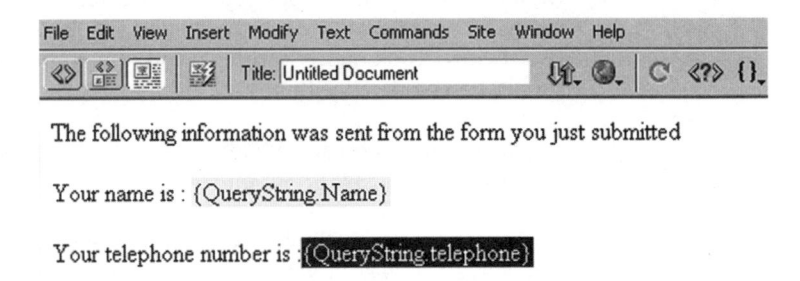

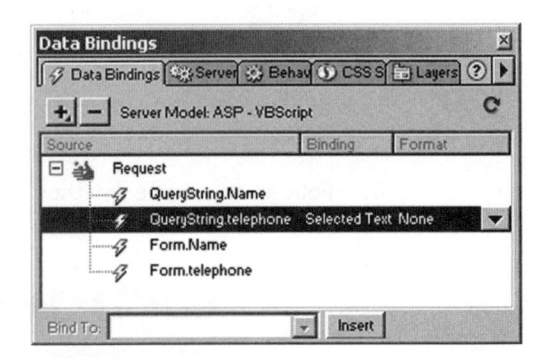

The downside of using the GET method is that the data in the URL is obviously not secure as any user can see the information you're sending just by looking at their URL window.

So far we've dealt with passing text field data from one page to another, but what about moving text between pages without using forms? Let's try it.

Passing Formless Data between Pages with GET

1. If you haven't still got it open from the last exercise, open your `create_form.asp` page again.

2. Type the words My Link to Read_Form somewhere on screen, and highlight them.

Moving Data between Pages 4

3. Bring up the Property inspector and click on the folder icon next to the Link box to bring up the Select File window.

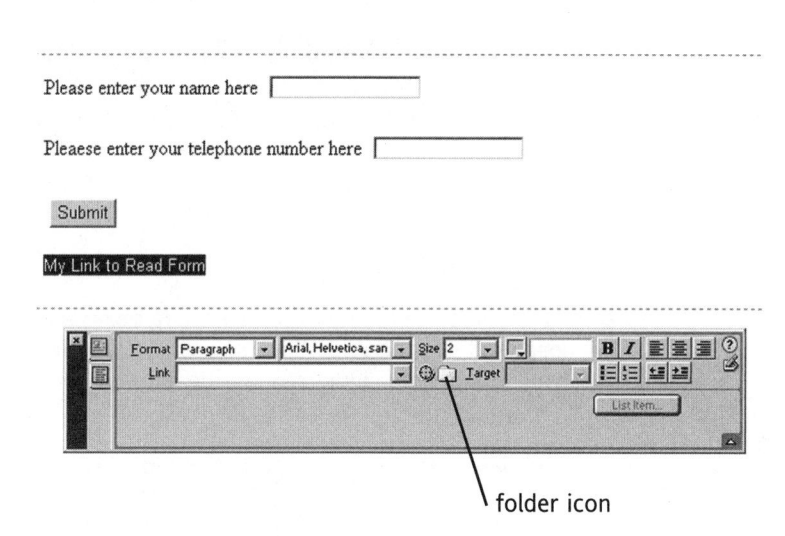

folder icon

4. Select the target page read_form.asp. Click the Parameters... button.

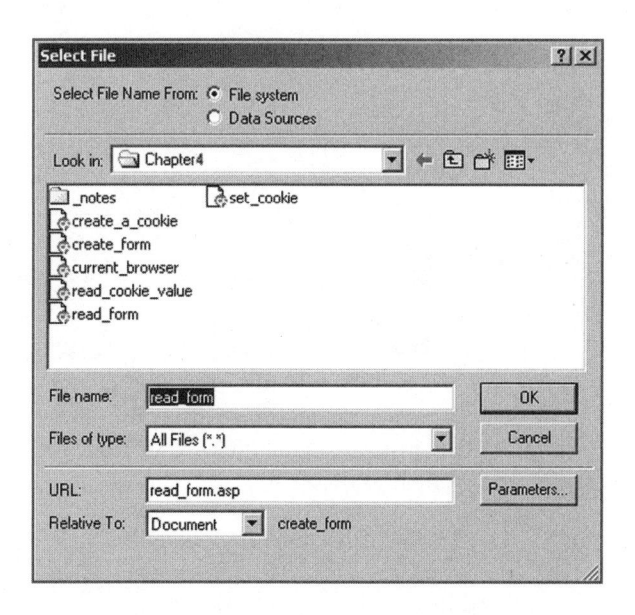

Foundation Dreamweaver UltraDev 4

5. Using the + button, add two parameters called name and telephone and add values of your own:

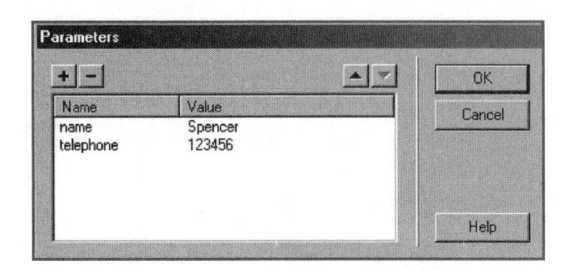

6. Press OK twice to close the two dialog boxes and your link to the read page will now be underlined so that it looks like a proper URL link. If you look at the Link box in the Property inspector, you'll see it's showing a full URL path with your variables included:

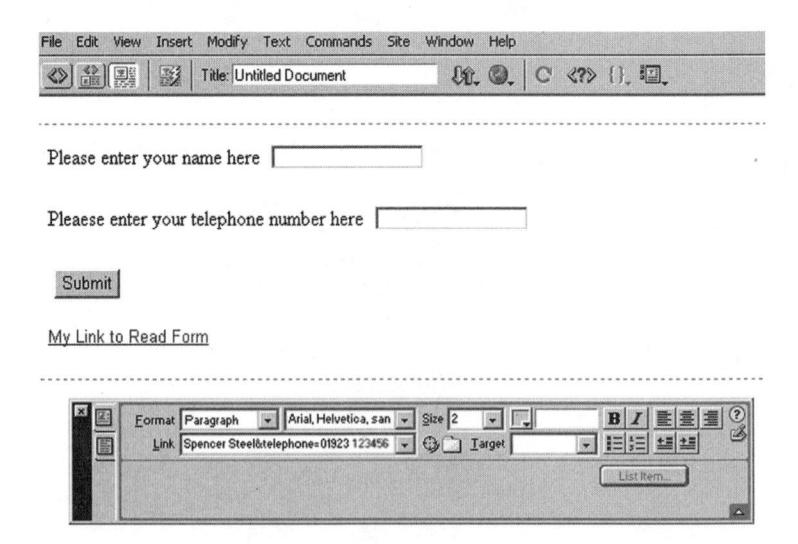

7. Save the page and run it from your browser. This time, ignore the form and just click your link. Note how the Request.Querystring has worked as before.

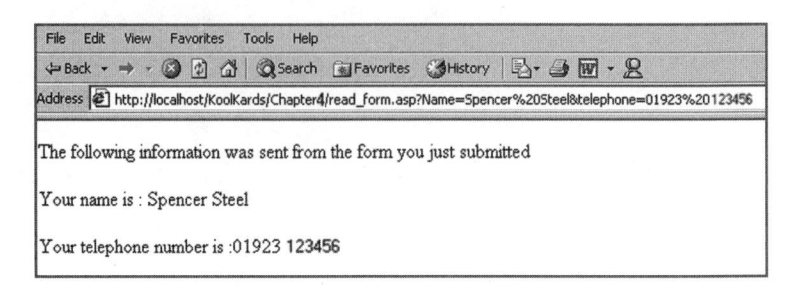

Moving Data between Pages

Obviously, this isn't the best method for moving telephone numbers and names around, because we have no way of entering them in the first place. There are no text boxes, but it can still be a powerful way of passing information around pages. For example, you could use it to provide a unique introduction to a page depending on which link someone had selected – you'd have a generic main page and several links reading "Gardeners click here," "Motorists click here" etc. The link could then send the details of a special offer in each category to feed into a header on your generic main page.

Because we're still using the `GET` method, everyone can still see our information in their URL windows. Next time you're browsing, and particularly at e-commerce sites, have a look at the URLs that are being created as you pass around a site.

As we've just seen, we can pass variables from one page to the next fairly easily, but they also lose their value very quickly. You were probably thinking 'well that's no good for what I had in mind – I need my web application to remember things for longer'. The answer to your problems is the **session variable**, which will hold a value for the whole of a session. We'll look at those next.

Session Variables

We'll start with a few definitions.

Session variables give you the ability to track the browsing habits of users and can be used to store all sorts of information, whether this is in the form of personal preferences or shopping carts. A session variable can be set anywhere within the site and starts when the user enters your domain, but will be destroyed after the user leaves.

Session variables won't work unless the client's browser has cookies enabled because they use a cookie called `SessionID`. This is how the server manages to keep track of many clients all using the same site. ASP session variables are very easy to use - if you want to store some data that you may want to use at anytime while the user is on the site, you can simply set a session variable with some code like this:

```
<% Session("Name") = "Robert" %>
```

Let's see how we create a session variable and then read it back on another page.

Using a Session Variable

We're going to go back to the two pages we've been using and use one of our text fields to illustrate the use of session variables. We've just told you that you should only use session variables when you need to keep hold of a value for a while over several different pages. With this in mind, we're going to pretend that you want to personalize your site by greeting your user by name on several different pages in a site and create a session variable to hold the user's name.

1. Open up `read_form.asp`. You need to go and select the `QueryString.Name` or whatever variable is currently next to the Your Name Is: text, and delete it.

2. Go to the code and add the following code at the very top of your page:

    ```
    <%@LANGUAGE="VBSCRIPT"%>
    <%
    ' set session to text name from previous Form using
    ➥ Querystring Session("session_name") =
    ➥ Request.Querystring("name")
    %>
    ```

    This creates a session variable called `session_name` and makes it equal to `name`, which we obtain from the URL `querystring`. Now that this session variable has been created, we can use it on any page.

    We need to put our session variable on our `read_form.asp` page. The best way of doing this is to create a data binding to our session variable and then drag and drop the data binding onto the page. This makes your session variables drag and droppable – it doesn't create a session variable for you.

3. Open the Data Binding window (CTRL+F10), and select +>Session Variable:

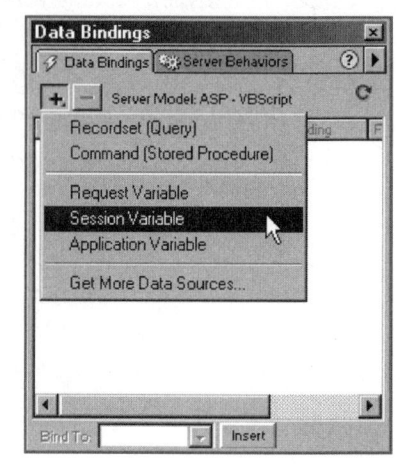

Moving Data between Pages   4

4. In the Name: box, type the name of the session variable we have already created – session_name. Take care, as this must exactly match the name of the session variable we created in our code:

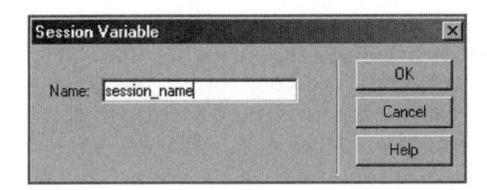

5. Click OK and your session is now drag and droppable from the Data Bindings panel.

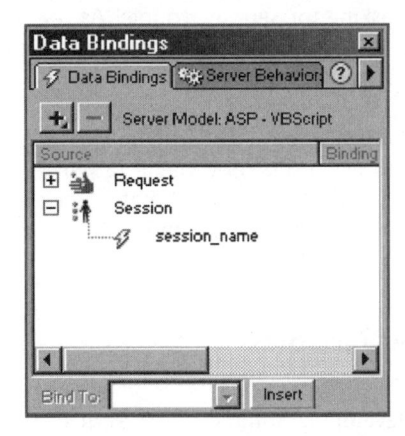

6. Drag your session variable out of the Data Bindings panel into your page, so that Your Name Is: just like our Request.QueryString and Request.Form variables were.

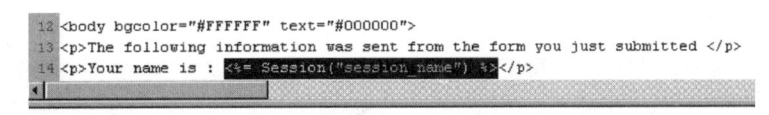

```
<body bgcolor="#FFFFFF" text="#000000">
<p>The following information was sent from the form you just submitted </p>
<p>Your name is : <%= Session("session_name") %></p>
```

The following information was sent from the form you just submitted

Your name is : {Session.session_name}

7. Save your page, and open the create_form.asp page in. Check that the text field after Enter your name here: is called name and go to your browser and open up create_form.asp. Everything should now work.

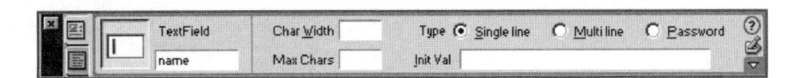

95

We're going to be using session variables at several points in the rest of the book, so you'll be seeing more of them. If you're really impatient to check out the power of session variables, then you can make another page to link to and see the value carry over from the first page to the third page in a way that our POST and GET methods don't allow for.

If you did an Internet search looking for information on session variables, you'd find a number of articles telling you not to use them. Session variables and cookies are synonymous, so if a user has set his browser not to accept any cookies, your session variables won't work for that particular user.

Please also note that an instance of each session variable that you use is created when the user visits the page, and these variables last for twenty minutes after the user leaves the page by default. If you put any large objects like recordsets or connections in the session variable you're asking for serious trouble. As the number of visitors increase, your server will experience a dramatic performance slump as a result of placing so many large objects in each session it creates.

If you have a variable that needs to be passed around to a lot of web pages, it may simplify things to use a session variable rather than passing the variable around through the QueryString. Just keep in mind that, used badly and unnecessarily, they can degrade the performance of your web site and irritate the occasional user who has their cookies turned off.

Request.ServerVariables

When you're developing commercial sites, it can be very useful to know which browser your visitors are using. If you've spent time trying to develop nice looking pages for both Netscape and Internet Explorer, you'll know that it's sometimes much easier to develop separate pages for each browser and this allows you to do just that. We can find out this information easily using the Request.ServerVariables collection, so let's try this out.

Detecting which Browser is Viewing your Page

1. Open current_browser.asp from the chapter folder and open the Data Bindings window. Select + > Request Variable and choose Request.ServerVariables from the drop-down menu. Type in HTTP_USER_AGENT under Name:

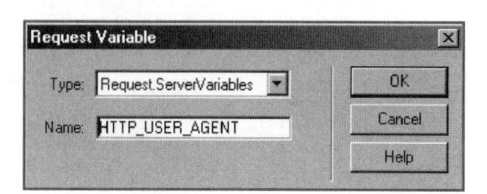

Moving Data between Pages

2. Drag and drop the request variable onto your page, after the Hello your current browser is text:

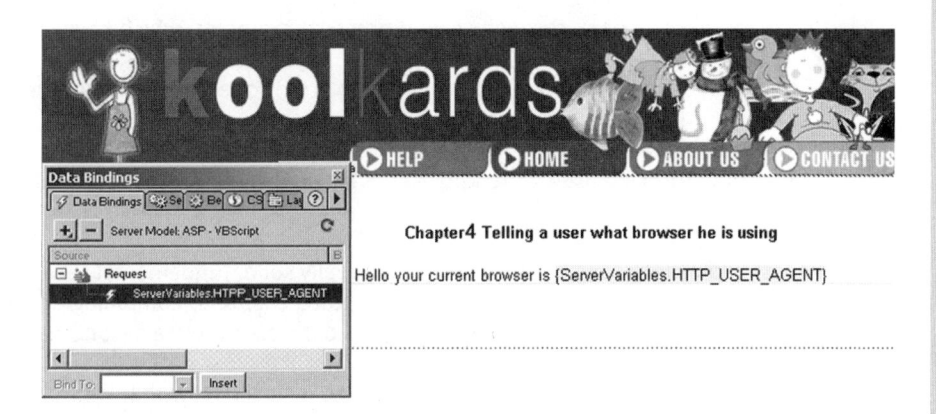

<image>

3. Save the page and open it in your browser. The page will now tell you what browser you are running. The output of a typical web page would look something like:

Mozilla/4.0 (compatible; MSIE 5.01; Windows NT 5.0)

MSIE stands for Microsoft Internet Explorer, so this isn't too difficult to interpret. For example, here's some code that you could use at the top of any page to redirect a user to a different page if they're not using a Microsoft browser.

```
<% If InStr(1,Request.ServerVariables
➥ ("HTTP_USER_AGENT"), "MSIE")
then
    Response.Write "You are using Internet Explorer"
Else
    Response.Redirect ("netscape_page.asp")
End If %>
```

We're using InStr (in the string) to check our line of output for the text 'MSIE'. We don't specify a number because each version of Internet Explorer ends with a different number. If the letters MSIE appear in HTTP_USER_AGENT, the user must be running Internet Explorer. If not, they need to be re-directed to the Netscape page.

You can use any of the other Request.ServerVariables in exactly the same way as HTTP_USER_AGENT. Try HTTP_REFERER, for example, to find out what page your user has just come from.

Foundation Dreamweaver UltraDev 4

Summary

In this chapter, we've been through several practical examples, which have shown us:

- The different ways of passing data from one page to another, and the advantages and disadvantages of each method
- How to make use of the `Request.ServerVariables` collection in UltraDev

In the last two chapters we have covered some really solid, fundamental server techniques and we'll be building on these techniques in future chapters, combining and expanding them until we're able to pass data from page to page as if it were second nature.

This chapter brings the first section of our book to a close. Now that we've gone through some basics, we can put our foot to the floor and start creating those really cool pages that manipulate our database data with add, edit, update and delete pages, shopping carts, e-mails, and all the other stuff you're just dying to get on with.

Moving Data between Pages   4

koolkards

5 Displaying your Database

What we'll cover in this chapter:

- Using **templates** to create and maintain consistent layout across our site, and **Live Data View** to see our pages as they develop

- Creating and displaying a **recordset** – returning information from our KoolKards **database**

- **Navigating** our records, keeping track and managing the size of our results pages

Foundation Dreamweaver UltraDev 4

Over the course of this chapter we'll learn how to display data from a database in various ways, and this will ultimately become part of our administration section for the KoolKards web site.

For the first time, we will be making full use of our database, which is a Microsoft Access database. We realize that you might be an expert on databases or a complete beginner, so we have provided a solution in each case. In Appendix B we have written a step-by-step guide to Access, from creating your first database and putting in data, to searching that data and specifying criteria.

> *Basically, if you're a beginner and don't know anything about Access, go read the Access tutorial now. If you're an expert, or at least know your way around Access already, don't.*

Before we start our dynamic pages, we need to spend just a little time getting to know the **schema** (structure) of our database, so let's have a look at it (and welcome back to those who've read the Access tutorial between paragraphs).

The Database

As we know, our database is an **Access** database called `koolkards.mdb`, residing in the database folder of our site. So let's open it and take a closer look.

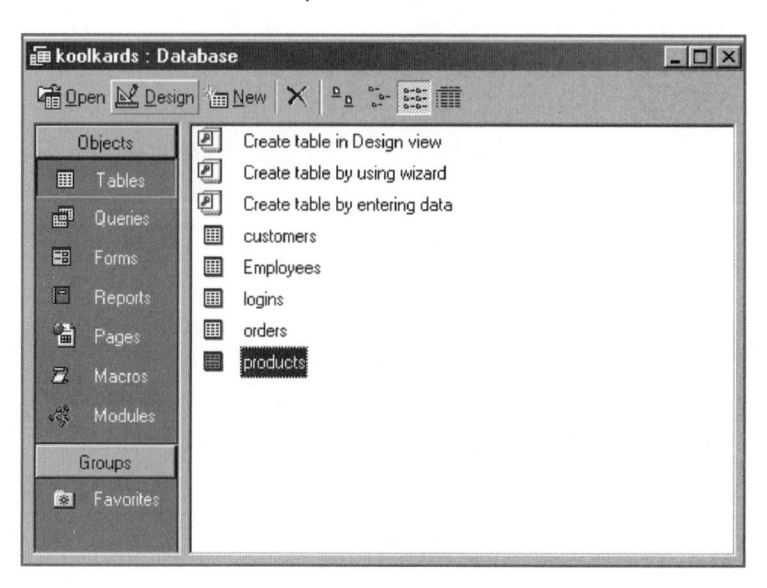

Displaying your Database 5

The table we're concerned with at the moment is the **products** table, just one of the tables found in the `koolkards.mdb` database. Click the Tables tab (down the left-hand side) to list the tables contained within our database; then highlight the products table and click the Design button along the top.

The database we've given you has about fifty records for you to work with; of course there could be any number of different types of products, it's is up to you.

Have a look how the table is put together. The next two screenshots show the structure and some sample data:

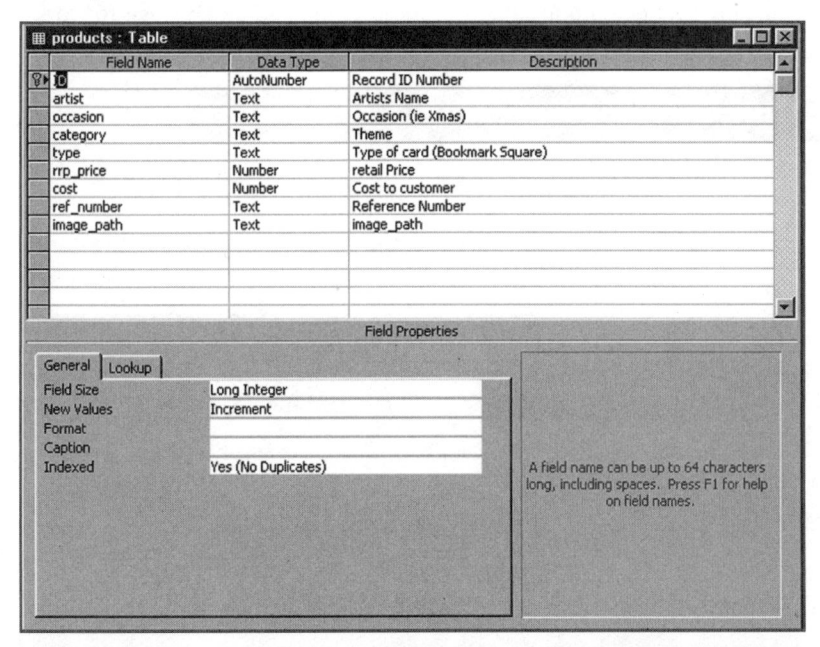

Field Name	Data Type	Description
ID	AutoNumber	Record ID Number
artist	Text	Artists Name
occasion	Text	Occasion (ie Xmas)
category	Text	Theme
type	Text	Type of card (Bookmark Square)
rrp_price	Number	retail Price
cost	Number	Cost to customer
ref_number	Text	Reference Number
image_path	Text	image_path

Field Properties

General | Lookup

Field Size	Long Integer
New Values	Increment
Format	
Caption	
Indexed	Yes (No Duplicates)

A field name can be up to 64 characters long, including spaces. Press F1 for help on field names.

products : Table

ID	artist	occasion	category	type
90	Kate Gardner	Sorry	Daydreams	Bookmark Range (63r
91	Kate Gardner	Sorry	Daydreams	Bookmark Range (63r
92	Kate Gardner	Congratulations	Daydreams	Bookmark Range (63r
93	Kate Gardner	Retirment	Daydreams	Bookmark Range (63r
94	Kate Gardner	Sorry	Daydreams	Bookmark Range (63r
95	Kate Gardner	Sorry	Daydreams	Bookmark Range (63r
96	Kate Gardner	Mothers day	Daydreams	Bookmark Range (63r
97	Kate Gardner	Get well soon	Daydreams	Bookmark Range (63r
98	Kate Gardner	Get well soon	Daydreams	Bookmark Range (63r
99	Kate Gardner	Birthday	Daydreams	Bookmark Range (63r
100	Kate Gardner	Congratulations	Daydreams	Bookmark Range (63r
101	Kate Gardner	Congratulations	Daydreams	Bookmark Range (63r
102	Kate Gardner	Valentine	Daydreams	Bookmark Range (63r
103	Kate Gardner	Valentine	Daydreams	Bookmark Range (63r
104	Kate Gardner	Birthday	Daydreams	Bookmark Range (63r
105	Kate Gardner	Birthday	Daydreams	Bookmark Range (63r
106	Kate Gardner	Birthday	Daydreams	Bookmark Range (63r

Record: 1 of 222

Foundation Dreamweaver UltraDev 4

We've assumed that as you're reading this book you have a basic understanding of Access. If you have some more expert Access knowledge, you may have a few things to say about our database. For a start it's not **normalized** – which means our database might contain a lot of repeated information (names of artists etc.). We took this conscious decision so as not to confuse you with too many new techniques at the start. However, we'll introduce the finished normalized database when we discuss **SQL Server** towards the end of the book.

So, let's talk about how we might collect the product data from the database and display it in a web page.

We've already connected our database, so now we need a new page to work on.

Creating a New Page from a Template

1. Open UltraDev if it isn't already.

2. We want to create a new page from one of the templates we've provided. To do this, look under File > New From Template.

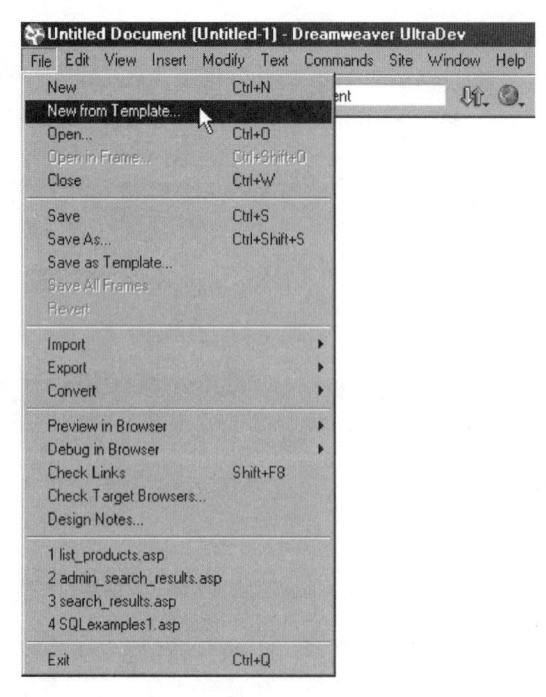

3. From the pop-up window, you can see two templates listed called master and admin. We've created these templates for you and they

Displaying your Database 5

contain the border designs we'll use for our two main sections throughout the site:

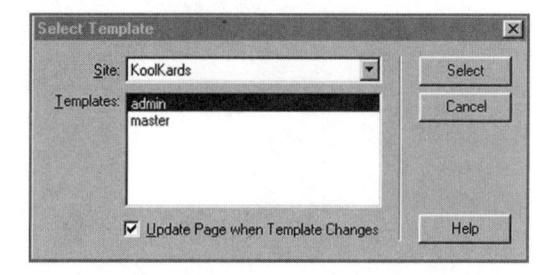

4. We'll use the master template for the pages our normal web visitors will use and the admin template for the pages which our administrators will log into, to create and change the records in our database.

> *Templates are a great way of maintaining consistency throughout the site. You can find more information in the online help under **Templates**.*

Over the next two chapters, we'll create an entire administration system where you can view, update and delete records, based on this new page. We'll use the Admin template to keep it consistent throughout – but remember, in your real-life web applications, you'll probably want to let your visitors and customers view these records in the same way.

The great news is that once you know how to do it, you can easily change the template to suit your needs. You can even apply a new template to your page after it's been completed – Modify > Templates > Apply Template to Page...

5. Once you've selected the Admin template, the page will be created for you with the overall design in place.

6. Save this page as list_products.asp.

Foundation Dreamweaver UltraDev 4

We now have a fresh page to work on – with an attractive Administration sidebar:

The first thing we need to create on our page is a **recordset**. In the next section, after a brief introduction, we'll get on to an exercise to create exactly that...

Recordsets

A recordset is an intermediary between our page and the database; it returns a certain subset of data based on what we ask it for. For example, we might only be interested in certain columns or tables; the recordset meets these criteria in 'fetching' just the information we have asked for.

And how do we ask for information in this way?

We use a **query** – we query the database and ask it to show us data based on our criteria. We'll cover queries in more detail (along with SQL, the language of queries) in Chapter 7, and we'll further discuss all the properties of recordsets as we progress through this one.

In our case, we just want to create a recordset that will return all the fields from our products table, so let's do it...

Creating a Recordset for the Products Table

1. In your new page click on the Data Bindings tab (you can also use CTRL+F10 to show/hide it).

2. Press the + sign and a list of options will appear. We've been here before when we covered the different types of variables in Chapters 3 and 4. This time, however, we need to select the first option: Recordset (Query):

Displaying your Database 5

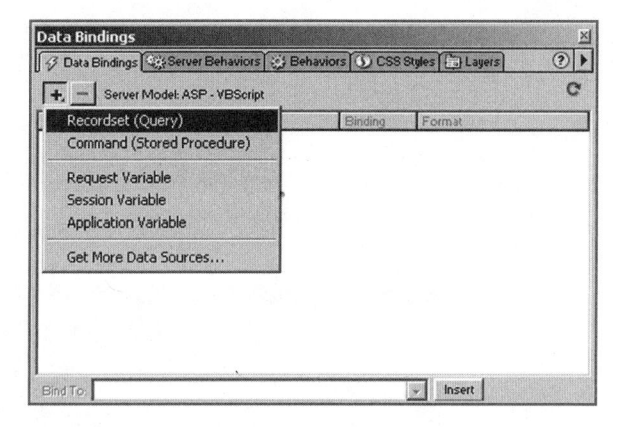

3. This will open up the Recordset dialog box:

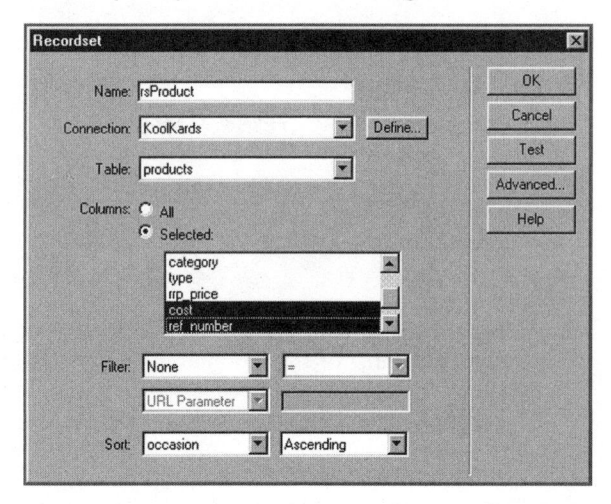

4. Don't panic – it's not that difficult to fill in. Let's just work through each option, step by step, where you'll see that each field in the dialog box has been numbered to correspond with the step that tells you what to enter.

> *Creating a recordset lays the foundations of your dynamic web pages; once you've done it a few times, it'll become second nature.*

5. Name: Here you fill in the name of your recordset; you can call it anything you want, but we'll give you a tip – keep the name short (you'll

see why later). Most ASP coders usually start the name with rs, standing for, you've guessed it, recordset, so why not call it rsProducts for now.

6. Connection: select the connection that you created for KoolKards.

7. Table: select the products table from the drop-down list. We're telling UltraDev that the information we need is contained in the products table of our database:

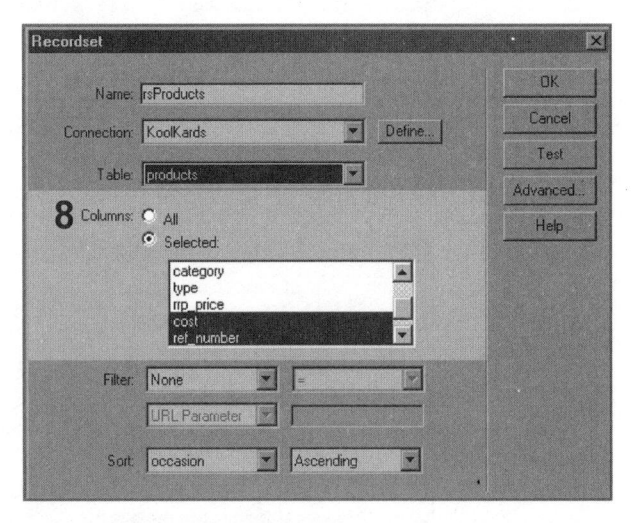

8. Columns: by default All will be currently selected, but we only need certain columns for the moment. Check the Selected option and select each of the following – artist, cost, occasion and ref_number (you can highlight multiple choices by holding down the CTRL button while you select each one).

It may be tempting to use All and then choose which fields to put on your page as and when you need them. However, this isn't a good idea, because the more data you return in a recordset the longer it will take to arrive at your web page. To make matters worse, the server temporarily holds the contents of your recordset for the duration of your session, so an unnecessary batch of data can slow down performance on a number of fronts.

So, plan ahead and only return the fields that you're going to use on each page. You can create a different recordset for each page, so if you need more fields later that won't be a problem.

Displaying your Database   5

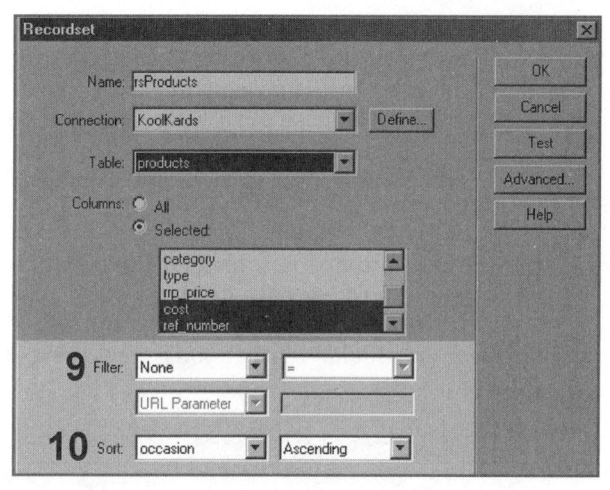

9. **Filter:** leave this set at None for now. Filtering is a method of taking out records that meet criteria. For example, we could only return cards designed by a specific artist or at a certain price. We'll be looking at some filters later on but, for now, we want all data to be returned.

10. **Sort:** set this to occasion and Ascending. The sort function allows us to... well... sort the data returned. Often you'll want your data pre-ordered alphabetically by name or numerically by number. In this example we're telling UltraDev to sort the records alphabetically by the occasion, thus giving us a grouping of like cards.

11. To check that everything is working OK click on the Test button. Your screen should look something like this:

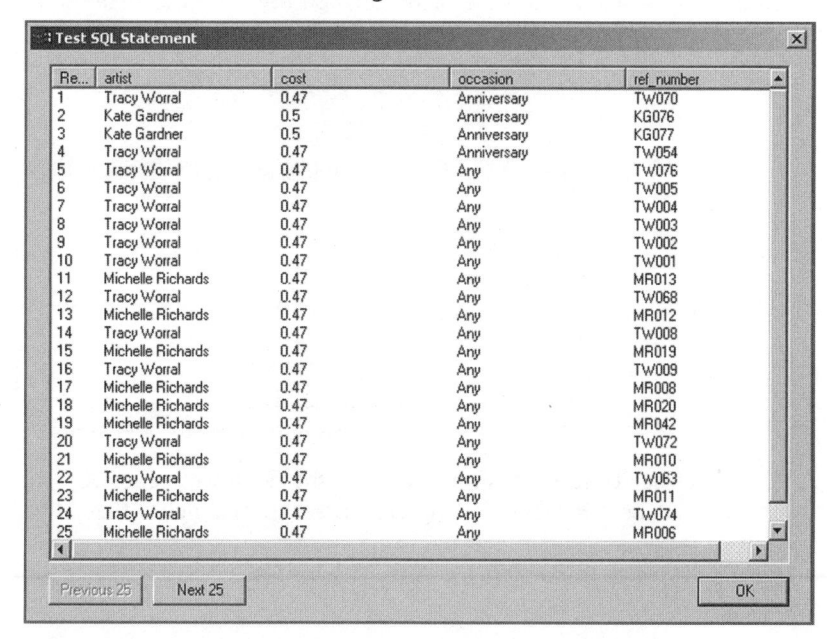

Re...	artist	cost	occasion	ref_number
1	Tracy Worral	0.47	Anniversary	TW070
2	Kate Gardner	0.5	Anniversary	KG076
3	Kate Gardner	0.5	Anniversary	KG077
4	Tracy Worral	0.47	Anniversary	TW054
5	Tracy Worral	0.47	Any	TW076
6	Tracy Worral	0.47	Any	TW005
7	Tracy Worral	0.47	Any	TW004
8	Tracy Worral	0.47	Any	TW003
9	Tracy Worral	0.47	Any	TW002
10	Tracy Worral	0.47	Any	TW001
11	Michelle Richards	0.47	Any	MR013
12	Tracy Worral	0.47	Any	TW068
13	Michelle Richards	0.47	Any	MR012
14	Tracy Worral	0.47	Any	TW008
15	Michelle Richards	0.47	Any	MR019
16	Tracy Worral	0.47	Any	TW009
17	Michelle Richards	0.47	Any	MR008
18	Michelle Richards	0.47	Any	MR020
19	Michelle Richards	0.47	Any	MR042
20	Tracy Worral	0.47	Any	TW072
21	Michelle Richards	0.47	Any	MR010
22	Tracy Worral	0.47	Any	TW063
23	Michelle Richards	0.47	Any	MR011
24	Tracy Worral	0.47	Any	TW074
25	Michelle Richards	0.47	Any	MR006

Note how UltraDev returns only twenty-five rows at a time. This prevents huge processing if you have a large database. You'll use a similar technique of returning a small amount of rows of data at a time on your web page as well – we'll look at this a little later.

Once you're happy that UltraDev has returned all the information you requested, press OK.

Our recordset is now finished. Click OK to exit the recordset dialog and return us to our page design.

If you look at the Data Bindings panel you'll now see our newly created recordset rsProducts ready for use:

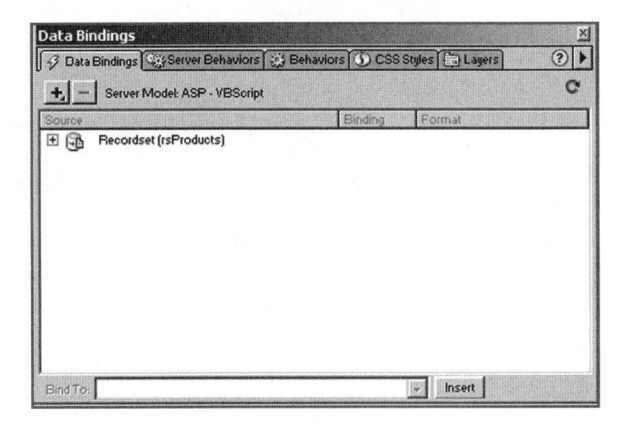

Click on the + and expand the recordset; you will see a list of all the fields you selected:

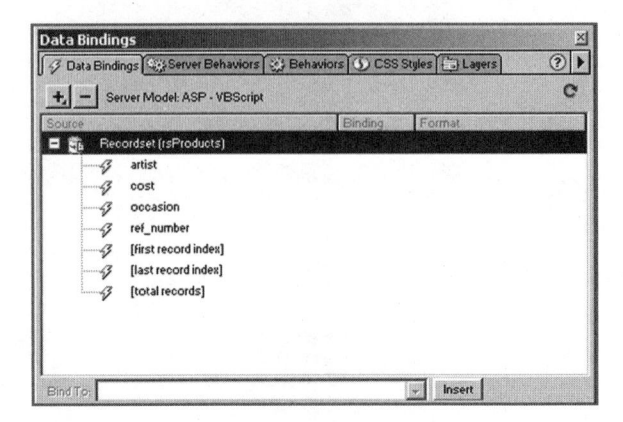

As you can see UltraDev has returned only the fields we requested – artist, cost, occasion and ref_number. However, there are three special fields that UltraDev has created

Displaying your Database | 5

automatically for us: [firstrecordindex], [lastrecordindex] and [totalrecords]. These are really useful and we'll show you how to use them shortly. See if you can guess what they will do for us.

Displaying the Recordset

We have the recordset created and we can now utilise the great drag-and-drop features of UltraDev to start displaying live, *dynamic* data on our web page. But before we do, we need to add a few more bits to our basic page template.

Firstly, we need somewhere neat for our data to be displayed, and for this we'll use a simple HTML table – such as the one we used in Chapter 3.

Creating a Table for the Recordset

1. From UltraDev's menus choose Insert > Table and enter the details as below... We'll create one row for our table headings and one row for our data, and since we have four columns of data in our recordset we'll need (you guessed it) four columns!

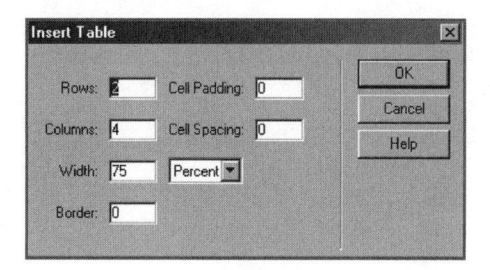

> "Only one now for our data?" you may cry – oh yes! Just build the table for now and we'll add some more UltraDev magic soon.

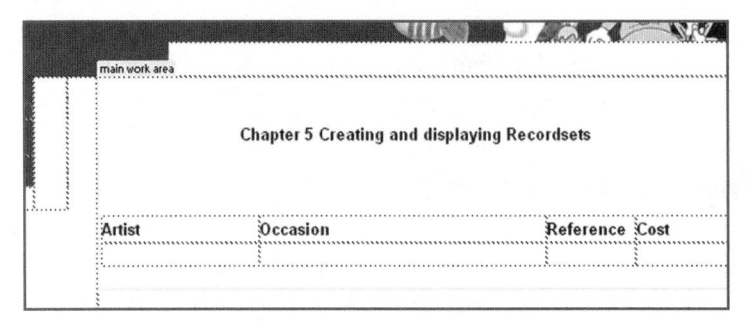

Anything similar to the screenshot should be fine.

2. Manually type the headings into your table. If you like, select your headings and press CTRL+B to make them bold, but don't get too hung up on matching our screenshots.

    Now, we need to get our fields from the recordset and place them into the appropriate cells in our table.

3. Expand your recordset by clicking the tiny + beside rsProducts in the Data Bindings window, and select the artist field. Holding the mouse button down, drag the field to the cell under the Artist heading.

> *If your cursor's in the right place already, you can just highlight **artist** and click Insert at the bottom of the Data Bindings window. This simply places the highlighted field where the cursor is.*

4. Now repeat this technique for the remaining three fields, until you've built your table to look something like this:

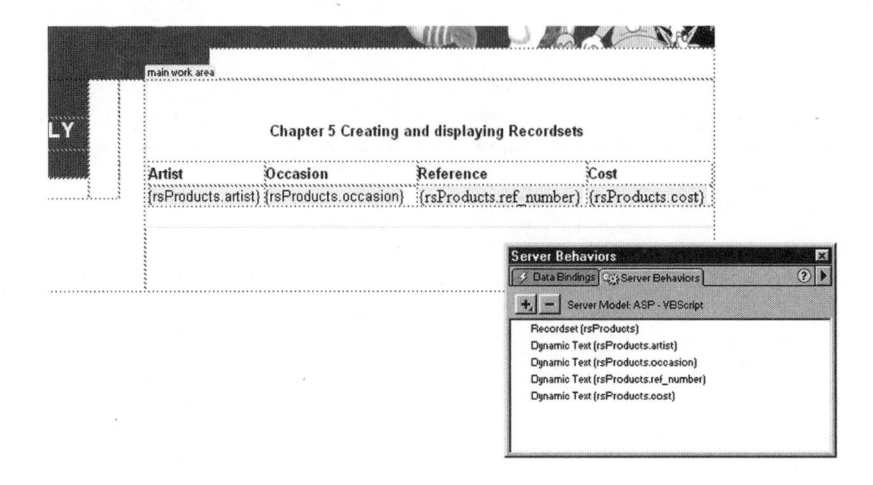

Displaying your Database   5

If you want to change the font, size, or background color of any of the fields, you can do this in just the same way as you would change normal text. You have total freedom on the look of your data and as your UltraDev design skills improve, you'll be finding new ways to attractively display your results.

Remember a while ago we mentioned about not giving your recordsets long names. We called our recordset rsProducts, which, if the truth were told, is probably longer than most developers would use... why? Well, as you can see your layout is being stretched to accommodate the field name. The cost cell is stretched to fit the word {rsProducts.cost} so we don't visually get the best representation of what our page looks like.

This is one of the few drawbacks of UltraDev – you end up with a non-WYSIWYG feature. Instead, What You See Isn't Exactly What You Get – your finished page will look the same in a browser but what you're seeing in the design view might be slightly out of proportion.

Normally, we'd suggest that you call your recordset rs1 or rs2 – not exactly user-friendly and can be a nightmare when you return to your sites after a long spell – but at least it avoids the above glitch. However, don't worry about it now, but be aware when you come to browse your page that your column widths won't necessarily be the same in your browser as they are in the design mode.

A few chapters back we mentioned something within UltraDev called **Live Data View**. It's a nifty feature that saves us hopping between our browser and program to see what our page will look like with data in it. We'll take a more detailed look right now.

Introducing Live Data View

We can fire up Live Data View from the menu View > Live Data (CTRL+SHIFT+R) or by clicking the icon on the main toolbar:

Once selected (and if set up correctly), you'll get something in your design environment similar to this:

Foundation Dreamweaver UltraDev 4

> *In order for Live Data to work correctly, a site definition must be set with the appropriate values in the **Local Info**, **Web Server Info**, and **Application Server** categories. The majority of errors encountered when attempting to view the Live Data window are attributable to errors in the settings of any of these three categories. Check all your settings and if you're getting an error or if this view isn't working for you go to www.macromedia.com/support/ultradev and search for 'live data', which will bring up all the latest known issues.*

There are a couple of important things to note here:

- Firstly and obviously, we're now looking at the first record from our database – *this is actual real-time data from our connection!*

- Secondly, it's likely that the column widths have changed if you called your recordset rsProducts. You may find your columns are a lot narrower than you expected, but whether you're happy or unhappy with the results, here's the great thing – you can visually resize them now while keeping the Live Data view on.

Once you've finished playing with the look of your table, switch back to normal Design View and watch the table cells grow back to accommodate your recordset names. You may like to flick back and forth just to confirm your changes are permanent – but remember to regularly save your work – especially when you're making a lot of changes.

OK, well, one record from our table isn't very useful – we need them all. So let's look at a way in which we can display all our data.

All we want is a way of repeating the recordset row of our table; once for each record. And that's exactly what we will do next, with a powerful **server behavior**.

Repeating the Recordset Row

Before we begin we must specify which region of the screen we want repeated. We need to highlight the cells in our table that contain the recordset fields, and for that we have a useful hint.

Selecting rows, cells and tables can be made easier by using the Tag selector at the bottom of your screen. Before we begin the main part of this exercise, follow these brief instructions and you'll see how easy selecting parts of your table can be.

Displaying your Database

1. Click anywhere in the table and look at the bottom of your page. Note you can now see four table <tags>:

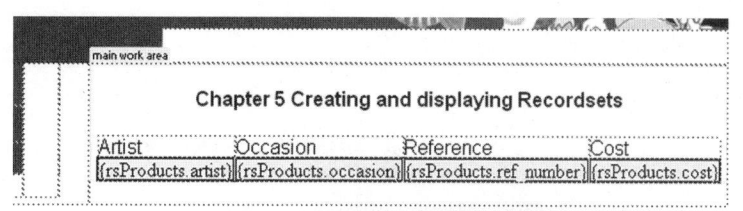

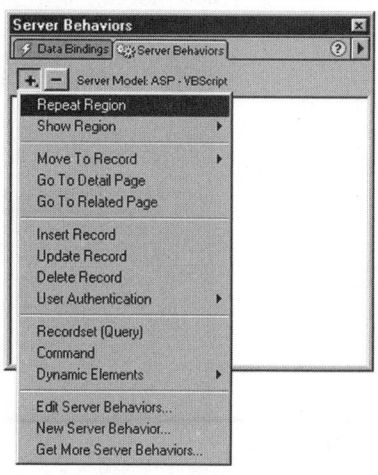

   `<mm:template> <body> <table> <tr> <td> <mm:editable> <table> <tr> <td> <font>`

   - `<tr>` = one table row
   - `<td>` = table data – which means one cell in the row
   - `<table>` = entire table
   - `<font>` = the text within the cell

2. Click on these tags one at a time and note how the areas are selected on your table (and in your code if you have Code/Design View enabled). This can make life a lot easier for you!

3. Select the row in the table that contains our recordset data (`<tr>`), bring up the Server Behaviors panel with CTRL+F9, and use that behavior.

4. Click the + on the Server Behaviors panel and on the drop-down menu you'll see an option called Repeat Region – the 'region' being the row in our table we want repeated.

Once you've done that you'll be presented with the Repeat Region behavior properties box:

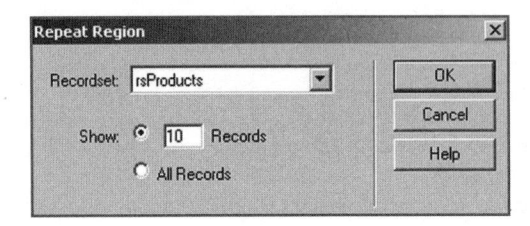

5. Select rsProducts from the drop-down box, and choose to show ten records per page.

> *Remember, one of the secrets of creating sites that users will return to again and again is **speed**. In the same way we've looked at optimizing our connection and only returning the fields we want in our recordset, it's important that we don't try to return too many records at once, or the page will be slow to load and unattractive to users.*

6. Once you've clicked OK you'll notice a small gray tab labelled Repeat on the top of your table row. This is just your visual guide (if you can't see it, go to View > Visual Aids > Invisible Elements):

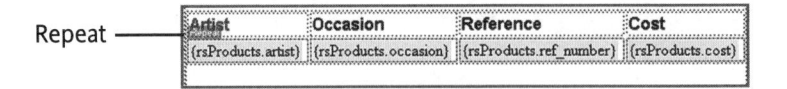

Repeat

Also note that our Repeat Region behavior is now listed in the Server Behavior panel from where we can amend the properties if we need to add more records per page.

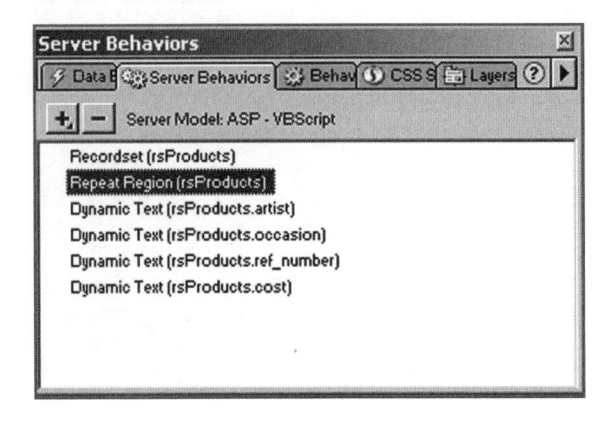

Displaying your Database

7. Save the page and test it out; in a moment we'll start to examine what's going on in the code.

   Hopefully you should be looking at something like this (remember you can test out your results either in the Live Data View or from within your browser.)

   Chapter 5 Creating and displaying Recordsets

Artist	Occasion	Reference	Cost
Tracy Worral	Anniversary	TW070	0.47
Kate Gardner	Anniversary	KG076	0.5
Kate Gardner	Anniversary	KG077	0.5
Tracy Worral	Anniversary	TW054	0.47
Tracy Worral	Any	TW076	0.47
Tracy Worral	Any	TW005	0.47
Tracy Worral	Any	TW004	0.47
Tracy Worral	Any	TW003	0.47
Tracy Worral	Any	TW002	0.47
Tracy Worral	Any	TW001	0.47

   Pretty cool – even if we're only displaying the first ten records!

Before we move on to creating navigation controls let's examine some of the code that has been written using these behaviors. Don't worry, we're not going to wade through it line by line, but once you know what it looks like you'll become more familiar with the functions it performs and it becomes easier to tweak and even to troubleshoot.

The Code

Once we applied the Repeat Region a whole load of Visual Basic code was written to our page. Take a look at the first part, which deals with the opening of the database connection and population of recordset data.

```
<%@LANGUAGE="VBSCRIPT"%>
<!--#include file="../Connections/KoolKards.asp" -->
<%
set rsProducts = Server.CreateObject("ADODB.Recordset")
rsProducts.ActiveConnection = MM_KoolKards_STRING
rsProducts.Source = "SELECT artist, occasion, cost,
➥ ref_number FROM X products ORDER BY occasion ASC"
rsProducts.CursorType = 0
```

```
rsProducts.CursorLocation = 2
rsProducts.LockType = 3
rsProducts.Open()
rsProducts_numRows = 0
%>
```

You should recognise the first five lines of code from Chapter 4 – we've declared our script language and created the connection. The highlighted line is particularly interesting:

```
rsProducts.Source = "SELECT artist, cost, occasion,
➥ ref_number from products ORDER BY occasion ASC"
```

This is known as an **SQL statement** – we mentioned we'd be giving SQL and queries full attention in the next chapter, but for now take a look at the statement.

Our SQL statement is just a piece of code that tells the database what information it wants. In this case we requested the fields artist, cost, occasion, and ref_number from the products table and we wished them to be in **ascending order** based on occasion.

```
rsProducts.CursorType = 0
rsProducts.CursorLocation = 2
```

The next two lines tells the database what type of cursor to open and where. The cursor in a database does just what a cursor in a word processor does. It simply specifies where we are in the recordset at any given point. There are four types (numbered 0,1,2,3) and ours is set to UltraDev's default, 0, which is a forward-only cursor – the simplest and fastest kind. For the CursorLocation, 1 = client-side and 2 = server-side (default). We don't want the entire contents of the database sent down the line for our computer to navigate, so we let the server do it.

```
rsProducts.LockType = 3
```

The LockType function determines how records can be updated; the default value of 3 means when we hit the Update button after changing a record (as we'll be doing in the next chapter), the record will be locked for the split-second that the update takes place, protecting our data.

We now have all the information we need to open our recordset, so the next line of code does just that:

```
rsProducts.Open()
```

You can easily change all of these parameters from within UltraDev. To access these, open the Server Behaviors box and click on your Recordset. If you open the Property inspector (CTRL+F3), you'll be able to make changes to the parameters we've just discussed, but for the moment you'll probably find yourself just accepting the UltraDev defaults.

Displaying your Database | 5

> When you're looking for small sections of code within a larger code block, you can use the **Server Behaviors** panel to help you. In our example we're looking for the code that manages the repeated regions, so we can simply highlight the **Repeat Region** server behavior in the panel whilst keeping our code view open. The relevant code will be displayed in your code window and highlighted!

OK, that's enough of the code for the moment. Most beginners never take the time or effort to go over any of the code UltraDev generates but it's a really useful exercise, one that should give you a solid understanding of what's going on. There will be many times when you need to understand the inner workings of your page, especially when it comes to debugging or trouble-shooting your own code. Also, reusing parts of Macromedia's code for your own routines is fairly common practice – so it's best to get an understanding of what's going on!

As a nice contrast to all that code, let's do something that's *drag-and-droppable*...

Recordset Navigation

Now we have ten records displayed on our page – but we know there are many more to look at. We need to create some way of moving to the next set of ten records.

This is a breeze for UltraDev and ready to go after a few clicks!

Remember in the first chapter where we used the Live Object Insert Record – well UltraDev has another useful Live Object called Insert Recordset Navigation Bar.

5 Foundation Dreamweaver UltraDev 4

Inserting a Navigation Bar

1. Look under the Live section of your Objects panel and find the Insert Recordset Navigation Bar button. Don't select it quite yet.

2. First of all, you'll need to place the cursor on your web page on the line beneath your table (this is where we want the bar to go).

3. Once in place, click the Insert Recordset Navigation Bar button and choose the Images option from the dialog box:

4. Click OK and check whether the screen shows what you see here. If you've placed your navigation bar in the wrong place, use the Edit > undo feature and try again.

Displaying your Database

You've just inserted a fully functioning recordset navigation system with about three clicks!

Our Navigation Controls in Detail

Let's take a look at what has been created here... UltraDev has inserted four buttons for us, and reading from left to right they are:

|◀◀| Move to the beginning of the recordset

|◀| Move to the previous record

|▶| Move to the next record

|▶▶| Move to the end of the recordset

The other clever function it has added is the ability to only show the appropriate buttons at certain times so that you don't have the |▶| button appear when you're at the end of the recordset.

This is a really cool time saving feature and perfect for building pages quickly and easily.

Test it out now in your browser. Look at how navigation buttons disappear when they're not needed.

If you're feeling adventurous, you may be wondering whether you can build your own navigation bars – you might have designs of your own, a particular site style or color scheme, or maybe only want certain functions. As we saw with the Insert Record Live Object, our navigation bar is really just a series of individual server behaviors 'wrapped up' for us.

It's possible to set all these up on an individual basis. If you look under the + symbol on the Server Behaviors panel you'll a Move to Record option which then gives you all the navigation options.

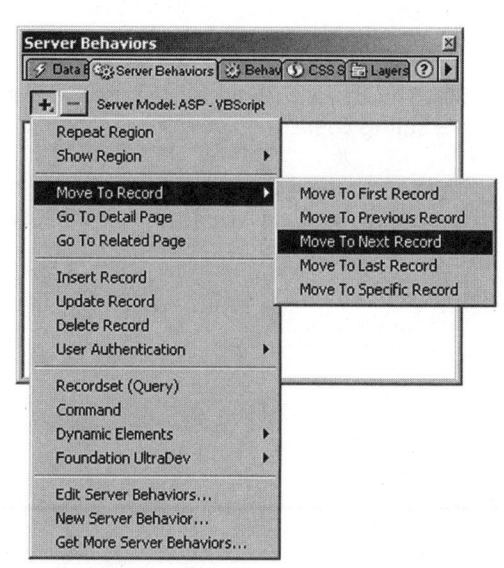

What about the way UltraDev cleverly hides the buttons if they're not needed? They are controlled by the Show Region options:

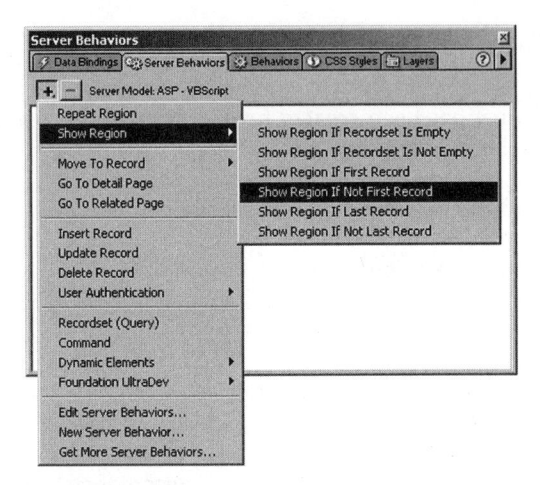

By applying these server behaviors to individual buttons or images, you can create your own navigation systems really easily – so you can quickly improve on the default ones UltraDev creates for you.

Why not delete the navigation bar created by UltraDev and see if you can create the same thing using individual images or text links? You'll soon get the hang of it.

You'll also be pleased to know that we are not going to dive into all the code that is produced by the live object. However, we suggest you take a look now and read it through. Although hard to reproduce, it's not that difficult to read and it's a useful exercise. We don't need to be able to write all this code, but it is handy to be able to understand it.

On your journey around the Web, a common feature that you'll have undoubtedly seen many times is a **record counter** – something like "You are looking at records 5 to 10 of 30". This is really useful for the user, as it gives them an idea of how many more records are still to come.

The good news is that this function is also built into UltraDev's Live Objects! We'll take you through a quick exercise to show how easy it is.

Displaying your Database 5

Keeping Track of our Records

1. Place your cursor on the page where you want the record counter to go (we suggest putting it directly underneath the navigation buttons); go to the Live Objects panel and click on Insert Recordset Navigation Status:

   You'll see the properties box, with not a huge number of options.

2. Make sure our recordset rsProducts is selected and click OK.

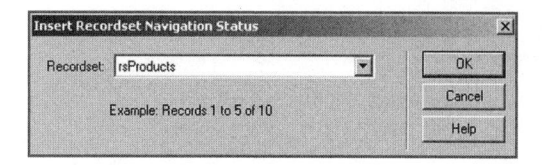

3. Your page will look something like this.

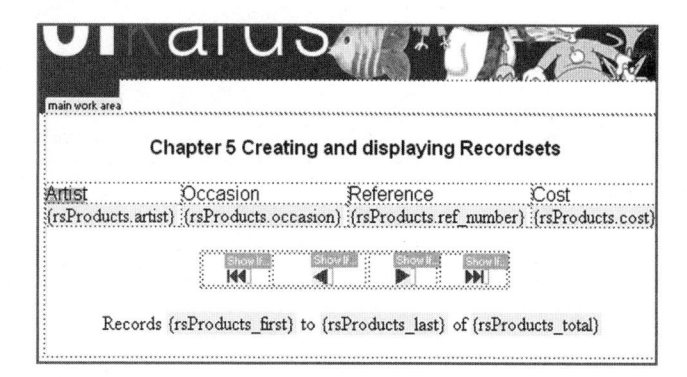

5 Foundation Dreamweaver UltraDev 4

See how UltraDev has placed a line in for us. The black-on-white text at the bottom is normal HTML text, which we could change. The black-on-blue text bits are special dynamic recordset fields. You may recognize these special fields {rsProducts_first}, {rsProducts_last} and {rsProducts_total} from the list of fields in our recordset.

> *If you have highlighting turned off in your application preferences, you won't see this! Turn to the back of the book for information on preferences and how to set them.*

Save and preview your web page again. Now it's really cooking. We have a full navigation system that tells us where we are in the recordset. Imagine how long that would have taken us to code by hand.

That's pretty much it for our viewing page – we've returned all the records from our database and put them inside a navigable table.

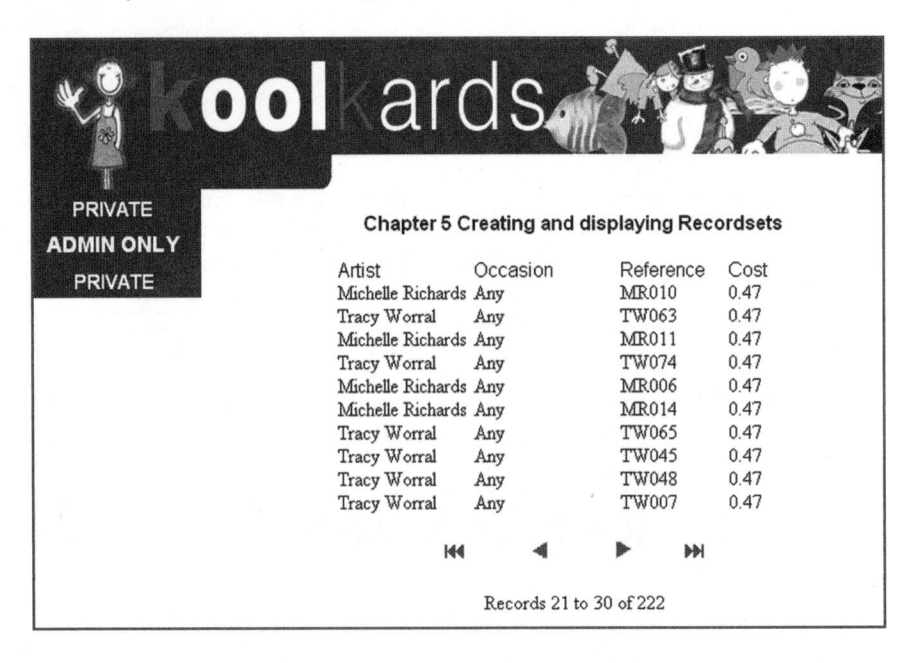

Chapter 5 Creating and displaying Recordsets

Artist	Occasion	Reference	Cost
Michelle Richards	Any	MR010	0.47
Tracy Worral	Any	TW063	0.47
Michelle Richards	Any	MR011	0.47
Tracy Worral	Any	TW074	0.47
Michelle Richards	Any	MR006	0.47
Michelle Richards	Any	MR014	0.47
Tracy Worral	Any	TW065	0.47
Tracy Worral	Any	TW045	0.47
Tracy Worral	Any	TW048	0.47
Tracy Worral	Any	TW007	0.47

Records 21 to 30 of 222

Displaying your Database   5

Summary

In this very hands-on chapter, we've laid the foundations of our dynamic web application by learning how to display and navigate our database. We've learned that:

- A recordset is a subset of information from our database, gathered according to our criteria.

- We can drag and drop recordset fields into our pages to show only the data we want, exactly where we want it, whilst with the Live Data View we can see our pages as they come alive.

- UltraDev's live objects allow us to insert commonly used but powerful features, such as a navigation bar, with a few clicks.

Now that we can view and navigate our records, in the next chapter we'll look at how to update, manage and even delete these records – all the things that only an administrator can do.

kool kards

6 Amending your Database

What we'll cover in this chapter:

- **Detail pages**: allowing our users to find out more about a particular record

- Creating **administration** pages which won't be seen by normal users

- **Updating** our database records and **deleting** unwanted or out-of-date records

- **Live Objects** – UltraDev's useful '**wizards**'

Foundation Dreamweaver UltraDev 4

Now we have a connection, a recordset to use, and we know how to display and navigate our records, what we need is something more *dynamic*.

In this chapter, we'll show you some of the ways you can truly interact with your data. Starting with detail pages – which allow you to click on an item to find out more – we'll then move on to pages which enable us to update and even delete records entirely!

These basic view, insert, update and delete pages are the real bread and butter of most data-driven web pages, and something you will find yourself creating time and time again with UltraDev.

What exactly is a detail page?

Detail Pages

If you bought this book from an e-tailer like Amazon, your search for 'UltraDev' might have brought up a number of books – but when you then clicked on *Foundation UltraDev*, it would have come up on a page of its own with more details and a picture. That's what a detail page is. From our results page, we need a way for our users to click on a product to find out more...

Setting Up your Page

1. The first step is to create a new page; call it `product_details.asp`. Use the Admin template again, so we can tie this exercise in with our administrator's tools later, although realistically you'd want these detail pages to be readily accessible by customers.

   Important; ideally, we would want all these pages (the results page, the detail page, etc.) to be in the same folder – this way the links are easier. So, we advise you save this new page in the Chapter 5 folder.

   Our page is going to display the details for a specific card, which the user will select from the table of results we created earlier. We basically want to provide all the other bits of information stored in our database relating to that product.

Amending your Database — 6

2. Continue by creating a new table; again it's just a simple table (Insert > Table), this time with eight rows and two columns; something similar to what you see here will do:

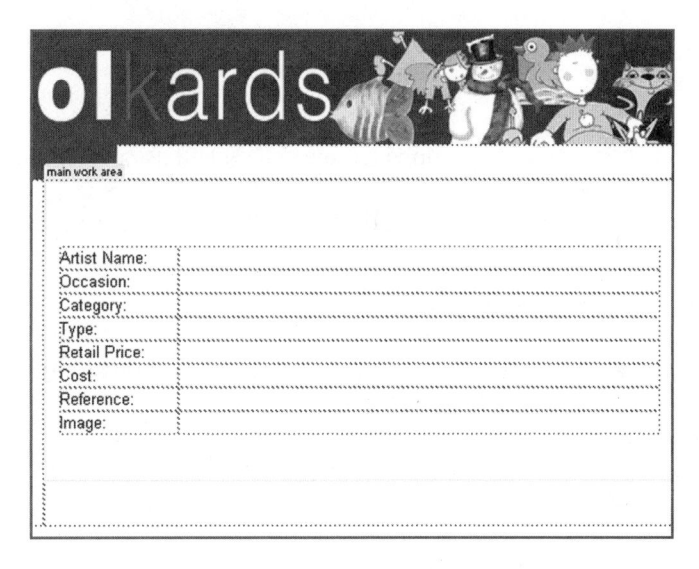

Make sure you save your new page.

3. Now we need to add the all-important recordset for our page – so just like last time open up the Data Bindings panel, use the + sign and select Recordset (Query) from the drop-down list. Once you have it open set the parameters to what you see here:

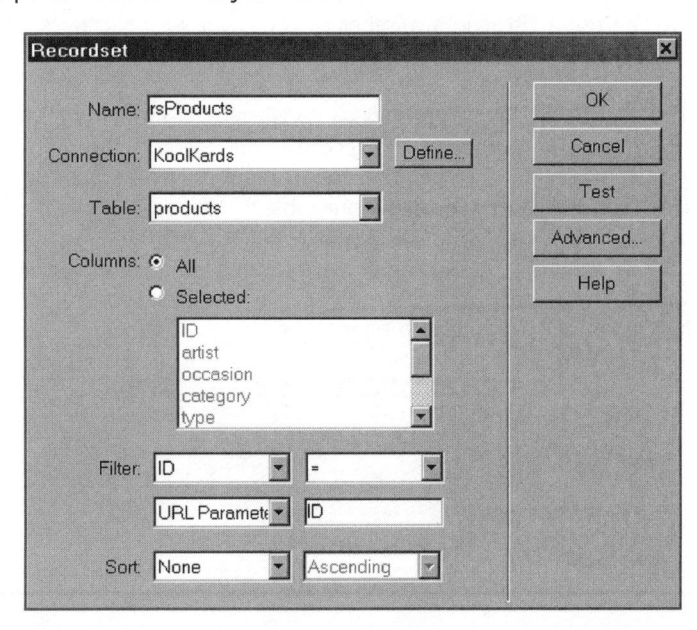

- In Name: **enter** rsProducts
- In Connection: **enter** KoolKards
- In Table: **enter** products
- In Columns: **ensure the All radio button is selected**
- In Filter: **enter** ID = URL Parameter ID
- In Sort: **enter** None

There are two things to note here:

- We really do want all the fields to be returned here, as we are going to display them on the detail page.
- This time we're using a **filter** – ID = (URL Parameter) ID, which will be explained below.

Filtering your Records

OK, so what record are we going to want to display? Simple – whichever one the user selects. However, we need a way of telling UltraDev this. It has no idea that we're creating a detail page – one page looks the same as any other to UltraDev!

We can use a **filter** in a number of ways, but we need ours to filter out all the records except the one selected from the results page.

The method we are using is to say to UltraDev, "Show me all the records in the database where the **ID number** of the record is the *same* as the number being passed from the **results page**." (Remember that the ID number is a *unique* number in our database – one that can identify any record in our table.)

Let's simplify this by clicking Test from our Recordset dialog. As UltraDev doesn't have a value to work with from a results page, it will ask you for one – to simulate what will happen in our working web pages.

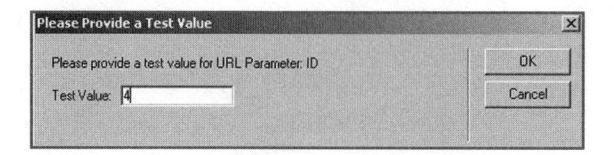

Amending your Database

Type in 4, click OK and see what happens.

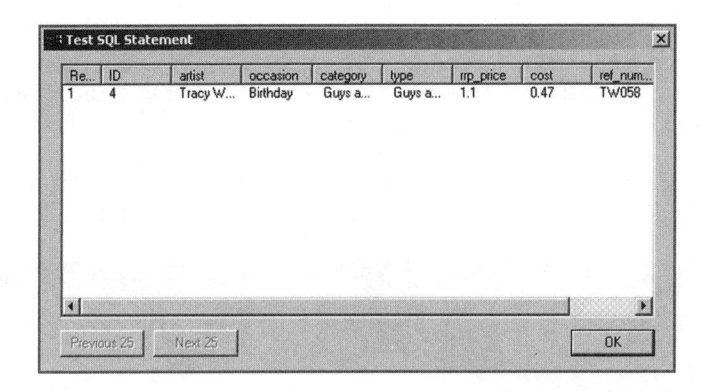

Only one record has been returned – the record with ID 4 – just the one we want. Click OK twice to close the test window and the recordset dialog box.

It's worth spending a moment here to have a look at what code has been written to achieve this. Go into Code View.

```
<%
Dim rsProducts__MMColParam
rsProducts__MMColParam = "1"
if (Request.QueryString("ID") <> "") then
rsProducts__MMColParam = Request.QueryString("ID")
%>
```

Remember back in Chapter 3 when we explained how we could pass details around through **URL parameters**. Do you recognise some of that code? How about...

```
Request.Querystring("ID")
```

You'll notice that the value of the ID is being placed in a variable called rsProducts__MMColParam. This value is then passed to the **SQL statement** in a variable called rsProducts.Source:

```
<%
set rsProducts = Server.CreateObject("ADODB.Recordset")
rsProducts.ActiveConnection = MM_KoolKards_OLEDB_STRING
rsProducts.Source = "SELECT * FROM products WHERE ID = " +
➥ Replace(rsProducts__MMColParam, "'", "''") + ""
rsProducts.CursorType = 0
rsProducts.CursorLocation = 2
rsProducts.LockType = 3
rsProducts.Open()
```

Foundation Dreamweaver UltraDev 4

```
rsProducts_numRows = 0
%>
```

See how the code has created a SQL statement (in bold) from the passed ID `QueryString`. Bit of a nightmare with all those inverted commas, but at least you can see how it works!

Now your recordset is up and running you can drag and drop the fields to the appropriate places on your page. But don't drag the last field Image just yet. Nice and easy this bit!

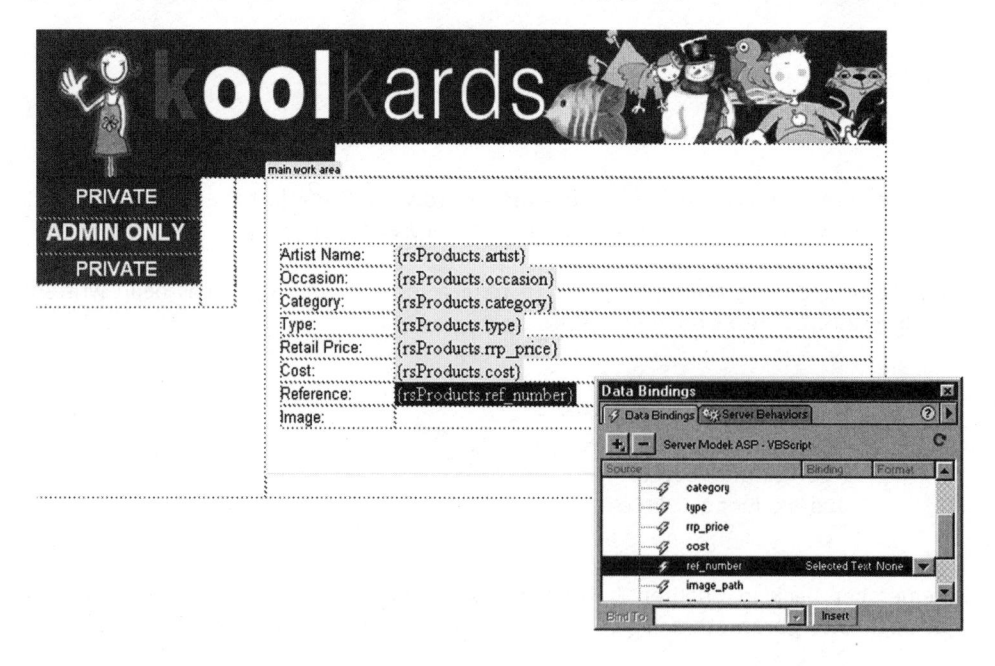

You may have noticed if you looked at the product table that we're not actually storing the images in the database. We're only storing the path to where the image can be found. Although storing a real image is possible in a database – you'll soon find your database swelling to unmanageable sizes. We need to create what's known as a **dynamic image** and in the next exercise we'll do just that.

Create a Dynamic Image

1. Place your cursor on your web page in the last row of your table – where you expected to drag the image field to.

Amending your Database   6

2. From your menu, choose Insert > Image or the Insert Image button from your Common Objects – just as you would insert a normal image for your web page.

3. This will bring up your file browser to select your image. However, select Data Sources from Select File Name From: near the top of the file browser:

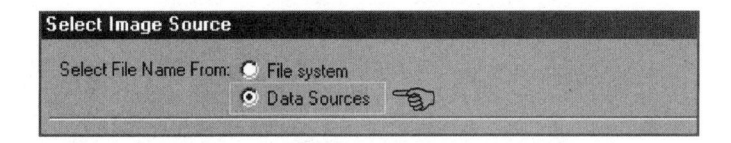

4. Once you've clicked Data Sources, you'll see the screen change to display all the fields in your recordset:

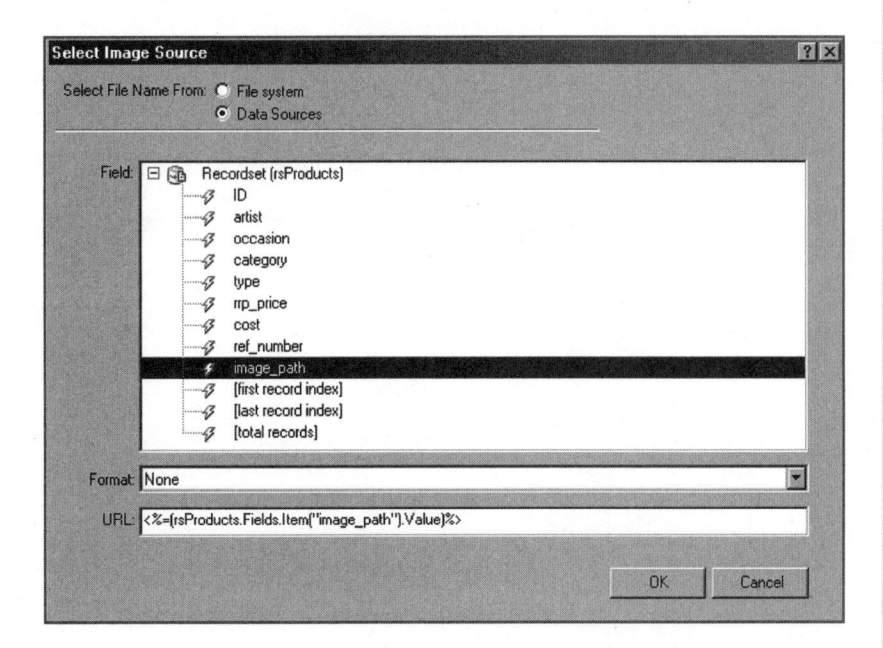

5. Click on the field called image_path this will replace the URL: with `<%=(rsProducts.Fields.Item("image_path").Value)%>`

6. Press OK.

Foundation Dreamweaver UltraDev 4

Your page should now look something like this:

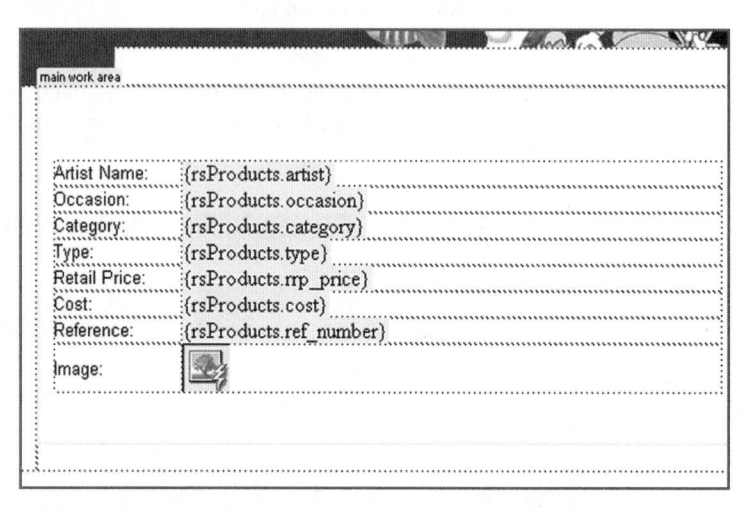

Now is a good time to use our Live Data Preview again – to see how a page might look with a full image in it.

7. Click the Live Data Preview button now and this is what you should see:

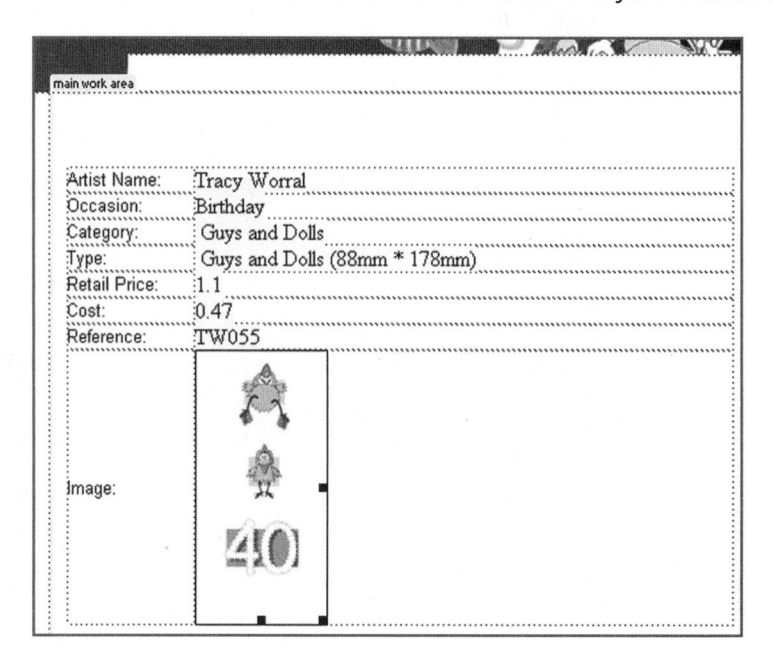

All we have to do now is link our results page to our details page. Save your work and close your web page.

Amending your Database   6

Linking Results to Detail

Let's return to our `list_products.asp` page. Looking at our results table, we are going to make the Artist's name a clickable link that will take us to the detail page of that particular record.

We need to make a couple of changes on this page first.

If you remember, in our detail page we've made a **filter** – one that will only work once an ID number is sent to it. What we need to do is somehow set up our results table, so when the user clicks our Artist hotlink the ID number is passed to the details page, which in turn can filter the results to only display this one record.

Making the Link

1. Double-click Recordset (rsProducts) under the Server Behaviors tab, this will launch the Recordset box again:

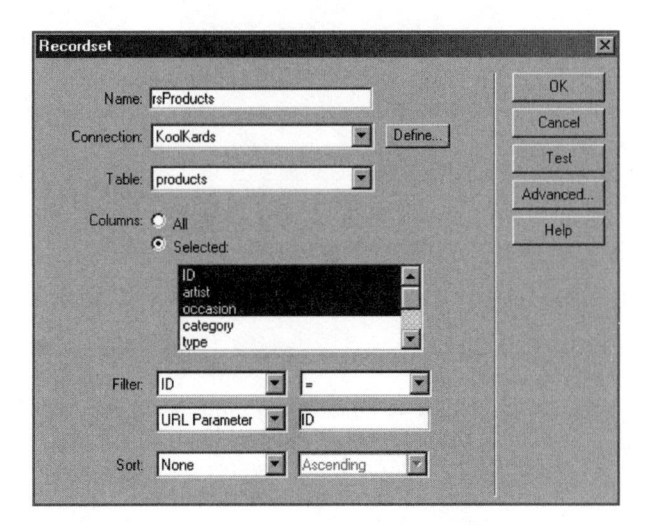

2. Under the Columns: Selected: press and hold CTRL to select ID and add it to the columns already in the recordset. You should now have ID, artist, occasion, cost, and ref_number selected.

3. Click OK to close the box.

   Now we're ready to introduce you to a new server behavior.

Foundation Dreamweaver UltraDev 4

4. Highlight {rsProducts.artist} from our web page:

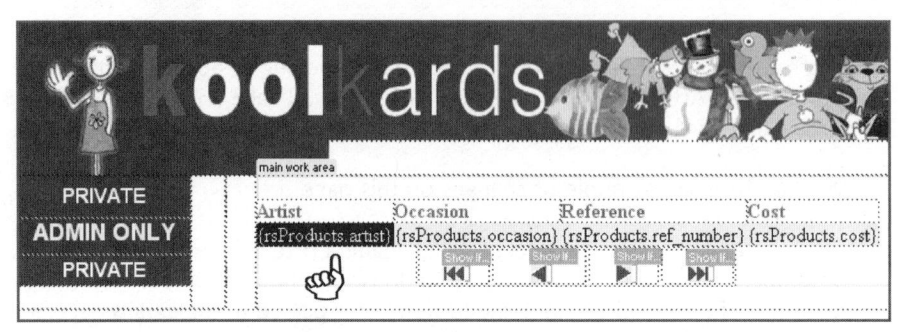

5. Insert the server behavior Go to Detail Page found on the Server Behavior panel:

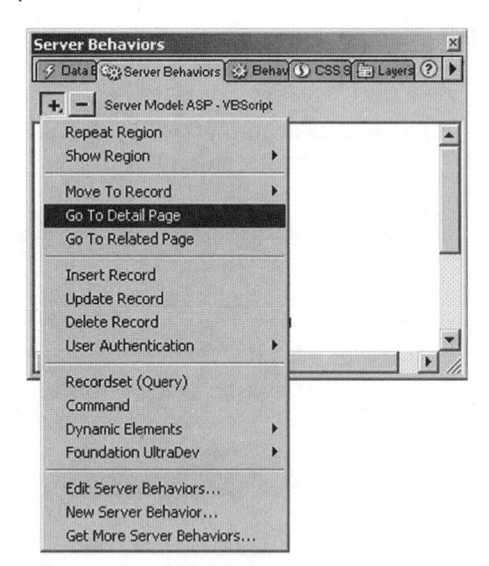

6. When the Go to Detail Page window comes up, the Link: box should be filled automatically if you highlighted rsProducts.artist correctly. Enter the name of your detail page or press Browse... and select your page from there. Either way, for now it's our product_details.asp page we want:

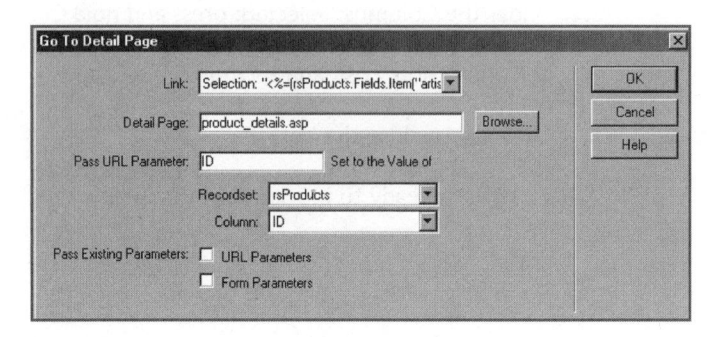

Amending your Database | 6

7. Pass URL Parameter: will contain a column value, referred to on the detail page – in our case this is ID since that's the column that contains our unique value.

8. The recordset is, of course, rsProducts, and from the drop-down box, select the column containing the value which will be passed to our parameter – our ID column again.

9. Press OK, and let's recap on what we've done here.

> *We created a parameter called 'ID'. This parameter gets its value from the field ID in the rsProducts recordset. We'll use this number to filter out all but the correct details page.*

10. Test the result in your browser. Now we're really creating some serious ASP pages.

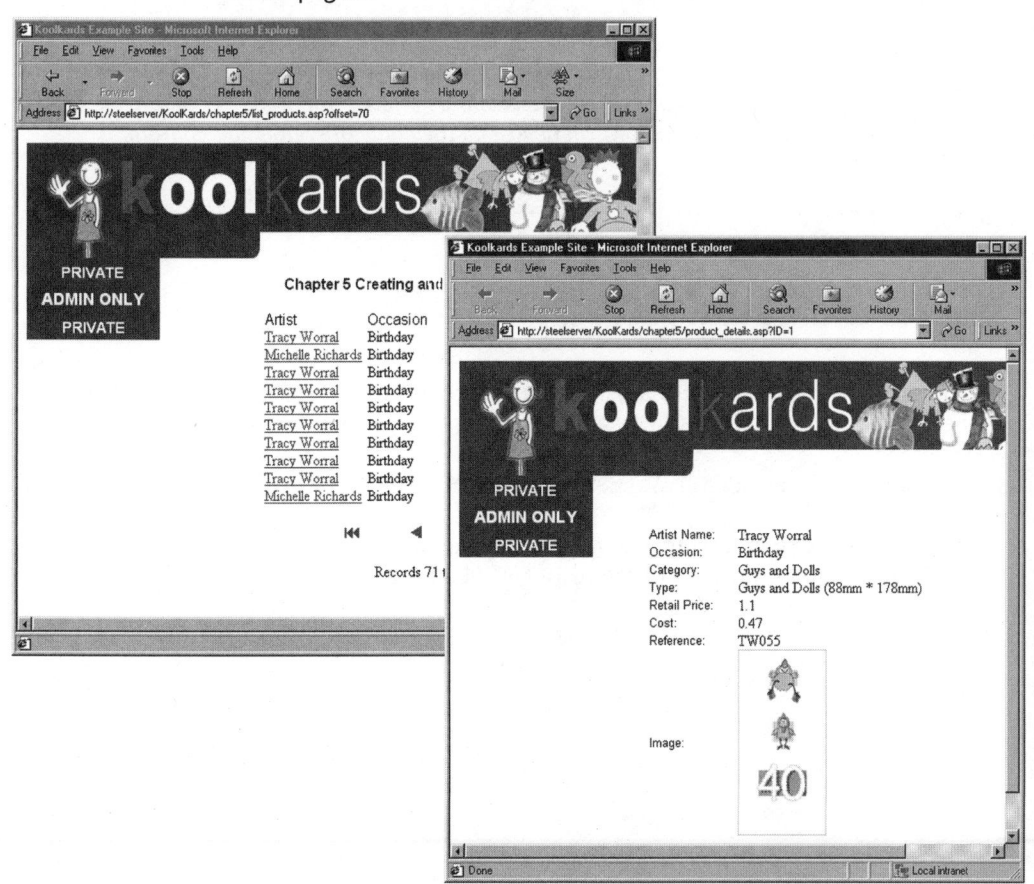

137

Into the Code

Time to take a peek at your code again. In particular let's look at the server behavior created by UltraDev on the results page:

```
<A HREF="product_details.asp?<%= MM_keepNone &MM_joinChar
➥ (MM_keepNone) & "ID="&rsProducts.Fields.Item
➥ ("ID").Value%>"><%=(rsProducts.Fields.Item
➥ ("artist").Value)%></A>
```

Looks like a bit of a nightmare – but it's just creating a link to `product_details.asp` and then adding our parameter `"ID="`. The `"artist"` part is just stating which column will be used as our hotlink.

Basically the final URL would look something like this in our browser

http://locahost/koolkards/chapter5/product_details.asp?ID=4

> If you pop up the server behavior **Go To Detail Page** again (double-click on it), you'll see the option to **pass existing parameters** – here we can keep passing our parameters between as many pages as we want. Remember if we don't, they will be lost as they only are remembered from one page to the next.

Shortcut to the Detail Page

You saw that UltraDev writes a fair amount of code to produce this behavior. You could have achieved the same result by adding this to your URL link:

```
product_details.asp?ID=<%=rsProducts.Fields.Item("ID").Value %>
```

If you're feeling confident, try deleting that Go To Detail Page behavior and add the above to the link in the properties of the Artist cell, like this:

Amending your Database 6

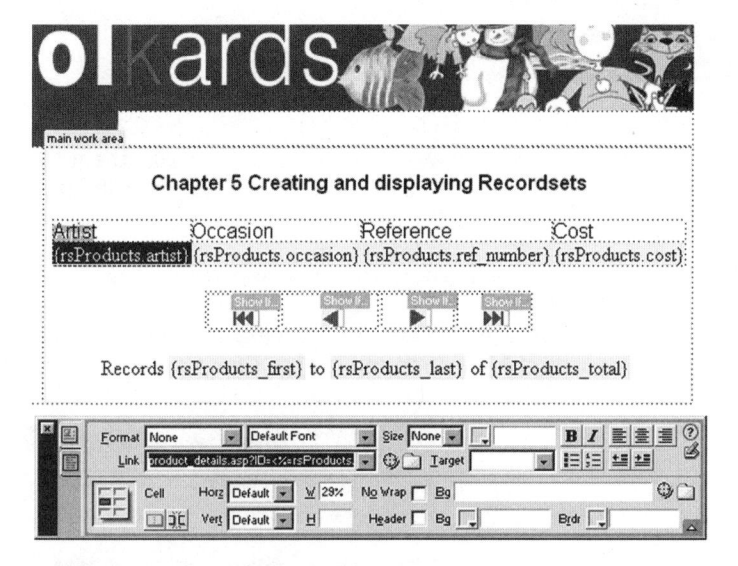

Sometimes pre-written server behaviors need to take all potential scenarios into consideration and therefore the code generated isn't always as streamlined as it could be. With a bit of understanding of ASP, you can create some smarter code, just like we have here. This is one of the reasons we encourage you so much to look at the code from time to time.

Go to Detail Live Object

If you prefer it when we give you shortcuts first, there's a chance you may be swearing at us in a few seconds, because we just spent all that time creating our results page and detail page separately, and *guess what*? Lurking in the background was a Live Object that would do most of the job for you!

The reason we didn't show you this first is we wanted you to learn how to put these pages together separately, so you would understand how it all fits together. It's no good letting all these wizards do the job for you, because soon enough you'll want to do something that is out of the wizards' reach, no matter how long their wands!

So, let's illustrate this point beautifully by using the Live Object to create the same results and detail pages – and see if you can anticipate the problem the wizard is going to have...

Foundation Dreamweaver UltraDev 4

Setting up a Master Detail wizard

1. Make two new blank pages – call them something like `MasterTest.asp` and `DetailTest.asp`; we'll not be using these pages after this demo – but this is a useful exercise to undertake.

2. Re–open your `list_products.asp` page.

   Make sure your Data Bindings panel is open, select the rsProducts recordset, right-click and choose Copy:

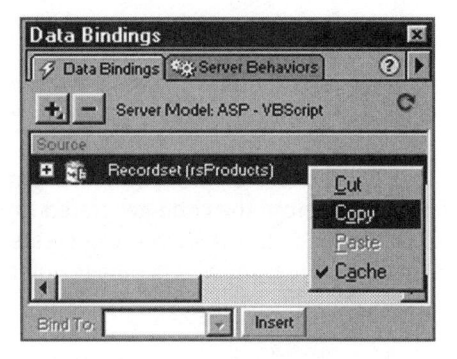

3. Open your `MasterTest.asp` page and open the Data Bindings panel – click the small > arrow in the top right corner and the Paste option will appear. Select this and you've just made an exact copy of the recordset from the previous page:

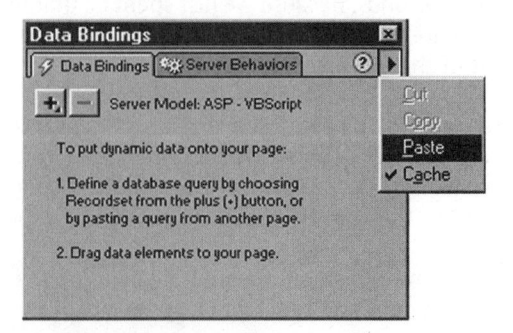

   This is a really great time-saving technique that will also ensure your recordsets are exactly the same.

Amending your Database 6

4. Click on the Insert Master–Detail Set from the Live Objects panel. You'll be presented with a large dialog box. Again, just follow the steps and the screenshots.

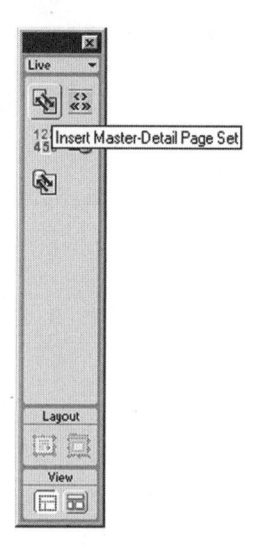

5. Select your recordset (rsProducts).

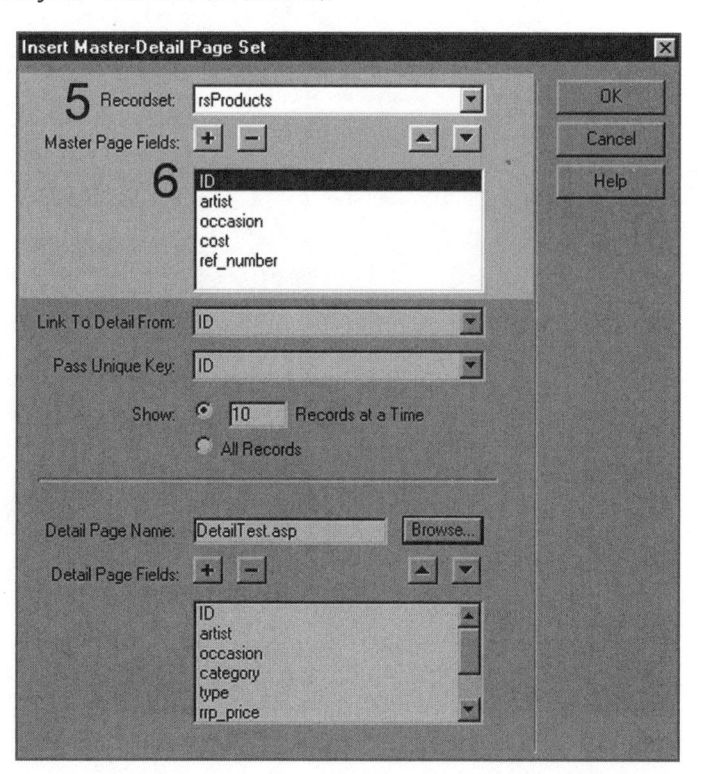

6. Select the fields you wish to display in the master page (that is the results/list page). You can do this by adding columns with the + (plus)

button and removing them with the – (minus) symbol. You can also decide in what order you would like the fields displayed by using the up and down arrow symbols. Remember to only include the fields you want in your results table/page.

7. Select the ID field for the Link To Detail From:

8. Select the ID for Pass Unique Key:

9. Accept the default 10 records to show at a time.

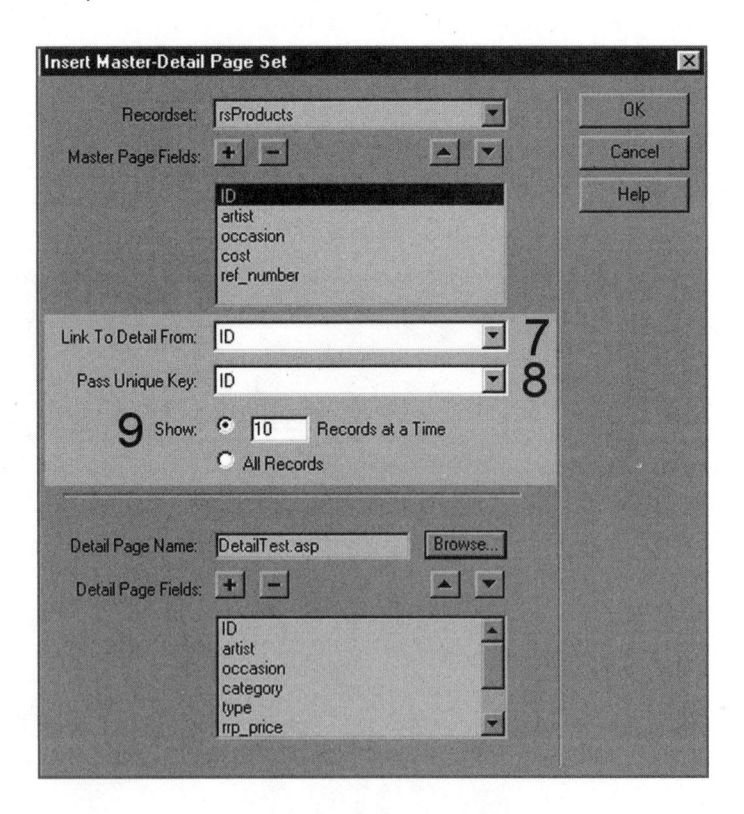

Amending your Database | 6

10. Select the details page (`DetailTest.asp`).

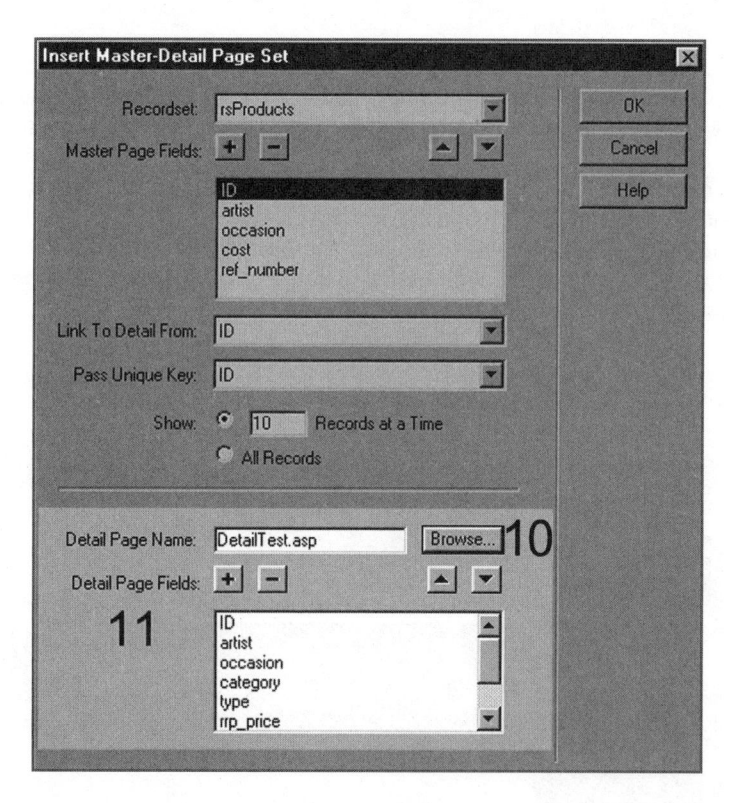

Insert Master-Detail Page Set

- Recordset: rsProducts
- Master Page Fields: [+] [-] [▲][▼]
  - ID
  - artist
  - occasion
  - cost
  - ref_number
- Link To Detail From: ID
- Pass Unique Key: ID
- Show: ● 10 Records at a Time
  - ○ All Records
- Detail Page Name: DetailTest.asp [Browse...] **10**
- Detail Page Fields: [+] [-] [▲][▼]

11
- ID
- artist
- occasion
- category
- type
- rrp_price

11. Again use the + and − symbols to select which fields you want displayed on the detail page. In our case we want them all so leave it as it is.

12. Click OK and watch the wizard go to work. Impressive stuff eh?

13. Now test and view your records – notice the difference?

    The wizard can't handle our dynamic image – just a path name.

Sure, we can do it manually as above – but only because we taught you the long way around. As with most things in UltraDev, it's best to learn the *whys* first – if you later find a wizard that saves you time, that's great, but wizards without understanding make for big headaches later down the (yellow brick) road.

Well, we've covered a lot in this chapter already. We've looked at creating a detail page manually, saw a nifty shortcut and then seen how UltraDev can do all it for us. It's now time to look at some more advanced pages that our regular users won't get to see – just us!

6 Foundation Dreamweaver UltraDev 4

Administration Pages

Our **Administration System** will be the password-protected part of the site, where employees of KoolKards can enter 'hidden' screens not seen by the average user. From here the Administrator can **view**, **add**, **update** or **delete** the cards from each range.

For example, if Christmas card prices are to come down in February, to protect us from having to go in to the actual database and change the prices within the tables, we'll create some user-friendly screens that enable the Administrator to make changes from the web. This also means that the Administrator can change the product range, prices, etc., from anywhere in the world, via any web-enabled computer!

We can link these admin pages to the full site using something like this AdminMenu screen (you'll find this in the Chapter 5 download – `adminmenu.asp`):

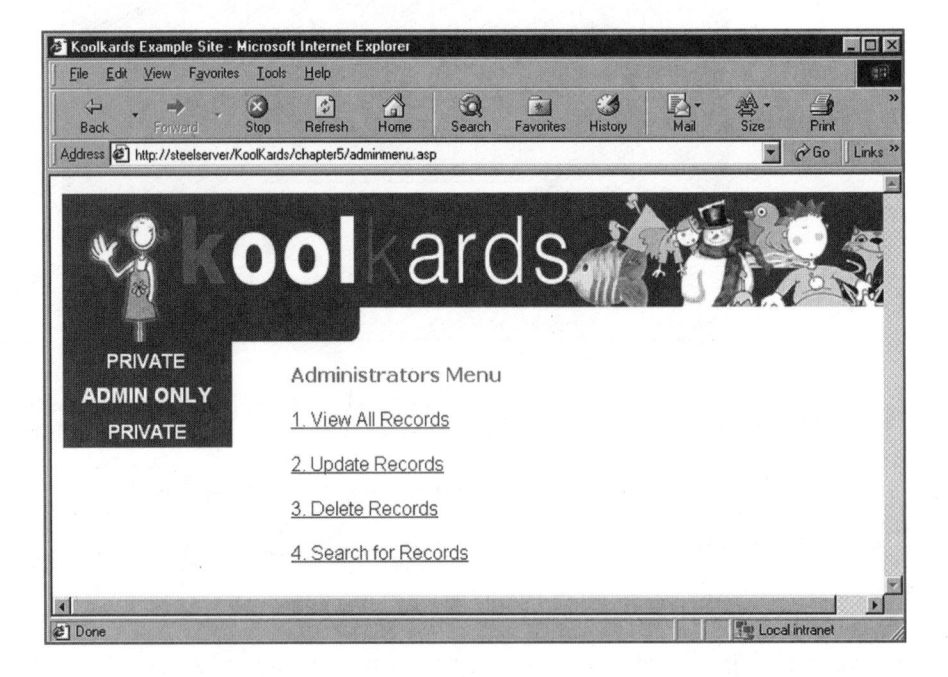

> Later in the chapter, we'll be combining some of the options – making an update and delete page – so you may well want to change your Admin menu to reflect these changes as we cover the topic. This Admin Menu is just a series of links – there is no 'right' or 'wrong' way of doing it and you should feel comfortable changing it as you progress with the chapter.

Amending your Database   6

So, at this stage the user can *view* all the information from their database but they can't do anything with it. What we need now is a way he or she can change the data in the database. This is commonly known as an **update** page, *a page where the administrator can update the data.*

After we've created our update page, we'll continue the chapter by looking at how a administrator can use a **delete** page – to delete any record.

Finally, we'll look at an advanced exercise, which they won't tell you about in the manuals! Creating update and delete functionality on the *same* page!

Update Pages

So far we have covered how to display our data ten records at a time in a list format or as individual 'detail' records. All this is great but we have been limited by 'viewing' only and really need a way in which our Administrator can change the data when they need to.

Like we've seen with many other things in UltraDev, you've got a choice. You can slowly and laboriously create your update pages manually, with lots of room for error and a greater understanding needed, or you can simply push a button on the Live Object panel and watch UltraDev do it for you. Guess which method we are going to use?

Oh yes! We're going to do it the *hard way*!

> *Actually, we will look at the Live Object version afterwards – but by that time you'll want to do it manually anyhow, promise!*

Most update pages work in a very similar way to our results/detail set of pages. The Administrator will find the records they want to edit, and then select them to view the data. However, instead of just viewing this extra data in static text, he or she will be able to edit the data and send it back to the server once they've finished with it.

We've covered how to create the first part already – how the Administrator can view all the records to find the particular record they want to update, so let's start by saving some time.

The page we will need will look more or less identical to our `product_details.asp` page, so from your site window, let's make a copy of it.

Copying a Page

1. Bring up your site window (F8), find the `product_details.asp` page and right click on the file. Select Copy:

2. Now highlight your Chapter 6 folder, right-click and choose Paste:

3. Finally, right-click on this new file, choose Rename and call your page `update_products.asp`.

   We'll make some changes to this page shortly to make the data editable by the user.

If you think about it, we should need to create another **master** list page – so the user can find the record and get to the update page. Indeed, this is what you'll see in your final downloaded site. But it seems a bit of a waste of time, creating all that when we know how it works now – so let's cut a few corners and just edit our existing `list_products.asp` page, and instead of linking it to the detail page we'll make it jump straight into the update page.

Redefining your Dynamic Link

1. Re-open your `list_products.asp` page.

   We need to change the dynamic link Artist in the table so it points to our new `update_products.asp` page.

2. Highlight the link and its details will appear in the Property inspector (CTRL+F3):

```
Format None    Default Font    Size None           B I
Link update_records.asp?<%= MM_keepNone    Target
```

3. Change the Link: to read `update_products.asp` instead but keep the dynamic code.

Once you have a connection between the two new pages, switch to the `update_products.asp` page and let's start to make the records displayed editable.

Amending your Database   6

Creating your Update Page

1. Move your cursor into the work area of your page and choose Insert > Form. See a small red-lined border appear? This is the boundary of your HTML form.

2. In the Property inspector, give your form a name like frm_Update. Don't worry about the Action and Method, as our update behaviors will take care of this.

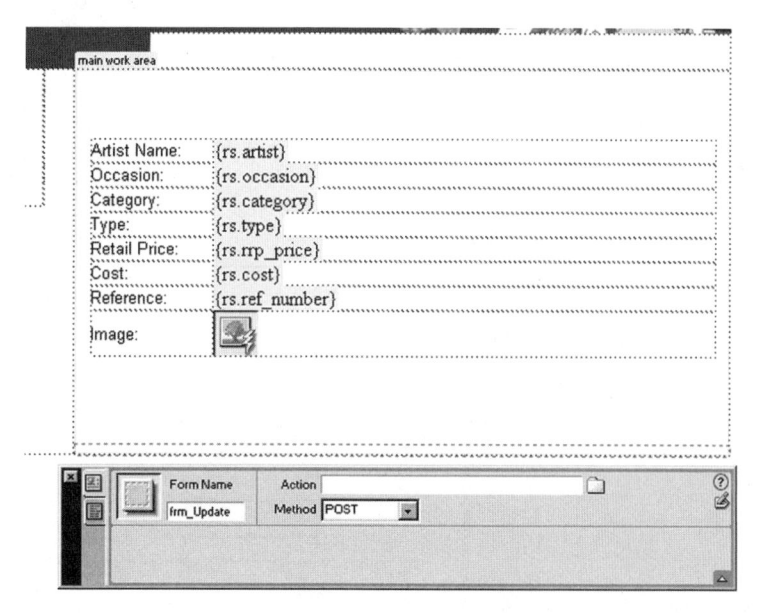

3. Now we need to cut and paste our table so it's inside our form boundaries (the red outline), and delete our dynamic data since it's non-editable.

4. Add our **edit boxes** – you'll find these on the Form Objects panel. Simply place the cursor on the page where you want your edit box and click the Insert Text Field button. For each of the fields in our table add a text box to allow the user to edit the contents.

    We need to give each text box an appropriate name – this will help us know which text box contains what information when we apply our Update behavior. You can rename your text boxes by highlighting the box and displaying the properties (F3). Change the name of each box so they read as in this list:

- Change Artist Name: to read frm_artist
- Change Occasion: to read frm_occasion
- Change Category: to read frm_category
- Change Type: to read frm_type
- Change Retail Price: to read frm_rrp_price
- Change Cost: to read frm_cost
- Change Reference: to read frm_reference

By the end of this step you'll have something like you see here:

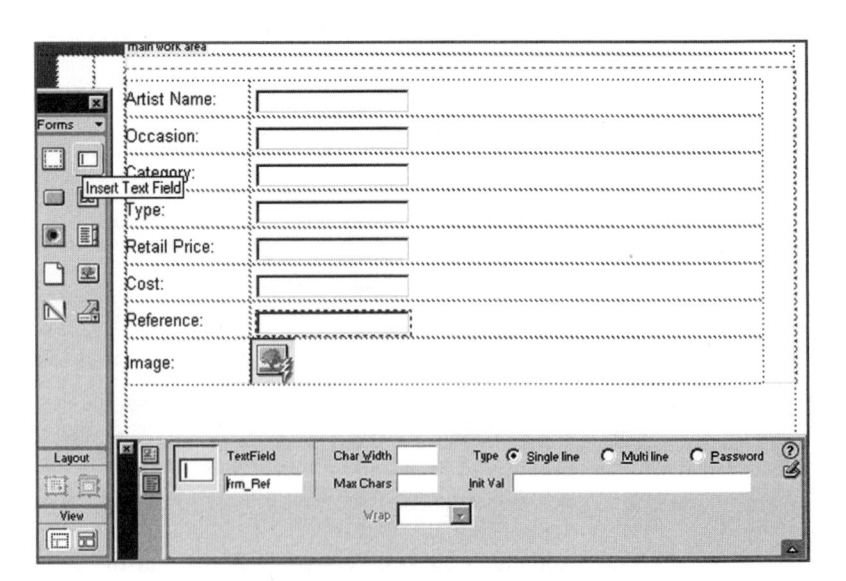

5. Once you've added a text box for each recordset field we need to set its initial value to the current value of the corresponding field from the database. You can do this by simply dragging the appropriate field from the Data Bindings panel and dropping it into the corresponding text box. If you've done it correctly, the dynamic fields will be nicely nestled in your text boxes like this:

Amending your Database 6

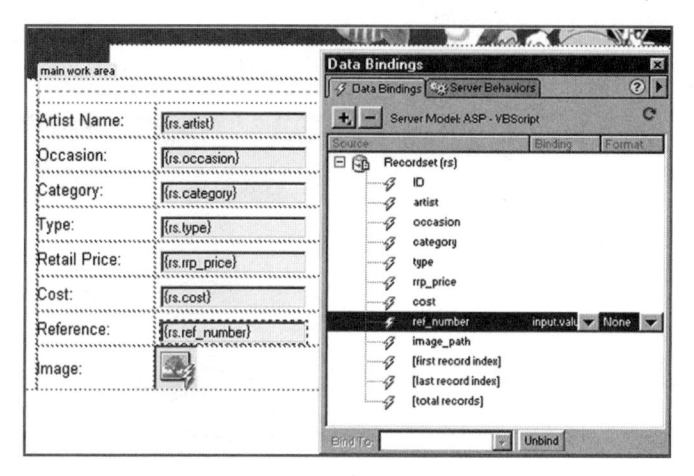

6. Add a Submit button to the form (Insert > Form Objects > Button).

7. If you wish, change the label of the Submit button by selecting the button, opening the Property inspector (CTRL+F3), and entering a new value in the Label box. In our example we've changed it to read Update Record.

Your finished form should now look something like this:

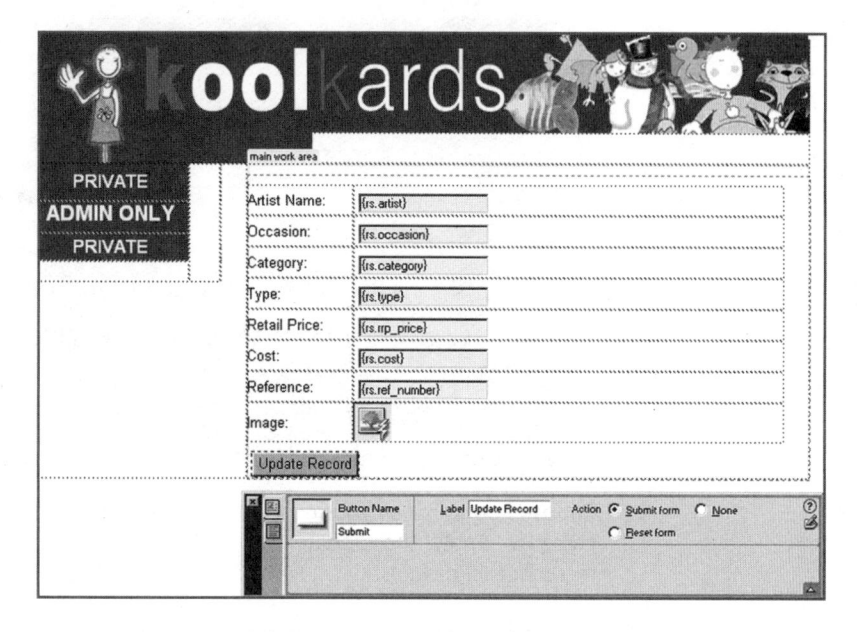

Our update form is complete and we are now ready to add the Update Server server behavior.

You can find the Update Record server behavior in the usual place on the Server Behaviors panel:

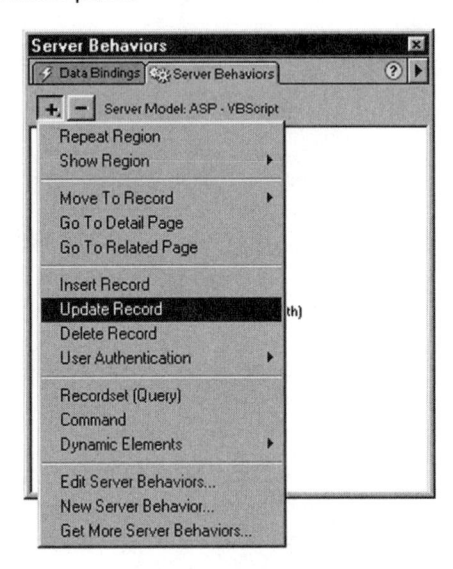

8. Select this and the Update Record dialog box will pop up:

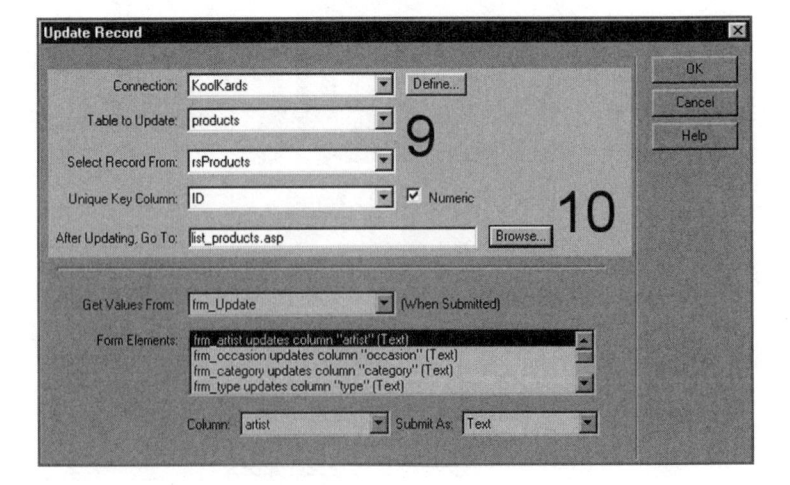

9. Choose KoolKards as your connection. The name of the table that we're going to apply the update to in this case is products. Select our recordset rsProducts.

10. You need to change the Unique Key Column to ID; UltraDev always defaults to the first field in the recordset as the Unique Column. After updating you need to decide where to direct the user. In this case we

Amending your Database   6

will simply send them back to the results page, so they can view the updated information.

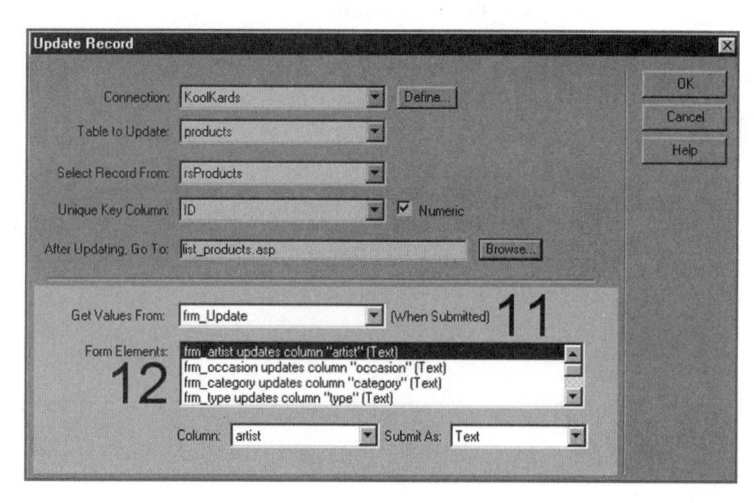

11. Get Values From: You need to select the name of the form that holds all the data. Remember when we renamed our red-lined box – that's the form name. It's possible to have more than one form on a page so make sure you choose the correct one (frm_Update).

12. Form Elements: In this section we are 'mapping' or 'marrying up' the parts of our form (the elements) with the fields in our database.

To do this, we select an element from the Form Elements section (highlighted in the above screenshot) and choose its respective field column in the Column drop-down menu. Finally we state what 'datatype' we Submit As (text, numeric, date, etc. etc).

Interestingly, if you call your form elements the same as the fields in your database (e.g. if you have a text box called frm_date_of_birth and a field in your database called date_of_birth) UltraDev will automatically marry the two. If you call your form elements something different however, you have to manually map the two parts.

Here's how the final mapping should be.

Form Element	Column	Submit As
Frm_artist	artist	Text
Frm_occasion	occasion	Text
Frm_category	category	Text
Frm_type	type	Text
Frm_rrp_price	rrp_price	Numeric
Frm_cost	cost	Numeric
Frm_Ref_number	ref_number	Text

13. Click OK and the behavior will be applied.

That's it! You now have a page that will update your record for you. Test it out and see how it works.

How the Update Behavior Works

Let's have a look at what exactly this behavior has placed on your page. The first thing we need to look at are the two **hidden fields** that have been created for us. Select the first one and look in the Property inspector.

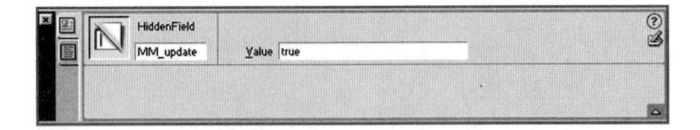

Note the first one is called MM_update. This hidden field contains a value that changes when the page is submitted. Only once the page realizes it has been submitted and comes back to itself, will it go away and do the update.

Let's look at the code that does this for us:

```
' *** Update Record: construct a SQL update statement and
➥ execute it

If (CStr(Request("MM_update")) <> "" And
CStr(Request("MM_recordId")) <> "") Then

  ' create the sql update statement
```

Amending your Database 6

Basically the above line says "If there is something in the MM_update box and there is a valid current record (MM_recordId) then do the update".

The other hidden form value is MM_recordId.

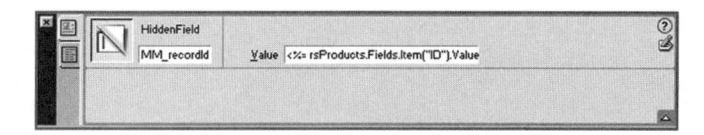

This means when the update is performed the page knows what record to update. It's essentially the hidden field that contains the **unique ID** from our database.

We could spend a lot of time looking at how the page constructs the update statement, but the part we want to introduce you to is the actual update statement itself.

```
<% Set MM_editCmd = Server.CreateObject("ADODB.Command")
   MM_editCmd.ActiveConnection = MM_editConnection
   MM_editCmd.CommandText = MM_editQuery
   MM_editCmd.Execute
   MM_editCmd.ActiveConnection.Close %>
```

The above code is responsible for the actual update. All it does is call one of the pre-written **Command Objects** that are embedded within UltraDev. A Command Object is a very clever routine that can be reused anywhere. UltraDev contains a lot of these Objects and if you were to break one open, you'd see an awful lot of very clever code. It takes more than 5 lines of ASP code here to update a database with data but UltraDev just calls upon its powerful Objects to do the work!

Now that we have looked at building our pages manually, let's get UltraDev to do it for us.

The Wizard Returns

1. Create a new, blank page within your Chapter 6 folder called `update_wizard.asp`.

2. Copy and paste the recordset rsProducts from the `list_products.asp` page, just like we did before to ensure the integrity of our recordset pages.

Foundation Dreamweaver UltraDev 4

You'll find the wizard, called Insert Record Update Form, in the Live Objects panel as usual.

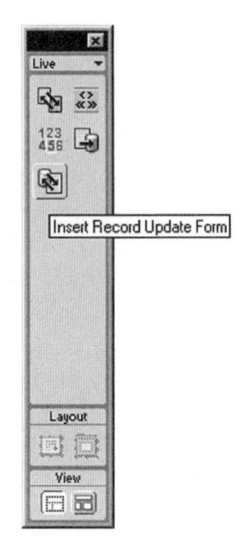

3. Click the Insert Record Update Form button and the dialog box will be launched:

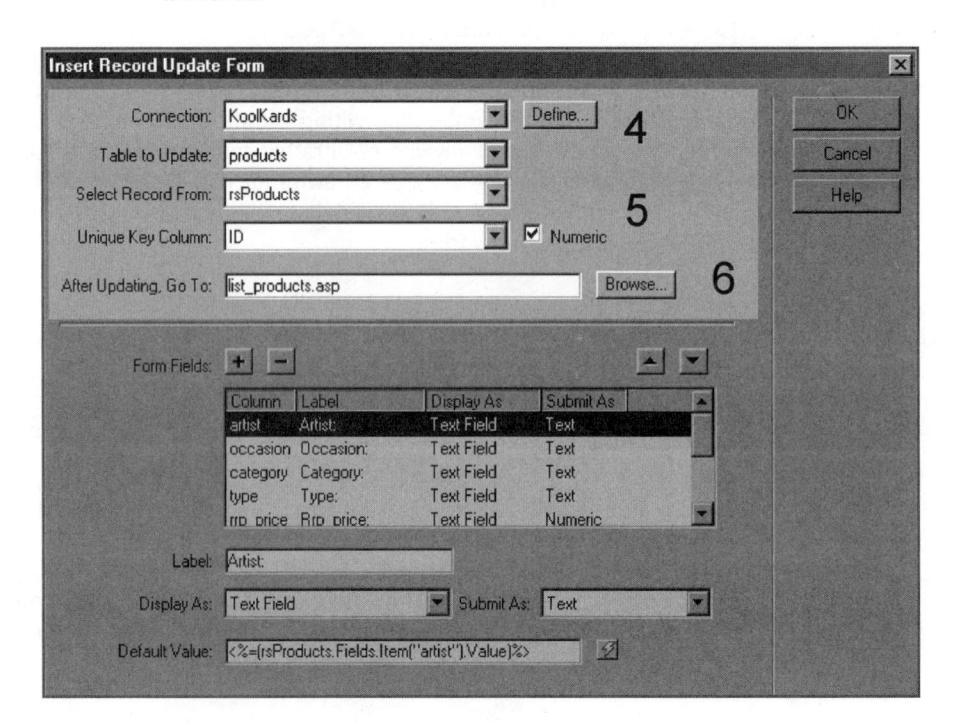

4. The Connection:, you've guessed it, is KoolKards and the table that you wish to update is products.

Amending your Database

5. In the Select Record From drop-down menu, specify the recordset that you wish to apply the update to which in this case is once again rsProducts. In the Unique Key Column menu, select the key column (ID) to identify the record in the database table.

6. After Updating, Go To: Enter the page to go to after the update has been performed – try bouncing back to `list_products.asp` again.

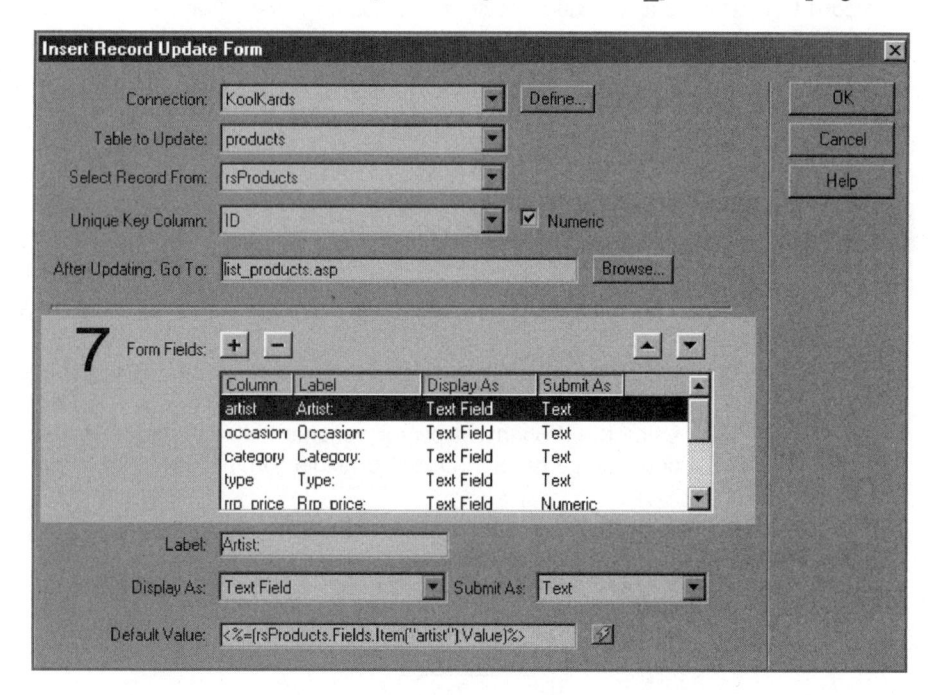

7. In the Form Fields area, specify the form objects you want to include on the update pages. By default, UltraDev creates a form object for each column in the database table. The only form object you wish to remove is the Unique ID as you certainly don't want to be able update this field.

   Everything else can be left as it is.

8. Press OK.

Yet again, UltraDev goes to work and creates us a robust update page. You may choose to use this feature to get you started when you create your first update pages. It's quick and efficient and gives you a great place to start from.

Now our Administrator is able to change the details of the records in our database – what happens if they want to remove one completely?

Deleting Your Records

Deleting a record in a fairly simple topic. As it's an 'all or nothing' action, it doesn't concern itself with individual fields in the database, just the entire records.

Again, in our finished application we might create another master list page, for finding our record to delete – but let's take the shortcut again, by making a copy of our details page and calling it `delete_products.asp`. Then let's link our dynamic Artist field on our current `list_products.asp` page to our delete page. We'll leave you to do the copying and renaming for yourself.

Creating a Delete Page

You should be on your renamed details page, now called `delete_products.asp`.

1. Firstly, remove the Update Record behavior from the server behavior list.

2. Using the Property inspector, rename the red-lined form to frm_Delete and change the Submit button label to Delete Record.

   Your page will now look something like this:

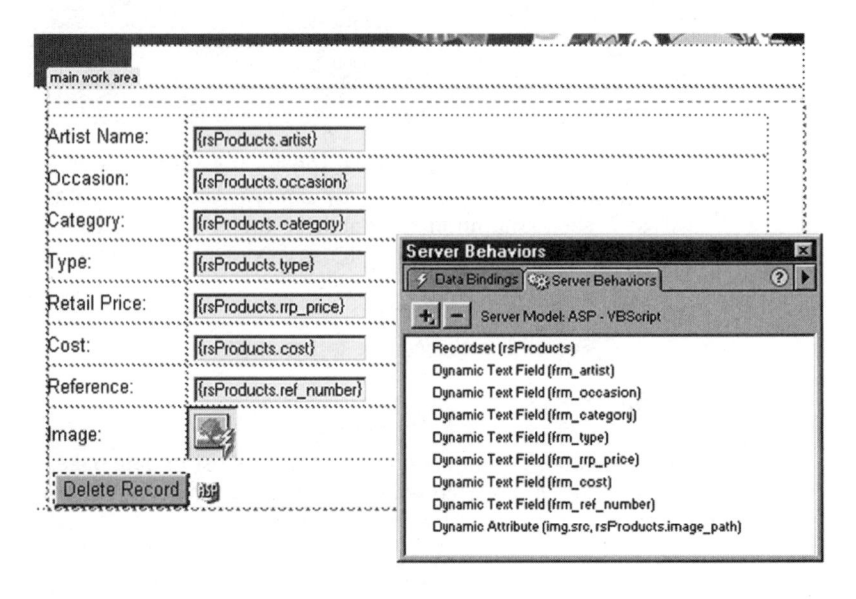

Amending your Database

Now, let's apply the Delete Record behavior.

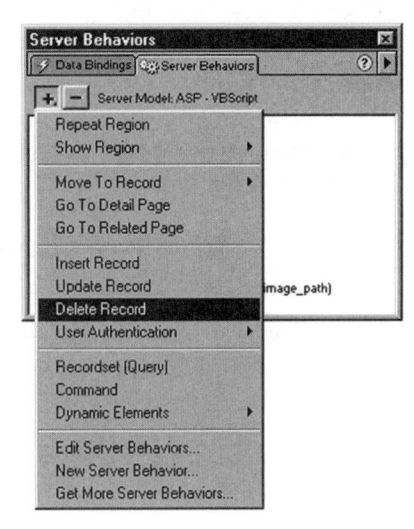

3. Let's look at the properties we need to set – you should be getting the hang of this by now.

    - Select your KoolKards connection
    - The table that you wish to delete the record from is products
    - Select your recordset (rsProducts)
    - Unique Key Column is set to ID again
    - After deleting you need to redirect the page so we suggest you refer the user back to the list_products.asp page
    - Choose the name of the form that is acting as the delete function (frm_Delete)

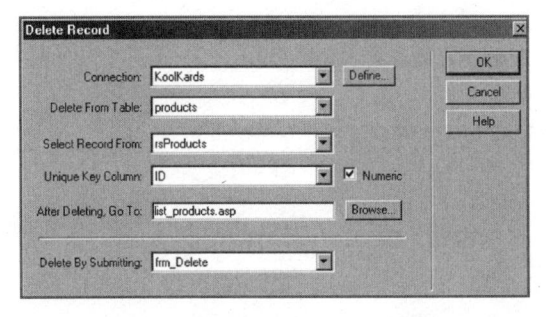

If you open the list_products.asp page, you should now be able to find a record, get to the details and click the delete button. The record should be deleted and you should be returned to the list_products.asp page, minus the record.

Foundation Dreamweaver UltraDev 4

How It All Works

The **delete** page works in a very similar way to the **update** page in that it places a couple of hidden text boxes on the page, which it uses to determine if the Submit button has been clicked or not.

We'll leave you to look at code and play with this one, as it should be fairly straightforward for you by this point(!)

You may be thinking something – if we were creating separate list pages for each of the detail/update/delete pages it would be getting a bit messy by now. What we could really do with is a way of updating or deleting on the same page!

The bad news is that if you try to put an update and a delete behavior on the same page, you'll run into problems – even if you use two separate forms on the same web page.

Well, what Macromedia won't do for you – we *will*...

Updating & Deleting on the Same Page

Let's look at making a much more streamlined update and delete page. To make our multi-functioned page, we'll need to hand-code the scripts.

1. Open our original `update_products.asp` page and amend it, to save us creating yet another page.

2. You need to add an extra button for the **delete**. Label it accordingly and assign the name but_Delete.

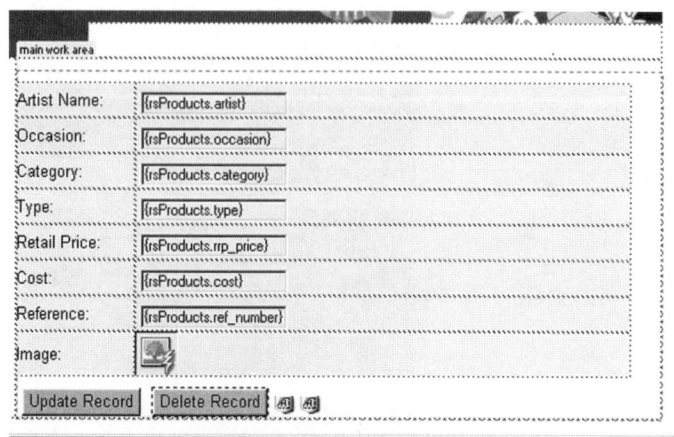

Amending your Database

3. Switch to Code View. Right at the top of the code, just after the...

   ```
   <!--#include file="../Connections/KoolKards).asp" -->
   ```

   ...you need to type the following...

   ```
   <%
   ' check to see if delete button is pressed
      If (Request("but_delete") <>"") Then
   Set MM_editCmd = Server.CreateObject("ADODB.Command")
      MM_editCmd.ActiveConnection = MM_Koolkards_STRING
   MM_editCmd.CommandText = "Delete from products where
   ➥ ID = " &Request.Form("MM_recordId")
      MM_editCmd.Execute
      MM_editCmd.ActiveConnection.Close
      Response.Redirect("list_products.asp")
      End If
   %>
   ```

   You'll end up with something like this:

```
1  <%@LANGUAGE="VBSCRIPT"%>
2  <!--#include file="../Connections/KoolKards.asp" -->
3  <%
4  ' check to see if delete button is pressed
5     If (Request("but_delete") <>"") Then
6  Set MM_editCmd = Server.CreateObject("ADODB.Command")
7        MM_editCmd.ActiveConnection = MM_Koolkards_STRING
8  MM_editCmd.CommandText = "Delete from products where ID = " & Request.Form("MM_recordId")
9        MM_editCmd.Execute
10       MM_editCmd.ActiveConnection.Close
11    Response.Redirect("list_products.asp")
12    End If
13 %>
```

If you save and test your page now, you should be able to update or delete each record accordingly. Powerful pages indeed!

Foundation Dreamweaver UltraDev 4

Summary

We've covered a number of powerful UltraDev functions here – if you managed the whole of this chapter in one sitting, you'll probably need a lie down now! Looking back, we learned that:

- A **detail page** can allow users to find out more about a product and is an integral part of any e-commerce web site

- UltraDev can be used to create **administration tools** – pages that regular users will not be able to access

- UltraDev helps us create pages that can **interact** with our database, **updating** it and **deleting** unwanted records, and using a combination of UltraDev's features and our knowledge of the code, we even created a **multi-functional** update *and* delete page!

- Although UltraDev offers '**wizards**' called Live Objects, it's very important – and sometimes more productive – for us to **know the code** and how it works

Before moving on to discuss how to password-protect our site, in the next chapter we'll look at how we can get to our data quickly and easily using dynamic **search pages**.

Amending your Database   6

kool kards

7 Searching your Database

What we'll cover in this chapter:

- *Adding **search** functions to our pages*

- *Using **Structured Query Language** to extract records for our search results*

- ***Altering** our page templates and defining editable regions on them*

- ***Advanced search functions** – dynamic list boxes, parameterized queries and joined tables*

7 Foundation Dreamweaver UltraDev 4

After the last two chapters you should be getting quite excited about what you can already develop with UltraDev. You may be tempted to put down the book and start building your own pages already, but don't do that just yet.

Searching for and getting to data is probably the most important thing in your database driven site. If a user has a bad experience searching for an item that they want to buy then they may give up or not come back. If we only gave KoolKards users the option to move through our database ten records at a time, we would probably only ever sell cards that begin with 'A' and would soon be out of business.

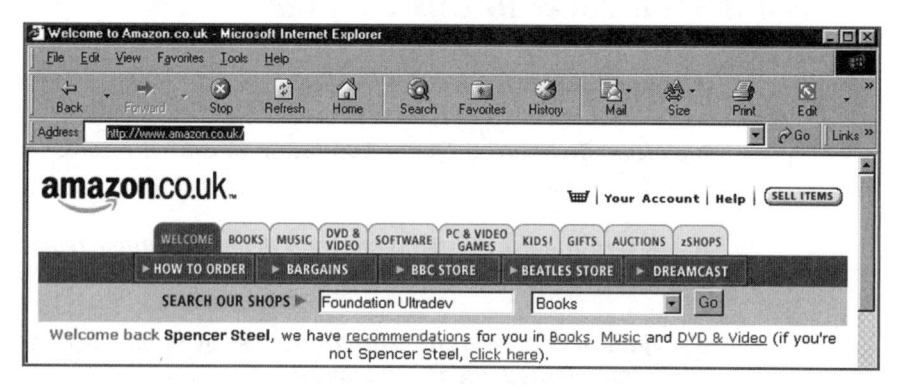

This is why almost every data-driven site has a searching capacity. Some are very simple, with maybe just a one-line box where you type in the name of the product you're looking for. Some sites feel that this won't be enough to guide their users to the correct product or area and are designed with drop-down boxes to help you narrow your search. Other sites are just purely search engines! We need to get our KoolKards user to their chosen type of card quickly and easily so that they buy our product, go away happy and come back again.

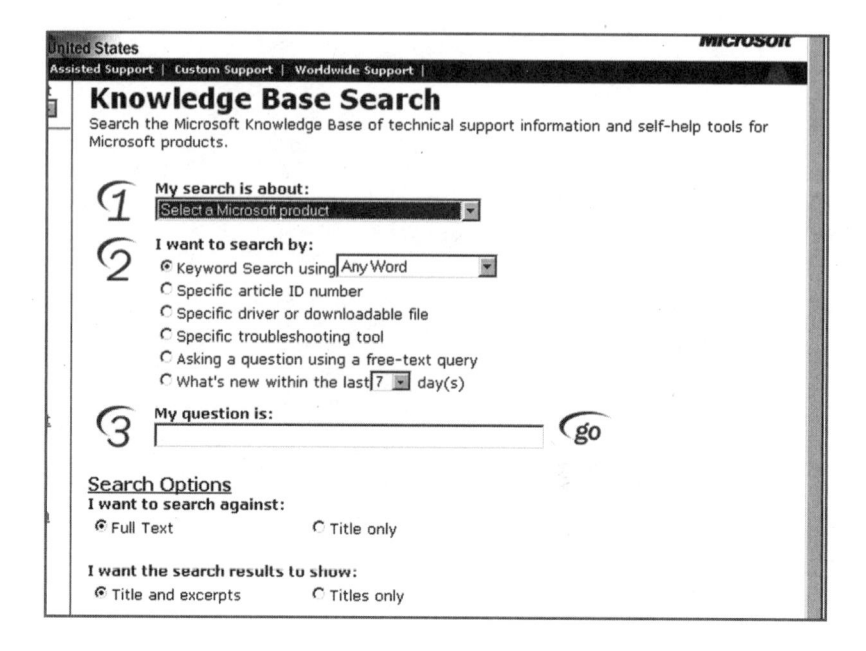

Searching your Database | 7

As you've probably guessed, UltraDev can help us do this. It works best using Structured Query language (SQL). In the detail page in the last chapter, we looked at how to filter out all records except the one the user had selected. A search is really nothing more than a function that filters out all records except those that match our criteria, so we're taking up where we left off.

What is SQL?

Structured Query Language is the universal language for interrogating (or querying) a database. UltraDev has already written loads of SQL statements for you. Every time that we've clicked a button which told UltraDev to do something or dragged a recordset out of the Data Bindings panel, UltraDev has written some SQL for us.

Every instruction that we use SQL for is called a query – we are literally querying the database for some information. We could write SQL to show us all the Christmas cards in the database – which would be our query. The information that SQL returned from our query would be our recordset, literally a set of records.

Generating an SQL Statement

Let's try this out. We're going to be querying a table called rsEmployees – a pretend table of all the people who might work for our company. (You might notice that we've borrowed this from Microsoft's sample Northwind database.)

1. Create a new page called SQLexamples1.asp and save it.

2. From your Data Bindings panel, start by creating a recordset called rsEmployees that connects to our Employees table:

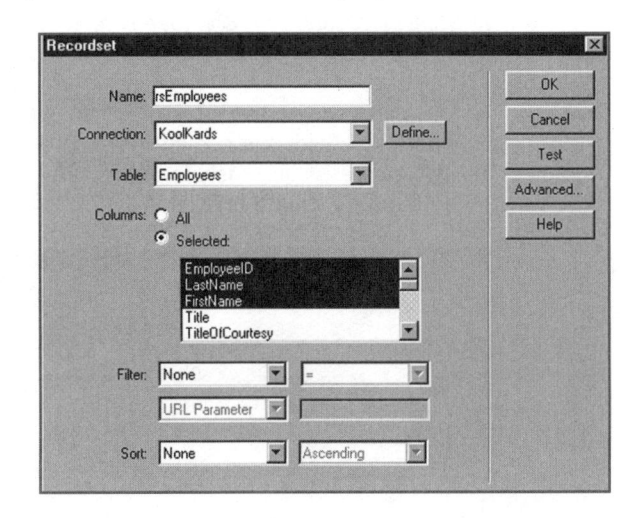

Foundation Dreamweaver UltraDev 4

3. Select the Country, EmployeeID, FirstName, HireDate, HomePhone and LastName columns from the Employees table, and click the Test button to check that everything is working. The results shouldn't surprise you — you'll see all the records, with just the seven selected columns shown:

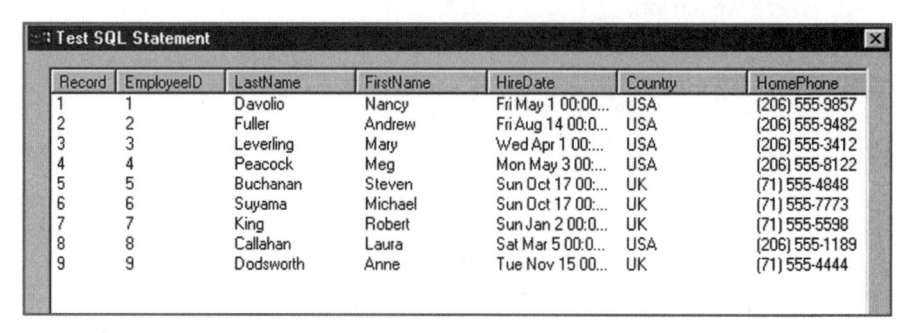

Record	EmployeeID	LastName	FirstName	HireDate	Country	HomePhone
1	1	Davolio	Nancy	Fri May 1 00:00:...	USA	(206) 555-9857
2	2	Fuller	Andrew	Fri Aug 14 00:0...	USA	(206) 555-9482
3	3	Leverling	Mary	Wed Apr 1 00:...	USA	(206) 555-3412
4	4	Peacock	Meg	Mon May 3 00:...	USA	(206) 555-8122
5	5	Buchanan	Steven	Sun Oct 17 00:...	UK	(71) 555-4848
6	6	Suyama	Michael	Sun Oct 17 00:...	UK	(71) 555-7773
7	7	King	Robert	Sun Jan 2 00:0...	UK	(71) 555-5598
8	8	Callahan	Laura	Sat Mar 5 00:0...	USA	(206) 555-1189
9	9	Dodsworth	Anne	Tue Nov 15 00...	UK	(71) 555-4444

4. In the RecordSet window, click Advanced (it's just under the Test button) to see how UltraDev compiled the SQL statement for you.

> The **Advanced** view shows more detailed information than the **Simple** view that you've just used to enter the fields you want to display, and you'll find yourself using this option more and more as you continue with UltraDev. UltraDev will usually let you switch between the two windows, but if you write a complex SQL statement it sometimes isn't possible to return to the **Simple** view.

This is the SQL query that UltraDev should have created for you:

```
SELECT Country, EmployeeID, FirstName, HireDate,
➥ HomePhone, LastName FROM Employees
```

You can see the use of SELECT to *select* fields and FROM to *define* where the fields are coming from. The only thing to note here is that field names which include spaces are a pain and you have to place them inside square brackets [ ].

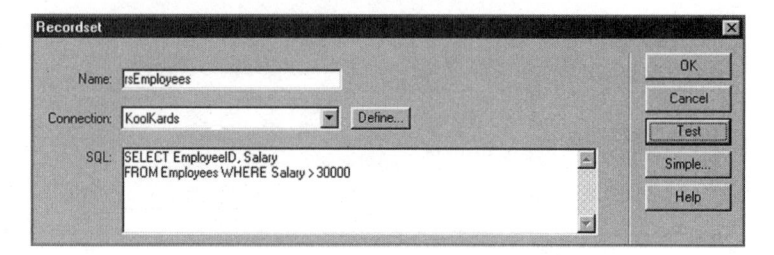

Searching your Database

5. Change the text in the SQL window to:

   ```
   SELECT EmployeeID, Salary FROM employees WHERE
   ↳ Salary > 30000
   ```

   This tells UltraDev to display the records of employees who earn $30,000 or more.

   > You'll probably remember the greater than symbol from doing math at school. Technically, these symbols are known as **relational operators** and SQL uses six of them:
   >
   > | | |
   > |---|---|
   > | = | Equal |
   > | <> | Not Equal |
   > | < | Less Than |
   > | > | More Than |
   > | <= | Less Than or Equal To |
   > | >= | Greater Than or Equal To |

6. Select Test, and UltraDev will test your SQL statement before you've even thought of creating a page to hold the results.

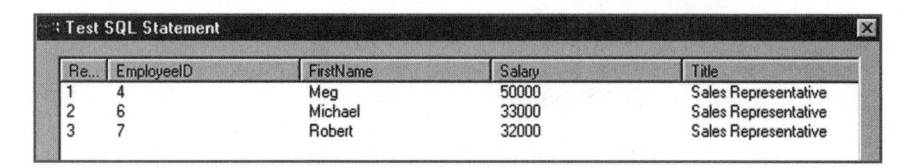

Re...	EmployeeID	FirstName	Salary	Title
1	4	Meg	50000	Sales Representative
2	6	Michael	33000	Sales Representative
3	7	Robert	32000	Sales Representative

7. Let's get a little more sophisticated and ask for a list of all sales representatives earning over $30,000. Change the text in your SQL window so that it now reads:

   ```
   SELECT EmployeeID, FirstName, Title, Salary
   FROM Employees
   WHERE Salary > 30000 AND Title = 'Sales
   ↳ Representative'
   ```

   The AND operator joins two or more conditions, and displays a row only if that row's data satisfies all conditions listed.

8. If we want more than one condition to be met, then we can use OR. So, to see all those who make less than $30,000 or work in the UK, we could use:

   ```
   SELECT EmployeeID, FirstName, Salary, Country
   FROM Employees
   WHERE Salary < 30000 OR country = 'UK'
   ```

9. We can even combine the two to find out all those who earn more than $30,000 and are either Sales Reps or work in the UK:

   ```
   SELECT EmployeeID, Firstname, Title, Country, Salary
   FROM Employees
   WHERE SALARY > 30000 AND Title = 'Sales
   ➥ Representative' OR Country = 'UK'
   ```

10. There's an easier way to do things, though – this will find all Sales Reps and Managers by using IN:

    ```
    SELECT EmployeeID, FirstName, Salary, Country
    FROM Employees
    WHERE Title IN('Sales Representative','Sales Manager')
    ```

11. This finds all records with salaries greater than or equal to $30,000, but less than or equal to $50,000 by using BETWEEN:

    ```
    SELECT EmployeeID, FirstName, Salary, Country
    FROM Employees
    WHERE SALARY BETWEEN 30000 AND 50000
    ```

    This is a lot of information to assimilate, but don't worry – we're going to be putting this into practice on our KoolKards site later in the chapter. There are just two more factors that we want to look at before moving on – asking for those records that fall outside of a set range, and asking for records without knowing the full details of what we're searching for.

12. We can use NOT to look for records outside of a set range – this statement returns all records for people who don't earn a salary of between $30,000 and $50,000:

    ```
    SELECT EmployeeID, FirstName, Salary, Country
    FROM Employees
    WHERE SALARY NOT BETWEEN 30000 AND 50000
    ```

Searching your Database   7

13. Searching databases is great, but what if we can't remember exactly what we want to search for? For example, suppose we want to find an employee that we'd met at a conference and we know their first initial from their business card, but not their first name. We can use LIKE just like this:

```
SELECT EmployeeID, FirstName, Salary, Country
FROM Employees
WHERE Firstname LIKE 'M%'
```

The percent sign (%) is a wildcard character and works in a similar way to the asterisk (*) wildcard we used earlier. It represents any possible character or set of characters that might appear after the M. We could even search for those people with an M anywhere in their name by using '%M%'. You might even have worked out that you could use NOT LIKE to display rows that don't have an M in them.

> *It's important to use single quotes, such as with '%M%' in our last example. You may see some books on SQL using double quotes but UltraDev will compile some complex code using your SQL statement. A lot of the time, UltraDev will have to put your quoted SQL statement within quotes of its own, so it needs the double quotes for its own use.*

Don't worry too much about absorbing all this material - we're going to use it for KoolKards before the end of the chapter.

Creating Parameterized Queries

The major flaw with our SQL statements was that they assumed that we knew exactly what data the user wanted. If you had a games shop on the web then you could have a number of buttons labelled Classic Board Games, Computer Games, Handheld Electronic Games and Adult Board Games and so on. When your user clicked the Computer Games button, you could use a query similar to:

```
SELECT * FROM tblGames WHERE gametype = "Computer"
```

However, most of the time, this type of search is far too limited. In the above example, we'd really want a user to be able to search all the games by a keyword like Donkey Kong or Twister.

What we need is a way of saying:

```
SELECT * FROM tblGames WHERE gametype = "What the user types in"
```

UltraDev is quite happy to deal with something that a user types in (technically defined as a search parameter). This is something that would be very useful for our KoolKards site. In the last chapter we left our administrator having to move through all the records every time they wanted to alter or delete a particular record. Now we can create a search page that allows our administrator to enter the reference number of a product and display that record.

This is an administrator's screen, so the user will know the reference number of the cards and we can use this to search by. We need two pages – a page with a form on it that allows the administrator to enter their search, and a page that displays the results.

Making a Search Page

Let's deal with the search page before adding the results page.

1. Close any open pages, create a new page from the Koolkards master template and save it as `admin_search.asp` in your Chapter 7 folder. Then create a new page from the master template called `admin_search_results.asp` and save it. You may think that the search page is quite complex, but most of the work will be done by the results page.

2. Our search page will pass information to the results page just as we passed information between two pages in Chapter 4.

3. Insert a form into `admin_search.asp` using the Objects toolbar and call this search_form in the Property inspector.

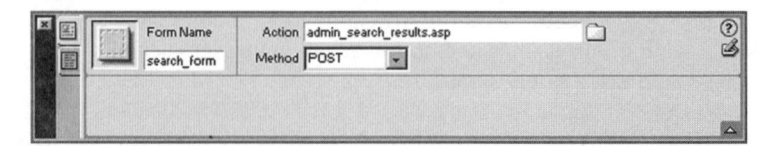

	Form Name	Action	admin_search_results.asp	
	search_form	Method	POST	

4. Still in the Property inspector, make sure that Method is set to POST and set the Action to `admin_search_results.asp`. This creates a direct link to our results page, which will be able to process the search parameter from the search text box.

   (Note this could be set to GET but there is a limit to the number of characters that can be contained in a URL – 8192 characters).

Searching your Database 7

5. Put a simple 2x2 table into the form area with Insert > Table. In the top left-hand cell of the table, enter the text Please enter the card reference number. In the top right-hand side, insert a text box and give it the name search. Drop in a Submit button underneath it. Your screen should now look like the one pictured.

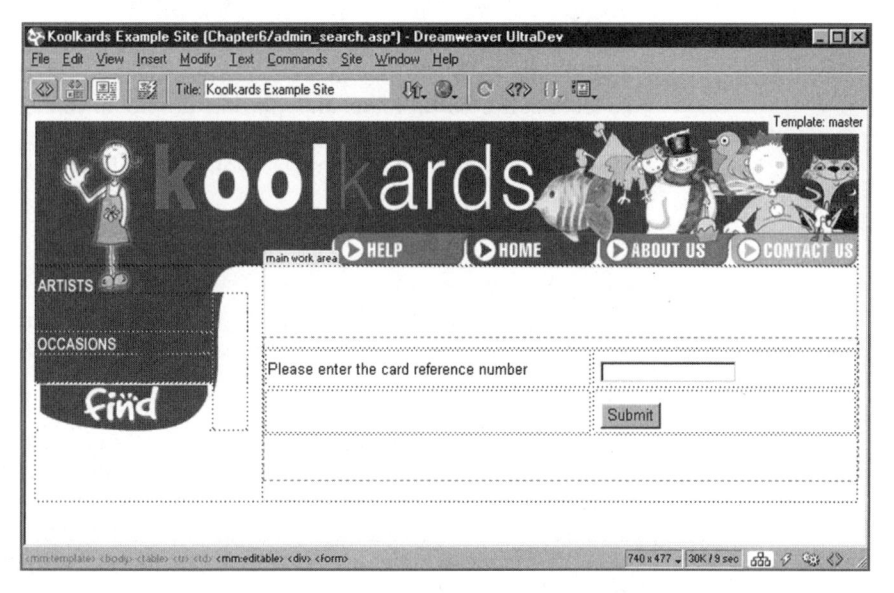

6. Save the page, and we've pretty much finished with our search page.

7. Open your admin_search_results.asp page and open up the Data Bindings window. Click on Recordset(Query) and set up your recordset as usual, this time calling it rsSearch:

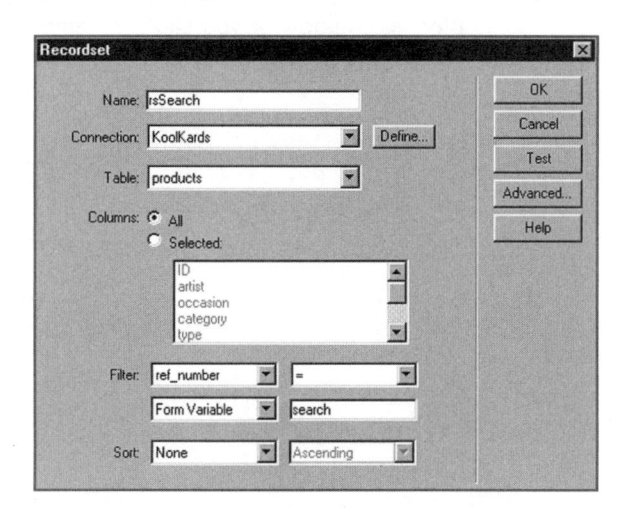

8. We want our results page to receive the search criteria from our search page and use it to form a query. To do this, we use the Filter option you can see on the left-hand side of the Recordset panel. Here, we need to tell UltraDev to show the records where [ref_number] = [Form Variable called search] so enter these into the panel, as shown.

   If you click the Advanced button and look at the Variables: window, you should see a Name of MMColParam. This is UltraDev's way of collecting the form value and placing it into a variable - anything marked MM is a Macromedia 'wrapper' around something. If you look at the code generated by UltraDev, you'll see this:

   ```
   <%
   Dim rsSearch__MMColParam
   rsSearch__MMColParam = "1"
   if (Request.Form("search") <> "") then rsSearch
   ➥   __MMColParam = Request.Form("search")
   %>
   ```

   This creates a variable called `rsSearch__MMColParam` and sets the value of the form text box search to it. It has already been given a value of 1, even though the user hasn't done anything yet. This is known as a **run-time** value, a value placed in the code to make it work before being replaced by the user's search parameter with the Replace keyword further down in the code.

9. Still in admin_search_results.asp, build an 8x2 table. Label the left-hand columns Artist Name:, Occasion:, Category:, Type:, Retail Price:, Cost:, Reference:, and Image:. Then drag and drop the corresponding fields out of the new rsSearch recordset displayed in your Data Bindings window. If you can't remember how to create the dynamic image next to Image:, just have a look back at the exercise in Chapter 6.

Searching your Database   7

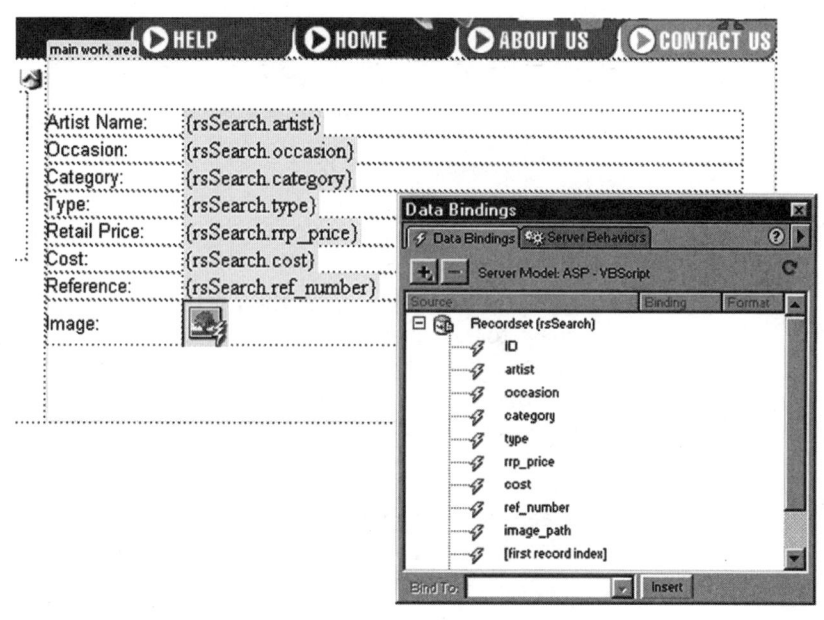

10. Save your pages and open up your search page in your browser. Try typing in a value that you know is in the KoolKards database, such as kg001 (take our word for it). You should be taken straight to your results page:

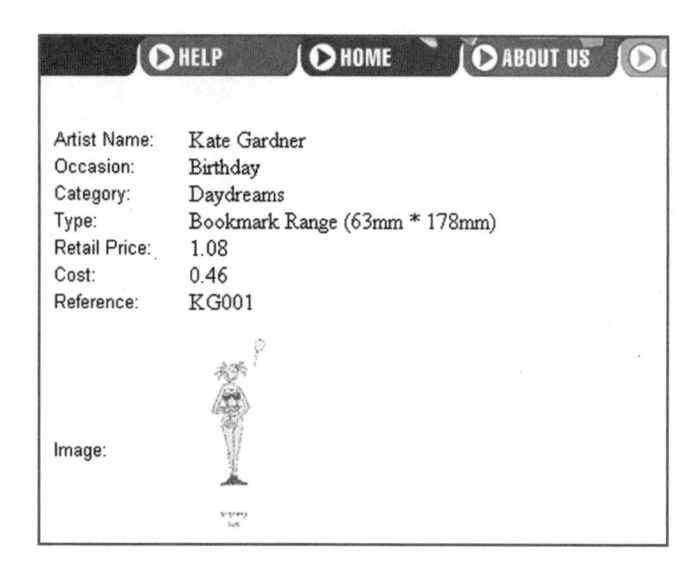

11. Return to your search page and type in a rogue value that's definitely not a reference number from our table, SS9999 for example. The result will be a nasty error message that isn't exactly user-friendly and would probably send our administrative staff into a blind panic.

Foundation Dreamweaver UltraDev 4

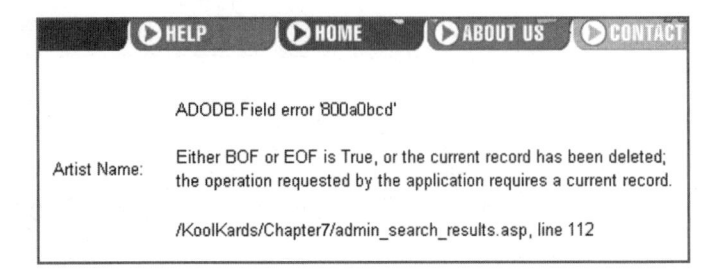

> ADODB.Field error '800a0bcd'
>
> Artist Name: Either BOF or EOF is True, or the current record has been deleted; the operation requested by the application requires a current record.
>
> /KoolKards/Chapter7/admin_search_results.asp, line 112

Our problem is simple; if there is no record to display, our table is going to fall over and produce a horrible error message. It sounds obvious, but the solution is to *not* display the table when there are no records. We can do this using a technique similar to the one that we used to create our hidden/showing navigation buttons in Chapter 5.

12. Select the whole table with the <TAG> selectors at the bottom of the screen (or you could click anywhere in the table and right-click Table > Select Table). Apply the Show Region > Show Region If Recordset Is Not Empty server behavior.

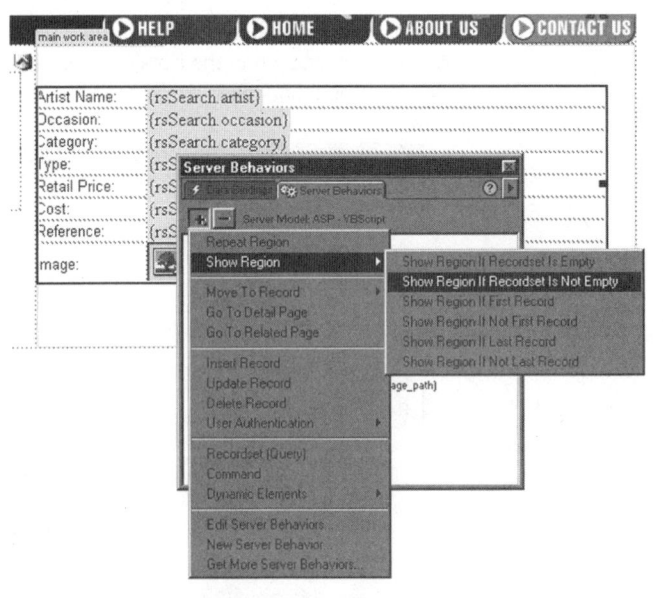

13. Select your rsSearch recordset, and click OK. Save your page and try entering SS9999 again. This time, you should just get a blank page.

> In the top left of our table, you should be able to see a small **Show If...** label to help you visually identify places where you've applied show/hide behaviors.

Searching your Database 7

The page is still not what we'd call user-friendly. What we'd expect is some sort of message telling us that there were no records found, rather that a blank screen. We need to create a message on our page by using a technique opposite to the one we've just used. This time, we want to show our message only when there is nothing in our table (in other words, the recordset *is* empty).

14. Still in `admin_search_results.asp`, type in a user-friendly message like Sorry - no results found just under the table.

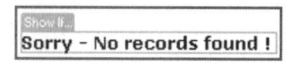

15. Highlight your message and apply the Show Region If Recordset Is Empty server behavior to it. After you've applied your behavior, you'll see the Show If... label around your text.

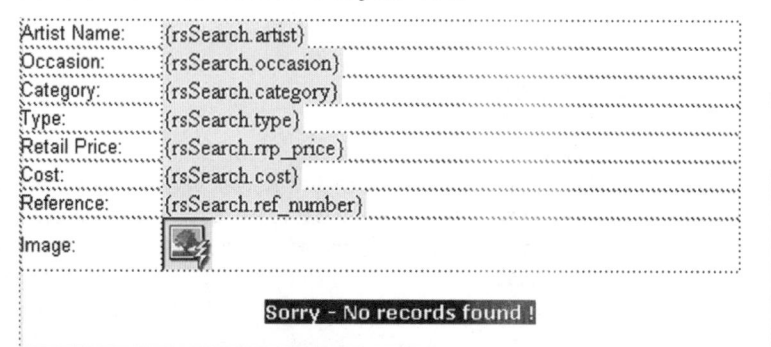

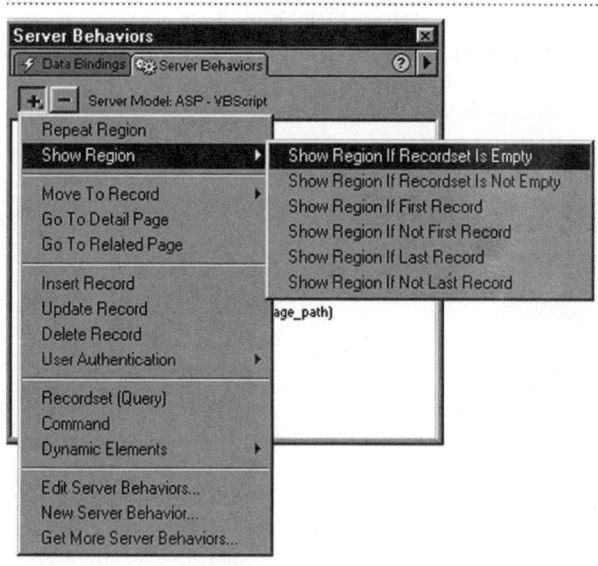

175

16. Save and test your pages yet again. You've now created a pretty perfect search and results page, so well done!

In the real world, we can start to mix and match the web applications that we're building. Our results page is fairly limited by itself, and we would need to add **update** and **delete** functionality to it. We've covered all the stages separately so you can go ahead and build the complete page yourself when you feel ready to – or just view our finished examples.

We've just looked at how to search by the contents of one text box. What if the user needs a list of items to select from? The answer to this is a multiple search where we can use drop-down boxes to limit the user's choices. You can see drop-down boxes in action on the final KoolKards site – the user can search for Artists and/or Occasions by using a drop-down box. These are perfect because the user is limited to the entries in the box whilst letting them create a more complex Artist and Occasion search in a user-friendly environment.

Time for a Database Change

Before we move on with our search page, you'll need to get the next version of the database. Replace your database with the newer version we've provided for you in the chapter folder. Rename your current database `old_koolkards.mdb` and then likewise rename the final database `koolkards.mdb`, making sure it resides in the same place as your previous database. Effectively, you've just replaced your database with another but we're keeping the same name. This way you won't have to recreate any connections!

Why are we replacing our database? When we first introduced our database schema, we said that it wasn't **normalized**. Well, the time has come to add some normalisation to it. Open your new database and take a look at the products table in Design mode. (If you're not too sure about the mechanics of Access, then take a look at the Access tutorial in the Appendix.)

Field Name	Data Type	Description
ID	AutoNumber	Record ID Number
artist_id	Number	Artist ID
occasion_id	Number	Occasion ID
category	Text	Theme
type	Text	Type of card (Bookmark Square)
rrp_price	Number	retail Price
cost	Number	Cost to customer
ref_number	Text	Reference Number
image_path	Text	image_path

Searching your Database   7

You might not spot the difference unless you have a very good memory, but we now have two new fields – `artist_id` and `occasion_id`, and these are number types. These replace `artist` and `occasion`, which were text types. We also have two new *tables* called `artists` and `occasions` unsurprisingly containing the artists' names and a list of occasions.

Field Name	Data Type	Description
artist_id	AutoNumber	
artist_name	Text	

artists : Table

If you look at the design of the `artists` table, you'll see that it's just an auto incremental field and a name field. Auto incremental fields, or **AutoNumbers** as they are called in Access, are numerical fields that assign numbers to our records starting at 1, increasing (or incrementing) by 1 with each new record. This ensures that no two records have the same unique number, which is critical. The `occasions` table is just the same as the `artists` table, with an auto incremental field and a text field.

If you now open up one of the three main tables (products, artists, occasions), you'll see that, rather than having the full name of the artist each time, we refer to the artist in our products table by using the `artist_ID` field. So, instead of Tracy Worral, we use 3.

If you think about the number of times we would end up typing Tracy Worral in a 10,000 record table this makes sense. There's huge scope for an accidental typo that would render our queries completely inaccurate, not to mention the time it would take to change the records if Tracy got married and changed her surname. By using **look-up tables** and **relationships** as we have done here, we only have to make one change in our `artists` table when the details change.

What we have created here is known as a **one-to-one** relationship, because each one product has only one artist and one occasion. You can also have a **one-to-many relationship,** which can be very powerful as a result of using a number reference to represent a field – say your name – across many fields.

Normalisation is fairly simple; if you find that data is repeated often, you need to take it out and make it reside in a separate table, and then create a relationship between the tables. If you think that the tables in your database might need normalising, you can always use the Tools > Analyse > Tables tool in Access, which will suggest better ways of organising your tables.

Foundation Dreamweaver UltraDev 4

Creating a Dynamic List Box

On the Koolkards site, it's possible to perform a search from any page. It's always a good idea to try to make sure a sale is never more than a click or two away – if your user is faced with a difficult navigation to get to the checkout, you may lose them.

We're going to build this feature into our main template. Make a copy of the `master.dwt` template before you start, and call it `old_master.dwt`. We're going to make quite a few changes to the `master` template and if you get these wrong this will give you the option of deleting the template and going back to the original. We've included an example of how the template should look once you have finished this chapter in the download as `master_final.dwt`.

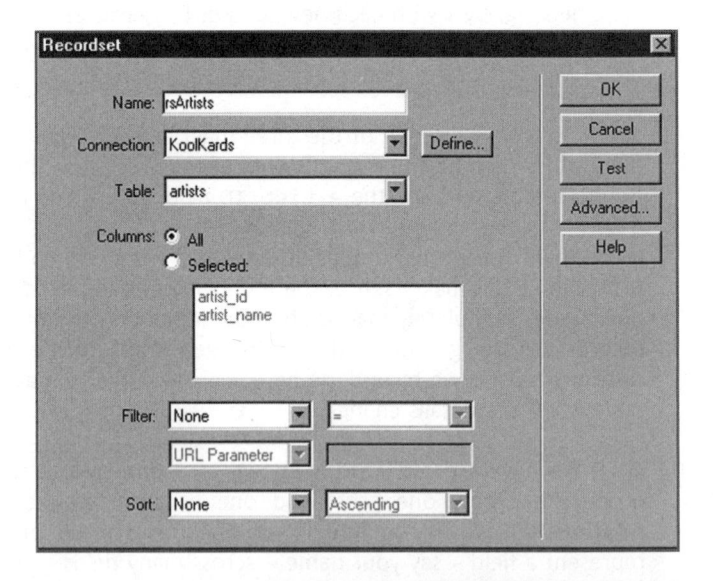

1. Open the `master.dwt` template from the Template directory. We need to create two recordsets based on our artists and occasions tables – rsArtists and rsOccasions. You'll need to go through the data binding routine for each recordset.

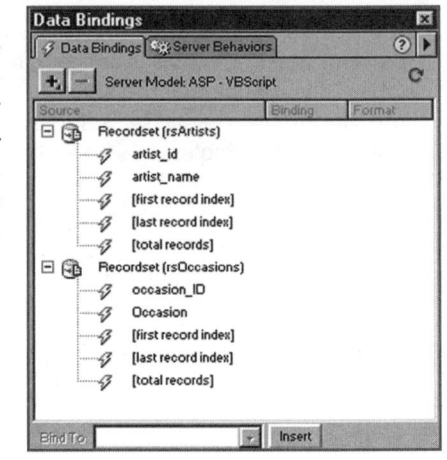

Searching your Database   7

After the user has selected the search criteria by using two drop-down boxes, they will need to click a Submit form button to fire off the search. As you can see, we have provided a Find graphic to achieve this. To get this to work we'll need to put a form on our template – so the information can be submitted.

2. Before we create the two list boxes we need to place a form around the sidebar. The easy way to do this is to place the `<FORM>` tags before and after the `<TABLE>` tags. Place the cursor anywhere in the search table (say, just below the ARTISTS label), as pictured, and click the table tag at the bottom of the page.

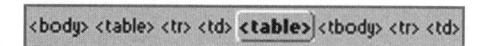

`<body> <table> <tr> <td> <table> <tbody> <tr> <td>`

This will select the whole table, and you'll be able to jump to your Code View and add the `<FORM>` tags easily.

179

Foundation Dreamweaver UltraDev 4

3. Go into your code, and your table code should be highlighted. Just before the <TABLE> tag, type <FORM>. Scroll down until you see the </TABLE> tag and type </FORM> on the line below. Your <FORM> tags should now be exactly surrounding your table.

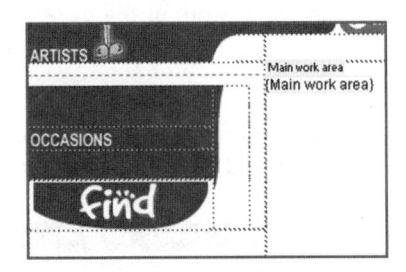

```
82    <td width="200" height="59" valign="top">
83      <FORM>
84      <TABLE height=94 cellSpacing=0 cellPadding=0 width=176 border=0 valign="top">
85        <TBODY>
86        <TR vAlign=top>
87          <!-- row 4 -->
88          <TD vAlign=center width=147 bgColor=#00527d>  </TD>
89
90          <TD width=29 rowSpan=4><IMG height=116
91      src="../images/Kt_r4_c02.gif" width=29 border=0
```

4. Place your cursor anywhere in the form and you'll see that you now have a <FORM> tag at the bottom of your page. Select this and use the Property inspector to give it a name of search and an Action of search_results.asp.

5. Now create the two drop-down boxes, they're on the Form Objects panel, and call them artist and occasion.

Searching your Database

6. Highlight the `artist` box and click the List Values button on the far right of the Property inspector.

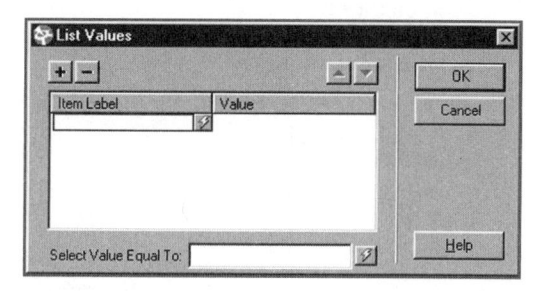

The Item Label is the text the user will see in the drop-down box. We could just type in values for the menu here but we want our list to be populated by the contents of a database table. The Value contains the value of the item, which UltraDev will use to create *queries*. In this case, we want the user to see the artist's name but the value passed back to UltraDev will be the ID number of that artist.

7. To set the Item Label click the lightning icon next to the label box. Once you've done that, you'll see all the possible fields available from all the possible recordsets. As we want the full artist's name to appear in our drop-down box, select artist_name. UltraDev will automatically generate some code in the Code: box at the bottom of the window. Click OK when you're done.

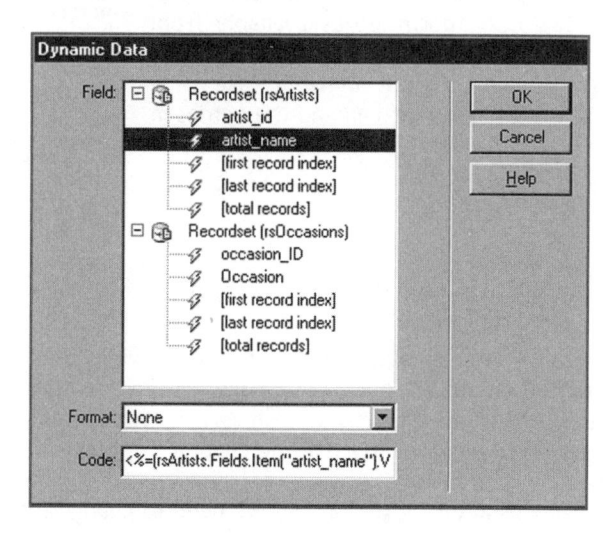

8. We need to set the field that will contain the value UltraDev will use in our queries. Put the cursor under the Value column, and click the

lightning icon. In the same way select artist_id from the chooser. Click OK again and your list box panel should look something like the one pictured:

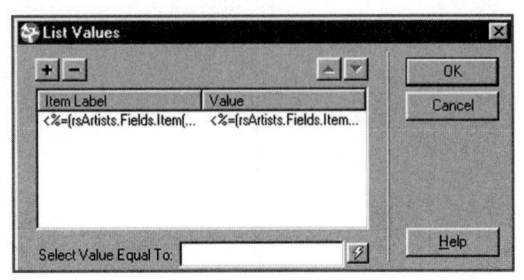

9. Press OK to close the list box panel, and you've now created a dynamic list for artists. Follow the same procedure for occasions, but apply it to the occasion list box using Item Label = Occasion, Value = Occasion_ID.

10. Save your files and create a new page using our master template. Save the new page as dyno_listbox.asp and test it from your browser. We now have two drop-down boxes available from every page and, because they're dynamic, we only have to amend the entries in our database to change them.

Let's recap – we're creating a template that provides us with a search feature. When the Find button is clicked, our search page will go to our search results. Currently, we're working on chapter 7 and will want our search results to point to the ../chapter7/search_results page in the chapter 7 folder.

What happens in our next chapter? We need to change the target results page, and each chapter will end up needing a different template destination. We need to alter the template to take account of this, but, as you've probably noticed, once the template is placed on the page there are parts of it you can't alter.

Searching your Database   7

Editable and Non-editable Regions of Templates

A template is a great way of creating standard-looking and -working web pages. Once created, they can be applied to any page and we can change the look of every page by updating one template. When you create a page using a template, you aren't allowed to make any changes to the parts of the page that were created by it.

When you create a template, all areas on it are uneditable. Having a template with a 100% uneditable area is fairly useless because the user wouldn't be able to make any further changes to their page, so UltraDev requires that we must create at least one editable region when we create our templates. On our template, this editable area is called Main Work Area and is marked in blue. This is the only region in which a user may add additional page components.

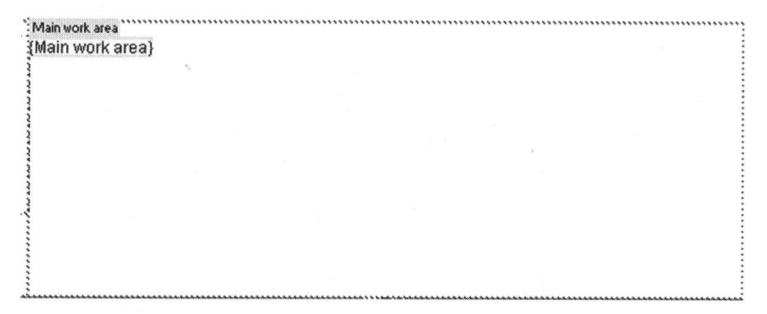

The problem that we have is one that you will come across at some point in your site-building career. We don't necessarily want every page created with our template to point to `chapter7/search_results.asp`. The easiest way to solve this problem is to make our new search form an editable region. Let's look at how we can do that.

Defining an Editable Template Region

Before we finish we need to place another editable region on to your template page. We need to make the form editable as we will be using the multiple copies of the `search_results.asp` page in different chapters so we need to make sure the form points to the `search_results.asp` that is contained within the chapter we are working on.

1. Place the cursor inside the form and then select the `<FORM>` tag at the bottom of your page.

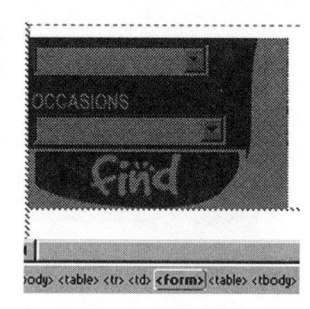

183

2. Select Modify > Templates > New Editable Region. Enter search_bar under Name and click OK.

3. Save your page, and if you look at your template, you should now have two editable regions (as shown by the blue highlighting).

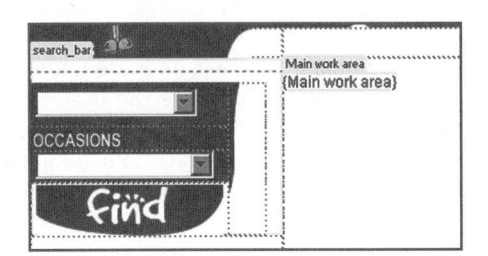

Building a Search Result Page

Now we have our drop-down boxes, we can carry on with our search pages. We have provided a page called search.asp in the chapter folder. Now we need to create a new results page to work with our dropdown boxes.

1. Create a new page using our updated master template. Save it as search_results.asp in your chapter 7 folder.

2. Click inside the Search form, click on the <FORM> tag and bring up the Property inspector. The Action will be pointing to /Templates/search_results.asp which of course is incorrect.

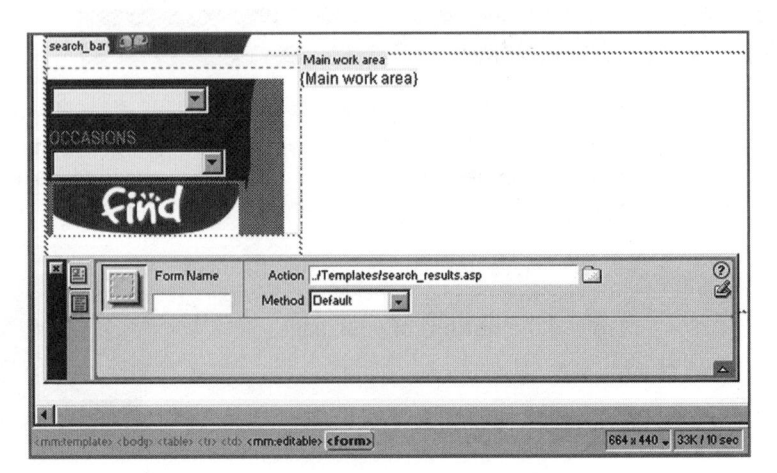

Searching your Database

3. Now that we've made this part of our template editable, we can change the Action to search_results.asp. The fact we haven't included a folder name in the path means UltraDev will look in the current folder.

4. As usual, the key to getting our results to work properly is creating a recordset. Now create a recordset called rsResults, which connects to the products table and returns all the results.

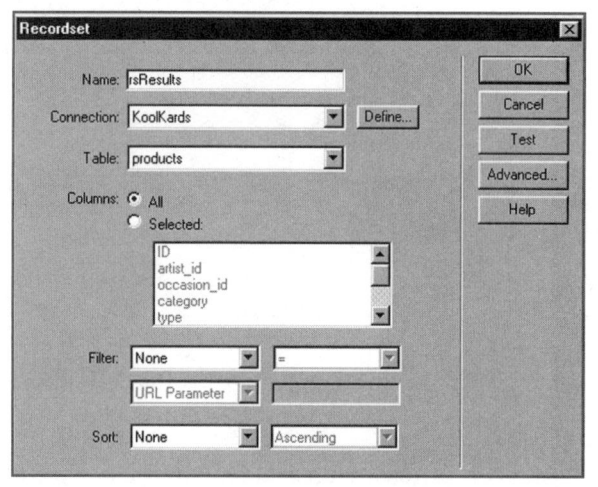

> *You'll notice that there are the two recordsets we created in our template already available. It's one of the great features of UltraDev that they're now placed here for our use whenever we want.*

5. Use the Test button to check your connection.

    There are two things we need to address before we dump our data onto our page. Firstly, imagine our results screen – under artist_id and occasion_id there will be some pretty meaningless numbers. We're also using two search parameters – one for occasions and one for artist but if you look at the Simple view of the Recordset panel, there's only room for one parameter under the filter.

6. To convert artist_id and occasion_id into something readable we need to do join the three tables together with a new SQL statement. Switch

to Advanced view in your Recordset and type in the following SQL statement:

```
SELECT products.artist_id, ID, ref_number,
➥ artists.artist_id, artists.artist_name
FROM artists Inner Join Products ON (artists.artist_id
➥ = products.artist_id)
```

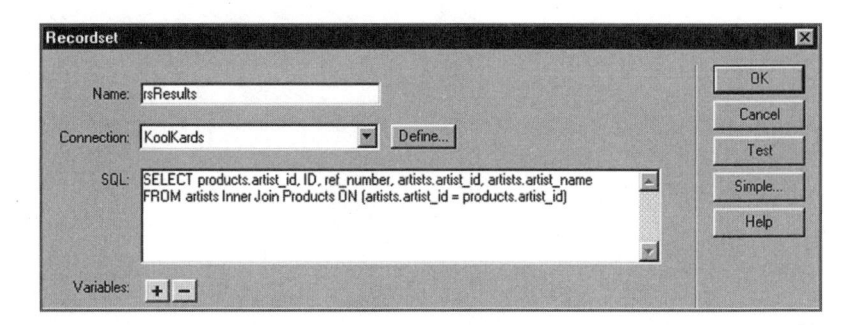

7. Try this out by pressing the Test button. You will see that we now have an artist's name column, which is far friendlier than just a number.

   You'll see something strange in our code called an Inner Join, which is what we used to join the three tables together. An Inner Join returns rows from either table only if they have a corresponding row in the other table. In other words, it ignores any rows in which the join condition specified in the ON clause isn't met. You may notice that each field name is prefixed with the table name – the two tables both have an identical field so SQL needs a way of identifying which field belongs to which table.

   You've probably taken a look at that Inner Join and started to get worried – it looks pretty complex. Fortunately, you can use Access to generate SQL code for you by using the graphic Query Designer (pictured) before selecting SQL View and pasting your code into UltraDev.

Searching your Database   7

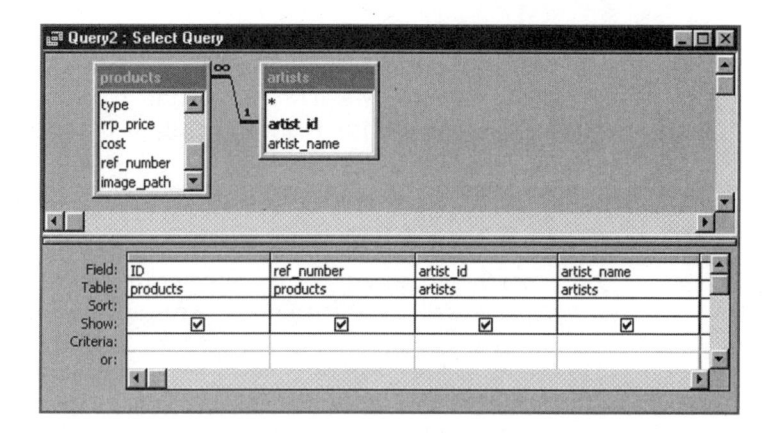

8. In the Advanced view of the Recordset SQL box, add the following statement. It's the same method as before, but with added fields from the Occasions table as well. If you're new to this or just want to try it out, you might want to open up your database in Access and design this in an Access query.

```
SELECT artist_name, Occasion, category, cost, ID,
➥ image_path, ref_number, rrp_price, type
FROM Occasions INNER JOIN (artists INNER JOIN products
➥ ON artists.artist_id = products.artist_id) ON
Occasions.occasion_ID = products.occasion_id
```

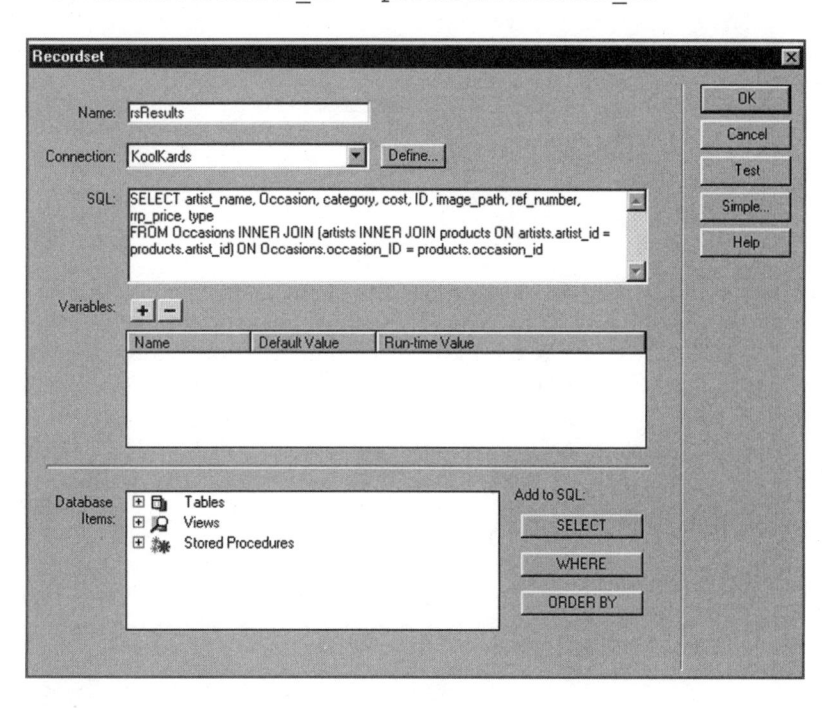

187

Foundation Dreamweaver UltraDev 4

9. Press the Test button again. We now have fields from all three tables being returned into one virtual table. Before we can start to drag these onto the form, we have to tell the recordset to expect our two parameters, one from each drop-down box. In the same way as we passed a form variable from our single search box earlier in the chapter, we need to pass two form variables to the recordset from our dropdown boxes.

10. From the Advanced view in our recordset, use the + button to add two variables called artistName and occasionType.

11. We named our two drop-down boxes artist and occasion and we now need to use the Request.Form method to pull the value from these. For the Run-time Values, we need to enter Request.Form("artist") and Request.Form("occasion"). Enter default values of 1 and 2 in the dialog box – this is for testing purposes, although UltraDev won't work unless there is a value there.

> Remember, even though the user sees the full artist's name in the drop-down box (the Label), UltraDev will be requesting the Value – which is a numeric value.

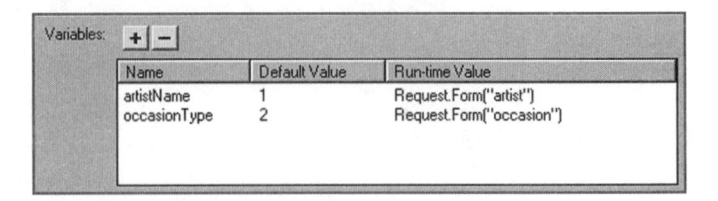

Variables: + –		
Name	Default Value	Run-time Value
artistName	1	Request.Form("artist")
occasionType	2	Request.Form("occasion")

12. We must now add to our SQL statement, so that we request the product details where the artist matches the value in the artist drop-down box and the occasion matches the value in the occasion drop-down box. Replace your code with thhis, which adds the WHERE clause:

```
SELECT artist_name, Occasion, category, cost, ID,
↪ image_path, ref_number, rrp_price, type
FROM Occasions INNER JOIN (artists INNER JOIN products
↪ ON artists.artist_id = products.artist_id) ON
Occasions.occasion_ID = products.occasion_id
WHERE products.artist_id = artistName and
↪ products.occasion_id = occasionType
```

Searching your Database

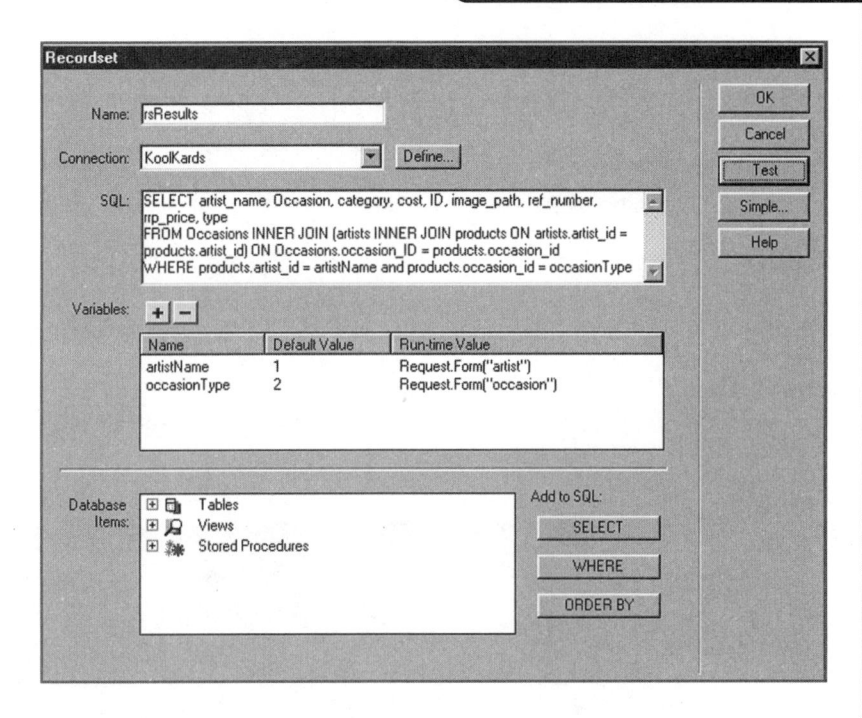

13. Test your advanced query. Remember we're using defaults of 1 and 2, so that if you look at your tables, you'll see that we're asking for all Anniversary cards (2) designed by Kate Gardner (1).

> *Remember, that if we were using a text field such as* Occasion *to search against, you need to return your **string**, or text, with the parameter name in single quotes. If you used this:*
>
> ```
> SELECT ...
> WHERE occasion = occasionType
> ```
>
> *with a parameter* occasionType *set to* Request.Form("occasion"), *then you'd get an error message reading **Too few parameters**. What you'd need to use is this:*
>
> ```
> WHERE occasion = 'occasionType'
> ```

14. To finish off, we need to design the layout of our page and decide on how many records we wish to display at a time. We'd suggest that you display five records at a time.

Foundation Dreamweaver UltraDev 4

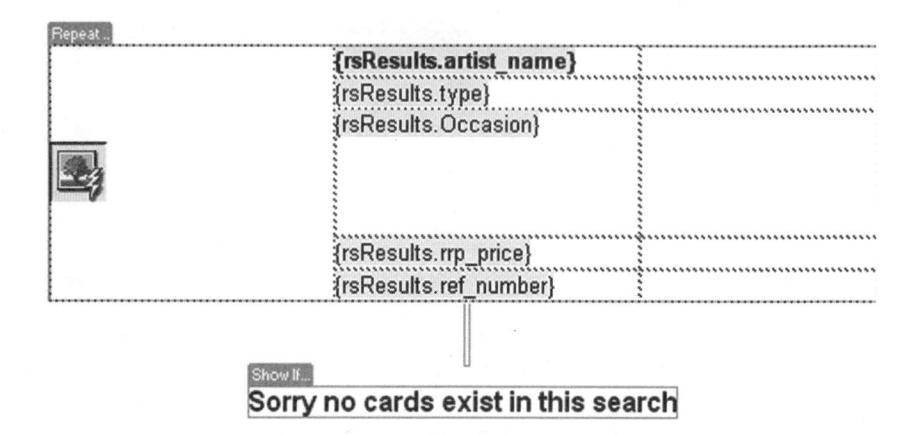

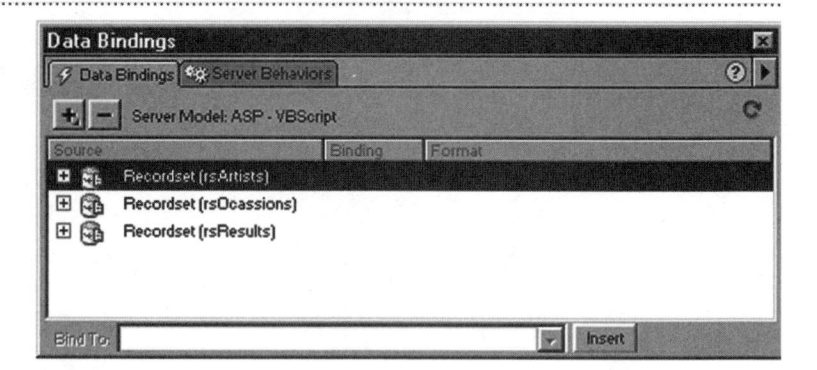

15. Now you need to set up some navigation buttons in case the search returns more than five records. More importantly, you need to set up a friendly message to appear if no records exist – error messages and blank pages annoy customers! We've covered how to do this already, so we'll leave it to you – but go back and check, or open up our finished version and compare it with yours if you get stuck.

I bet you didn't realise there were going to be that many steps to create your dynamic drop-down search! The good news is that we're now done, and the even better news is that once you've done this a few times few times, you'll fly through it passing those variables around without a second thought.

Now the recordset is complete, we must take the obligatory look at our source code. Go on – you know you want to. Highlight the recordset in the Data Bindings panel and the corresponding code will be highlighted for you in the Code View. Ignore the two recordsets that we've inherited from our template, and take a look at the block of code for the third recordset:

Searching your Database 7

```
<%
set rsResults = Server.CreateObject("ADODB.Recordset")
rsResults.ActiveConnection = MM_KoolKards_STRING

rsResults.Source = "SELECT artist_name, Occasion, category,
cost,
➥ ID, image_path, ref_number, rrp_price, type FROM Occasions
INNER
➥ JOIN (artists INNER JOIN products ON artists.artist_id =
➥ products.artist_id) ON Occasions.occasion_ID =
➥ products.occasion_id WHERE products.artist_id = " +
➥ Replace(rsResults__artistName, "'", "''") + " and
➥ products.occasion_id = " +
Replace(rsResults__occasionType, "'",
➥ "''") + " "

rsResults.CursorType = 2
rsResults.CursorLocation = 2
rsResults.LockType = 3
rsResults.Open()
rsResults_numRows = 0
%>
```

The part in bold is the SQL statement that is passed to the database. It's pretty much what you typed in to the recordset panel – the only difference is the use of the VBScript function REPLACE, which inserts the values from the parameters. Oh, and all those quotation marks, but we did warn you that UltraDev uses a few of these!

Searching for all with numerical values

One of the most annoying limitations of this type of search in UltraDev is that when we select all – as in all occasion cards by Kate or even all cards by all artists then we run into problems. This is because we're searching on the numerical ID field and there isn't a numerical wildcard we can use like the * we used on our text fields earlier. We're going to finish off the chapter by running through a solution for this.

Setting up a Search for *All*

1. Open your Code View in the results page and find the rsResults recordset. Once located you should see the following code just above the recordset near the top.

Foundation Dreamweaver UltraDev 4

```
<%
Dim rsResults__artistName
rsResults__artistName = "1"
if (Request.Form("artist") <> "") then
 rsResults__artistName = Request.Form("artist")
%>
<%
Dim rsResults__occasionType
rsResults__occasionType = "2"
if (Request.Form("occasion") <> "") then
rsResults__occasionType = Request.Form("occasion")
%>
```

2. You then need to replace this with the code shown in the screenshot. If you don't want to type all this in, we've provided it for you as a text file called `AllFix.txt` in the Chapter 7 folder.

```
35 <%
36 'Foundation UltraDev ALL fix
37
38 Dim sqlString
39 ' Set sql to this if no artist is chosen and a occasion is
40 If (Request.Form("artist") = "-1") and (Request.Form("occasion") <> "-1") then
41 sqlString =  "SELECT artist_name, Occasion, category, cost, ID, image_path, ref_numbe
42 End If
43 ' Set sql to this if no occasion is chosen and a artist is
44 If (Request.Form("occasion") = "-1") and (Request.Form("artist") <> "-1") then
45 sqlString =  "SELECT artist_name, Occasion, category, cost, ID, image_path, ref_numbe
46 End If
47
48 ' Set sql to this if both artist and occasion is set
49 If (Request.Form("artist") <> "-1") and (Request.Form("occasion") <> "-1") then
50 sqlString =  "SELECT artist_name, Occasion, category, cost, ID, image_path, ref_numbe
51 End If
52 ' Set sql to this if both artist and occasion not selected other way display all recc
53 If (Request.Form("artist") = "-1") and (Request.Form("occasion") = "-1")  then
54 sqlString =  "SELECT artist_name, Occasion, category, cost, ID, image_path, ref_numbe
55 End If
56 %>
57
```

It's a lot of code but it's not that complex – if you read the comment lines, you'll see that it's just four SQL statements that allow for all eventualities. We've created a dynamic WHERE statement, which is set depending on the criteria specified in the search.

3. We need to make our final amendments to the rsResults recordset. Open it up and alter the SQL statement to read like this:

Searching your Database 7

```
SELECT artist_name, Occasion, category, cost, ID,
➥ image_path, ref_number, rrp_price, type
FROM Occasions INNER JOIN (artists INNER JOIN products
➥ ON artists.artist_id = products.artist_id) ON
➥ Occasions.occasion_ID = products.occasion_id sqlstring
```

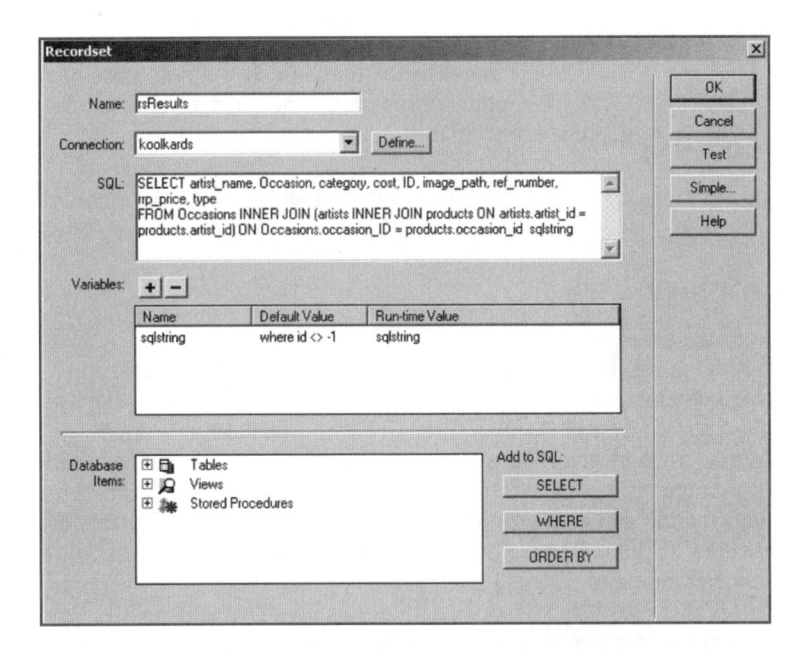

4. Add sqlstring as a variable by clicking +, and give it a Default Value of where id <> -1 and a Run-time Value of sqlstring.

    If you press the Test button you'll notice that all the records are returned – this is for test purposes only, and also because UltraDev insists on a default value setting.

5. It's time to move onto the list boxes, so open up the Artist list box by selecting the list values button. Add a new label called Choose Artist and assign a value of -1. This means that if any of the values in the dropdown box equal -1 then we need to select all for that table.

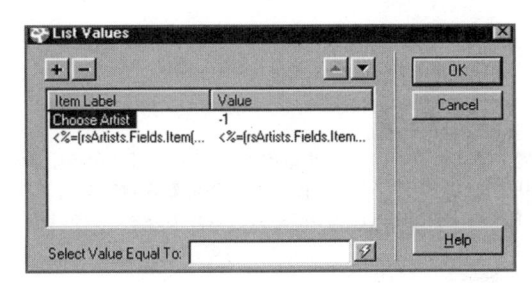

6. Go and do the same for the Occasion list box.

   Once our code routine has determined which combination of Alls (if any) we are using, it dynamically creates the SQL statement accordingly and holds the statement in a variable called `sqlstring`.

7. Make the same change to the `master.dwt` template. We couldn't apply the changes to the template in the first place because the list boxes are in an editable region, so the change wouldn't be reflected in the pages already created.

8. Test your page out, and all the searches should now work.

Summary

Although we've made the search pages for our Koolkards site, you'll be able to use exactly the same techniques for your own sites. If you've got this far, that's probably not too far off.

We've tried to give you a good grounding in SQL techniques and shown you that SQL statements are so powerful that you can use them to create almost anything that your imagination can come up with. Your brain probably really hurts now, especially if this was all new to you. Don't worry too much – the more you use UltraDev, the better your understanding of SQL will become.

For extra information, we've included a range of web resources at the back of the book.

In this chapter we saw:

- UltraDev can help us write some basic and some advanced **SQL** techniques, and we applied this to what we already knew about recordsets

- SQL allows us to create both simple and complex **searches**, and we can easily build search pages and results pages

- Using **dynamic list boxes**, we can offer and limit choices for our customers and the **parameters** of these boxes are quickly and efficiently passed on to our results pages

- UltraDev's **templates** can be altered to meet our needs and we can decide the extent to which they are **editable**

You now have the main ingredients for creating dynamic web applications – an understanding of basic coding techniques, how to query your data to create recordsets and how to manipulate the data on your pages. What you'll see in the next few chapters

Searching your Database 7

is how we can make these techniques work for us and provide not just another data driven web site, but a powerful web application. Keep reading, because these skills are what will really make you stand out from the crowd.

kool kards

8 User Login and Registration

What we'll cover in this chapter:

- *Building a **registration** page and **saving** your customers' details*
- *Understanding **logins** and how to define **access levels** for users and administrators*
- *Dealing with login problems and adding **server behaviors** to enhance functionality*

Foundation Dreamweaver UltraDev 4

Welcome to one of the hottest topics in dynamic web application software: securing your web pages.

Security and its related issues are crucial to your application providing different sections for different users. There would have been absolutely no point to in us creating the Administrator's section in the last few chapters if just *anyone* could enter those pages.

There are a number of solutions for securing parts of your web page. For instance, if you were using an intranet, IIS could allow only users that were authenticated by NT user groups to view certain pages.

UltraDev provides a solution for securing your web pages using a combination of very useful server behaviors. During this chapter we'll be building a login screen for users who want to use access the various parts of our site.

We'll want our normal visitors to register (with the promise of a discount). Remember, persuading users to register on your site is an excellent way of getting a mailing list together so you can provide your customer base with *targeted* product updates and information.

We also need secure Administration pages in our web site, which the normal users can't get into. We've already built those pages in the preceding chapters, but we'll now look at how UltraDev can secure the not only the Administrator's menu, but all subsequent pages.

Breaking down the Problem

Before we can start developing our solution let's look at some of the components of a login cycle. We'll need:

- A list of users that are allowed into the secure site – that is, a table within our database containing the names and passwords of 'authorized' personnel.

- A login page which will grant or deny access depending on the credentials (username/password) given.

- To be able to send different types of users to different menu pages.

- To properly secure all the pages in the Administrator's section in case the user correctly guesses the URL and bypasses the login page.

User Login and Registration | 8

The Login Table

To begin with, take a look at the table we've designed for you. It's called logins and can be found in the KoolKards database:

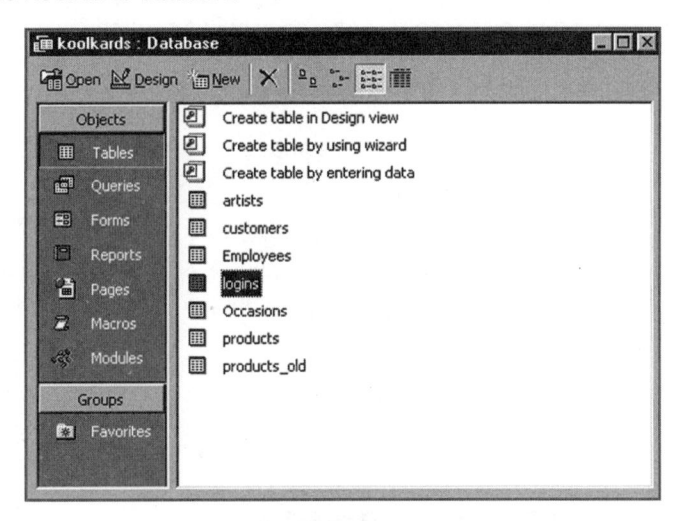

Let's start by taking a look at our data schema. Open up the logins table in Design mode (highlight logins and click the Design button along the top):

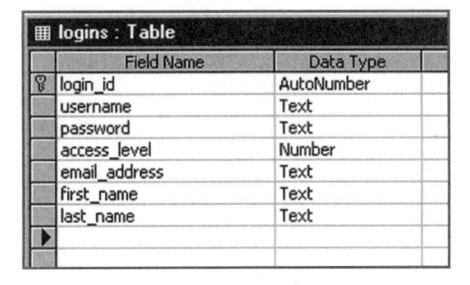

As you can see, our simple table is made up of nothing too scary – just text fields for the user's details and a password. The only special field is the access_level. We'll use this later but, as you can probably guess, the user's access level will determine which parts of the system they can access. Finally, we have a check box for newsletter, which we'll use later on.

If you open the table and see the contents, you'll see there is already an entry. We've already set up the Administrator with an access_level of 1. It will become clear later how we use this.

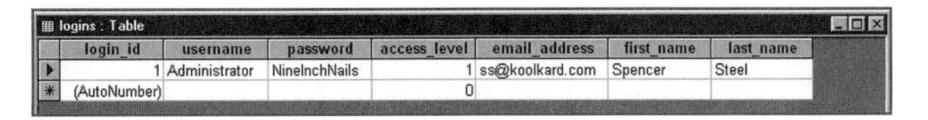

As we said in our introduction, we want users to have the option to register with our site. The benefit to them is that when they return to the site in future with a simple username and password, they won't have to go through the whole process of inputting their delivery address and credit card details again. You'll see this kind of approach on most large e-commerce sites. You can also monitor shopping trends with your database. Say, for example, you were running a record shop – you could extend the login table principle and hold tables of the type of music your customers listen to, and then recommend other similar types of music the next time the user logs on.

However, we'll start by keeping it simple – with the user just entering their basic details. We can always add the address and credit card info later on.

We can't make this mandatory in our final site – no one really likes registering without knowing a bit about your site (or after having made one successful purchase). However, we can entice people to register with a 10% discount on all orders – we'll look at how we handle the actual shopping cart later on.

Let's kick off by building the new user registration screen which will allow our users to register the first time they visit the site.

Building the Registration Page

1. Use the Master template and save your page as register.asp.

2. Remember, if you didn't properly alter your Master template in the last chapter, we've provided the finished version for you. Simply rename master_final to master and you can use that for this and future examples. We don't need to create a recordset at the moment – just get the page looking roughly right.

3. Create a form called register (with the Form Objects panel), with the Method set to POST, like this:

User Login and Registration 8

4. Create a table (Insert > Table) that has two columns and seven rows, just as you see here:

5. Your text fields (Form Objects > Insert Text Field) should have the following properties:

Display Value   **Text Box Name (Label)**

First name   first_name
Last name   last_name
E-mail address   email_address
Username   username
Password   password

And the following two special objects:

Special Objects

Hidden field   access_level – **value 3**
Submit button   Keep standard default settings

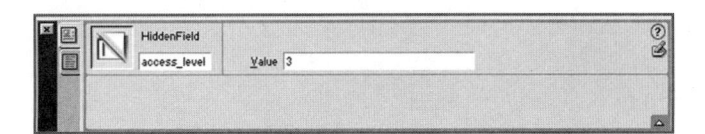

Levels of User Rights

You may not have realized this but the access_level dictates what rights and permissions each login will have. You can design your own schemes when you build your site, but here's what we've come up with:

- Level 1 – *Administrator* – can perform all functions.

- Level 2 – *Power Users* – user can perform some functions (in our site at the moment, we don't have any Power Users as such, but it's perfectly possible that you want some certain people to have the right to be able to view all the card details as the Administrators can, but not be able to permanently delete anything).

- Level 3 – *Customer Users* – can only use the customer part of the site and view and search limited product information, with no update or delete rights.

Now we have the page set up, we need to put in our **insert behaviors** – these will store these new customer details in our database permanently. It's no use people registering if our site forgets them as soon as they leave!

Adding Insert Behaviors

We've already looked at how we insert records into our database in chapter 1, so most of this will be old news. However, we'll be looking at a new technique, so let's take it from the top again.

1. Open up the Server Behaviors panel, click the + symbol and select Insert Record:

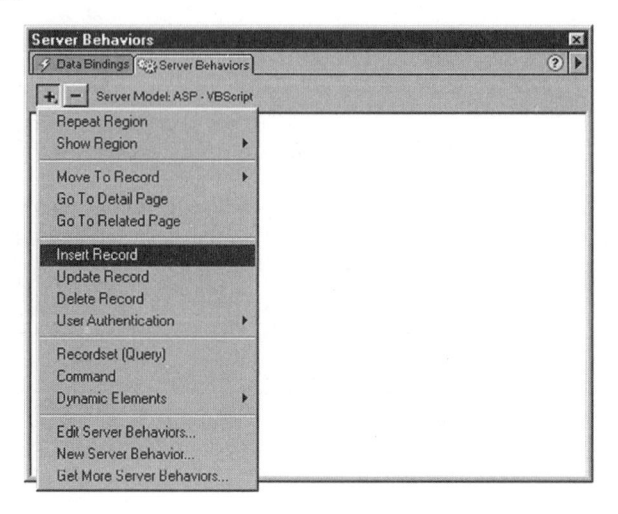

User Login and Registration   8

You should be able to walk through most of this by yourself by now.

2. The connection, as ever, is KoolKards.

3. Insert the records into the logins table.

4. Once you've inserted the record, go to thankyou_register.asp (we've provided this in the downloads).

5. Select register in the Get Values From: field. This is the name of the form. Remember we have two forms on our page now, because one is inherited from the template, so make sure you have the form called register selected. Now you can see why we should always call our forms something meaningful – most people would leave them as the default form, which isn't very helpful when you're working with multiple forms.

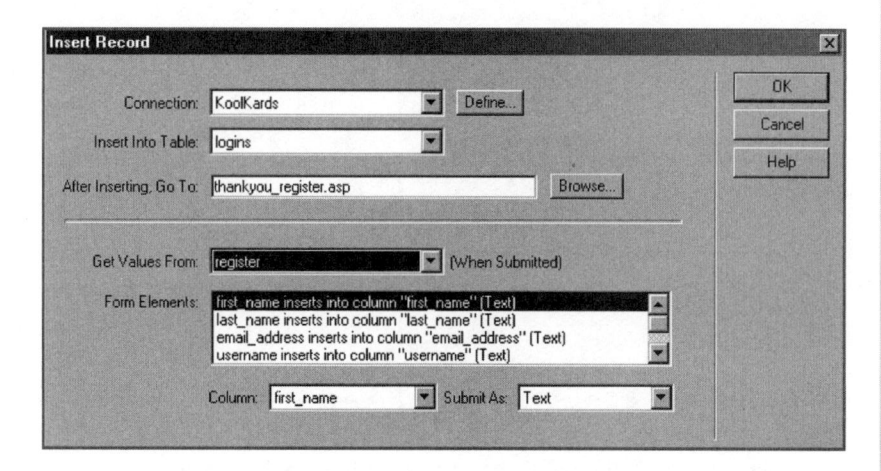

Note how cleverly UltraDev has anticipated what text box from our page will be inserted into which column in our database! Is it magic? Actually, no, it just looks for matches between text box names and column names from the table. If they're not matched exactly you'll have to do it yourself using the drop-down boxes.

Once your Insert Record behavior is filled in, we're all set to add the record.

6. Click OK.

Here's a thought. What happens if the new user chooses exactly the same username as someone else – not so likely if you choose Spencer_Steel but very much so if you choose Rob.

Duplicate Usernames

The best solution to this problem is to perform a search against the logins table and make sure the username doesn't already exist (in other words, the field username is *unique*).

You're in luck this time as we're not going to make you hand code this bit – there's already a handy server behavior that will do the job for us!

Return to your register.asp page, Open the Server Behavior panel and select User Authentication followed by Check New Username:

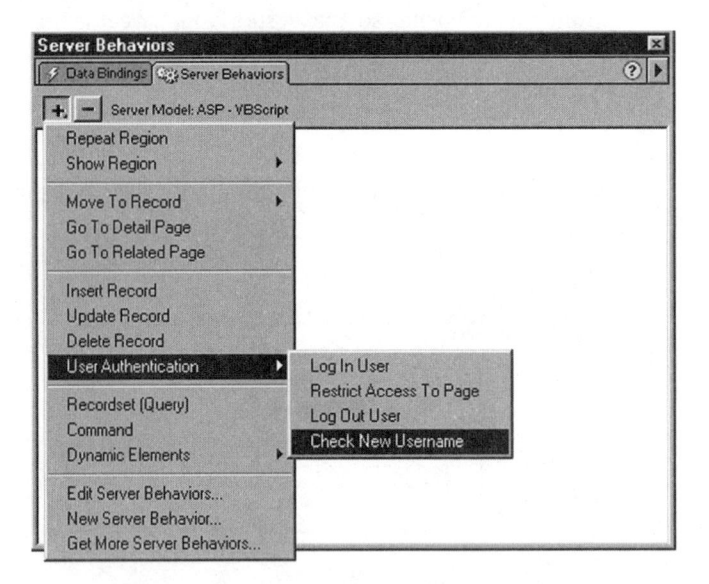

Select your username field from the list of fields available and select a page to go to if the user already exists. In our case we want to send it back to the registration page, so the user can try again. But for now let's just link it back to the same page.

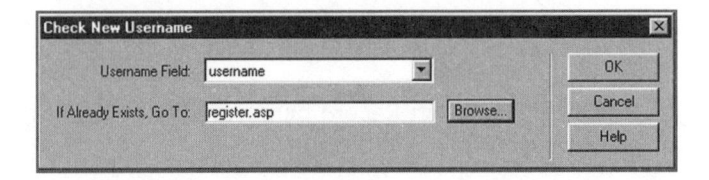

Well, we said we're not going to make you hand-code the routine, but instead let's take a look at the code it generated and see if we can make sense of it. It'll be about twenty lines down in your Code View:

User Login and Registration   8

```
19 <%
20 ' *** Redirect if username exists
21 MM_flag="MM_insert"
22 If (CStr(Request(MM_flag)) <> "") Then
23   MM_dupKeyRedirect="register.asp"
24   MM_rsKeyConnection=MM_KoolKards_STRING
25   MM_dupKeyUsernameValue = CStr(Request.Form("username"))
26   MM_dupKeySQL="SELECT username FROM logins WHERE username='" & MM_dupKeyUsernameValue & "'"
27   MM_adodbRecordset="ADODB.Recordset"
28   set MM_rsKey=Server.CreateObject(MM_adodbRecordset)
29   MM_rsKey.ActiveConnection=MM_rsKeyConnection
30   MM_rsKey.Source=MM_dupKeySQL
31   MM_rsKey.CursorType=0
32   MM_rsKey.CursorLocation=2
33   MM_rsKey.LockType=3
34   MM_rsKey.Open
35   If Not MM_rsKey.EOF Or Not MM_rsKey.BOF Then
36     ' the username was found - can not add the requested username
37     MM_qsChar = "?"
38     If (InStr(1,MM_dupKeyRedirect,"?") >= 1) Then MM_qsChar = "&"
39     MM_dupKeyRedirect = MM_dupKeyRedirect & MM_qsChar & "requsername=" & MM_dupKeyUsernameValue
40     Response.Redirect(MM_dupKeyRedirect)
41   End If
42   MM_rsKey.Close
43 End If
44 %>
```

Eek! Quite a chunk of code – don't worry, we're not going to wade through it all. In line 25, do you see something familiar?

```
MM_dupKeySQL="SELECT username FROM logins WHERE username='" &
➥ MM_dupKeyUsernameValue & "'"
```

It's an SQL statement that says "Show me all the records from logins where username is equal to the content of the edit box username". The previous line requests the form content of the edit box and assigns it to the variable MM_dupKeyUsernameValue. Obviously, if there are any records returned in this SQL statement then the user hasn't provided a unique name.

The last part of the code deals with what happens if there is a match:

```
' the username was found - can not add the requested username
MM_qsChar = "?"
If (InStr(1,MM_dupKeyRedirect,"?") >= 1) Then MM_qsChar = "&"
MM_dupKeyRedirect = MM_dupKeyRedirect & MM_qsChar &
➥ "requsername=" & MM_dupKeyUsernameValue
    Response.Redirect(MM_dupKeyRedirect)
```

UltraDev appends the username to the URL by using a querystring. This way the offending name can be returned to the user – in other words, it can tell you "Rob is already taken, please try again". Let's test it now.

Foundation Dreamweaver UltraDev 4

Testing your Page

1. Make sure that you have a thankyou_register.asp page set up in your Chapter 8 folder.

2. Enter a new user's details and choose a unique username:

   REGISTER NOW AND GET 10% OFF!

First name:	Rob
Last name:	Paddock
E-mail address:	rob@foundationultrade
Username:	Rob
Password:	

   [Submit]

3. Once you've submitted, you'll be taken to the thank you page.

4. Now try it again, but this time choose the same username as before. This time you'll be returned to the registration page – but check out the URL:

   Address: http://localhost/KoolKards/chapter8/register.asp?requsername=Rob

> Remember this makes it possible for us to use the Request.QueryString object to call this value. This means we could redirect the user to a page which says "The username {QueryString.requsername} is already taken – please try another".

Form Validation and Password Protection

There are still a couple of things wrong with our registration page.

- You can enter blanks in any fields – and that's no good. It's important to validate our form, to make sure we definitely get an entry in certain required fields.

- You can see your password as you type it in – no good for curious over-the-shoulder watchers (you'll have noticed most web sites disguise passwords as you enter them with *******).

User Login and Registration | 8

Although you could say forms have more to do with the Dreamweaver side of things than UltraDev, forms are so closely tied in with all this we thought we'd treat you to a couple of basic techniques.

Improving our Form

1. First pop up the Behaviors panel – not the Server Behaviors, but your normal, every day, run-of-the-mill Client Behaviors.

2. Press SHIFT+F3 to bring them up. As long as you have a form element on your page (as we do on our `register.asp`) – the Validate Form behavior will be available.

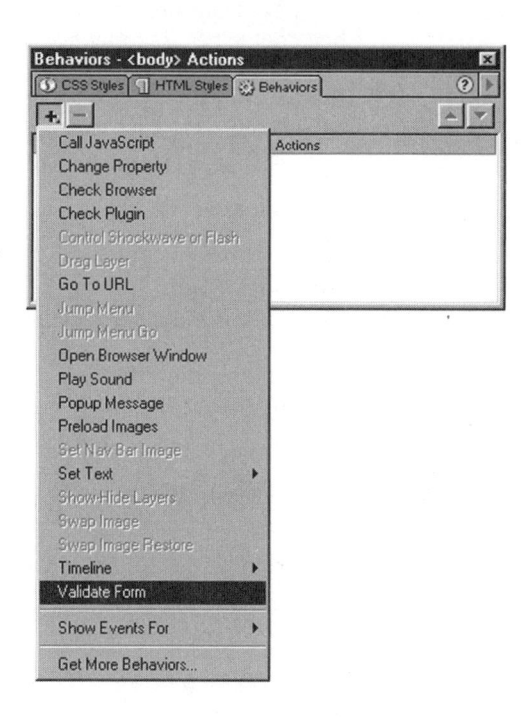

`<body> <table> <tr> <td> <div> <form>`

> *Before applying the behavior make sure the form is highlighted. This will make sure the behavior is applied when the form is submitted. If you apply the behavior without making sure the form is highlighted, it'll apply the behavior when the page first loads!*

Foundation Dreamweaver UltraDev 4

3. Select it and you'll see each form element on your page listed. One by one, highlight each of the Named Fields and choose what kind of validation you require from the list below. All of our fields need only the Required box checked, except the email_address field which needs the Email Address radio button checked as well as the Required box.

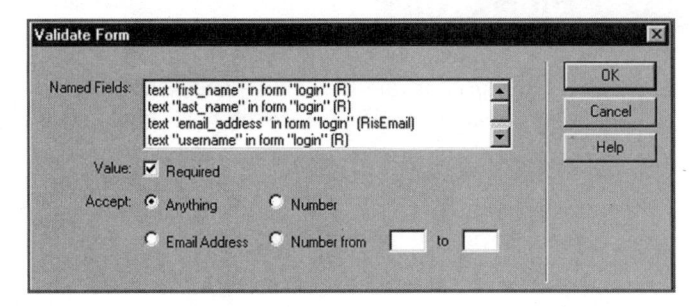

The form validation behavior will kick in as soon as the form is submitted on your page. Note that all form validation is done on the client-side. This takes the load off the server as the server only starts to do anything once the form has met the exact criteria, leaving it to work on other things.

So, that's the first problem solved...

The next slight problem is that it would be better if the password edit box couldn't be seen by everyone.

4. This is very easy – just highlight the edit box in question, bring up the properties and choose Password from the Type. This ensures as the user types each character only asterisks(*) are displayed on-screen.

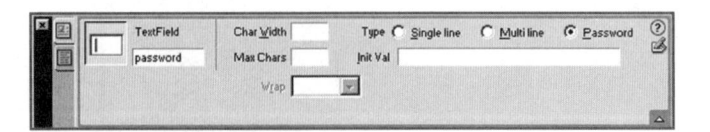

Here ends the form validation section. Test it out and see what happens if you don't supply all the credentials or input an invalid e-mail address.

Passing Back the QueryString

Now our page is 'error proof' and the form is validating nicely, what else do we need?

User Login and Registration

Well, it's a bit cold just being dumped back to the registration screen if the user name already exists. How about creating a user-friendly message that tells the user what the problem is?

Well, as we saw, if a username is already in the database, the behavior returns it in the URL. So, it wouldn't be too hard to extract this data using the Request.QueryString method to make a user-friendly message for our users.

Here's some code you can place on your page to display an error message.

```
<% IF (Request.Querystring("requsername") <> "") then %>
The username <%=Request.Querystring("requsername")%> already
➥ exists - please enter a different name.
<% End IF %>
```

See if you can get this to work for you. If you're a bit stuck as to where to place the code look at the screenshot below. All we've done is place our cursor in the empty cell to the left of the Submit button and opened our Code View:

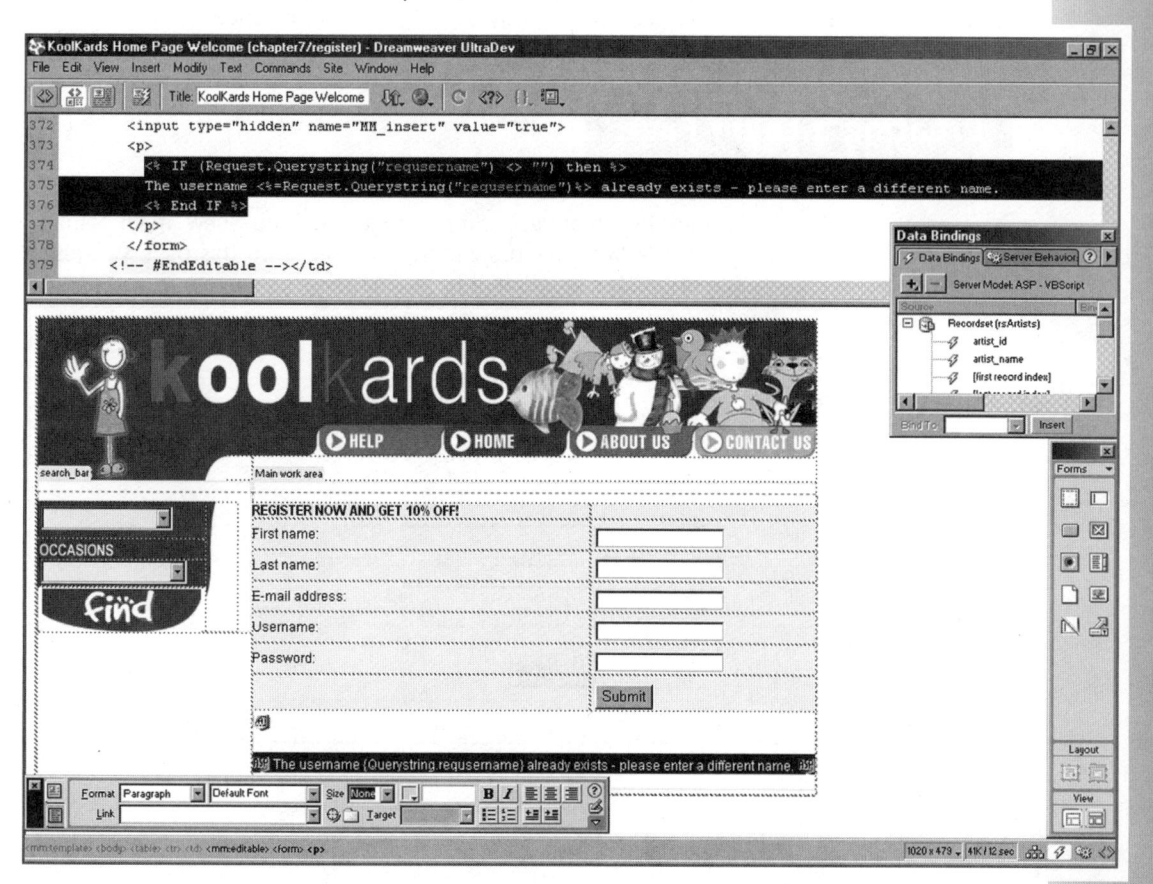

Foundation Dreamweaver UltraDev 4

The code that we've highlighted is basically saying:

> "If the QueryString 'requsername' is not empty, print on the screen "The user name {whatever you typed} already exists".

You should be able to test your fully user-friendly page. Perfect.

> *As we've said before, once you're more comfortable with UltraDev's functions and environment, you can start playing around to make your pages look better and better. For example, you might want to put the user-friendly message we just created in bold red.*

Right then, we've built our brand spanking new membership registration page. Moving on, let's now create the *login* page called `login.asp` that will verify the user who logs in and determine what rights they have whilst swiftly booting out any intruders!

Creating a Login Page

1. We'll start by creating a simple page from our new main `Master` template. We don't need anything too special on this page yet, just a couple of text boxes within a form – one for the username and one for the password:

```
Main work area
                    Registered Users Please Login
Login
Username:          [          ]
Password:          [          ]
                    [Submit]
```

User Login and Registration

2. Name your text boxes username and password. Make sure you call your form login and set the Action to point to the same page `login.asp`. Also, set the form's Method to POST.

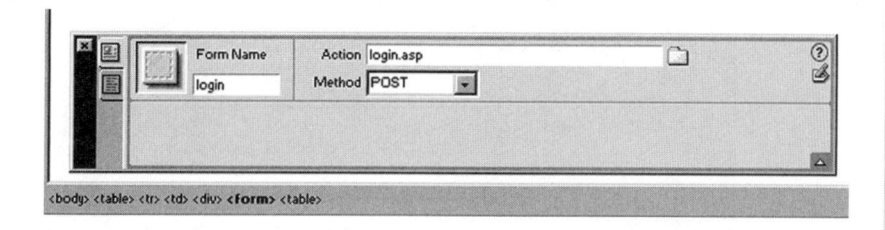

3. Now open up the Server Behaviors panel again, select User Authentication > Log In User:

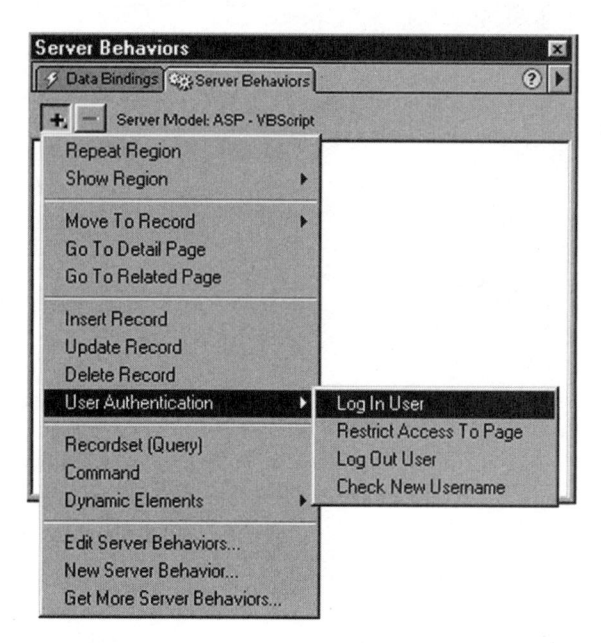

This will open the Log In User panel. Don't panic – there may seem a lot to fill in here, but it's pretty familiar stuff when you look at it.

Foundation Dreamweaver UltraDev 4

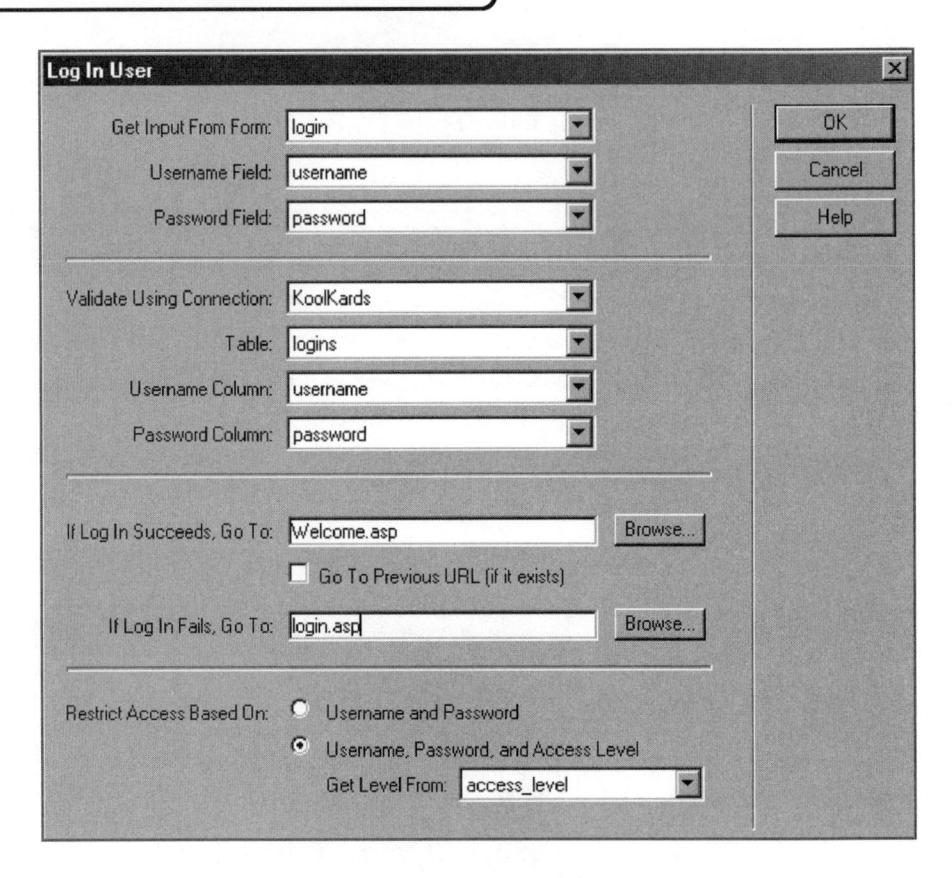

4. Work through all the options, step by step, following the screenshots:

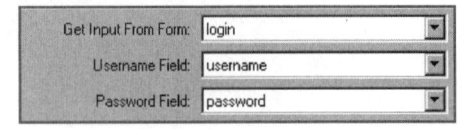

- Get Input From Form: select the login form.

- Username Field: choose username from the list of fields. Here we tell UltraDev which text box of our form contains the username string to match against the database.

- Password Field: choose password from the list of fields. Here we tell UltraDev which text box on our form contains the password string to match against the database.

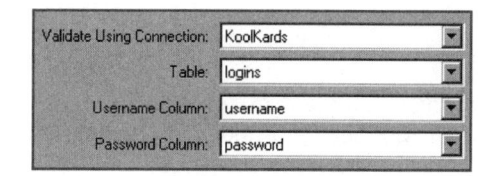

User Login and Registration 8

```
Validate Using Connection:  KoolKards
                    Table:  logins
         Username Column:   username
         Password Column:   password
```

- Validate Using Connection: **select the** KoolKards **connection**.

- Table: **select the** logins **table from the database**. We're just telling UltraDev where the details of registered users are kept.

- Username Column: **select your** username **field**. Here we tell UltraDev which column in the database contains the username, which it will attempt to match up with the form entry.

- Password Column: **select your** password **field**. This time, we tell UltraDev which column in the database contains the password.

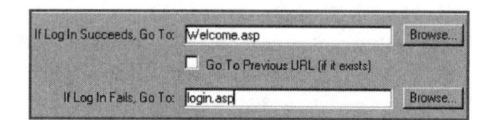

```
If Log In Succeeds, Go To:  Welcome.asp              Browse...
                            □ Go To Previous URL (if it exists)
   If Log In Fails, Go To:  login.asp                Browse...
```

- If Log In succeeds, Go To: **type in or browse to** Welcome.asp. This page will be for any user that successfully logs in. It has been provided for you with the chapter 8 downloads.

- If Log In Fails, Go To: **this needs to point back to your login page**. Of course you could redirect the user somewhere else but most sites just display a message Invalid login please try again. We'll keep it simple for now.

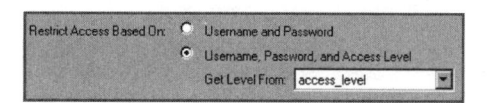

```
Restrict Access Based On:  ○ Username and Password
                           ● Username, Password, and Access Level
              Get Level From:  access_level
```

- Restrict Access Based on: **check the** username, password and access level **button**.

- Get Level From: access_level. We'll look at how we can use the access_level to give the administrator extra rights and privileges.

213

Foundation Dreamweaver UltraDev 4

Code Time

Go on – you know you want to see how it works – open your Code View again. No cheating now... it will help you understand what's going on. It seems quite intense, but we've highlighted the important bit:

```
' *** Validate request to log in to this site.
MM_LoginAction = Request.ServerVariables("URL")
If Request.QueryString<>""Then MM_LoginAction =
➡ MM_LoginAction + "?" + Request.QueryString
MM_valUsername=CStr(Request.Form("username"))
If MM_valUsername <> "" Then
  MM_fldUserAuthorization=:"access_level"
  MM_redirectLoginSuccess="Welcome.asp"
  MM_redirectLoginFailed="login.asp"
  MM_flag="ADODB.Recordset"
  set MM_rsUser = Server.CreateObject(MM_flag)
  MM_rsUser.ActiveConnection = MM_koolkards_STRING
  MM_rsUser.Source = "SELECT username, password"
  If MM_fldUserAuthorization <> "" Then MM_rsUser.Source =
➡ MM_rsUser.Source & "," & MM_fldUserAuthorization
  MM_rsUser.Source = MM_rsUser.Source & " FROM logins WHERE
➡ username='" & MM_valUsername &"' AND password='" & CStr
➡ (Request.Form("password")) & "'"
  MM_rsUser.CursorType = 0
  MM_rsUser.CursorLocation = 2
  MM_rsUser.LockType = 3
  MM_rsUser.Open
```

The first part requests all the information from the fields contained within your form (username, password). It also sets up where you want the pages to redirect to depending on the success of your login.

```
SELECT username, password"
  If MM_fldUserAuthorization <> "" Then MM_rsUser.Source =
➡ MM_rsUser.Source & "," & MM_fldUserAuthorization
  MM_rsUser.Source = MM_rsUser.Source & " FROM logins WHERE
➡ username='" & MM_valUsername &"' AND password='" & CStr
➡ (Request.Form("password")) & "'"
```

This is where the SQL statement is built and checked against the logins table to identify if the login is correct. This may look a bit chaotic with lots of IF statements, but basically it checks to see whether you've requested to use the access levels and if so it incorporates that access level field into the SELECT statement. Remember these routines have to cater

User Login and Registration 8

for all possibilities and therefore the code generated won't always be the leanest for your specific requirements.

Let's look at the next section of code:

```
If Not MM_rsUser.EOF Or Not MM_rsUser.BOF Then
    ' username and password match - this is a valid user
    Session("MM_Username") = MM_valUsername
    If (MM_fldUserAuthorization <> "") Then
        Session("MM_UserAuthorization") = CStr
(MM_rsUser.Fields.Item(MM_fldUserAuthorization).Value)
    Else
        Session("MM_UserAuthorization") = ""
    End If
    if CStr(Request.QueryString("accessdenied")) <> "" And
false Then
        MM_redirectLoginSuccess = Request.QueryString
("accessdenied")
        End If
    MM_rsUser.Close
    Response.Redirect(MM_redirectLoginSuccess)
End If
MM_rsUser.Close
Response.Redirect(MM_redirectLoginFailed)
End If
```

Here the code checks to see whether a record was returned after the SQL statement was executed. If no records were returned, the login must be invalid, so the appropriate redirect is used, depending on what you specified in the behavior. If there *is* a match, the routine sets up two session variables:

Session("MM_Username") = The User Name
Session("MM_UserAuthorization") = Access Level Granted

Foundation Dreamweaver UltraDev 4

Improving our Login Page

The completed page should look something like this:

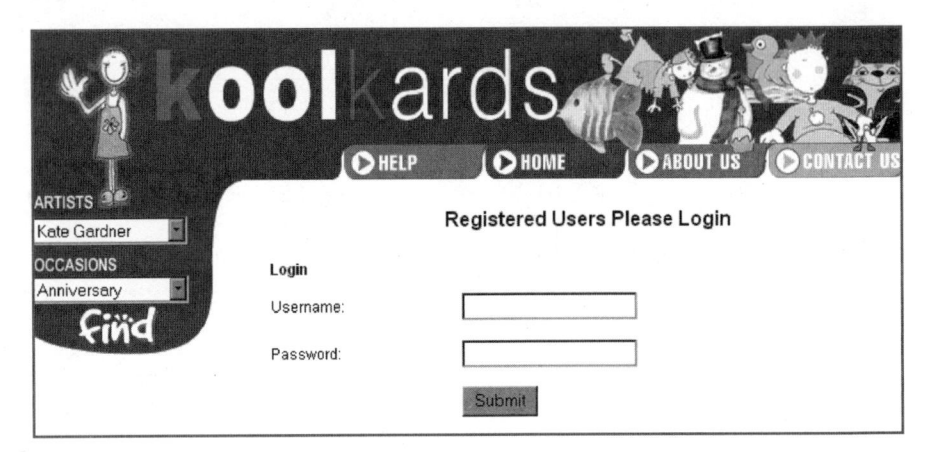

What improvements do you think we could make?

Well, for a start it would be nice to let the user know that they have entered the wrong information. This can be achieved in much the same way as we did with the user registration page.

The difference this time is the server behavior doesn't pass anything back to your login page telling you the login was invalid. We can solve this by putting a URL parameter after the login page URL.

Go back into the Log in User behavior and place the following code in the If Log In Fails, Go To field:

```
Login.asp?valid=false
```

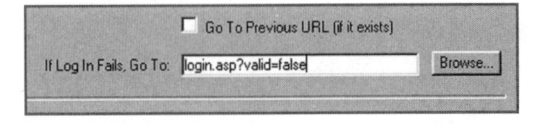

We're now sending back an extra URL parameter called `valid` – which we can extract and use to trap failed logins.

Click into the empty space under the form (or press RETURN to get some space) and bring up the Code View. From there we can add the following code:

User Login and Registration 8

```
<% IF (Request.Querystring("valid") = "false") then %>
You entered either an incorrect Username or Password
➥ please try again
<% End If %>
```

```
119          <tr>
120            <td height="35">
121 <% IF (Request.Querystring("valid") = "false") then %>
122 You entered either an incorrect Username or Password please try again
123 <% End If %>
124
125            <td height="35"><font face="Arial, Helvetica, sans-serif" size="2">
126              <input type="submit" name="Submit" value="Submit">
```

This would be the result you would get if login were incorrect:

Foundation Dreamweaver UltraDev 4

Remember Me?

Another cool feature we could add is a *Remember Me* option. Many sites use this option because it saves the user from having to type in their details every time they want to enter the site.

This can be achieved by writing a cookie to the user's machine to hold his login details. This would then enable the user's details to be automatically placed on the login page if the *Remember Me* feature was previously turned on.

Let's create one for ourselves.

Adding a Remember Me Check Box

1. Add a row to your table; just right-click in the cell next to the Submit button, and select Table > Insert Row:

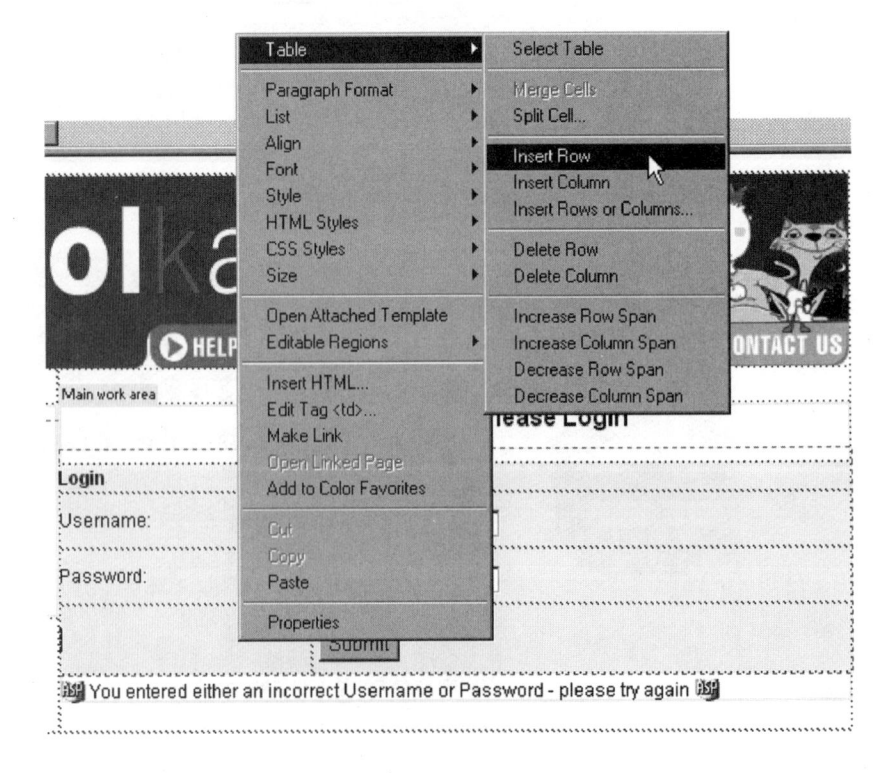

User Login and Registration

2. Now add a check box to your form using the Form Objects panel:

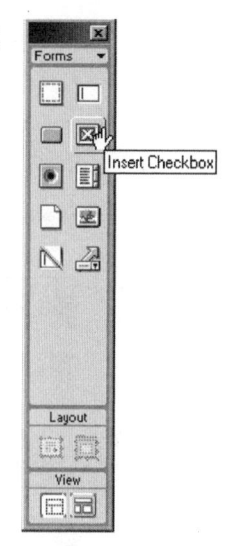

3. Using the Property inspector, name it remember and set its checked value to yes:

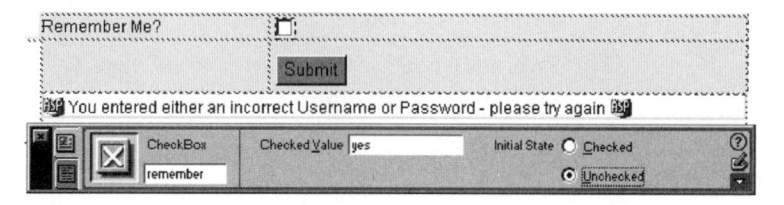

4. Place the following code at the start of your page just under the `<!--#include file="../Connections/KoolKards.asp" -->`

```
<% IF (Request.Form("remember") = "yes") then
    Response.Cookies("KoolKards")("username") =
    ➥ Request.Form("UserName")
    Response.Cookies("KoolKards")("password") =
    ➥ Request.Form("password")
    Response.Cookies("KoolKards").Expires = date + 90
End If %>
```

If the form object called remember is yes this sets two cookies, username and password, to the value of their respective form text boxes.

In the last line we've set the cookie to expire after 90 days. Feel free to set the time limit to whatever you want. The other thing you may remember from chapter 3 is that we've used the **dictionary** properties of a cookie to avoid having to write two cookies to a user's machine.

5. Now edit your login text fields to have an initial value set. The following code will now read the cookie values that where previously set:

```
<%=Request.Cookies("KoolKards")("username")%>
```

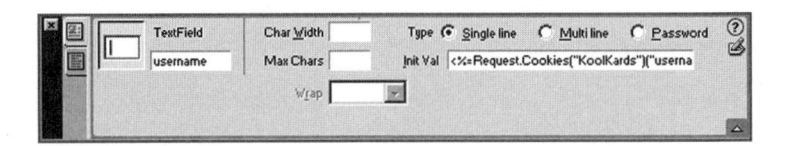

```
<%=Request.Cookies("KoolKards")("password")%>
```

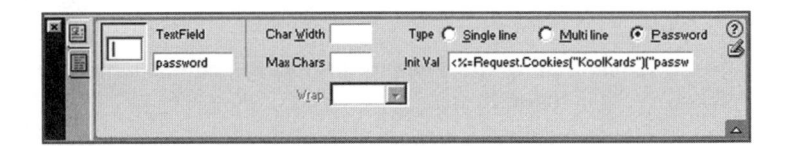

6. Save your page and test away. Your page will now remember your username and password when you return.

More Tweaking

Our page isn't perfect yet because there's no way to turn off the Remember Me. Once set, it stays for a whole 90 days.

To rectify this we need two things. First, we need the Remember Me state to be, er, *remembered* – so the user keeps the previous setting. If the user then turns off Remember Me the cookie is killed.

So, add the lines in bold to your existing code:

```
<% IF (Request.Form("remember") = "yes") then
   Response.Cookies("KoolKards")("username") =
   ➥ Request.Form("UserName")
       Response.Cookies("KoolKards")("password") =
       ➥ Request.Form("password")
   Response.Cookies("KoolKards")("rememberme") = "yes"
Response.Cookies("KoolKards").Expires = date + 90
Else
```

User Login and Registration | 8

```
        Response.Cookies("KoolKards").Expires = date -1
    End If %>
```

This kills the cookie if the Remember Me button is OFF the next time the user logs in, showing that they don't want the auto-login function.

= date -1 will effectively expire the cookie straight away.

All we need to add is a routine that makes our Remember Me box actually 'ticked' if the Cookie rememberme is yes.

Highlight the check box on the actual page, and make sure you can see the Code View. We're going to replace the code for the check box with a custom IF statement:

```
<input type="checkbox" name="remember" value="yes"
<% IF (Request.Cookies("KoolKards")("rememberme")="yes") then
➥ %> checked <%end if%> >
```

```
244         <td>Remember Me?</td>
245         <td>
246             <input type="checkbox" name="remember" value="yes"
247 <% IF (Request.Cookies("KoolKards")("rememberme")="yes") then %> checked <%end if%> >
248         </td>
249     </tr>
```

Note how we don't end the input type line with a > sign. Instead we leave the statement open and move down a line to apply some ASP.

What we are saying here is if the cookie (*"rememberme"*) = "yes" then make the check box checked. Checked is the way we can force the box to automatically tick...

We then close the check box with the > to finish our dynamic text box.

OK, now it's time to test your mini login application.

See how we've added some great functionality. The Remember Me stores your previous settings as long as you like – until you turn it off. Now that's user-friendly!

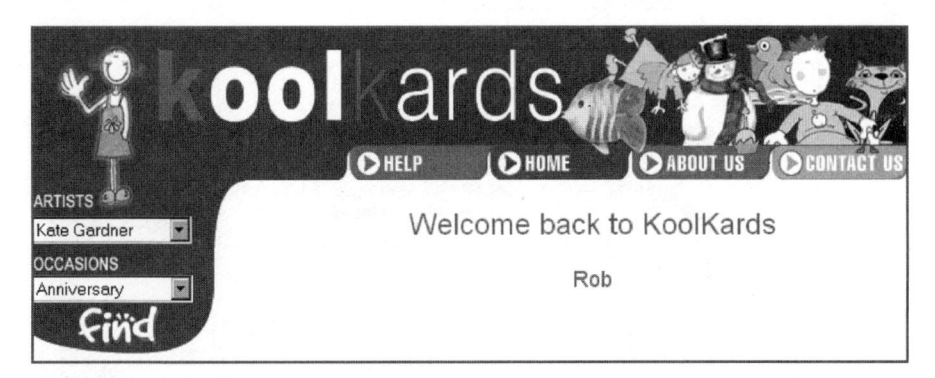

Foundation Dreamweaver UltraDev 4

Going to Pages Depending on Rights

Let's look at how we can push people with different access levels to different pages. Specifically, let's look at moving the administrator (level 1) onto their own menu page, from where they can access pages to edit the data in the database.

How do we redirect them to a page? Well – perhaps oddly, we need to take everyone to our Welcome page, and then divert off the people who shouldn't be there – very quickly. Basically, we want to deny the administrators access to the normal menu!

There is a server behavior that will help us with this: Restrict Access to Page.

Controlling Access

1. Pull up the Welcome page and apply the behavior:

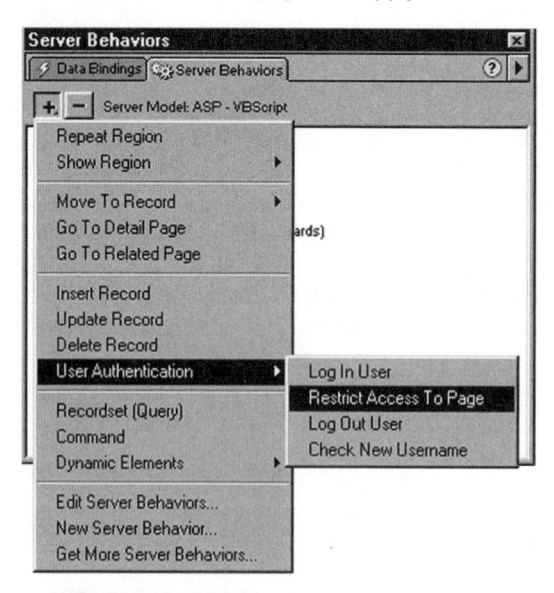

2. You'll be presented with an option of what method to use to restrict. We'll use the access_level:

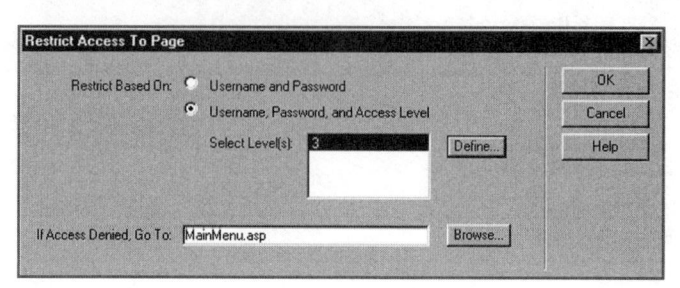

User Login and Registration

3. We need to tell the behavior what levels we have – and more importantly what levels are allowed in. If you Define the level, you can add as many levels as you want to remain on this page – we just need Level 3 people to stop here and Level 1 people to be denied.

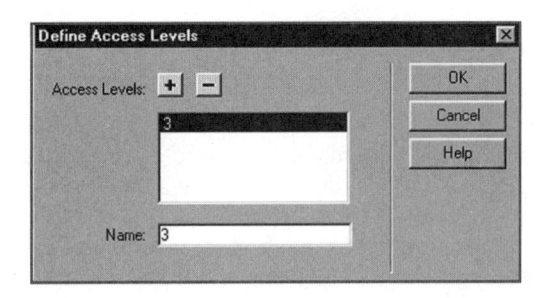

[Define Access Levels dialog box: Access Levels: + –, with "3" in list, Name: 3, buttons OK, Cancel, Help]

Thinking about what we've done here, we can see that we've gone about it in a rather funny and topsy-turvy way.

Remember our login page takes care of the 'intruder' situation – it won't let you through unless you have a valid username and password. Therefore, all valid users get passed on to our Welcome page.

Yet, administrators (level 1) don't want to be here, so we're going to *deny them* access – redirecting them instead to a place with more powerful options.

4. If you save your work and test this from the login.asp page, you'll see that if you login using the administrator account (if you haven't created one, try username=administrator and password=letmein), you'll fly through the Welcome page and end up at your administrator menu.

Further Discussion

What would happen if we had three or four groups of access? You would apply this behavior to each menu page like this:

Guestmenu   Apply behavior; only let in Level 4 and direct everyone else to...
UserMenu   Apply behavior; only let in Level 3 and direct everyone else to...
PowerUserMenu   Apply behavior; only let in Level 2 and direct everyone else to...
AdminMenu   Done!

Effectively, you could change the model and not have the login check on the login page. You could let everyone in, though unauthorized people would have no access level.

Therefore, on your admin menu page you could direct all other users (invalid users) to a Failed Login page.

Using these basic techniques, you should be able to push anyone to anywhere fairly easily.

Securing All your Pages

If you think about it, a malicious user who can see the basic structure and URL naming conventions of your site, might be able to guess the URL of a page deep within our site, for example: www.koolkards.co.uk/secure/admin/topsecret.asp.

Would our page be protected from someone guessing the URL and effectively leap-frogging the login screen? No – only those pages with the Restrict Access to Page behavior check for authorization.

So, you need to apply the behavior to every single page in the secure part of your site. You might want to do this individually, but we could just apply it to a template instead.

It takes a bit of planning but once your site 'levels' have been decided, make a template for each level and use the Restrict behavior to take users back to the login menu should they not meet security criteria.

Each page on that level that uses your security template would then have the behavior applied. You can see that we've applied the behavior to the `Admin` template in our final site – each page is checked for security.

Finally, there is also a server behavior called Log Out User. It's not a bad idea to use this in your administration sections as it kills the session, frees up some resources and generally makes the user feel more secure when leaving private pages.

Applying it to your page is easy – you get the choice of when the behavior kicks in, and where to go afterwards.

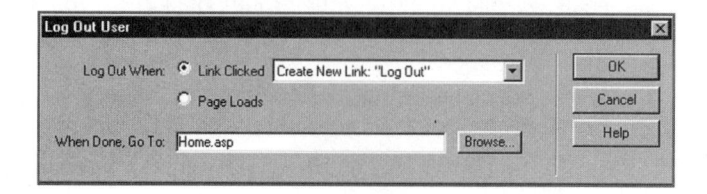

User Login and Registration 8

Summary

UltraDev provides us with the starting blocks to make some impressive login pages and secure our web sites. Hopefully, this chapter has also given you the burst of energy you need to take these much further.

By adding some code of our own, we've made a smarter application. You can change the model in a variety of ways for your own web application, but the principles will almost always remain the same.

We saw in this chapter:

- UltraDev has both the raw tools and the nifty wizards to let us create registration and login pages, saving the user information in a database and retrieving it when required.

- UltraDev's server behaviors allow us to add a range of useful security measures to our site, redirecting intruders and verifying passwords.

- We can set Access Levels to tell UltraDev who is allowed where.

- Using querystrings we can pass information, like duplicate usernames, around the site, while cookies enable us to 'remember' frequent users' details.

Next we'll be looking at possibly the most anticipated UltraDev topic: the shopping cart.

koolkards

9 Creating a Shopping Cart

What we'll cover in this chapter:

- Creating a **shopping cart**
- Altering the **quantity** of items in the cart
- **Clearing** the contents of the cart
- **Redirecting the user** if their cart is empty

Welcome to the nerve center of any dynamic e-commerce web application: the **shopping cart.**

Even as recently as a few years ago, sites rarely had full shopping cart functionality. Smaller outlets would just provide an e-mail link for you to express interest in a product. Sites that contained full shopping carts were hand coded by very clever people and there was certainly no such thing as a 'drag-and-drop' shopping cart. With UltraDev, and some handy behaviors though, all this has now changed.

Before we start to explore the functionality within UltraDev, let's look at other solutions that are currently available and what we really mean by a 'shopping cart'.

What Exactly is a Shopping Cart?

A shopping cart is nothing more than a temporary way of storing rows of data (items) from a table (products) and holding them until the credit card transaction (checkout), or in other words, a way that the server holds onto items until certain criteria are met (go to a checkout/empty the cart).

The user will be able to move throughout the site and add, remove or update items in the cart during his or her session.

Most people think of a shopping cart in terms of your typical Amazon.com scenario where the user picks products for purchase. However, if you think laterally, a shopping cart can be used for many other applications, such as:

- Job sites (store the jobs you're interested in as you go along, until you submit your CV at the 'checkout')

- Software or MP3 download sites (rather than download shareware files one at a time, your user could pick out all the items they were interested in and download them all at once)

You may find other uses for a shopping cart that don't necessarily entail a 'purchase' but use the same methodology.

By itself the cart is a fairly simple application, it's only when you add all the administration modules and ordering systems that it becomes more complicated.

Commercial Shopping Cart Solutions

We expect that as you're reading this, and interested in using UltraDev to the fullest, then you're probably considering developing your own shopping cart for your site. However, there are some alternatives. Let's take a brief look at what solutions are available.

Creating a Shopping Cart

Shopping Carts Purchased through Resellers

You may utilize an online shopping cart service as part of a turnkey (total solution) e-commerce package through your Internet Service Provider or web hosting company, although some turnkey solution providers offer packages for sale directly to merchants. If you have your ISP or web host build your store, you'll pay for the shopping cart feature as part of your payment plan for the overall e-commerce package.

Off-the-shelf Shopping Carts

The biggest advantage to buying ready-made shopping cart software is that you can change web hosts or other service providers without changing your entire storefront. Generally, the more expensive the package, the more sophisticated the features you'll find in terms of customization and back-end support.

While there is nothing wrong with the above two solutions, nothing will be better (and cheaper) than developing your own tailor-made shopping carts.

So, what does UltraDev provide us with to build shopping carts?

Nothing!

As it stands as an 'out of the box' package, there's nothing in UltraDev that will help you specifically develop carts. The KoolKards online site that you've been following throughout this book was all originally built with UltraDev without any specific cart behaviors. The original site was developed with SQL Server (Access's big brother) and Stored Procedures (think Access 'Queries'), and UltraDev provides the perfect environment to develop such sites, but there were no specific cart behaviors used.

We'll be looking more into SQL Server and Stored Procedures in Chapter 13, where we'll give you an insight into how a shopping cart can be built in such a way.

Ah, so we've got to hand code it all then?

Well... if you did a search on the Web for shopping carts in ASP I'm sure you would find plenty of examples of how to implement them, and it's a fair bet that a lot of hand coding would have to take place. Although we are used to looking at ASP code by now, we are probably not good enough to start writing full shopping cart functionality. So, what can we do?

Foundation Dreamweaver UltraDev 4

The UltraDev Shopping Cart

UltraDev Shopping Cart is a shopping extension written entirely for the UltraDev environment. Written by Rick Crawford specifically for UltraDev, it's possibly the greatest example of UltraDev's extensibility, as we said when we introduced server behaviors. Everything we'll use in this chapter was developed by a one-man third party (not Macromedia) and it perfectly shows how we can make UltraDev more powerful than it is out of the box.

> *The UltraDev shopping cart is available for download from* www.macromedia.com/exchange/ud_cart.html

However, nothing in life is that simple

It should be noted here and now that Rick's shopping cart was written in 90% JavaScript, therefore it will be beyond the scope of this book to really learn 'how' this cart was pieced together. However, the good news is that you can use the cart without any knowledge of JavaScript and get excellent results – as we shall see.

To make life even more difficult for us, UltraCart was written for the first version of UltraDev, which means we will have to make some changes to the code to get it to work in UltraDev 4. Although you may sigh heavily at this at least it's better than hand coding the whole lot!

Installing the Shopping Cart

We've already looked at the Macromedia Extension Manager and how to install a set of behaviors, so once you've downloaded the cart, just double-click the .mxp file and the Extension Manager will launch with your new package enabled:

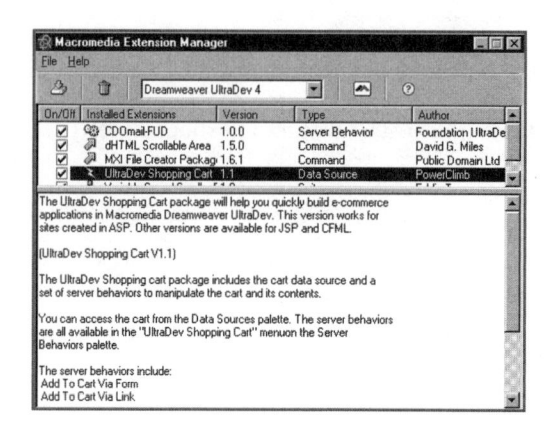

Creating a Shopping Cart | 9

In our KoolKards site, we have the perfect shopping scenario. The user will browse and pick out cards. Sometimes they will want more than one of the same card and they may wish to add, remove or update their orders. Finally, once the user has decided, it's time to move on to the checkout.

A Sneak Preview

Due to the nature of shopping carts you have to build a number of pages before you can really test or use one. Therefore, it will help you if you see or visualize the cart in action before you start building it. Below we've included the screenshots of a working cart – so you'll have an idea of what your final cart will look like in action. You may have to return to these screenshots to keep up with where you are.

The user searches for items:

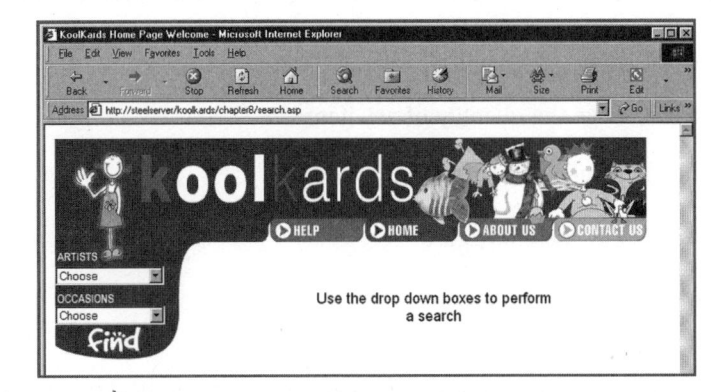

The results of the search are returned with the option to add items to the cart:

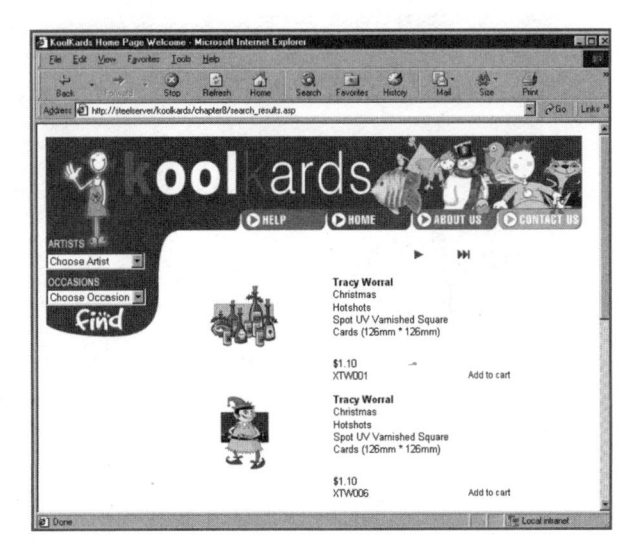

Foundation Dreamweaver UltraDev 4

After adding to their cart, the user is shown the cart's current contents:

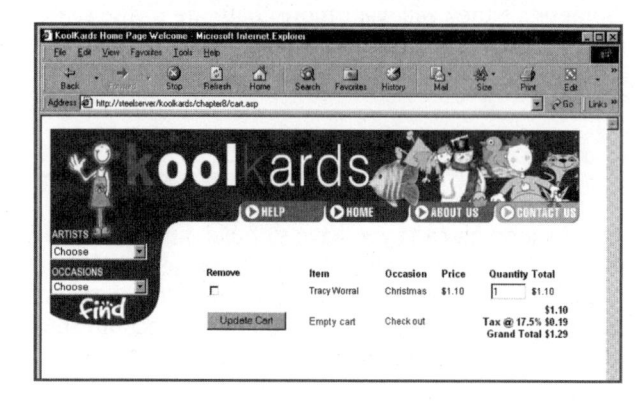

The user continues to shop, adding any other items they wish to purchase to their cart.

Notice that in our cart, the user can:

- Change the quantity of any item
- Remove any item from the cart
- Empty the entire cart
- Move to the checkout

There is also information about the total cost of any particular type of item, the amount of any sales tax to be added, and the grand total to be paid:

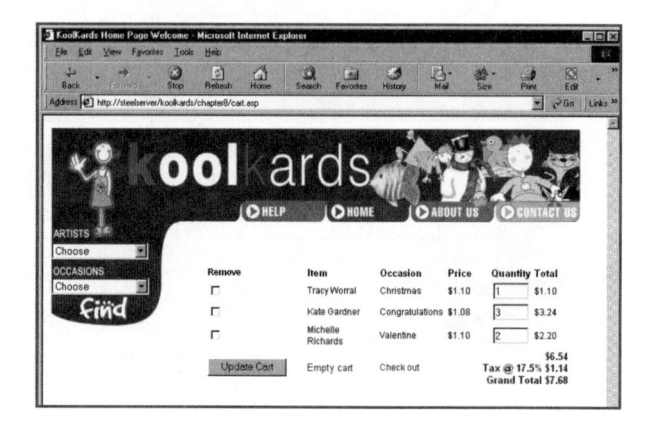

Creating a Shopping Cart

At the checkout, the user fills in their details:

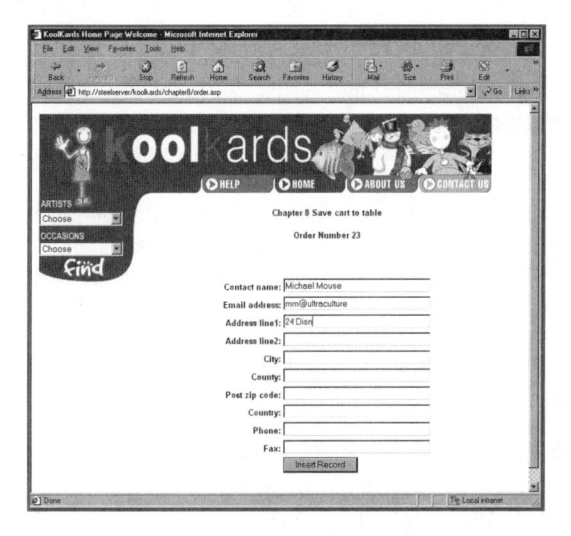

Finally, the user confirms the order and arranges payment:

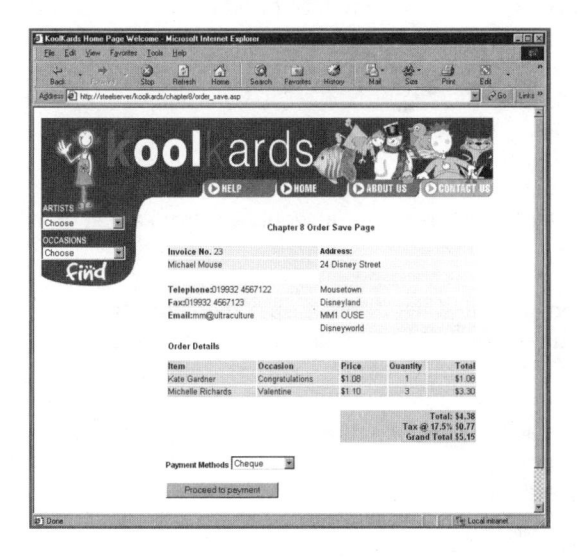

Payment Options

One of the largest misconceptions about the shopping cart is that it will enable you to 'take money' from customers, or help you build credit card transactions. The bad news is that it won't. With the variety of options that are available to you as a retailer, it would be beyond the scope of any single solution to take all your business needs into consideration.

What the shopping cart will do, however, is enable your users to browse the shop and write their orders to a database table. What you then do with that information is up to you. A small, low turnover business may wish to then process everything manually; larger retailers may use real-time credit card processing to finish the order.

Unless you're some sort of masochist, the easiest way of getting payment from your customers is by getting somebody else to do it. There are plenty of companies willing to take the hassle of the credit card transactions off your hands (for a small fee!).

Basically, these companies will instruct you where and in what format to send the credit card details. They then do the authentication and debiting from the card and credit your bank account, whilst sending back notification.

One common solution may be to use a secure server to take the credit card details from your customer and use an encryption program to send an e-mail to a company that runs the credit card transaction through for you.

They then decrypt your e-mail with a decryption program, which then allows the order to be processed.

This is often a good solution when you're first starting out with an e-commerce venture, as it's fairly cheap. You can find a myriad of companies, and even some web-space providers, who offer this service and will help you to get set up.

Let's have a brief look at the service you would get from a real time credit card transaction provider.

Firstly, your company would need to set up a merchant facility with a bank. Whether or not you already have a merchant account, you'll need to tell your provider that you need to be approved for Card Holder Not Present and Internet trading.

The funds from each transaction are normally then transferred direct to your bank account at the end of each day and credited to your account within about five days of the transaction taking place.

All transactions would be recorded and you can view your monthly transactions on the e-commerce provider's secure web site. This site allows you to refund a transaction, make further transactions, view your credit card status, and see how much money has gone through your merchant account.

This is a more complete solution, but perhaps only cost effective for larger e-commerce sites.

Creating a Shopping Cart

Right, we've talked about what the cart can do for you, and where it will stop. Let's get on with the tasks in hand.

Once you've installed the cart (and after restarting UltraDev) you can access it in the normal way through the Server Behaviors panel (CTRL + F9). Click on the + and expand the UltraDev Shopping Cart menu. Take a look at what you get in the package but don't select anything yet.

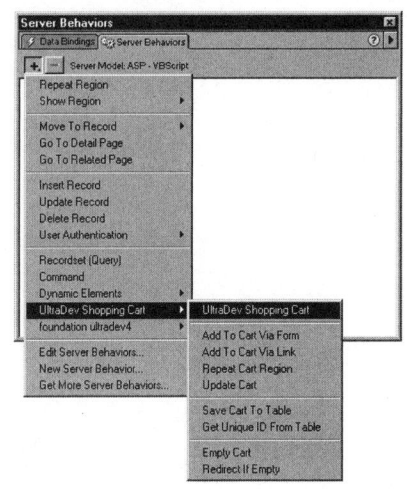

As you can see, you get a number of behaviors that make up the whole cart. We'll be looking at each component as we go along.

Building the Cart

Rather strangely perhaps, the first step in building the cart will be to build the main cart page, which shows the current items in the cart.

1. Let's start by creating and saving a new page called cart.asp based on the master template. Add a basic table and fill in some headers as you see here. Again, don't worry about it looking exactly the same as ours. To get the extra wide Grand Total box, select the two cells it spans and select Modify > Table > Merge Cells.

Item	Occasion	Price	Quantity	Total
			Grand Total :	

2. Once you've created the shell of our page to work on, select the UltraDev Shopping Cart from the menu on the Server Behaviors panel.

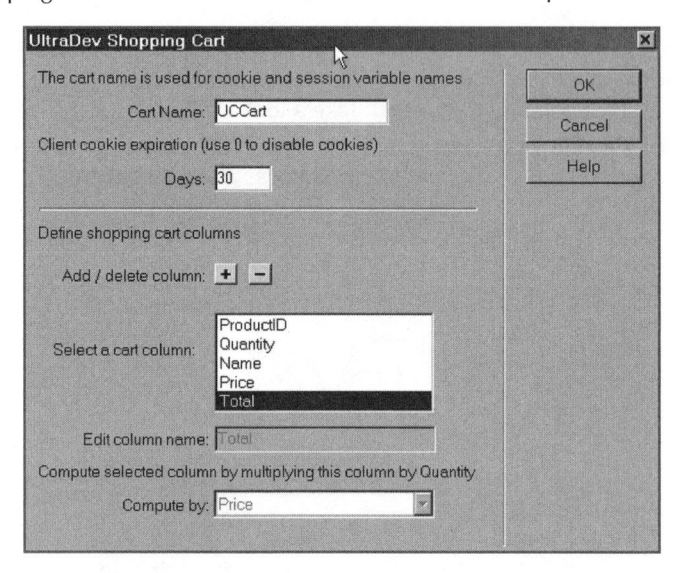

You'll be presented with quite a few options here. Let's go through them one by one as we set them up for our site.

3. Enter the name of your cart in the Cart Name text box; it's up to you what you call the cart, but for the moment best keep to the default as it's short and to the point.

One of the nice functions about a shopping cart built with this behavior is the ability for the user to start shopping on one day and come back and continue later on, knowing that the items they had put in their shopping cart are still there. It does this by writing cookies to the client, which we know all about by now. We suggest you set the number of days to 30.

4. Define your shopping cart columns. The UltraCart needs certain columns, whether you use them or not. The columns ProductID, Quantity, Price and Total can't be deleted. They're not coming from your database, they're inbuilt functions of the cart. Try to delete them and you'll see this message:

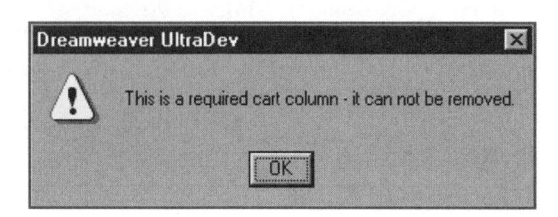

Creating a Shopping Cart

5. We now need to add an extra column: Occasion. To do this, highlight the Price column and press the + button. This creates a new column just above Price called Column1. Rename it as Occasion.

We'll use this to display the artist's name as well as the occasion of the card. It's not necessary but it will make the cart more understandable for our users.

Your own e-commerce sites may need to hold even more additional fields like weights, sizes, or colors.

Note that the UltraCart automatically creates a Total field. The total is worked out by the price of each item multiplied by the quantity – for example four copies of Foundation UltraDev at $29.99 each makes the total, er, hold on... where's the calculator?

The Compute by field tells UltraDev how to make these types of calculation. For example, if you highlight Total in the list of columns, Compute by will be automatically set to Price.

6. Press OK to finish.

As you can see, we pretty much accepted the defaults there (aside from adding our new column) and that's what you'll end up doing with the majority of your sites to begin with.

All ready...!

7. Have a look under the Data Bindings panel. You'll see a small shopping cart icon. If you expand this you'll see the fields that you have set up in the behavior. These behave in much the same way as the recordsets do, so you can drag and drop them onto your page. Just think of the cart as a special recordset. You'll just need to copy and paste it onto each page you want to work with.

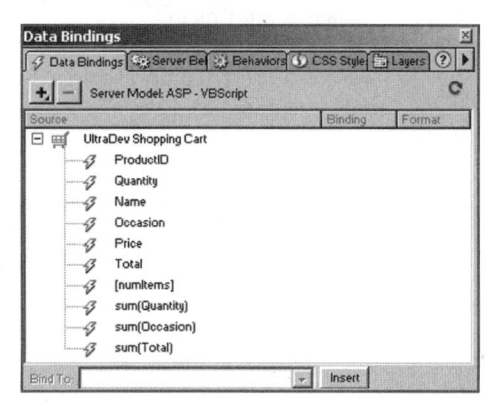

Foundation Dreamweaver UltraDev 4

In the same way a 'normal' recordset provided us with some time saving and handy extra columns like [first record index] and [total records] which we can use on our pages, UltraCart does something similar.

You can see UltraCart has created a sum[Total] column and a [numItems] column. You can drag these onto any page you like and it will display the total of your order so far, as well as how many items you are carrying (providing the cart is included in the Data Bindings panel)

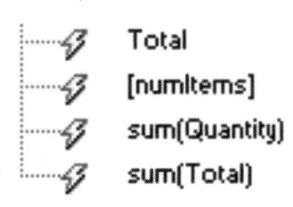

- Total
- [numItems]
- sum(Quantity)
- sum(Total)

8. Let's start by using the sum[Total] field. Drag it to our page next to the Grand Total row.

Grand Total : {cart.sum(Total)}

Formatting is the way we make data look presentable and understandable to us mortals. Take, for example, SQL Server (we've just chosen SQL Server as an example, it could be anything). It stores its unformatted dates like this:

2001-01-21 15:04:46.860

Nasty! So, if we returned this onto our page, we'd have to format it to something a little more readable. Using UltraDev's format tools, we can easily format the above date so it appears as:

Sunday, 21 January 2001

...which is a lot nicer.

There is a pretty comprehensive formatting selection that should cover most eventualities. Let's apply one to our Grand Total field.

9. Select the field on your page {cart.sum(Total)} and see how the Format drop-down box becomes available from the Data Bindings panel (you may have to resize the box or scroll along):

Creating a Shopping Cart   9

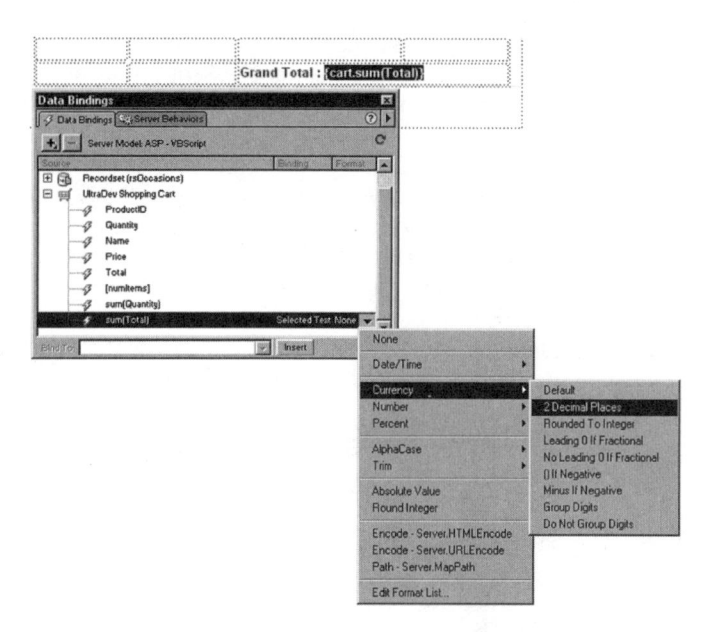

10. By using the drop-down box, we can see many different formats we can apply to our field.

For our purposes, select Currency and 2 Decimal Places.

This will make sure our currency always looks something like 29.99 or 45.00.

If you've applied your formatting correctly, your Data Bindings window will show Currency - 2 Decimal Places under the format column.

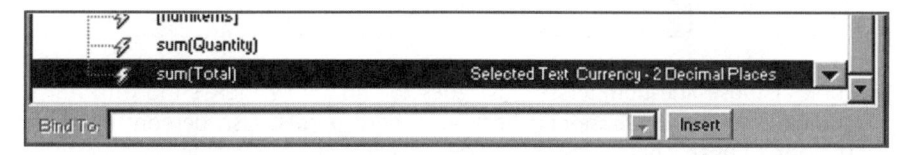

You may like to take this opportunity to look at the other formats available.

Before we move on let's just see what code has been written to our page to achieve this style.

```
<%=    FormatCurrency((UCCart1.GetColumnTotal("Total")),
➥2, -2, -2, - 2) %>
```

Foundation Dreamweaver UltraDev 4

As you can see it is a `Response.Write` statement with a `FormatCurrency` function added. `FormatCurrency` is a standard VBScript function. At some point in the future, you may wish to alter some of the parameters of this function to suit your particular environment.

As nice as it may be to have the item and price totals on each page there is a downside to this. The shopping cart would need to be applied to each page just so it could calculate the totals. This is a solution many people use, but we can do it using a much better method, with the help of a couple of cookies.

Before we add our cookie code, open up the code that's already on your page. Remember you can use the <> icon in the top left of your page to get a full screen of code.

Look at those line numbers! It just goes to show how there's more to ASP coding than adding a couple of `Requests` here and there. And it also demonstrates why we really shouldn't put this entire shopping cart on any more pages than we have to.

Creating the Number of Items and Total Cookies

Have you been to a site that tracks your total amount spent and the total number of items in your cart on every page? Maybe you haven't, but think about how cool it is to be able to see your grand total on every page, or the total items in your cart.

Creating a Shopping Cart 9

As we've seen, the cart is a weighty piece of code that we don't really want written to every page. Therefore it will make sense to write the total number of items and the Grand Total to a cookie that we could call up at any point.

Open the Server Behavior panel (CTRL+F9).

Apply the Server Behavior > Foundation UltraDev > Add cart totals to a cookie.

Remember, you'll be able to use this behavior on any of *your* carts!

Open your cart code and you'll see the new cookie code added.

```
628 rsOccasions.LockType = 3
629 rsOccasions.Open()
630 rsOccasions_numRows = 0
631 %>
632
633 <% 'set Totals and number of items to Cookies
634 Response.Cookies("cart_totals")("Num_items") = UCCart1.GetItemCount()
635 Response.Cookies("cart_totals")("total") = UCCart1.GetColumnTotal("total")
636 %>
637
638 <html>
639 <head>
640 <title>Koolkards Example Site</title>
641 <meta http-equiv="Content-Type" content="text/html; charset=iso-8859-1">
```

The behavior places this code just before the `<HTML>` tag, after all the cart code.

```
<% ' Set totals and number of items to Cookies Robert Paddock
➥ 22/01/20001

Response.Cookies("cart_totals")("Num_items") =
➥ (UCCart1.GetItemCount())

Response.Cookies("cart_totals")("total") =
➥ (UCCart1.GetColumnTotal("Total")) %>
```

This creates a dictionary cookie (see chapter 3) called `cart_total`, which is made up of `num_items` and `total`. We set `Num_Items` to equal the `Item Count` of the cart and `total` to equal the `Total` of the cart.

Now we can add them to any page we want (which we'll be doing later) by placing the following lines of code on our page.

```
<%=Request.Cookies("cart_totals")("Num_items") %>
<%=FormatCurrency(Request.Cookies("cart_totals")("total")),
➥ 2, -2, -2, -2) %>
```

Note how we still apply the `FormatCurrency` technique to the cookie.

Let's refresh our memory of where we're up to:

- We've created our basic cart in the Data Binding panel.
- We've created a Grand Total column.
- We've created two cookies; one for total number of items and one for Grand Total.

What we haven't yet done is put the cart columns on the page. We need to fill out the rest of the table with the correct fields.

Placing the Cart Columns

1. Expand the cart from your Data Binding panel.
2. It's just the same as displaying recordset data really, just drag and drop the fields into the appropriate places.
3. Set the Format for the Price and Total as you did above for the Grand Total.

   Your table should now look something like this:

Item	Occasion	Price	Quantity	Total
{cart.Name}	{cart.Occasion}	{cart.Price}	{cart.Quantity}	{cart.Total}
			Grand Total :	{cart.sum(Total)}

   Now is that it? No. Remember the cart behaves like a recordset so if we finished there the page would only display the first item in the cart.

Creating a Shopping Cart 9

So we need to apply the Repeat Region? Well, not quite. It's imperative that you apply the special Repeat Cart Region supplied with the cart package because although it performs the same function, it doesn't do it in the same way.

4. Highlight the row with your dynamic cart details (click in the row and select the <TR> (table row) tag from the status bar).

5. Open the UltraCart behavior menu.

6. Select Repeat Cart Region.

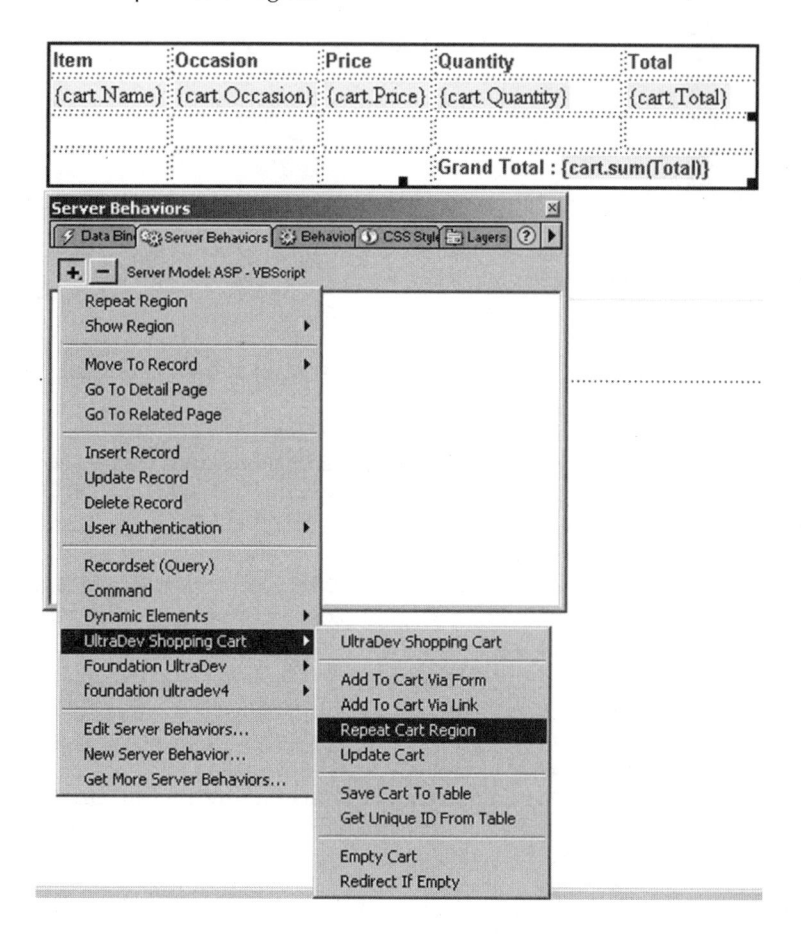

Your cart will now be repeated with one row for each item.

The Cart Code

We haven't explored the code written by the cart behavior much. The main functionality of the cart is written in JavaScript, which messes with our strategy really. However, there are parts of the cart that use VBScript so rest assured we'll investigate the code when we can.

The repeat region for the cart is one of those parts written in VBScript, so let's take a look at what has been written. The more you see the cart code the more you will become familiar with how it works.

```
776        </tr>
777
778        <% For UCCart1__i=0 To UCCart1.GetItemCount()-1 %>
779        <tr>
780        <td width="224"><font face="Arial, Helvetica, sans-serif" size="2"><%=(UCCart1.GetColumnVa
781        <td width="64"><font face="Arial, Helvetica, sans-serif" size="2"><%= FormatCurrency((UCCa
782        <td width="125"><font face="Arial, Helvetica, sans-serif" size="2"><%=(UCCart1.GetColumnVa
783        <td width="69"><font face="Arial, Helvetica, sans-serif" size="2"><%= FormatCurrency((UCCa
784        </tr>
785        <% Next 'UCCart1__i %>
786        <tr>
```

Remember, if you're having problems finding this code, you can open your Server Behaviors panel and highlight the Repeat Cart Region (with your code view open) and the cursor will jump to beginning of the code.

```
<% For UCCart1__i=0 To UCCart1.GetItemCount()-1 %>
<tr>
<td width="224"><font face="Arial, Helvetica, sans-serif"
➥ size="2"><%=(UCCart1.GetColumnValue("Name",UCCart1__i))%></font>
</td>
<td width="64"><font face="Arial, Helvetica, sans-serif"
➥ size="2">
➥ <%= FormatCurrency((UCCart1.GetColumnValue("Price",UCCart1__i)),
➥ 2, -2, -2, -2) %></font></td>
<td width="125"><font face="Arial, Helvetica, sans-serif"
➥ size="2"><%=(UCCart1.GetColumnValue("Quantity",UCCart1__i))%>
➥ </font></td>
<td width="69"><font face="Arial, Helvetica, sans-serif"
➥ size="2">
➥ <%= FormatCurrency((UCCart1.GetColumnValue("Total",UCCart1__i)),
➥ 2, -2, -2, -2) %></font></td>
</tr>
<% Next 'UCCart1__i %>
```

The highlighted code is the code written by the Repeat Cart Region behavior. The main loop will repeat for every item in the cart. This is achieved by placing a FOR NEXT loop around the area depending on the number of items in the cart. Very simply, the FOR NEXT loop says "For every item in the cart, display a row.", just as you would expect!

The items in the cart are displayed with a simple `Response.Write` statement in its shortened form.

```
<%=(UCCart1.GetColumnValue("Quantity",UCCart1__i))%>
```

Well here comes another brain expander. This line of code calls a JavaScript function `getColumnValue` to get the value for the quantity from the recordset and then writes it in VBScript, if that's the chosen language for your site. All this means you can then manipulate it with VB code if you wish, and later on we'll show you how to add some extra functionality to the cart.

Recap & Refresh

Now we have our cart in the Data Bindings *and* on the page. We have some totals and some cookies to use. We're making progress.

What other functions do we need to set up?

Refresh your memory by looking at the working cart screenshots. What else is needed on this page...?

- The ability to update and delete items from the cart
- The ability to empty the cart
- The ability to redirect from this page if it's empty.

Lucky for us UltraCart provides all these behaviors for us. Let's get going...

Updating the Cart

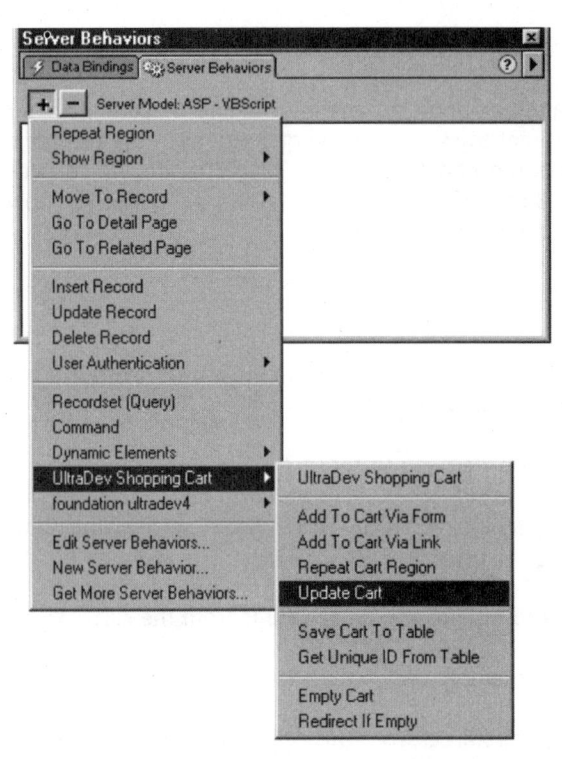

As it stands in our yet-to-be-designed 'add to cart' page, the user can add a single card to their cart. Now, this isn't exactly good for bulk ordering. If someone wanted to buy 25 Christmas cards, it wouldn't make sense to add 25 items.

Therefore, we can make the Quantity field *updatable* so that the user can type in a numerical quantity and 'update' their order. Let's build this in now. If you're still confused, check back to the screenshots at the beginning of the chapter to see how our user has put multiple orders of certain cards. The user would type in the number of the cards they wanted, click Update Cart and the cart would recalculate their order and totals.

Let's break down what's needed:

- A form on the page to let the user 'edit' some details
- To make the Quantity an updatable text box
- A Submit button
- To update the cart with the new Quantity values when the user clicks the Submit button

Creating a Shopping Cart   9

Creating the Form for our Cart

First we need to place a form element around the shopping cart table. Now we're getting up to speed with UltraDev, let's look at way of hand coding this efficiently.

1. Select your table on the page and open Code View. Your cursor should be just in front of the `<table>` tag.

2. Click in front of the tag, write `<FORM>` and then scroll all the way down through the cart code until you hit the closing `</table>` tag. Just after that, write `</FORM>`.

   You'll end up with this:

   `<FORM><table width="xxx" border="x">` {all the cart display code} `</table></FORM>`

3. Click back on the page and the red-dotted form will be positioned around your table. Once you get used to doing this, it can be the quickest and certainly most accurate way of getting your form around the correct parts of your page.

   Of course, if we were building the page from scratch again and knew we wanted a table surrounded by a form, the easiest way would be to use the Form Objects panel, drop the form on your page and nestle your table inside the red markers. However, the technique we showed you above can be very useful for placing form markers around items *after* you've placed them on your page (which can be tricky to do visually).

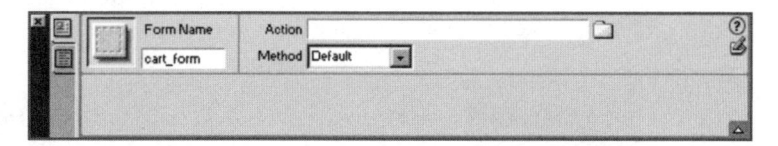

4. Before you move on, make sure you call your form something friendly in the Properties panel: cart_form. Leave the Method and Action for now.

We've now got a form around our table. The next thing we want to do is add the ability to change the quantities of each item.

Foundation Dreamweaver UltraDev 4

Making the Quantity Editable

To do this we need to make the quantity display field into a text box.

1. Delete the current Quantity field label and place your text field in its place (Insert > Form Objects > Text Field). Finally rename your text box text_quantity.

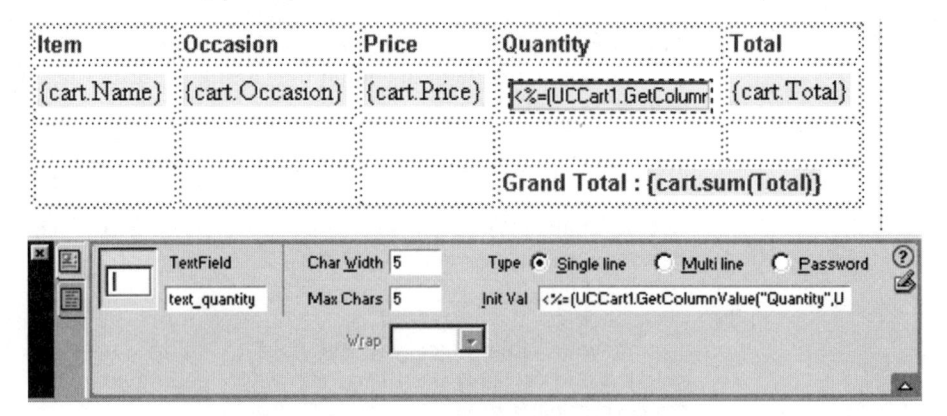

Item	Occasion	Price	Quantity	Total
{cart.Name}	{cart.Occasion}	{cart.Price}	<%=(UCCart1.GetColumn	{cart.Total}
			Grand Total : {cart.sum(Total)}	

TextField / text_quantity — Char Width 5, Max Chars 5, Wrap — Type ● Single line ○ Multi line ○ Password — Init Val <%=(UCCart1.GetColumnValue("Quantity",U

The initial value (Init.Val) of the box should be the quantity the user has ordered, so simply drag the Quantity field from the Data Bindings panel into the quantity text box. If you've done it correctly, it'll glow a nice bluey green color.

2. Next we need to add a Submit form button to the page to make sure it is contained within the bounds of the shopping cart form. Choose some appropriate names for the button name and label. The important thing is to make sure it's a submit button. Place it in the bottom left cell of your cart table.

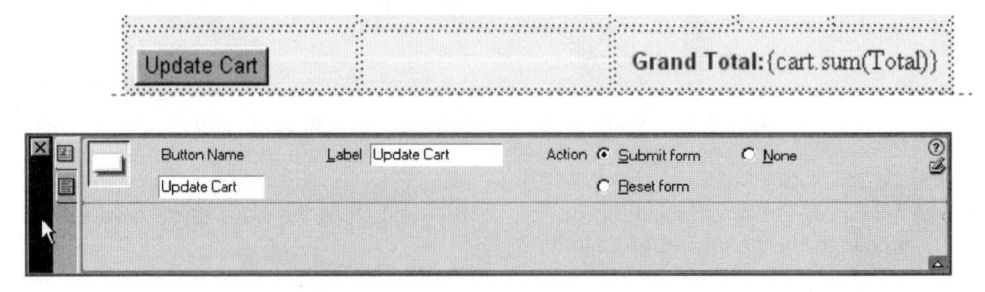

Update Cart			Grand Total: {cart.sum(Total)}

Button Name: Update Cart — Label: Update Cart — Action ● Submit form ○ None ○ Reset form

3. To apply the Update Cart behavior select the quantity text box on your shopping cart form, and then select the Update Cart behavior from under the UltraDev Shopping Cart menu:

Creating a Shopping Cart 9

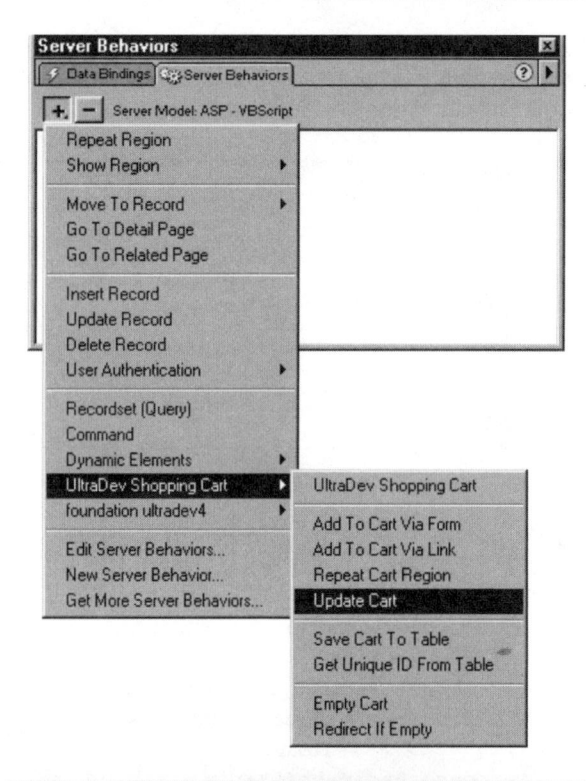

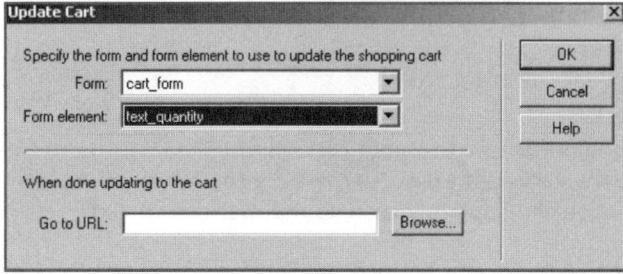

We're being asked by UltraDev to provide the form and the element from which the updated information will come. Remember that we have two forms on our page because of the template, so make sure you've got the cart_form selected.

For the form element you should have your text box automatically selected, as it's the only one.

For the redirect we want to return to the same page with our new amendments, so leave the entry blank.

Foundation Dreamweaver UltraDev 4

Great. We've done well, but the problem is we can't test this page at the moment because we still need to build a page to add items to the cart. We'll move onto this soon enough, but first, our obligatory look at the code.

```
633 <%
634 UC_updateAction = CStr(Request("URL"))
635 If (Request.QueryString <> "") Then
636   UC_updateAction = UC_updateAction & "?" & Request.QueryString
637 End If
638 If (Request.Form("quantity").Count > 0) Then
639   UCCart1.Update("quantity")
640   If ("" <> "") Then
641     Response.Redirect("")
642   End If
643 End If
644 %>
645
```

```
<%
UC_updateAction = CStr(Request("URL"))
If (Request.QueryString <> "") Then
 UC_updateAction = UC_updateAction & "?" &
Request.QueryString
End If
If (Request.Form("quantity").Count > 0) Then
 UCCart1.Update("quantity")
 If ("" <> "") Then
 Response.Redirect("")
 End If
End If
%>
```

The important part to note is the highlighted part. Here the code checks to see if there are any items in the cart – if there are (more than zero) then UltraCart will call the update function and apply any changes that were requested.

Right, we've nearly finished building our main cart page. However, it's always good to provide a way that customers can completely clear their cart with one click on either an image or some text. Fortunately, this is simple. We just need to create an Empty Cart text (or image) link and apply the Empty Cart behavior.

Applying the Empty Cart Behavior

1. Add a text link in the cell next to the Update Cart button – something like Empty Cart.

Creating a Shopping Cart

2. Make sure the Empty Cart link is highlighted.

3. Apply the behavior.

   As you would expect, you can find the behavior under the UltraDev Shopping Cart menu.

4. Select a page to go to now the cart has been emptied.

   We've provided a page called empty_cart.asp in your chapter9 folder. It simply displays a message telling the user their cart is empty. You may wish to redirect your user to a different page; it's entirely up to you.

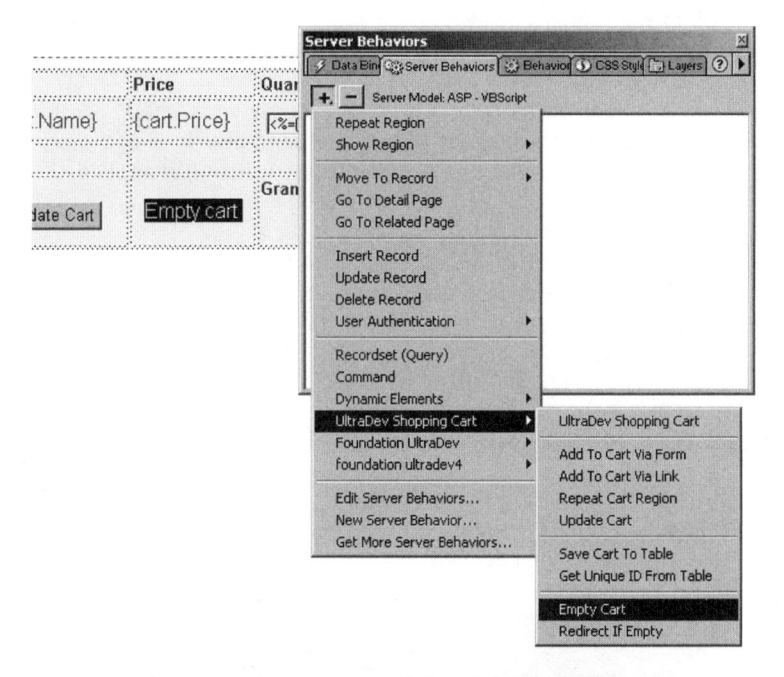

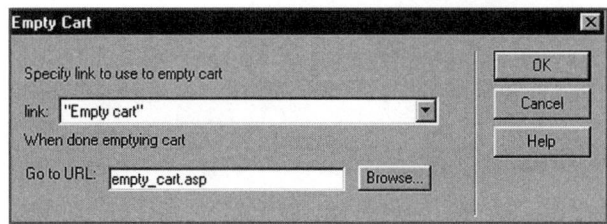

The Empty Cart Code

Below is a selection of the code that is written by the behavior.

```
UC_EmptyCart = CStr(Request.ServerVariables("URL")) &
➥ "?UC_EmptyCart=1"
If (CStr(Request("UC_EmptyCart"))) = "1") Then
UCCart1.Destroy()
➥ UC_redirectPage = "emptycart.asp"
```

The important part of this code is the call to the `UCCart1.Destroy` function. It does exactly what you think it would, obliterating the content of the cart before redirecting to another page.

Look in the Property inspector for the link that destroys the cart. Note how the link has been replaced with a special `<%=UC_EmptyCart%>` line.

If you now look at the code above you can see what `<%=UC_EmptyCart%>` represents. It's simply collecting the current URL of the page displayed and passing on a URL parameter. So when the page reloads, the destroy cart function is applied.

Now the cart is empty.

You've done very well, especially as we can't see any of this in action. Before we can build the add page and see things working, there's just one more simple feature to add to our main cart page.

Redirect if Empty

What shall we do if the cart is empty? If we don't have some code to check for this, it's more than likely the page will generate an error. This bit should be fairly straightforward.

All we'll have to do is apply the Redirect if Empty server behavior and choose the Redirect page.

Creating a Shopping Cart | 9

Applying the Redirect Behavior

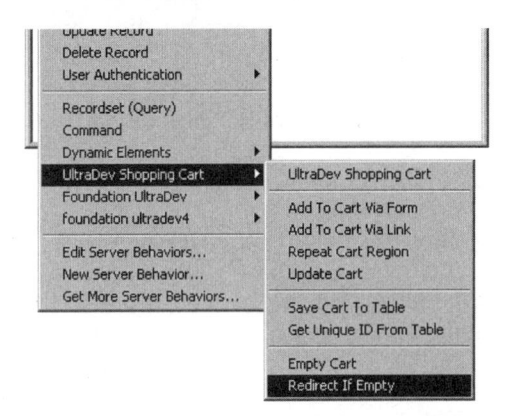

1. Select the Redirect If Empty behavior under Server Behaviors > UltraDev Shopping Cart.

2. Enter the name of your redirect page or browse for its location. We've created a page for you to redirect to if the cart is empty (empty_cart.asp).

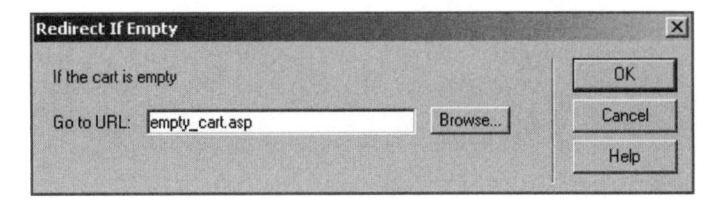

3. Press OK to finish.

   As far as the code goes, it's mercifully small!

   ```
   <% If UCCart1.GetItemCount() <= 0 Then
   ➥ Response.Redirect("empty_cart.asp") %>
   ```

If the number of items in the cart is less or equal to zero, then redirect to your chosen URL.

Foundation Dreamweaver UltraDev 4

Summary

Congratulations. You've just built a feature-rich shopping cart. Let's recap on what we've achieved in this chapter:

- We've created a main page, which displays the items in the cart
- The quantities of items in the cart can be changed
- The content of the cart can be cleared
- We can redirect the user to another page if they try to go to the checkout with an empty cart

Now, if we only had some items in the cart...

This is what we'll address in the next chapter, where we'll add some great features, which will add real functionality to the cart.

Creating a Shopping Cart 9

koolkards

10 Adding Cart Functionality

What we'll cover in this chapter:

- **Adding** and **removing** items from our cart
- Creating a pop-up **reminder** picture
- Adding a way of **calculating sales tax**
- **Writing** the cart to a database
- Inserting a **customer** into the database

10 Foundation Dreamweaver UltraDev 4

We're now going to expand the capabilities of the cart we built in the previous chapter.

To familiarize yourself with how we're going to encourage our customers to add their items to their cart take a look back at the screenshots at the beginning of the previous chapter.

You should be able to see that once the card results are given back to the user after a search, they have the option to Add to Cart, whereupon the page we've just built, our main cart page, is launched with one of the cards already in the cart.

Now we've taken stock, let's forge ahead and build our Add Items pages. We previously built pages for our site that let us search the database for specific cards and display the results. This is where we need our Add Item to Cart button, which would, obviously, add the item and link directly to our main cart page which we've designed already.

Adding Items to the Cart

1. Open up the search_results.asp from the chapter7 folder.

2. Save it in the Chapter 10 folder as the same name.

3. If you used a graphic 'First/Previous/Next/Last' for the navigation system you need to copy these GIF files into Chapter 10 too: First.gif/Last.gif/Next.gif/Previous.gif.

4. Copy the cart to the search_results.asp page.

   Now we're ready to learn a nifty technique of copying the cart, which is the safest way of making sure your cart is consistent across all your pages.

5. Open your cart.asp page. and open the Data Bindings panels. (CTRL+F10)

7. Select the UltraDev Shopping Cart behavior, right-click and select Copy:

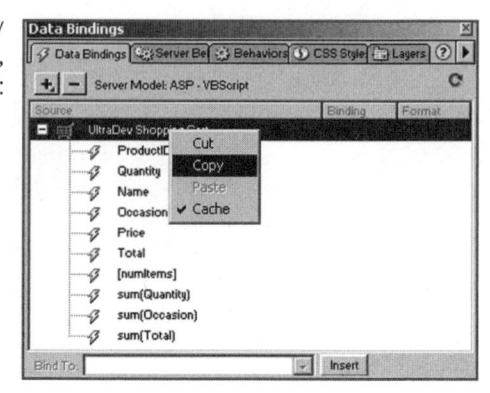

Adding Cart Functionality   10

8. Return to your search_results.asp page.

9. Open the Server Behavior panel (CTRL+F9).

10. Select Paste - or click the small ▶ arrow on the Server Behaviors tab that brings up any cut and paste options available:

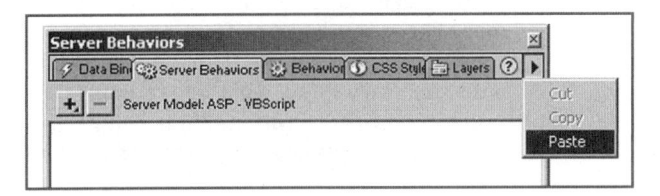

You now have an exact copy of the shopping cart. Use this technique whenever you use a cart on any page. When you create your own sites do as we've done and create the main cart page first, then copy and paste the cart to subsequent pages.

Making the Add to Cart Link

Let's create the link from our items to the cart.

1. Place the text Add to Cart in the repeat region of the table. You could use an image if you liked, as the procedure is the same.

2. Highlight the text or image

3. Select the Add To Cart Via Link behavior from the Server Behaviors > UltraDev Shopping Cart menu:

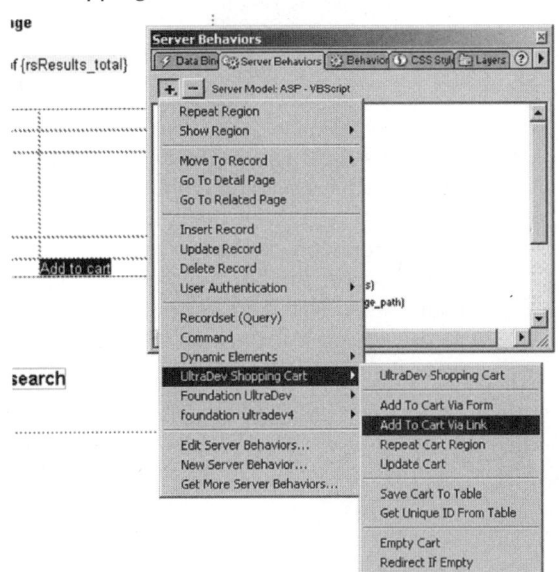

259

As you can see, there are two ways to add the item to the cart, either by a hyperlink (Add to Cart via Link) or by submitting a form (Add to Cart via Form).

Because we have a repeat region on our page, if we used the Add to Cart Via Form option we would have a number of submit type buttons on the page - one for each item. This is a bad idea as browsers don't really like more than one form on a page. To stress the point, it's never a good idea to put more than one form element on a page at any time until you really know what you're doing. Trust us - if you're using the Add to Cart feature with multiple results, use Add via Link. However, if you're only displaying one detail of an item, it's fine to use Add via Form.

4. Select Add to Cart via Link and you'll be presented with these options:

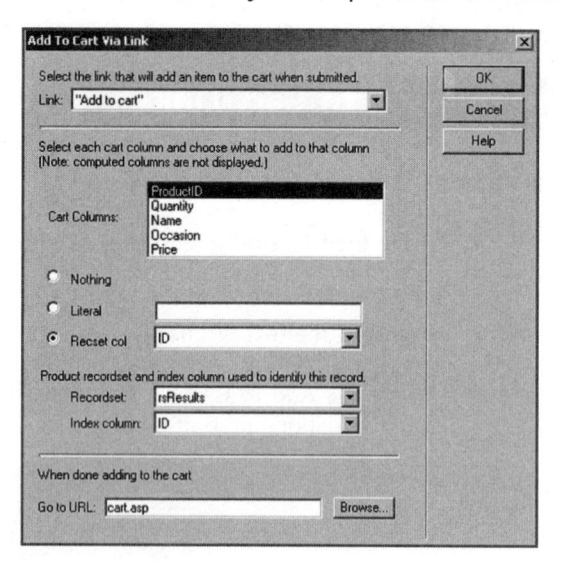

5. In the first field choose from the drop-down menu the text or image link that you've highlighted, that is "Add to cart".

In the Product recordset and index column used to identify this record field (towards the bottom of the screen), select the correct source for your Recordset and Index column. Remember we have three recordsets on our page so it's important to make sure it's set to the rsResults recordset and the Index column is set to ID.

Adding Cart Functionality 10

6. Select each cart column and choose what to add to that column. Now go through each cart column and identify where the information you wish to place in the cart is coming from, be it from our database, in which case we need to supply the column name, or a literal value. Add the values as we've shown here:

Cart Column	Source
ProductID	Recordset col = ID
Quantity	Literal = 1
Name	Recordset col = artist_name
Occasion	Recordset col = Occasion
Price	Recordset col = Price

   Be careful of the Quantity, it's a literal value!

7. The last setting is the When done adding to cart field. Most sites normally take you to the page that displays your shopping cart. If you leave it blank, it defaults to the page you're currently on. For our purposes select cart.asp.

8. Save your page.

We won't be looking at the Add to cart code, because it's written in JavaScript, very long and pretty confusing, which is probably the last thing you need right now.

However, we'll need to change one line of code as we have a slight issue. Forget the code and let's break down how this cart works:

1. User clicks Add to Cart..

2. Page gets the unique ProductID.

3. Page reloads and returns entire recordset of all products from the products table.

4. The page then finds the match of the ProductID with the item in the recordset.

5. The item is added to the cart..

This is a very unusual way of working. Returning the entire recordset and then performing a search is quite cumbersome. Remember when we lectured you on returning small recordsets of exact fields wherever possible. Well, this should be no exception. Unfortunately we didn't write this part of the cart. Our database is about 50 odd products so pulling the whole recordset back isn't really a problem, but large sites with 30,000+ records will effectively be using the entire recordset to add one item. All that said, if you're building your first small e-commerce site and are not anticipating huge traffic loads you'll be fine. Rest assured, there are plenty of sites out there already using this cart successfully.

However it does present us with a small code problem. Our solution with our drop-down boxes was ultra-lean and ultra-fast and only returned one record. We now need to undo all our good intentions and return the whole recordset so the cart can manipulate it. The next short exercise will show you how to make that change.

Altering the Add to Cart Code

1. Open your code view.

2. Find the line 647 and make the change that you see highlighted here:

```
646  ' Build a WHERE clause that asks for a specific Artist and a Specific Occasion
647  If (Request("artist") <> "-1") and (Request("occasion") <> "-1") and (Request.Querystring("UC_AddID") ="")then
648     sqlString = " WHERE products.occasion_id = " & Request("occasion") & " and products.artist_id = " & Request("artist"
649  End If
650
```

```
' Build a WHERE clause that asks for a specific
Artist and a Specific Occasion
If (Request("artist") <> "-1") and
➥ (Request("occasion") <> "-1")
➥ and (Request.Querystring("UC_AddID") ="") then
sqlString = " WHERE products.occasion_id = " &
➥Request("occasion") & " and products.artist_id = " &
➥Request("artist")
End If
```

This says "*If we have some records on our page (results) and the Add to Cart button has been pressed (UC_AddID="") then use the default Artist and Occasion (-1) - which will return all the records*". This will enable the cart to continue to work.

After all that we can finally save all our work and test it out.

Testing our Shopping Cart

1. Open your browser.

2. Open your search.asp page from your Chapter9 folder.

3. Perform some searches, add items, delete them.

4. Try changing the quantity of the items and see how the totals work out.

Adding Cart Functionality 10

What happens if you put in 0 (zero) as a quantity?

> It's always a good policy to do this kind of thing when you complete a page. Pretend you're the visitor for a little while, click the buttons and browse the pages. That way, you should come across any major errors long before your customers do!

Display shopping cart

Item	Occasion	Price	Quantity	Total
Tracy Worral	Baby	£1.10	3	£3.30
Michelle Richards	Birthday	£1.10	1	£1.10
Tracy Worral	Get well soon	£1.10	2	£2.20

Update Cart   Clear Cart   Grand Total £7.76

How was it for you?

We may have had a few grumbles with the way it was designed - but as you can see, it's working well and has saved us a lot of hand coding!

However, there is more we could do - we've just got the basics in place. We could improve the look of the cart page by adding some nice images in place of the submit button and text link but let's look at some more functionality now.

Additions to our Cart

What else could we add to our cart?

- A tick box to delete an item rather than having to enter 0 in the quantity text box

- We could make the artist name a link that opens a pop-up window with a picture of the card in it, to remind the customer of which card each one is, especially as the customer is far more likely to have bought on a visual whim

- We might need a tax calculation.

Let's build these functions to make our cart even better.

One of the most popular extensions to this cart enables us to create a check box to remove an item from the shopping cart. Hopefully, you've realized you need to put in a 0 (zero) to remove the item from the cart, but most people agree that a separate 'remove' check box would be a lot more user-friendly.

Let's look at how we do that.

Creating a Check Box Delete Function

We'll need to go through two stages for this. First we'll need to create a basic check box on our page, then apply the Delete Item from Cart behavior.

1. Using this screenshot as a guide, add a column to your table and place a check box in the repeat region of your cart (Insert > Form Object > Check Box):

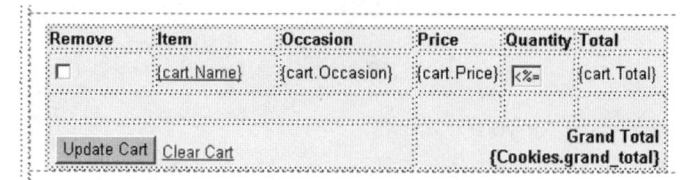

2. Give your checkbox a name - remove- and set the Checked Value to 0, with the initial state being set to Unchecked:

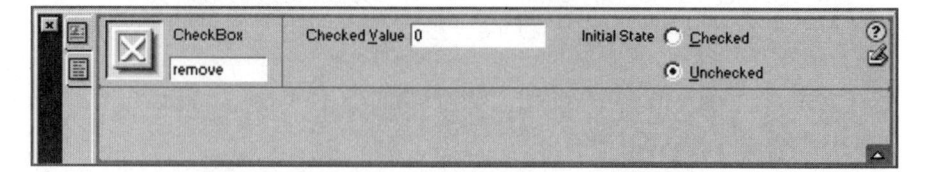

   With the check box created we need to find the extension we need as part of the Foundation UltraDev suite under Delete Item From Cart.

3. Highlight the check box and select the behavior Delete Item from Cart.

4. In the Delete Item from Cart window fill in the values that you see here:

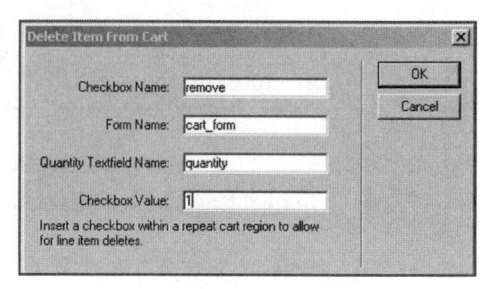

Adding Cart Functionality 10

5. Click OK and the behavior will be applied

6. Save and test your page.

Let's take a peek at the code.

The Check Box Remove Code

```
<input type="checkbox" name="remove" value="1"
 onClick="document.cart_form.quantity<%If
UCCart1.GetItemCount() >
➥ 1 then Response.Write("[" & UCCart1__i &
➥ "]")%>.value='0',submit()">
```

The code uses a client-side, JavaScript `onClick` (when the mouse is clicked) event to set the quantity of that item to 0, as if you had physically typed in zero in the quantity box yourself and then quickly submitted the update form, which of course deletes the appropriate item. Neat.

Creating a Pop-up Reminder Picture

Imagine going shopping in the store and every time you added an item to your trolley, you had to put it in a black box, where you couldn't see it again but you could view a list of what was in there. You'd soon get very confused. People tend to work much better with visual aids and therefore to make our shopping cart more intuitive we need a way for our user to be able to see the cards they've already added to their cart.

What we ideally need is a link on the item name which, when clicked, will open a new browser pop-up window, with the image in it. Like this for example:

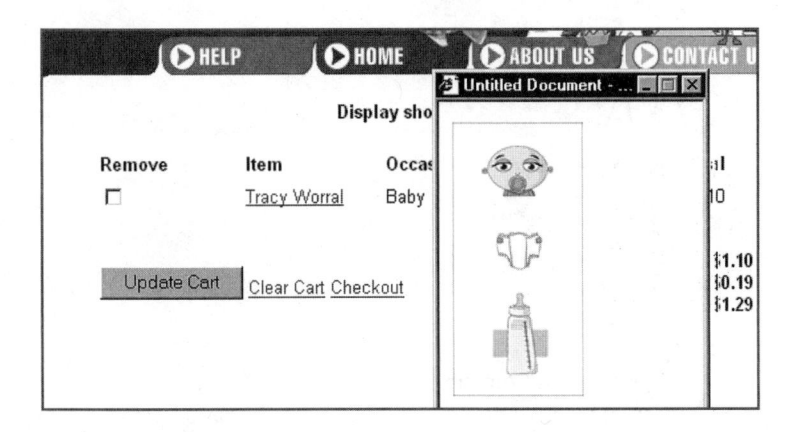

Foundation Dreamweaver UltraDev 4

Any card in our cart could be 'clicked' and a neat pop-up picture would appear in a separate browser window.

Hopefully, it's fairly obvious by now that we to use the Product ID as the parameter on our new pop-up page. We'll need:

- To create a link from the Item on the cart page to a new browser window.
- A pop-up web page to put in our new browser window. We've created this for you as `display_card.asp` in your Chapter 10 folder.
- The pop-up page to only display the item requested from the cart page (`ProductID=theitem`).

Let's start at the beginning.

We want to create a hyperlink on the {cart.Name} column which isn't quite as easy as you may think. If you just highlight the column and bring up the properties, you'll get the ASP properties of the column, *not* the normal 'text' properties from where you can normally set a link. We need to somehow make our {cart.name} field a hyperlink, because we'll want it to go to our pop-up new browser window.

Linking the Cart Page and New Browser Window

1. Highlight the {cart.name} field on your cart page.

2. Bring up the properties (CTRL+F3).

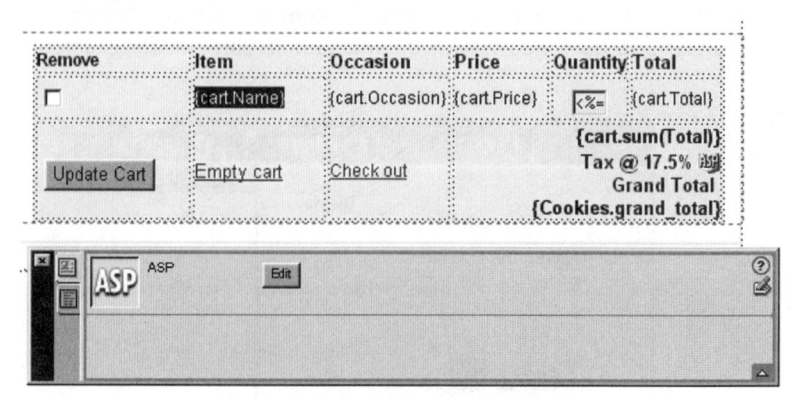

3. Click the Edit button.

Adding Cart Functionality 10

4. Add the hyperlink tags to the beginning and the end of the line, as shown here:

   ```
   <a href="#"> <%=(UCCart1.GetColumnValue("Name",UCCart1__i))%> </a>
   ```

   ```
   <a href="#"><%=(UCCart1.GetColumnValue("Name"
   ➥,UCCart1__i))%> </a>
   ```

5. Click OK. Once this has been entered successfully, your {cart.Name} column will become a hyperlink, indicated by it being underlined:

   Item
   {cart.Name}

We've just added a NULL hyperlink (#) to our {cart.name} field. There is now a link – but with no destination. We'll sort that out next.

This may not be the most conventional of ways to add HTML to your code, but it's another shortcut we thought you might like to know about!

The next time you click the ASP button, your newly added HTML tag won't be editable. It's still there in your code view and still working, but this ASP editor only returns, funnily enough, ASP code. So if you need to make changes you'll have to do it manually.

Now we have a hyperlink from our {cart.name} field in our cart. We can link to our pop-up browser window.

Opening a Browser Window

1. Highlight (by clicking) the {cart.Name} on your cart page.

2. Apply Behavior (SHIFT+F3) (not Server Behavior), and select Open Browser Window:

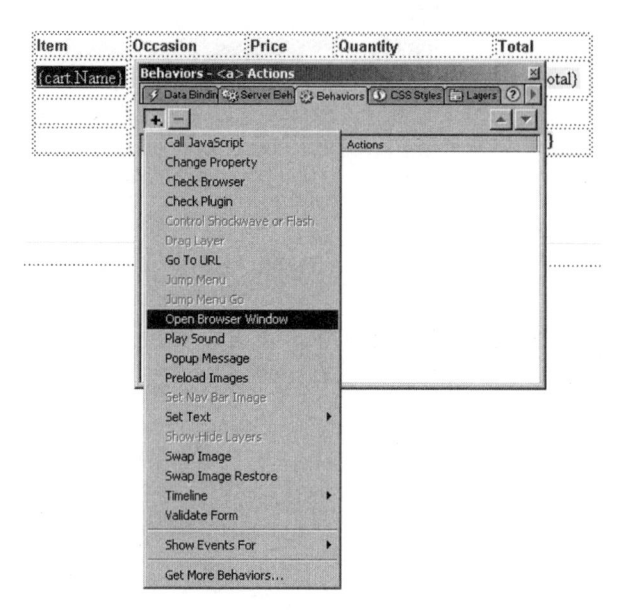

3. Fill in the properties as below, but don't click OK yet:

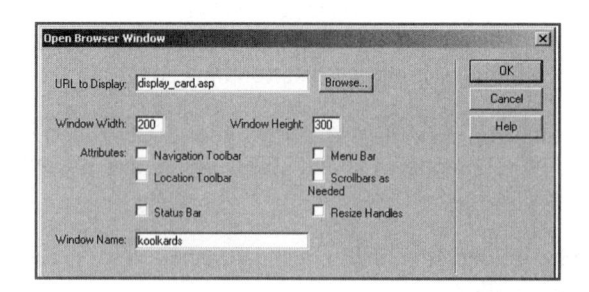

Most of this should be self-explanatory, especially when you see the final test. You might want to come back and play with some of the options later, to see what effect they have on our browser window but for now, keep the settings the same as our screenshot. The only thing to note is that we give our new browser window a name, which is how the ASP code on our page will refer to it, so we'll keep it user friendly as it helps us when we're reading our code.

Before we close the Open Browser Window behavior we need to set up the ProductID parameter to pass to our new browser window, so it only shows the selected card from the cart.

Adding Cart Functionality   10

4. Click the Browse button on the URL to Display property.

5. Select the Parameters button.

6. Create a parameter called cartid and give it a value of the ProductID from the shopping cart:

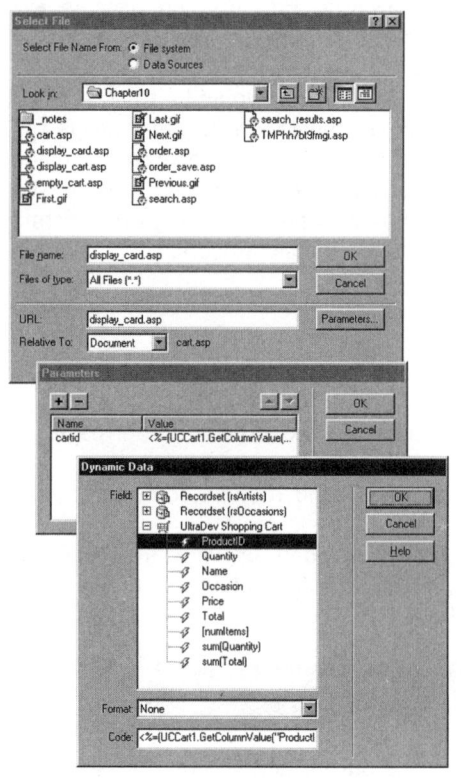

7. Press OK to apply the QueryString to your URL.

8. Press OK to close the Behavior window.

We're now saying "*When the link is clicked, open a pop-up window based on display_card.asp, and pass a parameter called* cartid *which has the ID of the item just clicked*".

Now go and test your page. Try the new pop-up window feature - very cool if we say so ourselves. It probably needs to be labeled better from the cart page, but we're not so concerned about the cosmetics, but how it all works. We hope you find this kind of technique useful in your own shopping carts.

Foundation Dreamweaver UltraDev 4

Adding Tax Calculations

Here's a subject that we all hate talking about - tax.

We get a lot of requests on how to add Sales/Value Added Tax calculations to the UltraCart - some from as far away as Hawaii - and because every country has a different tax percentage, it's an issue that crops up again and again.

The lazy way around the problem would be to add the tax to your prices in the database. No need to hand code anything then. This may be OK for some sites but quite often your clients will like to display the tax as a separate calculation, especially if they're going to print out their receipt and attempt to claim it back. We're not quite sure what kind of taxman would be happy with people writing off Christmas cards as a legitimate expense, but let's look at how we can make it work.

We need:

- The total sum figure from our cart
- To hand code our tax addition on our page
- To update our Grand Total based on this figure

UltraCart has already provided us with the total sum figure in the form of the UCCart1.GetColumnTotal("Total") column so that'll be our starting point. That's one less thing to worry about

Hand Coding the Tax Value

We need to hand code our tax addition on our page.

Once you've seen how it works for the British tax system (17.5%), you'll be able to customize the code for your region.

1. Bring up your Code View.

2. Place the code below just before the `<html>` code:

   ```
   <% ' Calculate Tax and place new grandtotal in a cookie

   Dim rate, Grand_total
   rate = .175 * (UCCart1.GetColumnTotal("Total"))
   Grand_total = (UCCart1.GetColumnTotal("Total"))
   ➥+ rate
   ```

Adding Cart Functionality

```
        Response.Cookies("grand_total") = grand_total
%>
```

```
<%
'Add 17.5% tax
Dim rate, grand_total
rate = .175 * UCCart1.GetColumnTotal("Total")
Grand_total = UCCart1.GetColumnTotal("Total") + rate
Response.Cookies("grand_total") = grand_total
%>

<html>
<head>
<title>Koolkards Example Site</title>
<meta http-equiv="Content-Type" content="text/html; charset=iso-8859-1">
<script language="JavaScript">
```

Now we need to edit the page so it can incorporate our new values. This final screenshot shows what we need. Let's see how we can achieve this.

> Total: {cart.sum(Total)}
> Tax @ 17.5%
> Grand Total
> {Cookies.grand_total}

Possibly the easiest way is to do this directly in the Code View.

3. Scroll down to the bottom of the Repeat Cart Region code and add the changes to the HTML code that you see here:

```
        </tr>
        <% Next 'UCCart1__i %>


        <tr>
          <td colspan="3"> </td>
          <td width="67"> </td>
          <td width="55"> </td>
          <td width="70"> </td>
        </tr>
        <tr>
          <td colspan="3">
            <input type="submit" name="cart_update" value="Update Cart">
            <A HREF="<%=UC_EmptyCart%>"><font face="Arial, Helvetica, sans-serif" size="2">Clear Cart</font></A></td>
          <td colspan="3">
            <div align="right"><font face="Arial, Helvetica, sans-serif" size="2"><b>Total:
            <%= FormatCurrency((UCCart1.GetColumnTotal("Total")), 2, -2, -2, -2) %><br>
            Tax @ 17.5% <%= FormatCurrency(rate , 2, -2, -2, -2) %><br>
            Grand Total <%= FormatCurrency( Request.Cookies("grand_total") , 2, -2, -2, -2) %></b></font></div>
          </td>
        </tr>
      </table>
```

```
<td colspan="3">
  <div align="right"><font face="Arial, Helvetica,
➥sans-serif" size="2"><b>Total:
  <%= FormatCurrency((UCCart1.GetColumnTotal("Total")),
2, -2, -2, -2) %><br>
```

Foundation Dreamweaver UltraDev 4

```
            Tax @ 17.5% <%= FormatCurrency(rate , 2, -2, -2, -2)
         %><br>
            Grand Total <%= FormatCurrency(Request.Cookies
         ("grand_total") , 2, -2, -2, -2) %></b></font></div>
         </td>
```

The highlighted code is what will display the tax and grand total calculations.

If you test out your cart again, you'll see the new tax system working. It looks professional and is a much better solution than just adding your tax to the prices in the database. Hopefully, by following the method above, you'll easily be able to add your own tax routines.

Well - we've accomplished an awful lot. It's not exactly easy this is it? However, you've done very well – don't underestimate what you've achieved in a short space of time. Although this may have seemed tricky we've created a fully working shopping cart feature with some great additional features.

But we're not done yet. We need to process the order - and for that we need to get the orders into a database.

If you've been working hard to get through the last section we suggest taking a break now before coming back, as the next part will require just as much attention to detail.

Writing the Shopping Cart to a Database

So far our user has hoppefully now filled their cart with many items.

We need to:

- Collect the user's information (name, address)
- Write this information to a database
- Write the shopping cart to a related table
- Take the user to a confirmation page
- Take the payment method from the user

Refer back to the screenshots at the beginning of the chapter if you need to refresh yourself with what we're going to build.

However, before we can do any of this we'll need to investigate our database schema.

Adding Cart Functionality | 10

Databases

Before we start building the pages to allow the user to complete their order we need to go back to the database and introduce some new tables to take the order information.

From your Site window (F8) double-click the `koolkard.mdb` database in the database folder. This should launch Access with the database ready for you to investigate

Let's look at the four tables that we've built for you.

The customers: table holds the customer details:

Field Name	Data Type
Customer_id	Number
contact_name	Text
email_address	Text
address_line1	Text
address_line2	Text
city	Text
county	Text
post_zip_code	Text
country	Text
phone	Text
fax	Text

The orders: table contains orders and payment details:

Field Name	Data Type
OrderID	Number
CustomerID	Number
Payment_Method	Text
order_date	Date/Time
completed	Yes/No
deleted	Yes/No

The orderdetails: table contains the information on each item:

Field Name	Data Type
orderid	Number
productid	Number
unitprice	Currency
quantity	Number

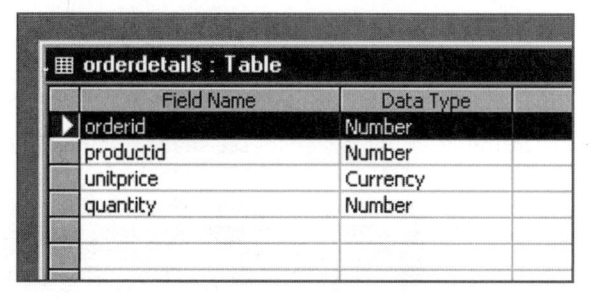

There's also a special get_orderID: table, used to get the next order number, which we'll look at separately.

Foundation Dreamweaver UltraDev 4

The relationship between these three tables is fairly complex, but try and follow this. The best way to explain it is to imagine you've entered your details and purchased four different cards.

In the customer table there would be one row for you. Simple enough. You would have a unique customerID.

The order table would have one row for your order. It would contain your customerID, so your details could be looked up, and a unique orderID

The orderdetails table would contain four rows for your order. Each row would be for the separate items and contain the cost. However, each row would have the same orderID, so it could be referred back to the order table, which in turn could be referred back to the customer table.

It may help to look at this hypothetical set of table screenshots:

customers : Table

Customer_id	contact_name	email_address	address_line1	address
1	Robert Paddock	robp@webbiz-s	19 SomeWhere	Some St
2	Spencer Steel	ss@ultraculture	24 Glademere (	St. Alban
0				

On the customers table we have two customers: Rob and Spencer. Spencer is customer 2 - let's see what he's bought:

orders : Table

OrderID	CustomerID	Payment_Method	order_date	completed	deleted
4	1	Cheque	28/01/2001	☐	☐
1	2	CC	26/01/2001	☑	☐
2	2	CC	26/01/2001	☑	☐
3	2	Cheque	26/01/2001	☐	☐
0	0			☐	☐

On the order table we can see that CustomerID 2 (Spencer) has made three purchases - orders, 1, 2, & 3.

orderdetails : Table

orderid	productid	unitprice	quantity
1	3	£1.10	1
2	5	£1.10	2
3	6	£1.10	1
4	9	£1.10	3
0	0	£0.00	0

Adding Cart Functionality   10

On the orderdetails table we can see that Spencer's orders 1,2, & 3 are productID 3,5, & 6. We would then look into our list of products to see what products 3,5, & 6 were.

Overly complicated?

Well, we could have just had one long table with all the details for everything in one row, but if you ordered lots of items, we would repeat ourselves and create a bit of a headache later on.

Our method is the tried and trusted method for e-commerce sites. When you start developing your own, you'll find you'll need to follow the same outlines.

If you'd like a little more information on this take a look at the Access Primer in Appendix B. The principles are exactly the same.

The relationship between the orders and the orderdetails is a very common one. One table contains the individual item information and one table contains the orders. As we briefly discussed in earlier chapters, this relationship is known as **one-to-many**. That is to say, for each order in the order table there can be many items from the orderdetails table. This saves us rewriting the same item information over and over again in the order table.

Get_ID table

What is perhaps slightly unusual is the use of a Get_ID table. We'lll see how this works with a special cart behavior in a moment. For now, look at how our table is just one non-incrementing numeric field and nothing more. Just one solitary number, sitting in a table of its own:

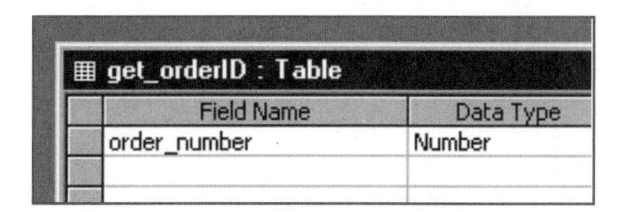

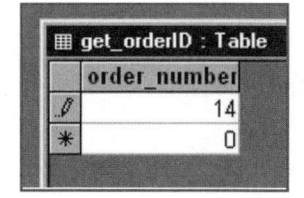

Field Name	Data Type
order_number	Number

get_orderID : Table

order_number
14
0

The important part to note about this table is you need to have a number in the table to start with. We've chosen '1', though it could have been any number we wanted. We'll see how the cart uses this number next.

Get Order ID

We now need to start the order process. We want each order to be unique so we'll need a unique order number. If you've used Access or similar before, your immediate thought would be to use an autonumber. However, if we think logically, if more than one card is purchased we'll need several rows in the order table for each order. We'll also need this number in the orderdetails table. As an autonumber is only assigned once the record has been written, this means that it's just not suitable. All of this will become clearer once you've seen how the cart works.

For now, take it from us, we need to get a unique number from somewhere else, which is why we have a separate table called get_orderID.

Here's the method the cart follows:

1. Order starts
2. Customer fills in details
3. Customer is added to table
4. Unique customer number is generated
5. Cart gets unique order number from get_id table
6. Cart write order to orders and orderdetails tables using number from get_id table and customerID
7. Cart increments the get_id by 1
8. Cart is ready for next order

OK, let's get this underway.

The Customers Details Order Page

As preparation for the next exercise, close down Access and return to UltraDev site window.

Open up the page called order.asp, which is in the Chapter9 folder.

Adding Cart Functionality 10

You can see we've provided you with the form for the user.

The form is based on the customers table and it's here that the customer will register the details about themselves. We thought we'd give this page a kick-start, as we want you to focus on the cart elements only. Now we have our order form, or parts of it, let's break down exactly what we'll need to do:

- Get a unique number from our Access table
- Insert the customers record into the database using this number
- Write the items ordered to an orders table using the UniqueID number

The first server behavior we want to apply is Get UniqueID From Table, which will go and retrieve our unique number. Once it's retrieved, the cart writes this number to a session variable for use in its calculations. As you know, we're generally against session variables, but that's the way it's been designed, so that's the way it is.

Applying the Get UniqueID Behavior

1. Make sure you're still on your order.asp page.

2. Apply the Get UniqueID From Table server behavior:

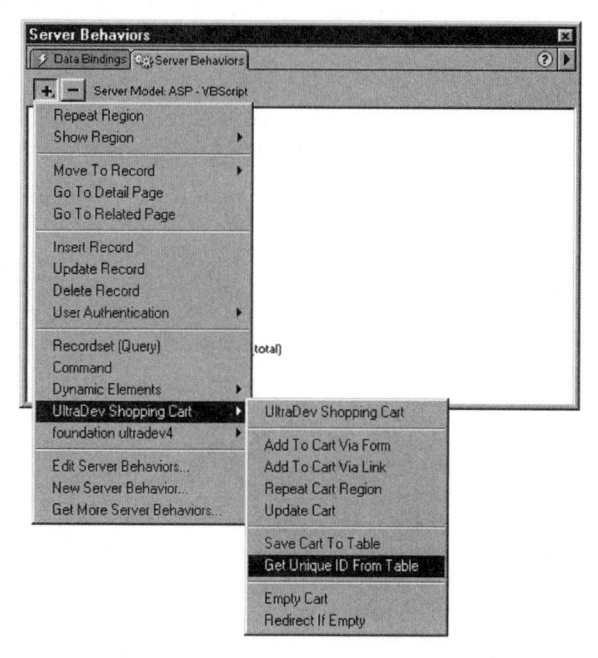

Foundation Dreamweaver UltraDev 4

This will open up a window for this behavior:

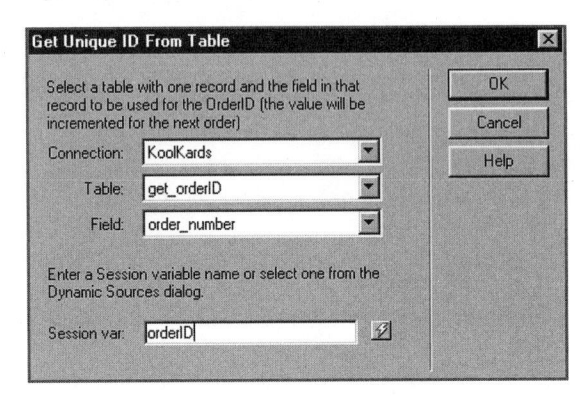

3. Select your connection as KoolKards.

4. Choose the table which will contain our unique number system: get_orderID.

5. Choose the Field: order_number.

6. Choose the name of the session the behavior will create for us: orderID.

7. Click on OK.

The GetID Code

Let's have a very brief look at the code that was written for this behavior - just skim read it and note the two lines in bold as we'll be investigating them later:

```
<%
UC_OrderIdSessionVar = "order_number"
If Session(UC_OrderIdSessionVar)="" Then
 ' Get a unique OrderID number and save to session.
 UC_tableName = "get_orderID"
 UC_fieldName = "order_number"
 UC_sql = "select " & UC_fieldName & " from " & UC_tableName
 tmp = "ADODB.Recordset"
 set UC_rsId = Server.CreateObject(tmp)
  UC_rsId.ActiveConnection = ""dsn=KoolKards;""
 UC_rsId.Source = UC_sql
 UC_rsId.CursorType = 0 ' adOpenForwardOnly
 UC_rsId.CursorLocation = 2 ' adUseServer
  UC_rsId.LockType = 2 ' adLockPessimistic
```

Adding Cart Functionality   10

```
 UC_rsId.Open
  Session(UC_OrderIdSessionVar) =
UC_rsId.Fields(UC_fieldName).value
  UC_rsId.Fields(UC_fieldName).value =
Session(UC_OrderIdSessionVar) + 1
  UC_rsId.Update
  UC_rsId.Close
  set UC_rsId = Nothing
End If
%>
```

This code checks to see whether there is an OrderID already held in session. If not, it gets the number contained in our get_id table and sets the session variable to that number.

It then proceeds to increment our unique record by 1, thus making available another unique number for the next order.

There are three important things to note here:

What if two users happen to be checking out at the same time, wouldn't they both end up with the same orderID?

The answer is no. Remember when we talked about the different locking types for recordsets, we mentioned the **LockPessimistic** option. This type of lock takes complete control of the specified table and will let no other user have access to this table until it's released. It only takes microseconds, so no one should be locked out for very long.

The routine then uses a different update technique to increment the unique ID. Normally, we write an SQL statement and pass it to the Macromedia COMMAND object, the prewritten object that makes life easy for us. However, the UltraCart uses a different method to update the record: UC_rsId.Update. Don't get too hung up on this, it's just that the developer has chosen to code without using the Macromedia objects.

And finally, the most important thing to note about this behavior is that *it won't work with UltraDev 4*. Why? Look closely at this line:

```
UC_rsId.ActiveConnection = ""dsn=koolkards;""
```

Just to make our life very awkward indeed, the UltraCart was written with UltraDev 1. In the release of UltraDev 4 the developers changed the way the connection strings are written and someone forgot to update the cart! In this version the code will look for a DSN entry for KoolKards.

Foundation Dreamweaver UltraDev 4

In UltraDev4, as we know, the connections are stored in the Connections folder and are used by calling the appropriate `include` file. Therefore, we need to add the `include` line to our code, as well as changing our Active Connection line.

If it isn't there already (you can check by right-clicking and use the Find option), place this line of code towards the top of your page:

```
<!-#include file="../Connections/koolkards.asp" -
```

Whenever we want to make a connection to our database, we can just use the following `MM_koolkards_STRING` command, so, change your Active Connection line now, so it reads:

```
UC_rsId.ActiveConnection =MM_koolkards_STRING
```

As if doing all this wasn't ugly enough for you already, once you've altered the code, the GetID behavior will no longer appear on your list of applied behaviors. But at least it will work!

We hope you see why you need to get to know your way around the code in UltraDev.

You probably feel very uneasy about all this hacking around, so let's prove it's working so far. We can prove it all works by displaying the number that our customized behavior has got from our table. It will be useful for our customer to be able to see their order number, in case they want to write it down. We're going to do this by adding a session variable: so that thing go like this:

- User goes shopping - goes to checkout
- Cart gets a unique number and stores in a session called OrderID
- User is taken to the customer detail page - let's display the session on the page

We can set up a session variable from the Data Bindings panel, so we can drag and drop it anywhere on the screen, or simply add the code in the code view.

Adding a Session Variable

You should still have `order.asp` open.

1. Open the Data Bindings panel (CTRL+F10).
2. Click the + button and choose Session Variable:

Adding Cart Functionality   10

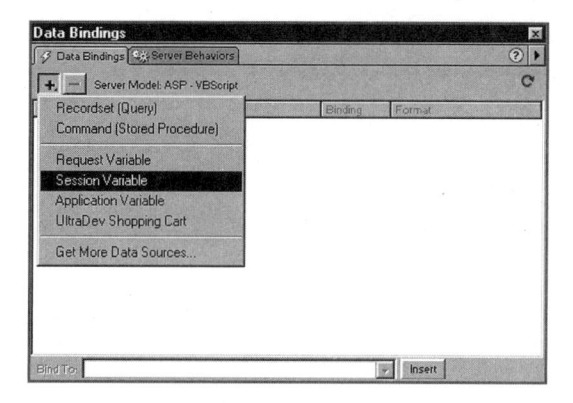

3. Name the session variable order_number:

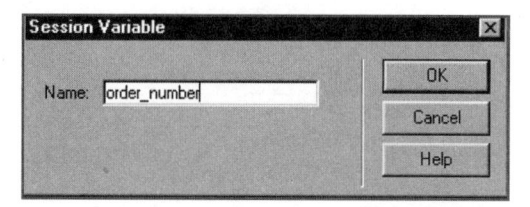

You can now drag the session to any point on your page:

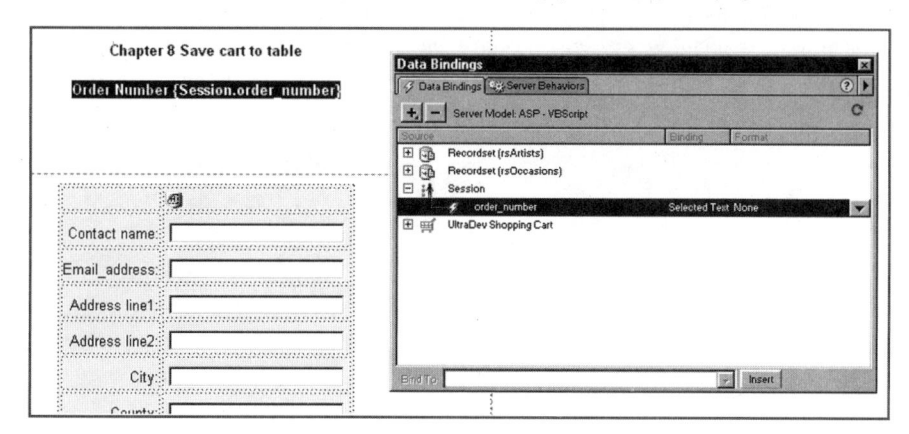

Alternatively, you could add the raw code to the page yourself:

```
Order Number <%= Session("order_number") %>
```

One thing we're missing is the link from the cart page to the customer details page.

Let's create a link from our cart page to this order form page now, then we can see whether our GetID is working with our cart.

Foundation Dreamweaver UltraDev 4

Linking to our Customer Details

What we need to do before testing things is pretty simple:

1. Save `order.asp`.
2. Open `cart.asp`.
3. Create a standard link to `order.asp`.
4. Save `cart.asp`.

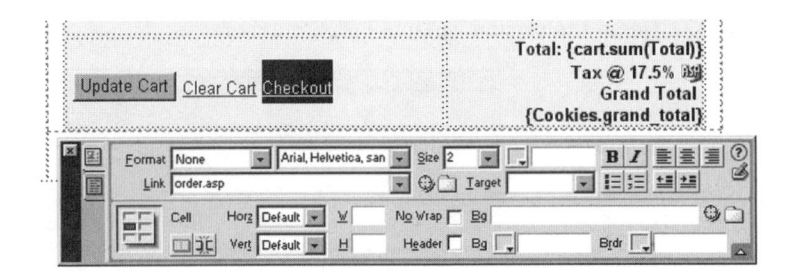

Test our new system out by searching and adding some items to our cart, then going to the purchase page, where you should have your unique number displayed at the top of the page. Now, repeat the process and the number should have been incremented by one:

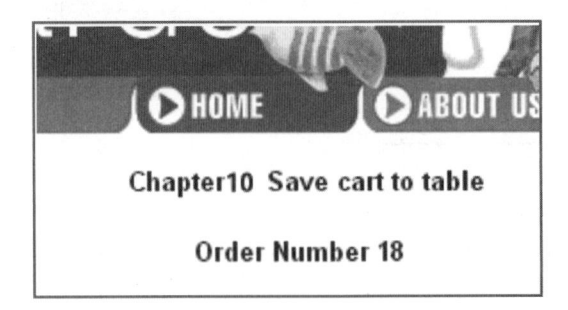

Okay, we have one more step, then we're home and dry.

Let's return to our `order.asp` page and steam through to the end.

We created *most* of the customer form for you but we've left out one important part, inserting the customer into the database.

Adding Cart Functionality 10

We need to:

- Use the Session value (the UniqueID) as the CustomerID
- Insert the customer's record

How do we do this?

We need to place a hidden field on our page and set its value to the session variable. From here, we can use it when we insert the form data to our table.

Inserting the Customer into the Database

1. Open up `order.asp`.

2. Place a hidden field on the page (Insert > Form Objects > Hidden Field) - anywhere will do, but somewhere it will stick out in future is best.

3. Bring up properties (CTRL+F3).

4. Name the hidden field Customer_id.

5. Set the value to `<%=Session("order_number")%>`:

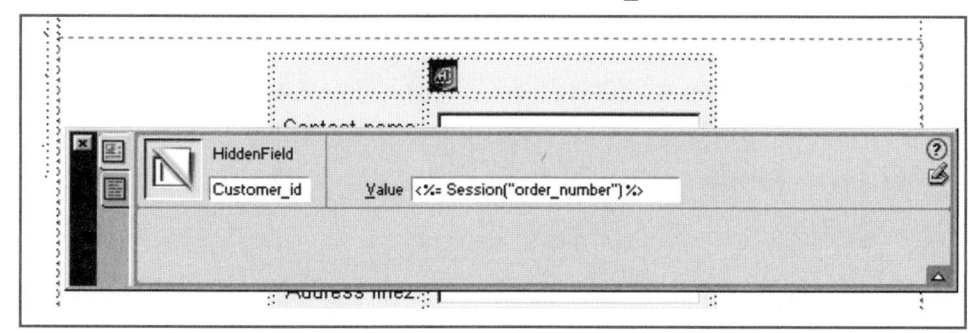

Now we can insert this unique number into our customer table, using a standard Insert behavior.

6. Select the Insert Record behavior.

7. Make sure that the field Customer_ID gets its value from the newly created hidden field customer_id on the form.

8. Make sure the other text boxes on the form insert into the correct fields in your database table.

9. Make sure you've set the After Inserting, Go To page to `order_save.asp`.

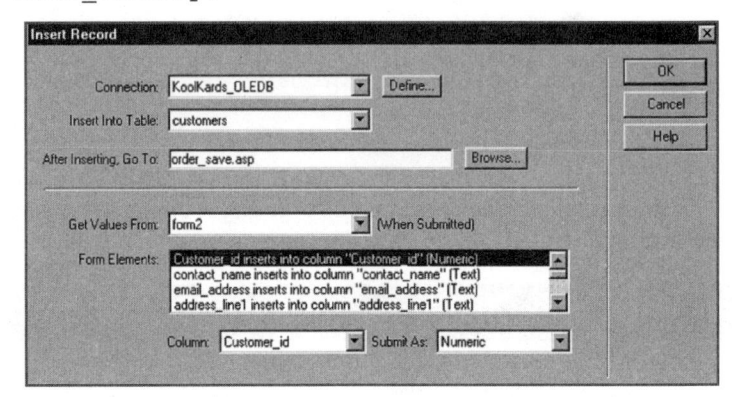

10. Save your pages and test.

Recap

Where are we up to now?

- We've got a working cart and an order link.
- From there we open a customer details page.
- Our customer is assigned a new unique number.
- The customer fills in details and is inserted into a database of customers, using our unique number.

What do we do next?

- Write contents of our cart to a orders table.
- Make sure the cart uses the customer's related unique number with the order, so we can reference who made the order.

Now we have all the customer information and a unique order number, we're finally ready to dump the contents of our cart to the orders table.

Open the page we've started for you - `order_save.asp`.

Again, we've done the layout for you so that all you need to build is the cart-specific parts:

Adding Cart Functionality   10

Invoice No. {Session.order_number}				
{rsCustomer.contact_name}		{rsCustomer.address_line1}		
		{rsCustomer.address_line2}		
Telephone:{rsCustomer.phone}		{rsCustomer.city}		
Fax:{rsCustomer.fax}		{rsCustomer.county}		
Email:{rsCustomer.email_address}		{rsCustomer.post_zip_code}		
		{rsCustomer.country}		
Order Details				
Item	Occasion	Price	Quantity	Total
{cart.Name}	{cart.Occasion}	{cart.Price}	{cart.Quantity}	{cart.Total}
			Total:	{cart.sum(Total)}
			Tax @ 17.5%	
			Grand Total	{Cookies.grand_total}

As well as writing the cart to the table, this page is going to act as a summary and final payment page. It's very good practice to show the user what they're actually ordering and the contact information they have supplied you with.

The next thing we want to do is display the current customer's information. Let's look at a different way of doing this.

We now know that our session variable order_number contains the details of our customer as that was the number used as the customer_ID value, so let's create a recordset and try to pull that record back.

Writing the Contents of the Cart to the Orders Table

1. Copy and paste your entire cart from the `cart.asp` page to this new `order_save.asp` page to make sure it's consistent.

2. Create a new recordset called rsCustomers.

3. Create a parameter called CustID.

4. Make the parameter equal the session variable value:

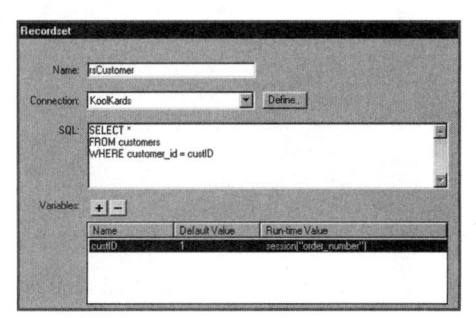

   Recordset
   Name: rsCustomer
   Connection: KoolKards
   SQL: SELECT *
        FROM customers
        WHERE customer_id = custID
   Variables:
Name	Default Value	Run-time Value
custID	1	session("order_number")

Test it out again. If everything is working, after you've entered your details on the order page, you'll be taken to our order_save page. The same details will be displayed, this time by querying the database for a matching record with a session variable.

We can start to populate the order table.

The details we need to insert into our order table are: OrderID, CustomerID, payment_method, and order_date.

Remember, we've created a customer table already and therefore need to make sure we use the related customerID.

Populating the Order Table

We've created the form object for you, called insert_order:

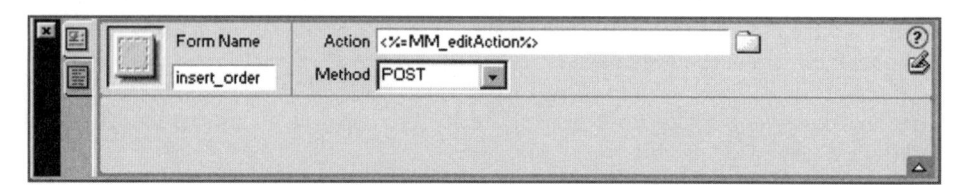

1. Create three hidden fields on your page. We suggest keeping them together so they stand out when you come back to develop on your page.

   Set them to the values as shown below:

   Hidden Field: OrderID –
   Value: `<%=Session("order_number") %>`

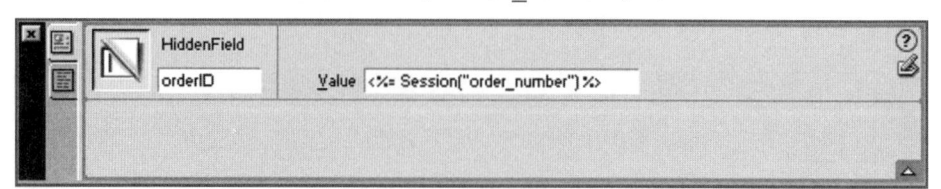

   Hidden Field: customerID
   Value: `<%=Session("order_number") %>`

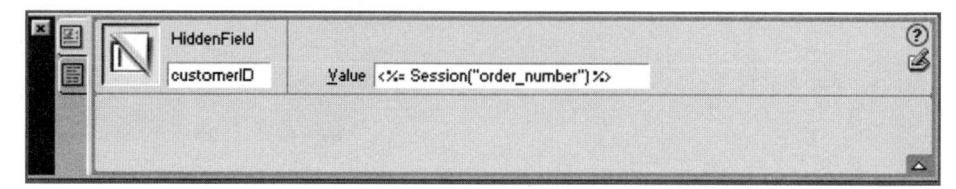

Adding Cart Functionality 10

Hidden Field: order_date
Value: <%=date%>

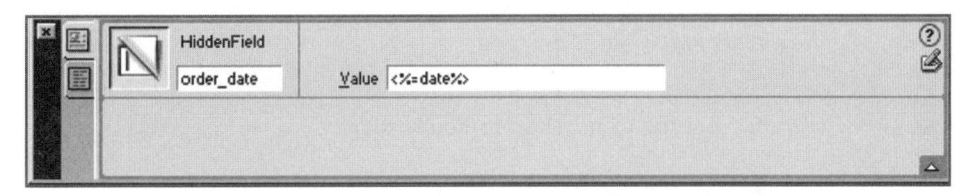

2. Apply the Insert Record behavior. We're going to write the order to the orders table.

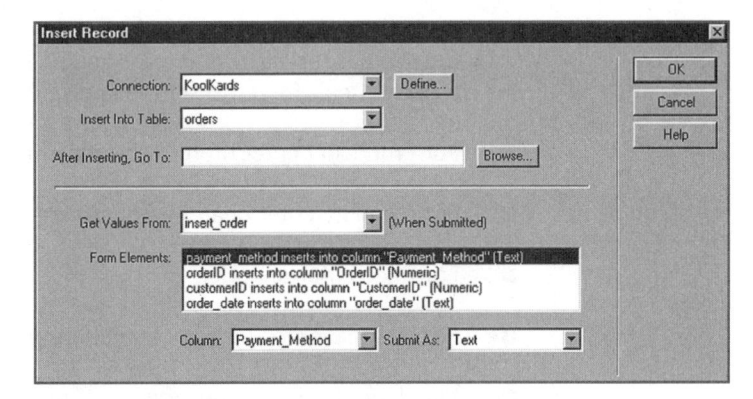

3. Apply the Save Cart to Table behavior now and let's look at the information required. This is where we put the final piece of this rather complicated jigsaw together.

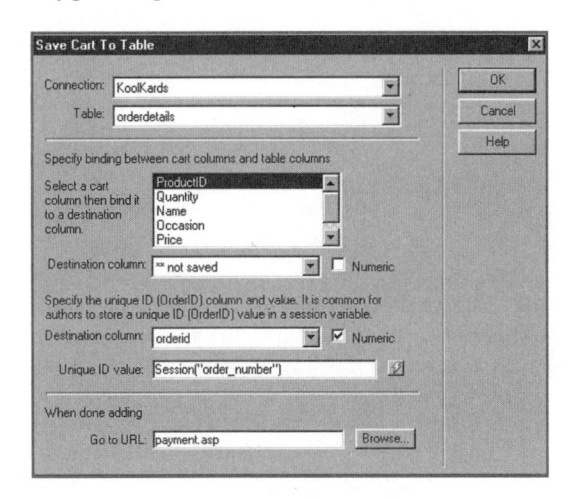

Foundation Dreamweaver UltraDev 4

> *As you fill in these properties, you may be presented with some horrible JavaScript errors. Ignore all of these, they are not critical, just some glitches in the UltraCart code.*

4. Set the Connection to KoolKards.

5. Set the Table to orderdetails.

6. Under specify binding…

    Select a cart column, then select the Destination column in the database. Do this for each column in the cart that is to be inserted into the database. Don't forget to set the appropriate fields to numeric.

    - For ProductID enter productid - **numeric**
    - For Quantity enter quantity - **numeric**
    - For Price enter unitprice
    - For Destination column enter orderid
    - For Unique ID Value the session variable enter Session ("order_number")
    - For Go To URL, enter payment.asp

7. Again we need to go into the code and alter the database connection string.

```
746 <%
747 If InStr(1, MM_editAction, "?", vbTextCompare) = 0 Then
748   MM_editAction = MM_editAction + "?UC_SaveCartToTable=1"
749 Else
750   MM_editAction = MM_editAction + "&UC_SaveCartToTable=1"
751 End If
752 If (CStr(Request("UC_SaveCartToTable")) = "1") Then
753   set UC_connCart = Server.CreateObject("ADODB.Connection")
754   UC_connCart.Open ""dsn=KoolKards;""
```

Line 754 needs to change to:

UC_connCart.Open **MM_koolkards_STRING**

8. Test your page.

Adding Cart Functionality 10

Add some items, fill in your customer details, and select your method of payment:

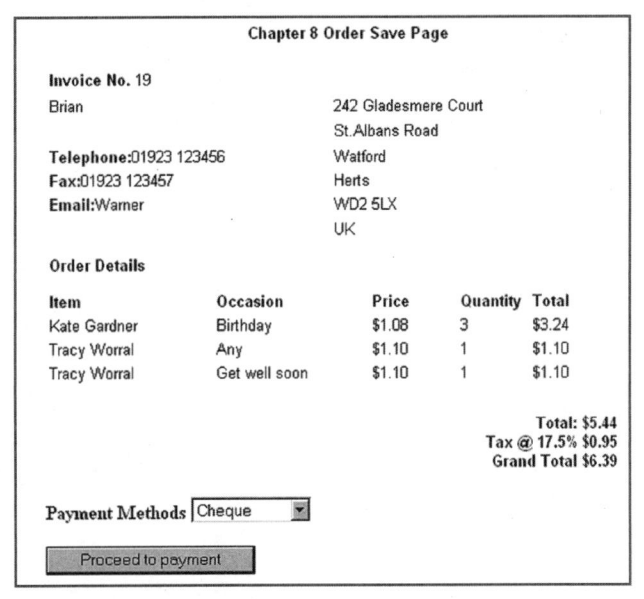

```
Chapter 8 Order Save Page

Invoice No. 19
Brian                                    242 Gladesmere Court
                                         St.Albans Road
Telephone:01923 123456                   Watford
Fax:01923 123457                         Herts
Email:Warner                             WD2 5LX
                                         UK

Order Details

Item            Occasion         Price      Quantity   Total
Kate Gardner    Birthday         $1.08      3          $3.24
Tracy Worral    Any              $1.10      1          $1.10
Tracy Worral    Get well soon    $1.10      1          $1.10

                                             Total: $5.44
                                     Tax @ 17.5% $0.95
                                     Grand Total $6.39

Payment Methods  [Cheque ▼]

[ Proceed to payment ]
```

It might be a good idea to open your Access database and look at what's been inserted into the three tables.

Perhaps the most useful aspect of this is the fact we've created a View Orders page for our admin team. In the next chapter we'll be looking at a better way of alerting our admin team to new orders. For the time being, though, you can see how we can nicely pull all the order information you've entered into a user-friendly page by opening the `view_order.asp` page provided.

Summary

In this chapter you've created a very powerful part of your application. When you come to create your own shopping cart, take it easy and take it slowly. Our example is about as complex as could be due to the multiple dynamic searches that we used. However, by doing this we think we've covered most issues that you'll come across in your applications.

If you keep looking at the Macromedia pages and third-party support groups you, may find that a new release will iron out a lot of the niggles. We imagine the next version of UltraDev will make life even easier, but the principles will always remain the same. Although it will always take some time to get your cart exactly as you want it, with time and practice you'll manage without any real difficulties.

kool kards

11 E-mail in UltraDev

What we'll cover in this chapter:

- **Sending e-mails** and presetting some of the content
- More **advanced e-mail options**, including **contact** and **feedback** forms
- How to browse for and **upload new files** to your server

Foundation Dreamweaver UltraDev 4

In this chapter we'll be looking at the various ways that we can send e-mails to people. "That's easy," you cry, "You just open Outlook..."

Well, not quite. What we're going to look at is how to collect information from forms and databases and get our server to generate automatic e-mails. Your inbox is probably full of mails that are auto-generated. If you become a new member of a web group, you'll probably have to fill in your details and choose a password, then your details are usually e-mailed back to you for confirmation.

After we've covered how to do this, we'll look at the frightening process of sending files from your hard-drive to the server. We'll be using all of this in our KoolKards site. There are a couple of places where we need e-mail confirmation of actions, the most obvious being in our shopping cart. Our purchaser needs a receipt with their order number and the items they purchased.

When we look at how we send files to the server, we'll move back into the Admin section and build a way for our administration team to be able to add new cards to the database. This will include sending a graphic preview of the card from their browser to the server.

We're going to start off with a couple of exercises that use the `mailto:` feature, before moving on to some more complex stuff. If you've used HTML before, you'll probably recognize some of this.

E-mailing Someone from within our Web Application

1. Go back to your Chapter 9 folder and open the `display_card.asp` file (this was the page that displayed the image of the card in a popup box).

2. Under the image placer, type *for bulk ordering, click here*:

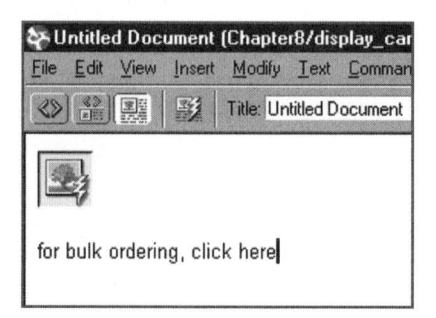

3. Highlight the text and bring up the Property inspector. In the Link property box type mailto:bulkordering@koolkards.co.uk. It's important that you don't leave a space after mailto: as this causes the e-mail

E-mail in UltraDev

address to come out incorrectly. You can do all this by highlighting the text and using Insert > E-mail instead if you prefer.

4. If you press F12 to view your single page locally, the default card from the recordset will display, saving you from going through the search and results process.

5. Click the hyperlink. It should launch and create a blank e-mail with the new address.

   This isn't too complicated, but let's see how we can make it even better.

6. Go back to the page and change the `mailto:` so that it now reads like this:

   ```
   mailto:bulkordering@koolkards.co.uk?subject=Bulk Order
   Enquiry for:
   <%=(rsCard.Fields.Item("ref_number").Value)%>
   ```

7. Test this by pressing F12 again. This time your link should be a little more 'dynamic'. As well as specifying the address for the customer, we've specified the subject and used some ASP to add in the reference number!

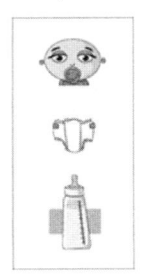

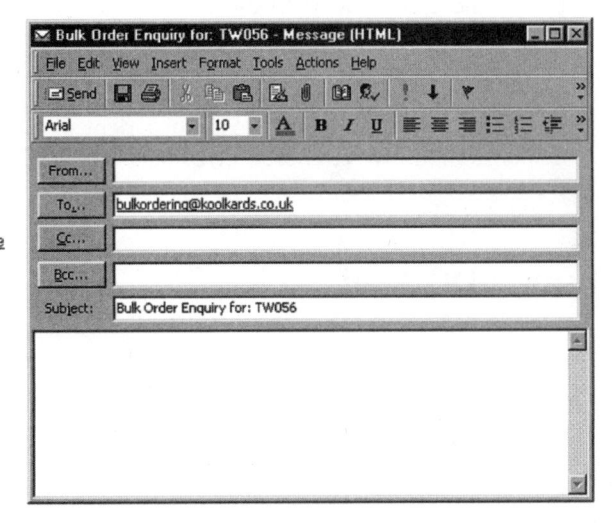

8. We can also add the cc (carbon copy), bcc (blind carbon copy) and even the body of the mail using this technique. Change that `mailto:` link so it reads like this:

   ```
   mailto:bulkordering@koolkards.co.uk?subject=Bulk Order
   Enquiry for:
   <%=(rsCard.Fields.Item("ref_number").Value)%>&cc=admin
   @koolkards.co.uk&body=I am interested in a bulk
   purchase of card ref:
   <%=(rsCard.Fields.Item("ref_number").Value)%>
   ```

9. Test this out again. You should have an entry in the cc and some body copy as well now!

The great thing about using the `mailto:` system is that it is simple, quick and effective for short mails that you want to prompt people with. You can go as far as requesting form variables and session variables in the e-mail like this:

```
mailto:<%=Request.Form("the_recipient")%>
```

```
mailto:<%=Session("the_recipient")%>
```

This would let you include information typed into a form by a user in an e-mail.

The disadvantages are - well, for all you know, your visitor may not have an e-mail client, or may not have an e-mail client set up properly to work with their browser. This may seem unlikely, but is possible. The method (`mailto:`) also leaves too much for the user to do. Launching an e-mail client in the middle of a web application can be off-putting, especially on a slower machine when it takes time. It's much better to build the copy in a form and mail it automatically.

As we've begun to see here, using `mailto:` can get more complicated as you start wanting to add more content. With these factors in mind, we recommend only using `mailto:` when you have to. So, let's move on to an even better way of doing things.

There are numerous ways to send e-mails using ASP and most follow a very similar technique. There really is no particular right or wrong way but for the purpose of our demonstrations, we've chosen CDO mail. This is both the most commonly used way and the Microsoft solution.

Using CDO Mail

CDO mail is just one part of the Microsoft CDO (**Collaboration Data Objects**) component, which lets you do all kinds of stuff with MS Office products. If you've ever

E-mail in UltraDev

used Outlook, you know that it's not designed just for e-mail. There are appointments, calendars, journal entries, reminders, and so on. CDO is like that too. You can use CDO to send people reminders and accomplish other MS Office-related tasks.

Added functionality does equate to increased size and a decrease in efficiency, so many people will tell you that CDO is bloated and slow. It's not as fast as other ASP components like ASPmail or Abmailer, but it's still not a bad mailer. You won't notice a speed difference between the two methods until you start sending out more than a few hundred mails a day.

CDO comes free with NT and will only run on NT Server. Unfortunately, this means that if you're running PWS you won't be able to do these exercises. This doesn't mean that you should stop reading, though – this is useful stuff and you're unlikely to end up hosting your web application on a system using PWS, even if that's what you're using at the moment.

Your ISP will be able to give you further information about whether or not you can use the CDO Mailer component. Plenty of hosting companies are perfectly happy with it, but if they insist on using a different mailer, it won't matter. Most mailers are the same, give or take some slightly different syntax.

Let's go back to where we left our shopping cart scenario in the last chapter. We had reached the end of the transaction, yet there was no receipt for the customer unless he printed out the page. This is problem number one. Problem number two is that the retailer needs to be made aware of the fact that the order has been made in order to process it.

The retailer could use a `view_cart.asp` page like the one we made earlier, but that would mean the retailer would constantly have to check for new orders. This wouldn't be very good if they want to do something else other than sit in front of their computer watching, yet still respond in the quickest way possible to incoming orders. In the real world of e-commerce sites, this wouldn't be good enough. Usually, after methods of payment have been dealt with, the user will receive an e-mail with confirmation of what they've ordered and the retailer will receive an e-mail with the details of the order.

CDOmail uses the **SMTP (Simple Mail Transfer Protocol)** mail service. This is installed by default when you install Internet Information Server (IIS) and takes care of sending and retrieving e-mail in accordance with SMTP.

Whenever you send e-mail from your e-mail client, you use SMTP and it's a great way of sending automated e-mail messages from your web site. The service can support sending thousands of e-mail messages a day. Later on we'll be using it to show you how to construct a newsletter to send to all of your customers (well, those who want it!)

It's worth noting that, traditionally, hosting companies use Unix-based systems for mail services. CDO won't talk to Unix, so some hosting companies disable CDO. It goes without saying that you don't want to be using one of those Unix servers in combination with CDO. If you have access to your server, you can check to see whether SMTP service is installed by opening up the Internet Service Manager and seeing if the Default SMTP Site appears in the Internet Information Server folder:

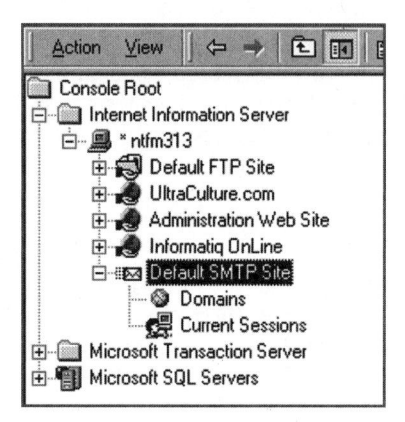

To make sure our SMTP Service is set up and configured correctly, open check.asp from this chapter's folder and run it. If a blank page is displayed, you can use CDO. Otherwise you'll get an error message reading Failed to create object error (which means you can't!)

Sending an E-mail Using CDO

1. To create an instance of a CDO object in your ASP code, you need to use some code like this:

   ```
   <%
   Dim objCDO
   Set objCDO = Server.CreateObject("CDONTS.NewMail")
   %>
   ```

   This creates a variable called objCDO then sets objCDO to a server CDOmail object and calls it NewMail. Once this has been written, we can refer to our CDOmail component as NewMail.

   Now you're ready to send off those e-mails! **CDONTS.NewMail** has a list of properties that you can apply to your mail, the most obvious ones being who the mail is to, from, and the cc, bcc, subject, and body, all of which you would expect to see in an e-mail.

2. Open up a new blank page and add the following code at the top (you don't need to actually do this exercise, as long as you know what it does – we've got a server behavior coming soon that will do it for you!):

E-mail in UltraDev

```
<%
Dim objCDO
Set objCDO = Server.CreateObject("CDONTS.NewMail")
objCDO.To = "INSERT AN E-MAIL ADDRESS"
objCDO.From = "YOUR E-MAIL ADDRESS"
objCDO.cc = "INSERT ANOTHER E-MAIL ADDRESS"
objCDO.Subject = "E-mail using CDO"
objCDO.Body = "This is my first e-mail"
objCDO.Send
Set objMail = Nothing
%>
```

3. If you test the page out nothing will appear but it will send the e-mail out 'behind your back'! I'm sure you can see how it's working from the code example. It's the same fields you would fill in if you were using your own e-mail client.

   The last two lines are important. The Send property speaks for itself. It's only when we reach this line that the mail is sent, so we could prepare the mail and not send it until, say, a button is clicked.

   The final line is where we close the object. This frees up resources on the server and is good coding practice in ASP.

   There are additional properties available for your use, one being the importance of a message.

   `objMail.Importance="x"`

   Add the line above to your code, before the Send command, but replace the **x** with either 0,1 or 2. This will set the importance of your e-mail.

   1=HIGH
   2=LOW
   0=NORMAL

4. Try setting the importance to high and watch your e-mails be sent with an exclamation mark.

   Now you know how to hand code it, you'll probably get a bit bored creating the objects each time, so we've created a little server behavior for you to use instead.

5. Start another new page and choose the Foundation UltraDev menu from the Server Behaviors panel and look for Simple CDO Message.

This will launch the CDO Behavior, which is really mimicking what you would do with your own mail client.

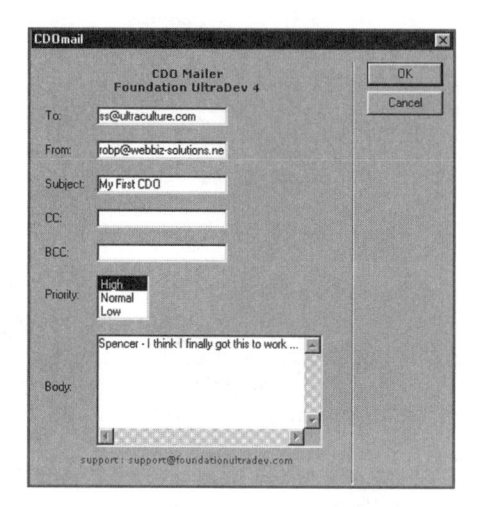

Now if you open your Code View, you'll see the simple CDO code, just like what you saw earlier:

```
<%@LANGUAGE="VBSCRIPT"%>
<%
' CDOmail Server Behaviour by Spencer Steel for Foundation UltraDev4
Set objMail = CreateObject("CDONTS.NewMail")

objMail.From = "robp@webbiz-solutions.net"
objMail.To = "ss@ultraculture.com"
objMail.CC = ""
objMail.BCC = ""
objMail.Subject = "My First CDO"
objMail.Body = "Spencer - I think I finally got this to work ..."
objMail.Importance="1"

objMail.Send()

Set objMail = Nothing

%>
```

You may find this useful in certain circumstances, but it's not really very 'dynamic'. One good use of this 'standard mail' is a reporting tool that e-mails administrators when certain conditions are met. The content isn't as important as the fact you get an e-mail!

E-mail in UltraDev

However, most of the time, we'll need something a little more powerful than our simple CDO example.

Let's look at some ways of using CDO to enhance our dynamic web site.

Creating a Contact Form

Have you ever wanted to have a user fill out a form and get the results automatically e-mailed to you? Perhaps the user is filling out a form for more information on your product line, or filling in a survey. Another common use for this process is a site 'feedback' form. It sure would be nice to get the results in e-mail format as soon as the visitor was finished.

This next section will show you how we can build a contact form for our users to fill in and submit. As soon as they do, an e-mail will be generated and sent to the relevant person in the administration team. Although this is only a simple contact page, once you've been through the process once, you'll see how you could have created a much bigger form with far more questions.

You'll find a 'contact us' page under the Chapter11 folder (`contact_us.asp`). This is a simple form that a user might fill in to request more information:

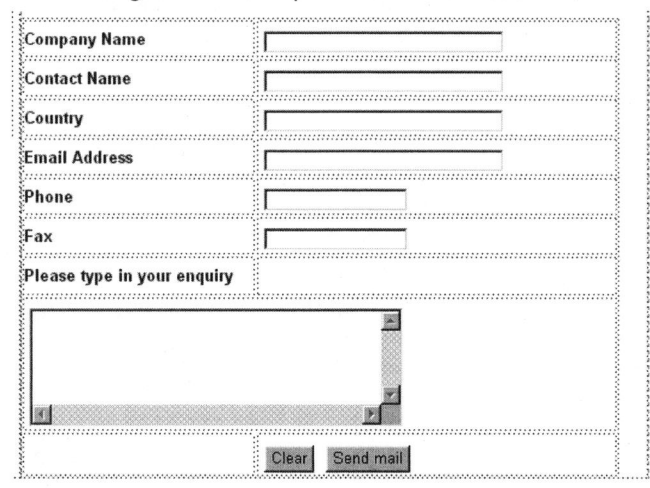

Look at the Method of the form and see that it's set to POST, with the Action set to `mailer.asp`:

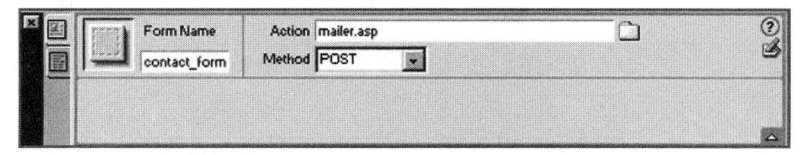

Foundation Dreamweaver UltraDev 4

As you may have guessed, all we're going to do from this page is POST the information to a new page, which will do the actual mailing for us. So, we're going to create a new page called `mailer.asp`.

Creating a Form Mailer

We've saved you some time and created you a server behavior that will take the content of any form you design and e-mail them to you. We'll have a look at the code that reads the form values in a moment, but first let's try the behavior out.

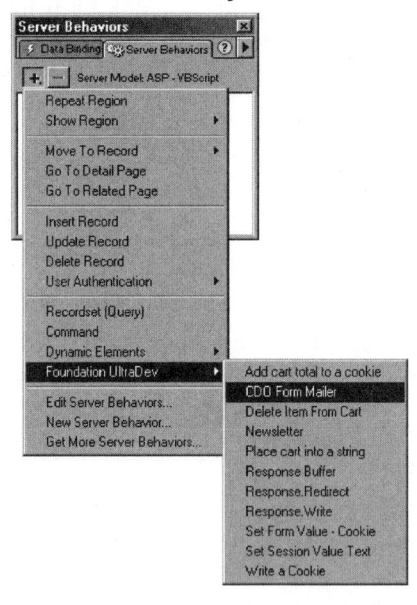

1. You'll find the behavior under Server Behaviors > Foundation UltraDev > CDO Form Mailer:

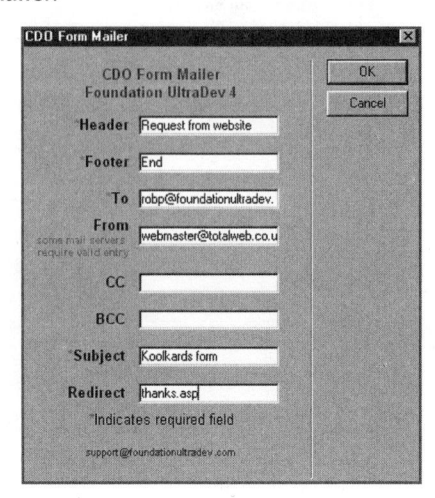

E-mail in UltraDev

2. Fill in the options that you require. The ones marked with an asterisk * are essential to the correct functionality of the behavior. Redirect to the `thanks.asp` page we've provided to thank your customer for their feedback.

> You'll notice that there is a **From** option. Setting the origin of the e-mail may seem like a pretty strange thing to do but some hosting companies require a valid origin in order to stop unscrupulous people using their servers for spamming people.

3. Save your page as `mailer.asp`, open your browser and try your pages out. If you have CDO set up correctly you should receive a mail looking something like this:

   FORM submitted at 27/01/2001 20:49:03

   CompanyName: Webbiz Network Solutions Ltd
   ContactName: Robert Paddock
   Fax: 0117 1234567
   Country: UK
   E-mail Address: robp@foundationultradev.com
   Phone: 07970 123456
   Enquiry: Test e-mail
   Mail: Send mail
   The end

4. Let's examine the code that performs this for you:

```
' CDO Form Mailer Created by Robert Paddock (Robp)
➥26/01/2001 ver 1.0
➥'The header/footer for the e-mail
Const Header = "Just because you sent this don't
➥assume you will get an answer"
 Const Footer = "The end"
  ' read all the form elements and place them in the
➥variable mail_body
Dim mail_Body
mail_Body = Header & vbCrLf & vbCrLf
mail_Body = mail_Body & "FORM submitted at " & Now()
➥& vbCrLf & vbCrLf
 Dim form_element
For Each FormElement in Request.Form
mail_body = mail_body & FormElement & ": " &
Request.Form(FormElement) & vbCrLf
```

```
Next
mail_Body = mail_Body & vbCrLf & Footer
'Create the mail object and send the mail
Set objMail = CreateObject("CDONTS.NewMail")
objMail.From = webmaster@totalweb.co.uk
objMail.To = r.paddock@btconnect.com
objMail.CC = ""
objMail.BCC = ""
objMail.Subject = "Form from website"
objMail.Body = mail_Body
objMail.Send()
Set objMail = Nothing
'Send them to the page specified if requested
Dim rp_redirect
rp_redirect = "thanks.asp"
If (rp_redirect <> "") then
Response.Redirect rp_redirect
End If
%>
```

The great thing about this piece of code is that no matter how many form elements you have on a page, it will e-mail them all to you. This is done by placing a FOR NEXT loop and putting them all together into the mail_body variable. You should recognize the middle section of code by now. We've created the CDO mail object and filled in the relevant properties. The last section deals with the optional redirect.

Sending the Shopping Cart via E-mail

Now we've played with the CDOmail object, we can look at the steps involved in mailing the shopping cart to the retailer *and* a confirmation to the customer. This is what we need to do:

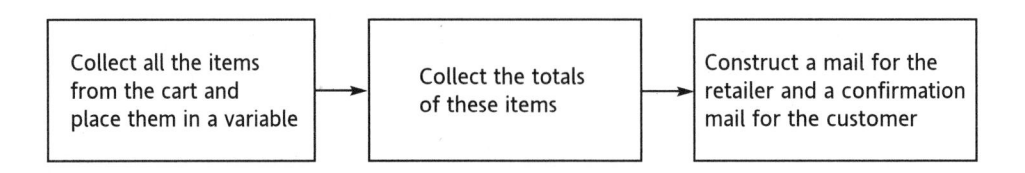

| Collect all the items from the cart and place them in a variable | → | Collect the totals of these items | → | Construct a mail for the retailer and a confirmation mail for the customer |

Before we do all this, we need to make yet another small adjustment to the shopping cart. At the end of the order_save.asp page where the cart was written to the database, the cart was completely erased and the sessions wiped.

E-mail in UltraDev

We still need our session variables. Remember, they hold our number of items and our total, so we need to take out the code that 'erases' the cart and sessions. This is good practice because it ensures that the sessions are destroyed after the cart was written to the database. However, we now need to take this out and get the cart to output the e-mails that we want before deleting itself.

Preparing to Mail your Cart

1. Open the `order_save.asp` page from Chapter 10.

2. In the code view, look for the `this.Destroy()` command under the `SaveToDatabase` function using the Find option (you can get at this by right-clicking in the Code View):

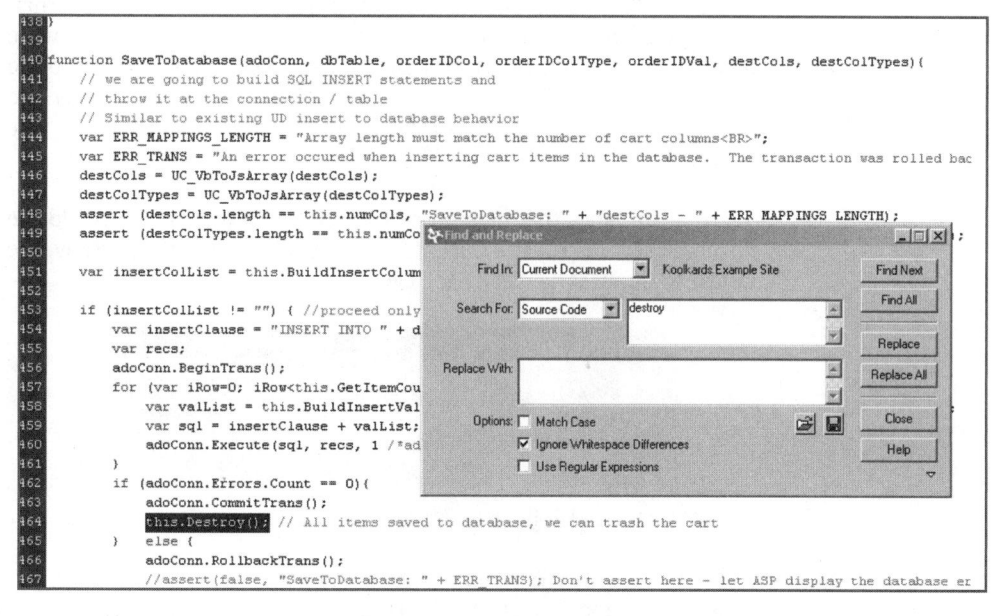

```
function SaveToDatabase(adoConn, dbTable, orderIDCol,
➥ orderIDColType, orderIDVal, destCols, destColTypes){
➥    if (adoConn.Errors.Count == 0){
            adoConn.CommitTrans();
            this.Destroy();         // All items
➥saved to database, we can trash the cart
       }      else {
            adoConn.RollbackTrans();
```

3. We need to disable the Destroy statement for the moment rather than remove it completely because we'll want to use it again later, once we've sorted out our e-mails. We can do this by turning the statement

into something that we can read but that the server won't process. This can be called a **reminder** or a **comment**. As this is a client-side JavaScript routine, we have to use the JavaScript reminder marker, simply two forward slashes // - so amend the line to read like this:

```
// this.Destroy();
```

4. Save your page and the cart will still be live and functional for writing to a CDOmail.

5. While you're here copy the shopping cart from the Data Bindings panel. Now go to our Chapter 11 `thanks.asp` page and paste the shopping cart to Data Bindings.

    The next step is to output the shopping cart to some sort of text format so that we can mail it. To help you along we've created you a simple server behavior that will collect all the items from your cart and place them into a variable called `mail_cart`. You can find this under the Foundation UltraDev menu in the Server Behavior panel called Place cart into a string.

6. Open it up and the name of the cart on your page should be automatically displayed. Click OK and you've finished possibly the easiest to apply server behavior ever!

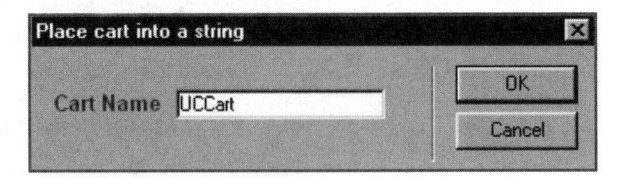

7. This will place the following code onto the page:

```
<% ' Place the contents of the cart in to a string
Robert Paddock (robp) 27/01/20001
  For UCCart1__i=0 To UCCart1.GetItemCount()-1
  'loop through each item in the cart
  For each myElement in UC_CartColNames
  mail_cart = mail_cart &
(UCCart1.GetcolumnValue(myElement,UCCart1__i))
  mail_cart = mail_cart & "   "
  next
mail_cart = mail_cart & vbcrlf
Next 'UCCart1__i %>
```

E-mail in UltraDev

What's this code doing? Well, basically it's visiting every item in the cart and writing it to a string, followed by a carriage return. A carriage return has the special name **vbcrlf** (Visual Basic Carriage Return Line Feed) in VBScript because it's a special keyboard function.

The whole string is held in a variable called `mail_cart`. Effectively, what you end up with is a long string that's just a text file of your cart and looks something like this:

```
Tracy Worral Baby $1.10 2 $2.20
Tracy Worral Christening $1.10 1 $1.10 ...
```

8. We then need the total of all the items, the tax and the grand total from our cart. We need to tack this onto the end of our text file. Place this code directly after the code that's just been added by the behavior – which will work them out separately in case tax goes up!

```
<%
Dim rate, grand_total
rate = .175 * UCCart1.GetColumnTotal("Total")
Grand_total = UCCart1.GetColumnTotal("Total") + rate
mail_cart = mail_cart & "Total : " &
UCCart1.GetColumnTotal("Total") & vbcrlf
mail_cart = mail_cart & "Tax :" & rate & vbcrlf
mail_cart = mail_cart & Grand_total & vbCrlf
%>
```

```
645  rsCustomer_numRows = 0
646 %>
647 <% ' Place the contents of the cart in to a string Robert Paddock (robp) 27/01/2000
648 For UCCart1__i=0 To UCCart1.GetItemCount()-1
649   'loop through each item in the cart
650   For each myElement in UC_CartColNames
651     mail_cart = mail_cart & (UCCart1.GetcolumnValue(myElement,UCCart1__i))
652     mail_cart = mail_cart & "           "
653   next
654 mail_cart = mail_cart & vbcrlf
655 Next 'UCCart1__i %>
656
657 <%
658 Dim rate, grand_total
659 rate = .175 * UCCart1.GetColumnTotal("Total")
660 Grand_total = UCCart1.GetColumnTotal("Total") + rate
661 mail_cart = mail_cart & "Total : " & UCCart1.GetColumnTotal("Total") & vbcrlf
662 mail_cart = mail_cart & "Tax :" & rate & vbcrlf
663 mail_cart = mail_cart & Grand_total & vbCrlf
664 %>
665
666
667 <html>
```

That completes the `mail_cart` string, containing all the information about your cart. Now we just have to dump it out somewhere.

We now need to set up our CDO objects to e-mail this information to the customer and the retailer.

Setting up the Cart E-mail

1. Create a recordset query that will pull the customer's e-mail address and name so we can use the fields to construct an e-mail and call it rsCustomer. Use the session variable `order_number` as the parameter value. This will return the customer details that you need to construct your e-mail.

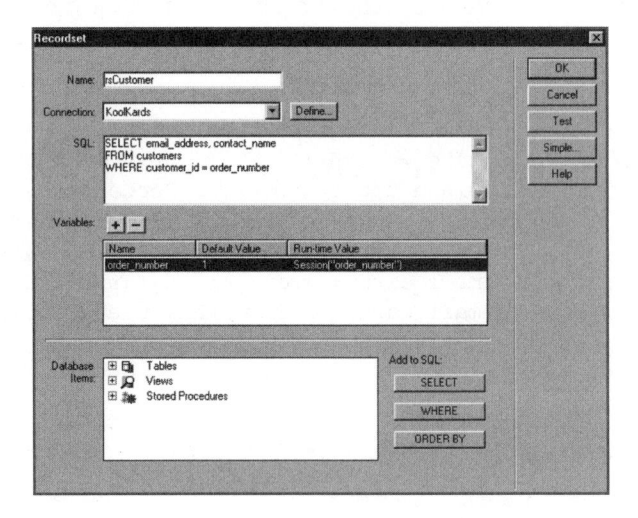

2. To build the e-mail, place this code directly after the code you've just been writing:

```
<%
' Create an e-mail to send to a customer
Set objMail = CreateObject("CDONTS.NewMail")
objMail.From = "orders@koolkards.co.uk"
objMail.To = rsCustomer.fields("e-mail_address").value
objMail.Subject = "Confirmation of your order"
objMail.Body = "To " & 
rsCustomer.fields("contact_name").value & mail_cart
objMail.Send()
Set objMail = nothing
%>
```

E-mail in UltraDev

3. The last piece of the jigsaw is to e-mail the order to the retailer. We've already opened the mail object, so we can just construct another e-mail by placing this code after the code we've just entered:

   ```
   <%
   ' Create an e-mail to send the retailer
   Set objMail = CreateObject("CDONTS.NewMail")
   objMail.From = "webmaster@totalweb.co.uk"
   objMail.To = "orders@koolkards.co.uk"
   objMail.Subject = "Order from Koolkards Website " & Date
   objMail.Body = mail_cart
   objMail.Send()
   Set objMail = nothing
   %>
   ```

4. We've completed our mailing so let's destroy the cart session as the transaction is finally complete. Add this line below what you've just added:

   ```
   <% UCCart1.Destroy ()%>
   ```

   You final code should look something like this:

   ```
   656 <%
   657 Dim rate, grand_total
   658 rate = .175 * UCCart1.GetColumnTotal("Total")
   659 Grand_total = UCCart1.GetColumnTotal("Total") + rate
   660 mail_cart = mail_cart & "Total : " & UCCart1.GetColumnTotal("Total") & vbcrlf
   661 mail_cart = mail_cart & "Tax :" & rate & vbcrlf
   662 mail_cart = mail_cart & Grand_total & vbCrlf
   663 %>
   664 <%
   665 ' Create an email to send to a customer
   666 Set objMail = CreateObject("CDONTS.NewMail")
   667 objMail.From = "orders@koolkards.co.uk"
   668 objMail.To = rsCustomer.fields("email_address").value
   669 objMail.Subject = "Confirmation of your order"
   670 objMail.Body = "To " & rsCustomer.fields("contact_name").value & mail_cart
   671 objMail.Send()
   672 Set objMail = nothing
   673 %>
   674 <%
   675 ' Create an email to send the retailer
   676 Set objMail = CreateObject("CDONTS.NewMail")
   677 objMail.From = "webmaster@totalweb.co.uk"
   678 objMail.To = "orders@koolkards.co.uk"
   679 objMail.Subject = "Order from Koolkards Website " & Date
   680 objMail.Body = mail_cart
   681 objMail.Send()
   682 Set objMail = nothing
   683 %>
   ```

5. You should now be able to test out your working cart with e-mail confirmation back to the company.

We've gone about sending these two mails in two very straightforward steps. One completes and ends; the next completes and ends in the same manner. It's possible to build several e-mails at the same time when using your own routines, as long as you call them different things. Here's the same code as the two parts previously written in the same section. It's not too hard to work out, but handy to know for later on in your development life.

```
<%
' Create an e-mail to send to a customer (objCustMail) &
retailer (objRetailMail)

Set objCustMail = CreateObject("CDONTS.NewMail")
Set objRetailMail = CreateObject("CDONTS.NewMail")

objCustMail.From = "orders@koolkards.co.uk"
objCustMail.To = rsCustomer.fields("e-mail_address").value
objCustMail.Subject = "Confirmation of your order"
objCustMail.Body = "To " &
rsCustomer.fields("contact_name").value & mail_cart

objRetailMail.From = "webmaster@totalweb.co.uk"
objRetailMail.To = "orders@koolkards.co.uk"
objRetailMail.Subject = "Order from Koolkards Website" &
Date
objRetailMail.Body = mail_cart

objCustMail.Send()
objRetailMail.Send()

Set objCustMail = nothing
Set objRetailMail = nothing

%>
```

Creating a Simple Newsletter

Newsletters have become part and parcel of every good web site today as a great way of keeping in touch with your users. If you've been online for any amount of time, you'll probably get a couple of newsletters every week telling you about new products or keeping you in tune with what's going on at your favorite sites.

E-mail in UltraDev 11

We'll now take a look at how we can use our knowledge of CDOmail to send a simple newsletter to all the people in a database. In Chapter 8, we created a user registration system encouraging our users to register with our site to get a discount on their orders. It's highly possible that we would want to send them a newsletter telling them about further special offers, or new products. All the information we need for the newsletter is stored in the logins table:

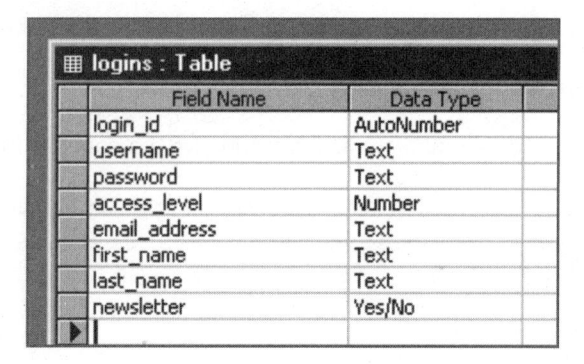

Field Name	Data Type
login_id	AutoNumber
username	Text
password	Text
access_level	Number
email_address	Text
first_name	Text
last_name	Text
newsletter	Yes/No

The first stage is to create an Admin page from where we can send out e-mails to all the users on our mailing list at once. We must remember that some users may not wish to receive e-mails from us, so we've added an extra column to our login table where we can flag any users who request not to receive any e-mails. We can do this by having newsletter as a *Boolean* yes/no value. If you're using the Chapter 7 database this will already be done for you.

Sending a Newsletter

1. Create a new page from the admin template and call it newsletter.asp.

Newsletter Admin Page

Subject :

Message :

send

2. Add a form called newsletter and set the Action to newsletter.asp. Also check that the Method is set to POST:

3. Add a text box and give it a name of subject.

4. Add a multi-line text box and give it a name of Message.

5. Add a hidden field, call it RP_Flag and set its value to true:

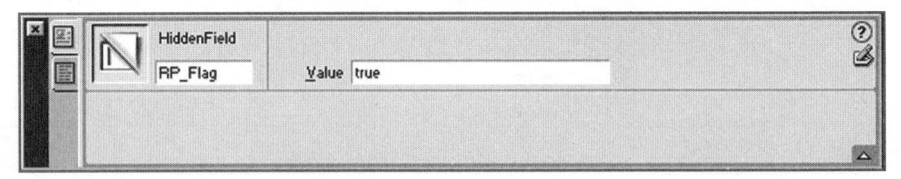

6. Add a form Submit button.

7. Set up a recordset query that will return the first name, the last name, and the e-mail address of any user that wishes to receive a newsletter by e-mail. We don't want to include any people in our list whose newsletter field is set to 0. In Access 0 is false, and -1 is true. In other words we need to create a recordset where newsletter = -1 (true):

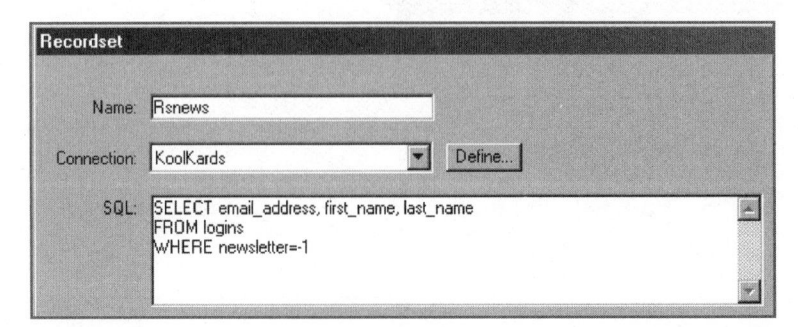

```
Name: Rsnews
Connection: KoolKards
SQL: SELECT email_address, first_name, last_name
     FROM logins
     WHERE newsletter=-1
```

8. You're now ready to use our Newsletter behavior. You'll find it in the usual place under Server Behaviors > Foundation UltraDev > Newsletter.

E-mail in UltraDev

9. Fill in the Newsletter options as we have here:

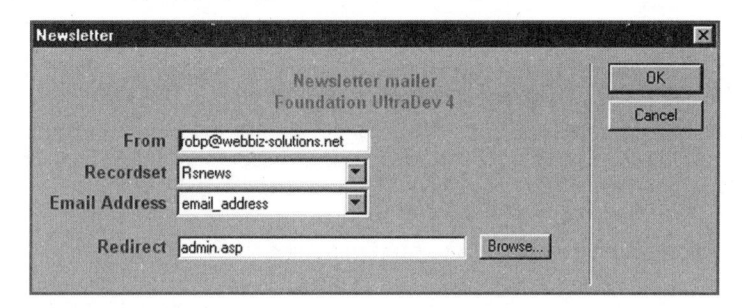

10. Press OK. Your page is ready to test.

11. If you look at the code, it should look like this:

```asp
<% ' Newsletter Behavior Robert Paddock 29/01/2001 v.1.0
' Check to see if form already submitted
If Request("RP_FLAG") ="true" then
Dim subject, message,no_sent
subject = Request.Form("subject")
message = Request.Form("message")
While Not Rsnews.EOF
Set mail = Server.CreateObject("CDONTS.NewMail")
mail.From = robp@webbiz.solutions.net
mail.To = Rsnews.fields("e-mail_address").value
mail.Subject = subject
mail.Body = message
mail.Send
Set mail = Nothing
rs.MoveNext
Wend
rs.Close
Response.Redirect "admin.asp"
End If
  %>
```

There's nothing in this code that we haven't covered before. The basic element is a While Loop that sends the message until there are no more records left in the recordset.

Having got a good grasp of CDOmail, we're going to move onto the issue of uploading your files to a server.

Sending Files from the Browser to the Server

Have you ever been to a site that's asked you upload a file? There are quite a few jobs sites that give you the option to send them your CV through a form uploader. An upload simply means that your computer sends information to the web server. For the user it's a simple and seamless exercise, and a lot nicer than telling you to manually attach a CV to an e-mail.

Normally the user will see something like this:

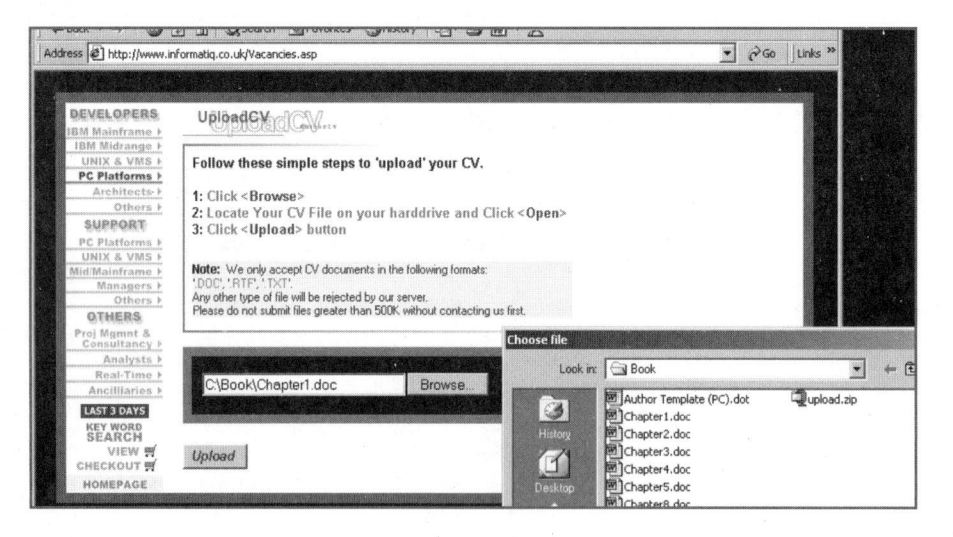

They're provided with a File object, from which they can browse their own hard drive and choose a file. Once they've chosen their file, the Submit button will send the file to the server.

Once the file is on the server, a number of things can happen depending on the type of application written. In our job application scenario it's probably best to send a CDOmail back to the company, attaching the uploaded file, for consideration. In the KoolKards site, we have a good reason to send a file to the server and for it to stay there. We need for our administration team to be able to add new cards to the database and to upload a small picture of the card (in GIF format) to the server.

There are a number of solutions for sending files from a browser to a server, as we want to happen here. To the user, most methods are identical. The user finds the file and then clicks upload. From our design point of view, there are different ways of doing this. The solution we're going to look at is a pure code solution. It's free and needs no customization to work first time. It comes pre-written as a server behavior and is ready to use.

E-mail in UltraDev 11

There are other, more robust solutions designed for heavy use that you can purchase. The advantage of these are that they are prewritten COM objects designed for file uploading that sit on the server and take most of the code and hard work away from the client's page. We'll look briefly at one of the best examples of this.

Pure ASP File Send

This is our 'free' solution. The technique is known as a **pure ASP upload** and it's a very clever thing indeed. As the title suggests, it's a solution that relies on ASP code only and no COM objects or additional software components are needed. Its only drawback is the amount of code it generates on a page. You won't notice any performance downgrade in comparison to pre-written COM object solutions when you first start using this solution but if you need heavy file capacity, you may start to notice the overhead.

There's a fair amount of code to be generated and some work to be done to the existing behaviors in UltraDev to make them work with a file uploader, so this isn't an easy job. However, the complete solution has been provided for us in an excellent server behavior called Pure ASP Upload which you can find in the Chapter 9 download.

The server behavior was written by George Petrov, and other examples of really useful similar server behaviors can be found at www.Udzone.com, one of the better 3rd party extension and support groups. The version we're using is version 2 beta 1 but if you go and check there's a chance you'll get an even better version. If you're publishing your sites to a remote NT server during these exercises and then browsing from there, you'll need to set up the rights on the folder where you send the files to. For information on how to do this, see the SA file discussion at the end of this chapter.

We're going to start with a single page example, so that we can see the behavior in action, before moving onto our KoolKards site. We won't be keeping these initial pages, so there's no need to spend a lot of time on them.

Pure ASP Upload

1. Create a new page, call it `pureasptest.asp` and save it in your Chapter 11 folder.

2. Under the Chapter 11 folder from your Site window create a new folder and call it uploads. This is where we'll store the files that our users will upload.

Foundation Dreamweaver UltraDev 4

3. We need a File Field and a Submit button. A File Field is the file browser that the user will pick a file from their hard-drive with. Go to the Form Objects panel and drag one of these onto your page:

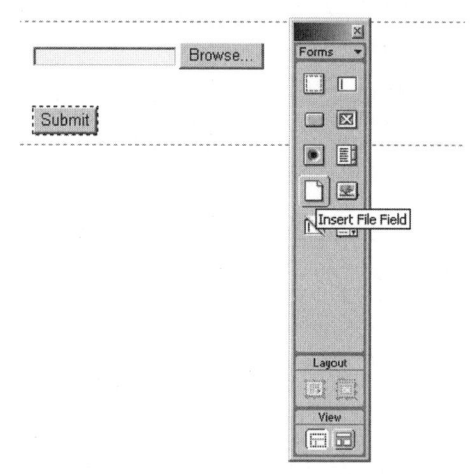

4. We now need to apply our new server behavior. It's called Pure ASP File Upload. Select it now and you'll be presented with the following properties panel:

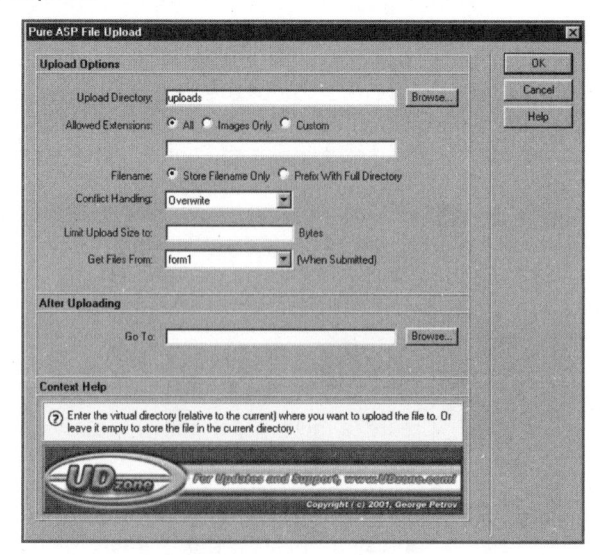

5. Beside Upload Directory enter uploads as this is the path to the folder we created earlier from your current location in the file directory. The rest you can leave as it is, although we'll be using some of the other features in our more advanced KoolKards example.

E-mail in UltraDev   11

6. That's it. If you save and test your page you should now be able to upload any file from your hard-drive to the uploads folder. Once the upload is complete you'll be returned to the same page and you can check the uploads folder (from your site file) to see if the file arrived safely.

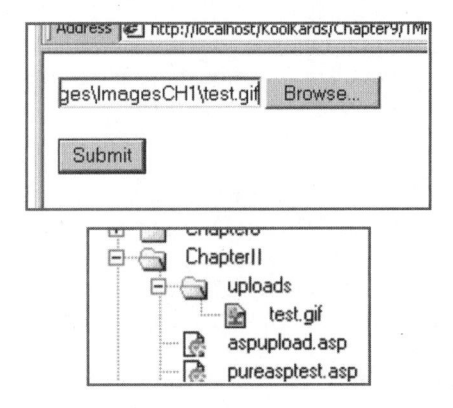

Upload Code

Have a look at the code that did this for us:

```
    GP_value = UploadRequest.Item(GP_curKey).Item("value")
    GP_valueBeg = UploadRequest.Item(GP_curKey).Item("ValueBeg")
    GP_valueLen = UploadRequest.Item(GP_curKey).Item("ValueLen")

    if GP_valueLen = 0 then
      Response.Write "<B>An error has occured saving uploaded file!</B><br>
      Response.Write "Filename: " & Trim(GP_curPath) & UploadRequest.Item(C
      Response.Write "File does not exists or is empty.<br>"
      Response.Write "Please correct and <A HREF=""javascript:history.back(
        response.End
      end if

    'Create a Stream instance
    Dim GP_strm1, GP_strm2
    Set GP_strm1 = Server.CreateObject("ADODB.Stream")
    Set GP_strm2 = Server.CreateObject("ADODB.Stream")

    'Open the stream
    GP_strm1.Open
    GP_strm1.Type = 1 'Binary
    GP_strm2.Open
    GP_strm2.Type = 1 'Binary

    GP_strm1.Write RequestBin
    GP_strm1.Position = GP_ValueBeg
    GP_strm1.CopyTo GP_strm2,GP_ValueLen

    'Create and Write to a File
    GP_curPath = Request.ServerVariables("PATH_INFO")
    GP_curPath = Trim(Mid(GP_curPath,1,InStrRev(GP_curPath,"/")) & "uploads
    if Mid(GP_curPath,Len(GP_curPath),1) <> "/" then
      GP_curPath = GP_curPath & "/"
    end if
    on error resume next
    GP_strm2.SaveToFile Trim(Server.mappath(GP_curPath)) & "\" & UploadRequ
```

Foundation Dreamweaver UltraDev 4

How do you fancy trying to learn that lot? Thought not! To be honest, the code is beyond the scope of this book. This behavior uses many advanced techniques, including rewriting the Macromedia standard update and insert behaviors if they are used on the same page, as we'll soon find out.

Now we want to incorporate this into our KoolKards site. We need to create an Insert New Card page for our Admin team. This would mean that they could fill in the details of a new product and upload the image of the card to the server with no knowledge of UltraDev or the site.

We need to store the final file path to the uploaded image on the server in the database records so that when our HTML pages need to display the image on the page, they can do so. As we mentioned earlier, the Pure ASP Upload server behavior modifies the standard update and insert behaviors that UltraDev provides. This means that we have to place our standard update and insert behaviors on the page first.

If you ever use this behavior on another project, the best way to do things would be to create your page without the upload section, and make sure all update or inserts are working correctly as before adding the Pure ASP Upload behavior. We've started the page for you by sorting out the standard form elements, so the only thing for you to do is add the behavior.

Uploading a New KoolKard

1. Open the `insertnewcard.asp` page from the Chapter 11 folder. This will open a basic insert form, with the additional File Field in place:

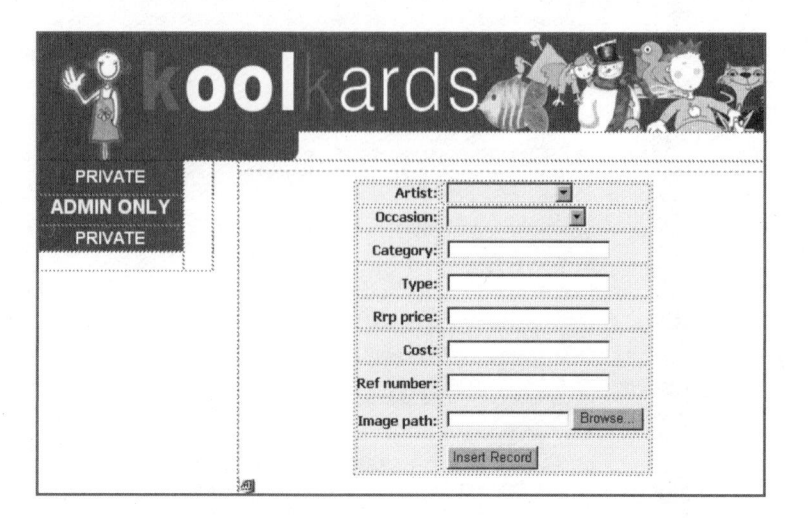

E-mail in UltraDev

2. Check to see whether this is working for your site by saving your file and loading up `insertnewcard.asp` in your browser. You can enter the details for an imaginary new card (make sure that you use numerical values for the money fields) and choose an image to represent it.

3. Click on Insert Record and then load up the KoolKards/chapter8/search.asp page. Use the drop-down boxes to search for the type of card you just entered and you should be returned to your results, although the image won't be there.

   Now that we've got everything else sorted, we need to apply our Pure ASP behavior.

   If you look at the screenshot, you'll see we need to specify several choices:

4. This time we want to upload to the images folder, so we need to set this under Upload Directory. You'll need to select Browse and move one step up the directory tree to find this.

5. Under Allowed Extensions, we want to specify GIF, JPG, JPEG, BMP, PNG to ensure that the only files uploaded are image files. This is a very useful option. You might choose only to let `.doc`, `.txt` and `.rtf` files be uploaded (on a CV/job site for example), for example), using Custom to specify your own file extension types.

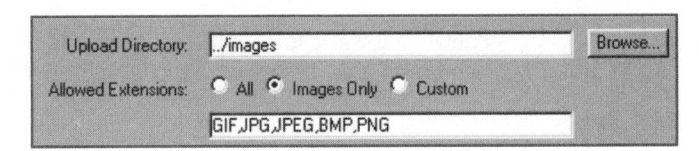

> *The step up the directory tree is always represented by a ../ prefixing the folder name.*

6. Under Filename, select the Prefix With Full Directory radio button. This means that the filename will be stored in our database with the whole path, rather than just the filename. This means that, for example, `inetpub/wwwroot/mysite/myfolder/uploads/image.gif` would be entered into our database rather than just `image.gif`.

7. We want to set Conflict Handling to Overwrite. This option allows you to specify what happens if two people upload files with the same name (say, `mycv.doc`). As we're only going to have two images called the same if we're renewing the image for a card, we can safely overwrite:

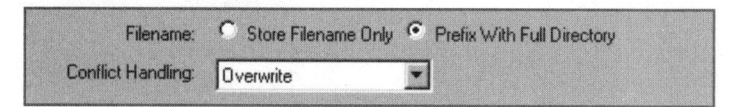

8. We've set Limit Upload Size to 100,000 bytes, or 100Kb, which is plenty for our images. This option is quite useful for stopping people from uploading huge files and taking up all your server space.

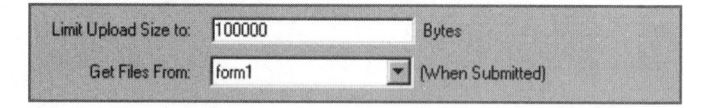

9. Under Get files From to state the name of the form that the file browser is on, form1 in this case. Apologies – we had had a momentary lapse and forgot all our resolutions about meaningful names when we were preparing the source files!

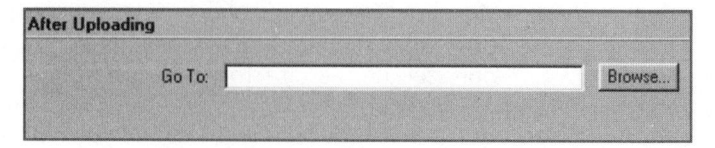

10. In the After Uploading Go To: field you can redirect to another page from here after the upload as our users may want to enter another. We'll leave it blank.

    Phew! That was a lot of options. Hopefully, you can now see the reason behind all that code and exactly why this is such a useful behavior.

E-mail in UltraDev 11

We're now ready to test it out again, so save your file and load it up in your browser.

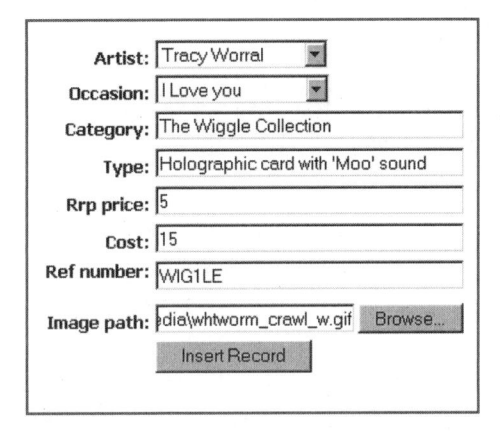

11. Once the file is loaded into your browser, you can enter some details and upload your file. Try an animated GIF for some fun. You can then browse the `chapter8/search.asp` page and search for your entry.

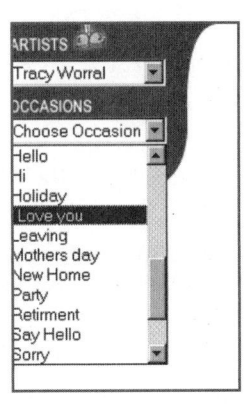

Before we move on, we're going to have a quick look at how our database has stored our filename.

12. Save and close any open pages in UltraDev before returning to your site window (F8). Launch Access by double-clicking on the `koolkards.mdb` file. Find the products table, open it, and scroll down to the last entry. This should be the entry that you've just added.

rrp_pric	cost	ref_numb	image_path
1.1	0.47	TW052	../images/TW052.gif
1.1	0.47	TW053	../images/TW053.gif
1.1	0.47	TW054	../images/TW054.gif
5	15	WIG1LE	/koolkards/chapter9/../images/whtworm_wiggle_w.gif

> The file name should be something you see in the screenshot, that is very long. This is because, as we said when setting the **Filename**, it contains the fullest path to the image. This is no bad thing, particularly as you can upload to folders on other sites, while still holding the full path. You do need to take care when you're designing your database table, though. If you set the **datatype** of the field that will hold this information to the default text value, it will only be able to store 255 characters. You can see that this could cause some problems with a long path, so you need to set the **datatype** to **Memo** instead, as we have here.

This ends our look at ASP uploading and we're going to have a quick look at a non-ASP alternative before we finish this chapter.

Field Name	Data Type	
ID	AutoNumber	Record ID Number
artist_id	Number	Artist ID
occasion_id	Number	Occasion ID
category	Text	Theme
type	Text	Type of card (Bookmark
rrp_price	Number	retail Price
cost	Number	Cost to customer
ref_number	Text	Reference Number
image_path	Memo	image_path

E-mail in UltraDev 11

SAFileUp

As we said, the only drawback with ASP uploading is that it uses a lot of code and becomes a little slow compared with other commercial solutions, particularly as volumes increase. If you're after a more robust file sender, we'd suggest that you take a look at the Software Artisans solution **SAFileUp**.

SAFileUp is a server-side control written to handle file sending, which allows file upload from any browser to IIS and can be controlled with ASP. The only snag is that you'll have to pay about $180 for it. If your site is dependent on file sending and downloading, this is probably worth it. We're going to have a quick look at it here, but there's a 30-day trial version available from their site (http://www.softwareartisans.com) if you want to take a closer look.

SAFileUp needs to be installed on the server itself, no client software is needed and you pay per server. Installation is straightforward. The components will self-extract to the right location on your NT Server and there's no need to reboot. Using SAFileup is also pretty easy. We're going to look at a simple example to finish this chapter with. We don't expect you to enter this code or test it out, but we thought you could have a look at some of the code to see how easy it is to use SAFileup. Of course, if you have access to your NT Server, IIS and have the SAFileup component installed, then you're welcome to test this out.

Advanced Uploading using SAFileUp

1. To carry out a basic upload, you need two pages (these are in the Chapter 11 folder as `SAFileUpBrowse.asp` and `SAFileUpUpload.asp`). The `SAFileUpBrowse` page contains a standard File Field and a form that submits to the `SAFileUpUpload` page, while the `SAFileUpUpload` page will save the file as `uploadtest.txt` in a folder called uploads.

2. Create the uploads folder and give it Read, Write, and Delete NTFS permissions for the anonymous or authenticated user so that SAFileUp will be able to write files in that directory. You can do this by selecting the properties of the Internet Explorer folder on your hard-drive and selecting Web Sharing and Share this Folder. You also need to set the share name to whatever is specified in the SAFileUp path /Uploads and set the permissions to Read and Scripts. Be careful not to select Execute here, as this would let people run programs directly on your server.

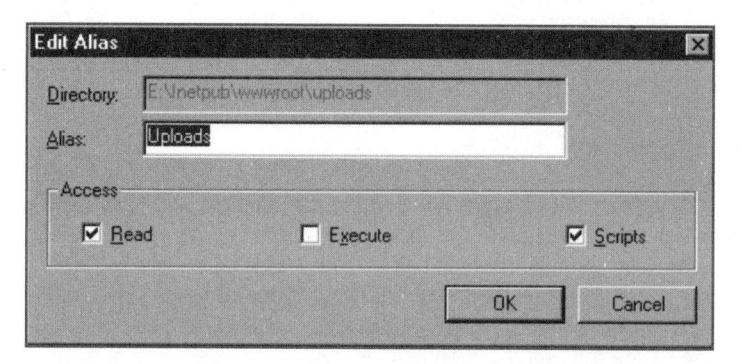

3. You're now ready to test the pages, so choose a file to upload and click Submit:

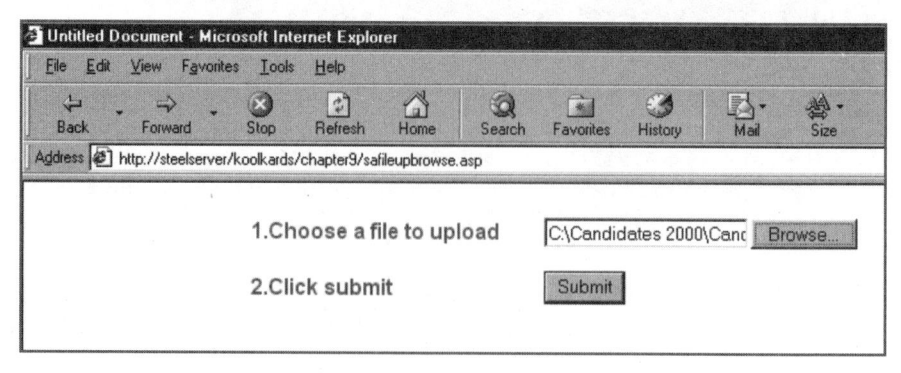

4. The file is then uploaded to the server on page 2. You can see how our page has renamed the file to upload.txt and placed it in the /uploads folder on the server.

E-mail in UltraDev

5. Let's have a look at the code on the second page that actually performed the file uploading:

   ```
   <% Set upl =
   Server.CreateObject("SoftArtisans.FileUp")
   upl.Path = Server.Mappath ("/uploads")
   upl.SaveAs "UPLOADTEST.txt"%>
   ```

6. Three tiny lines is all that was needed to perform a simple upload. That's the beauty of **COM** objects; they take all the processing power away form the page itself. Of course, in our example we can only upload one file at a time because it renames our file, but there's a myriad of options you can develop for use with your SAFileUp component. These include unique renaming and don't overwrite if exists options as well as multiple uploads on a page and a funky progress bar.

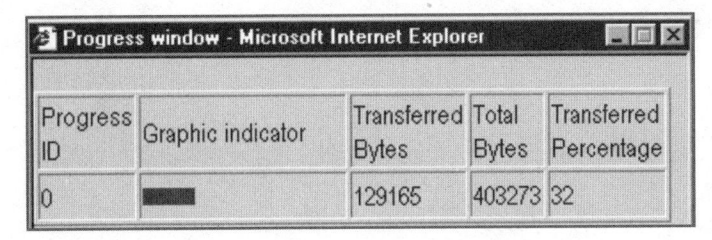

Progress ID	Graphic indicator	Transferred Bytes	Total Bytes	Transferred Percentage
0	▬	129165	403273	32

Summary

In this chapter we've given you some real world examples of both e-mail and sending files, but there are many more uses for them. As you start to build more dynamic web applications, you'll come across ways of using automated e-mail again and again. From the obvious Hot Products sales letter, simple upload your CV to us options through to complex intranet document and file management systems, the principals remain the same.

We've learned that:

- Nifty pieces of code can allow us to pre-enter parts of an e-mail in a standard HTML `mailto:` field

- CDOmail allows you to send forms and feedback information, made easier by UltraDev's extensibility

- We can use ASP to upload files to our server from a simple, user-friendly web page.

A good starting point for your interactive web applications...

koolkards

12 Server Behaviors

What we'll cover in this chapter:

- How to create our own **server behaviors**
- How to **package** these server behaviors so others can use them
- How to include our server behaviors into **UltraDev menus**

Foundation Dreamweaver UltraDev 4

Throughout our guided tour of UltraDev, we've been making good use of the in-built server behaviors and we've also imported some that we wrote especially for you. You may have wondered how these server behaviors work and what lies behind them, or even how easy it is to create your own. Well, you're about to find out.

A **server behavior** is a pre-written script that generates code on our page after asking for certain bits of information. That code then performs a function for us, like prompting a login or planting a cookie.

In a simple example, a server behavior might ask for your name and write the code `Response.write("Spencer Steel")` to the page after you clicked OK. Obviously there are more complex behaviors, but the principles remain the same. There are certain properties that the user must provide, and then the code generated is modified to reflect your property settings.

To edit or view the code in an existing server behavior, pull up the Server Behavior panel from any of your pages and drop the menu down to Edit Server Behaviors. Select it and you'll get a list of the server behaviors for each server model.

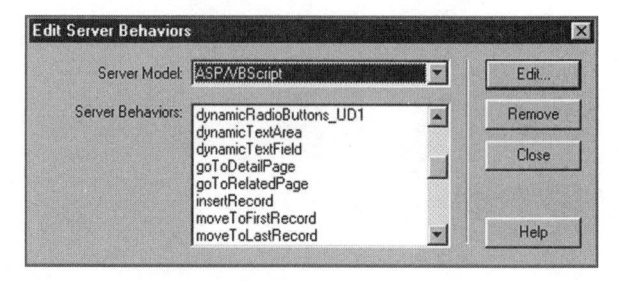

UltraDev supports multiple server models, so the author of the code has to specify which server model the behavior is for, although some behaviors are cross-platform and will work with all models. The ASP/VBScript model that we've been using is currently the most popular choice but there's a wealth of behaviors written for other models.

If you select the Newsletter behavior we used in chapter 11 and select the Edit button, you'll be taken to the Server Behavior Builder window, where you can see the code in the Code Block window.

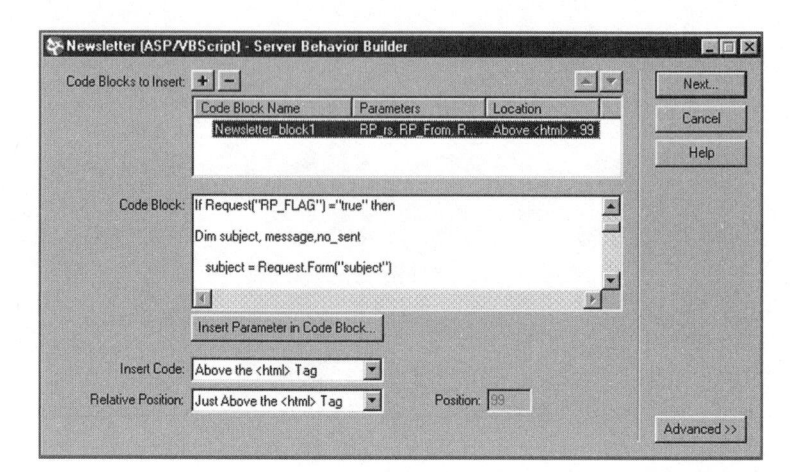

Server Behaviors

The Newsletter behavior sends a text e-mail to every person in a table of recipients. When we use the behavior, we're asked for four pieces of information:

- Who the mail is from
- Which recordset contains the recipients
- Which field in the recipients table contains the e-mail addresses
- Where to redirect to afterwards.

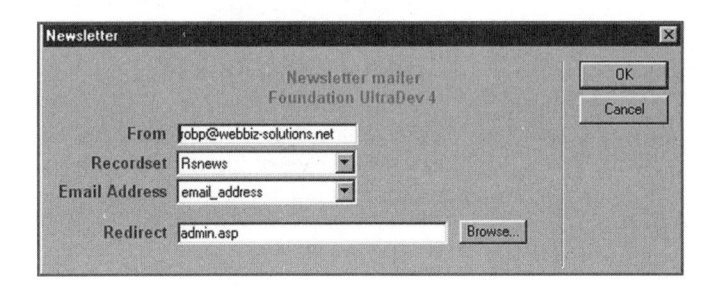

These four pieces of information become parameters in our code:

```
@@RP_from@@
@@RP_rs@@
@@RP_emailaddress@@
@@RP_Redirect@@
```

Armed with these four pieces of information, UltraDev can generate the code needed, replacing all the @@parameters@@ with your values. If you look at the final code generated on the page and compare it to the server behavior code, you'll see that this is exactly what has happened. The code is exactly the same, except it's replaced the @@parameters@@ with the values we entered.

User Interfaces

When we typed those four values into the panel to set up the newsletter behavior, we did so into a fairly standard looking gray window. UltraDev automatically creates a rather ugly pop-up panel when we build a behavior, but we can make these look a whole lot nicer.

Open Windows Explorer, find your Macromedia Folder and drill down to Dreamweaver UltraDev4\Configuration\ServerBehaviors\ASP. You'll see some HTM files that are effectively the pop-up panels from our behavior. Right-click on the newsletter.htm file, choose Edit with UltraDev and you'll be able to change the look and feel of the pop-up in UltraDev.

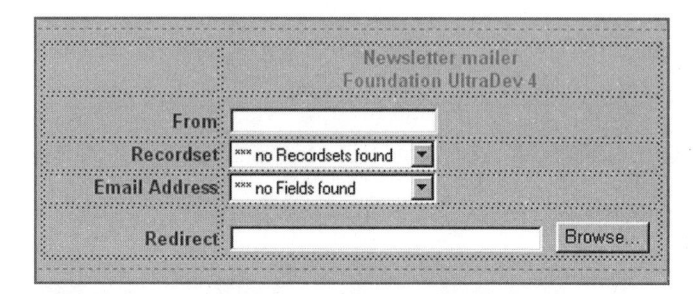

If you go to Dreamweaver UltraDev 4\Configuration\ExtensionData you'll find the blocks of compiled XML code used in a behavior. These XML files contain lots of clever code and the search pattern used to see if there's a behavior on your page already. Don't forget where these files are kept, because once we've finished making our server behavior we need to find the files we create in order to put them in a special UltraDev packaged file in order for others to use it.

Creating your own Server Behaviors

Let's create our own server behavior. Well actually, let's create two complementary behaviors, one to write text to a text file and another to read text from a file and display it as HTML. Our server behavior is quite a complicated and powerful one, and one that we're asked for often.

We don't expect you to understand all of the code. It's not that long but is a lot more complex than we've seen so far. We've offered a brief explanation so that you can see roughly what's happening but if you don't get it, don't worry because the point here is how we go about building the server behavior. Once done, you'll easily be able to apply the same principles to your more simple Response.Write type behaviors, as well as having a useful set of behaviors to use whenever you want.

Imagine a web site with a Daily News section maintained by a manager with admin rights. Rather than updating the HTML news page every day or creating a database file, we're going to create a simple form with a multi-line text box for our manager to enter today's news into. Once the manager has entered the news and clicked OK, a plain text file will be created on the web server with their text.

Unfortunately, this is another exercise where we need IIS for things to work. If you're using PWS, it's still worth looking at the exercise to see how it's done. As we said in the last chapter, you're extremely unlikely to end up using a server with PWS to host your site, even if you're stuck with it while you're learning UltraDev.

Server Behaviors 12

Creating a Server Behavior

1. Make sure the user has the necessary permissions to write to a file in your web space folder. If you're using an NT Web Server, check with your system administrator. If you're using IIS and you have access to the administration screen you can set the permissions yourself. Go into the MMC (Microsoft Management Console) for IIS and expand the folders until you find chapter12. Right-click and select Properties, and check the Write box. (If you have problems, right-click Default Web Site in the left-hand IIS pane and select All Tasks > Permissions Wizard.):

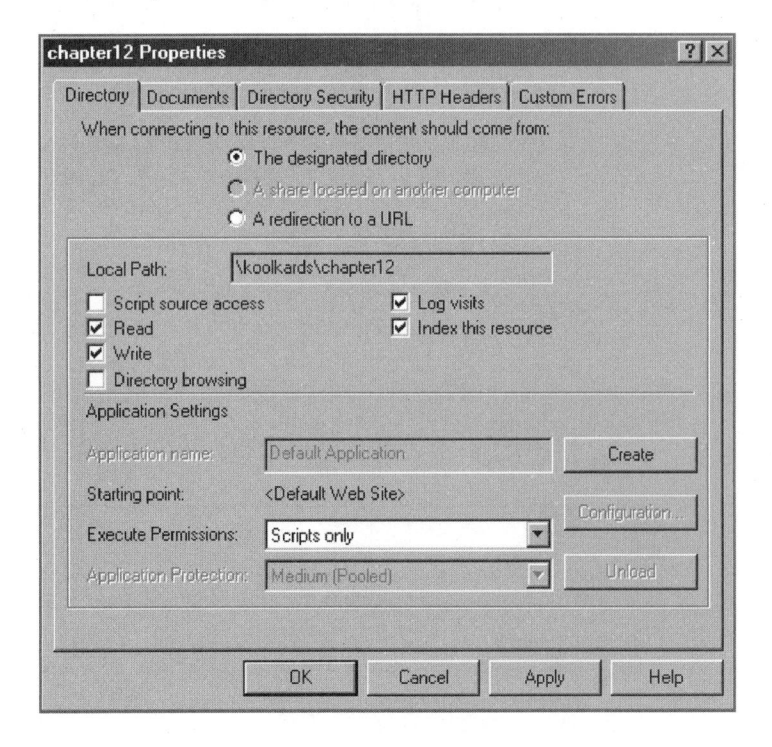

   Before we can create any server behaviors, we need to write some good, solid code and test it. Once we're happy that it's robust and it's working, we can put it into our server behavior.

2. Open a new page and save it as Write_Text_Test.asp. We're going to create and test our initial code here.

3. We now have to enter some code into the top of our page, above the <html> tag. To write to a text file, we need to introduce you to the

`FileSystemObject` and `TextStream` object. As with all objects, you must first create an instance of the `FileSystemObject`:

```
<% 'Write to a text file test

Set MyfileObject=Server.CreateObject("Scripting.File
➥ SystemObject")
```

4. Next, we need to call the `CreateTextFile()` method of the `FilesystemObject` to return an instance of a `TextStream` object. We've included the full path to the text file, so if you have your KoolKards folder in another location, change the path to suit:

```
SetMyTextFile=MyFileObject.CreateTextFile("c:\inetpub
\wwwroot\koolkards\chapter12\write.txt")
```

5. The most important part is to write some text to the file, which is done using the `WriteLine()` method of the `TextStream` object:

```
MyTextFile.WriteLine("This is my first time writing
➥ to a text file")
```

6. As with all good coding practices we need to tidy up:

```
MyTextFile.Close

%>
```

```
1  <% 'Write to a text file test
2
3  Set MyfileObject=Server.CreateObject("Scripting.FileSystemObject")
4  Set MyTextFile=MyFileObject.CreateTextFile("c:\Inetpub\wwwroot\KoolKards\chapter12\write.txt")
5  MyTextFile.WriteLine("This is my first time writing to a text file")
6  MyTextFile.Close
7
8  %>
```

You're probably wondering what has hit you after that. We've included a description of the code for you to see roughly what's going on, because as we said at the beginning of this exercise, the point here is that you see how to create a server behavior. Any bit of the code that you might understand is a bonus.

Server Behaviors

7. Run the page and then go and have a look in your chapter12 directory. You should see a text file called write.txt. If this didn't work, check that the folder path is correct in the second line of your code. If it's wrong, write.txt is probably lurking somewhere else on your hard-drive. Secondly, check the permissions on the folder; do you have the *write* permissions for that directory?

   If this behavior was used on another page, both the destination of the file and the actual text would change. We need two variables to hold these values so that we can change them in our behavior. One variable will hold the name of the multi-line text box (we'll call this @@TextField@@) and one will hold the path to the directory and the name of the file you wish to write the text to (we'll call this @@path@@).

   Our behavior will look something like a box into which we can type our text and hit a Submit button to upload the text to an appropriate folder when we've finished typing. Therefore, we'll need to have two separate blocks of code – one to write the main server-side code and the other to place a hidden field in the form so that we can check when the page has been submitted.

8. Open the Server Behavior panel and select New Server Behavior:

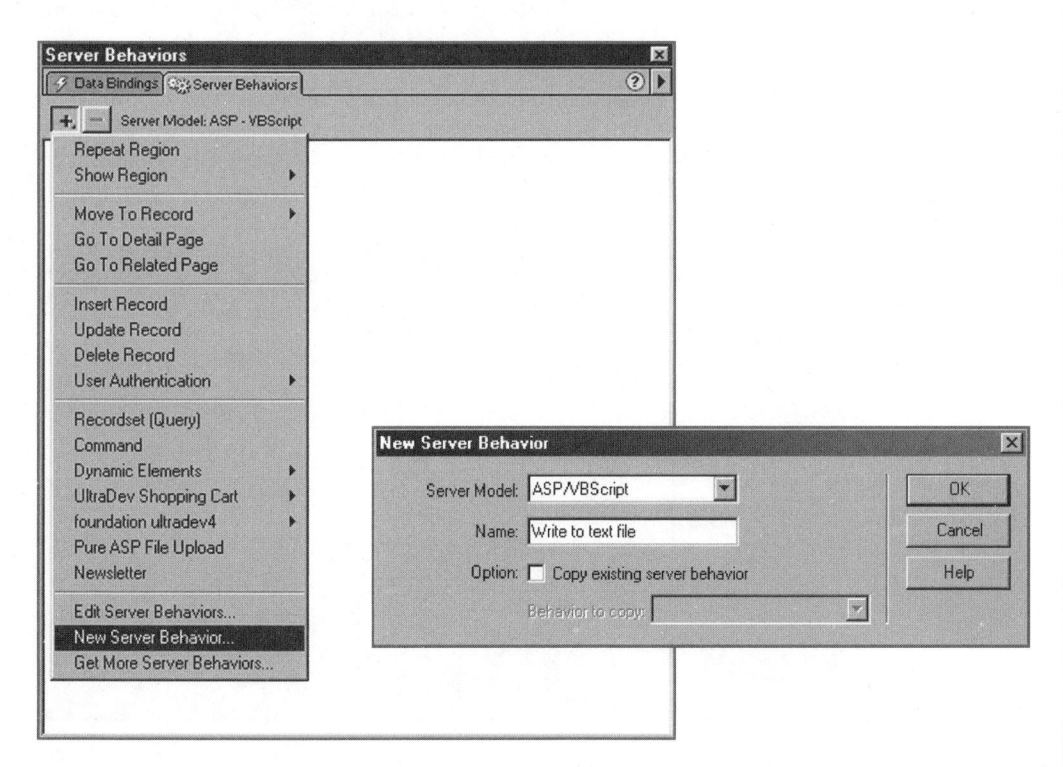

331

9. Select the server model you're using and call your extension Write to text file; click OK and the Server Behavior Builder window will appear:

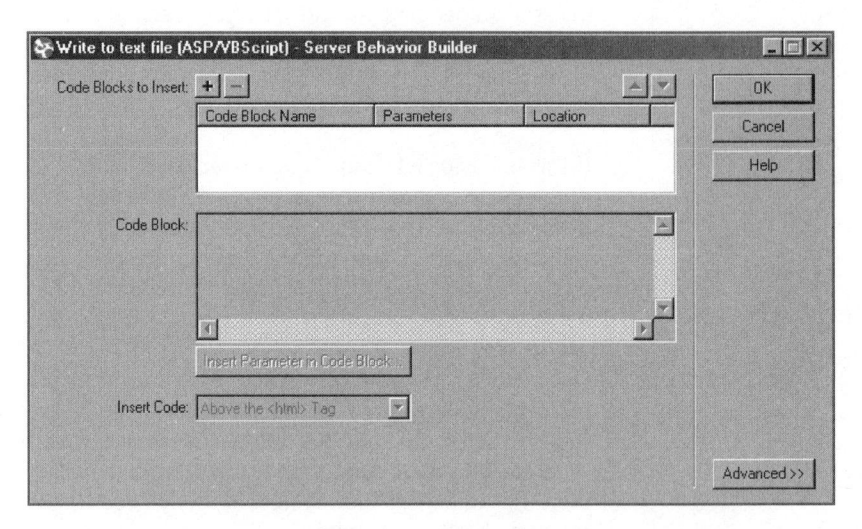

10. Click the + symbol next to Code Blocks to Insert. This will launch the Create a New Code Block panel. Macromedia use a naming convention of NameofBehavior_NameOfBlock so, as we're going to initialize our variables in the first block of code, call it Write to text file.ini.

11. We need to add the code that performs the text write to the Code Block part of the Server Behavior Builder. We can cut and paste the code that we wrote and checked earlier into this and then change it to take care of the parameters:

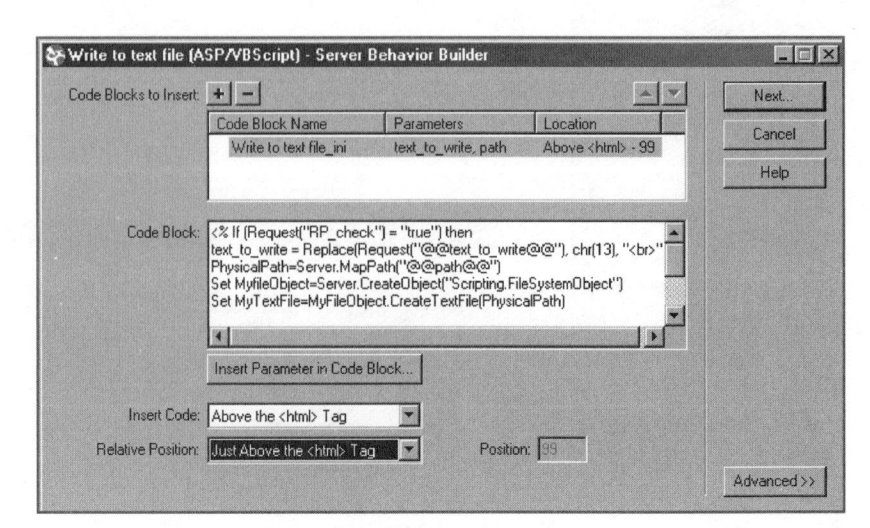

Server Behaviors 12

12. Here's the code you'll need to add, with the parameters in bold:

    ```
    <% If (Request("RP_check") = "true") then
    text_to_write = Replace(Request("@@text_to_write@@"),
    ➥ chr(13), "<br>")
    PhysicalPath=Server.MapPath("@@path@@")
    Set
    MyfileObject=Server.CreateObject("Scripting.FileSystem
    ➥ Object")
    Set
    MyTextFile=MyFileObject.CreateTextFile(PhysicalPath)
    MyTextFile.WriteLine(text_to_write)
    MyTextFile.Close
    end if %>
    ```

13. With the first block of code complete, we need to tell the behavior builder where to position the code on our ASP page. Under the Code Block window, you've got the option to select where to Insert Code. We want this behavior to run before any other behaviors, so select Beginning of the File.

> *UltraDev assigns weights to its code, with 1 at the top and 99 at the bottom of any given page. Whenever you place a recordset on your page, UltraDev will place the code block directly in the middle at 50. You'll notice the weight change to 1 when you select **The Beginning of the File**.*

14. Time to insert the second code block. Click the + button and insert a new code block called Write text to file_check.

15. Place this code into the code block. Delete the <% %> markers, as this is HTML and not ASP:

    ```
    <input type="hidden" name="RP_check" value="true">
    ```

Foundation Dreamweaver UltraDev 4

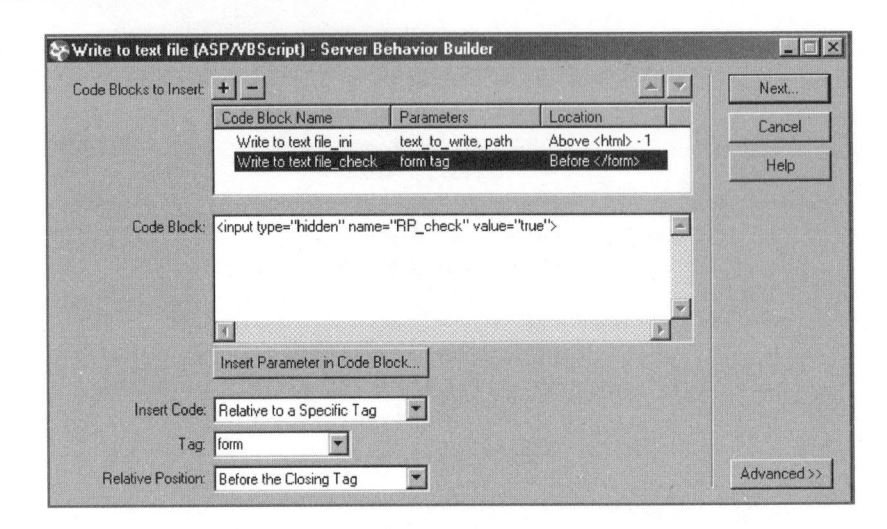

16. At the bottom of the Server Behavior Builder panel, set the Insert Code box to Relative to a Specific Tag, the Tag to form and the Relative Position to Before the Closing Tag. We're creating a hidden element on any page where this behavior is applied. This means that we can use the same method that we've used before to detect when the page is submitted.

17. Press the Next button, and the Generate Behavior Dialog Box will appear. UltraDev has read through our code and realized that there are three @@parameters@@ in it, so it loads the Generate Behavior Dialog Box to let us specify how the user will input these parameters. Pretty clever stuff, really.

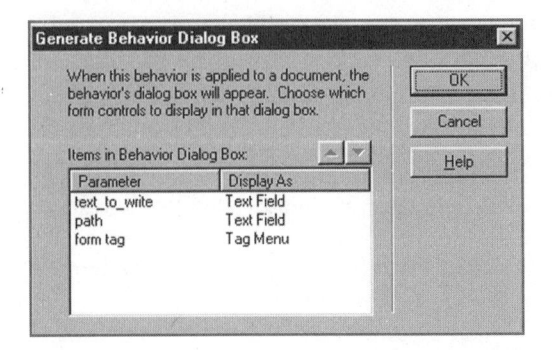

18. Here, you can change the order in which the parameters will appear on your behavior as well as choosing what type of form the user will use to apply your parameters. The one we need to change is the path. Getting users to type something like //myserver/mysite/uploads can be

Server Behaviors

a bit of nightmare. It's far nicer to have a Browse option than a plain text field, so change the Display As next to path to URL Text Field and click OK.

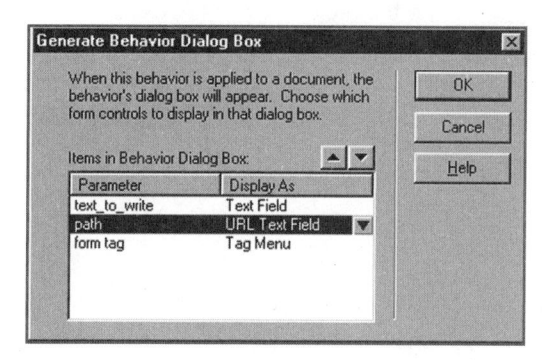

It's taken a while, but your server behavior is now complete and ready to use. Well done!

19. Test your new behavior out by creating a new blank page, dropping in a multi-page text box, and adding a Submit button before applying your shiny new behavior:

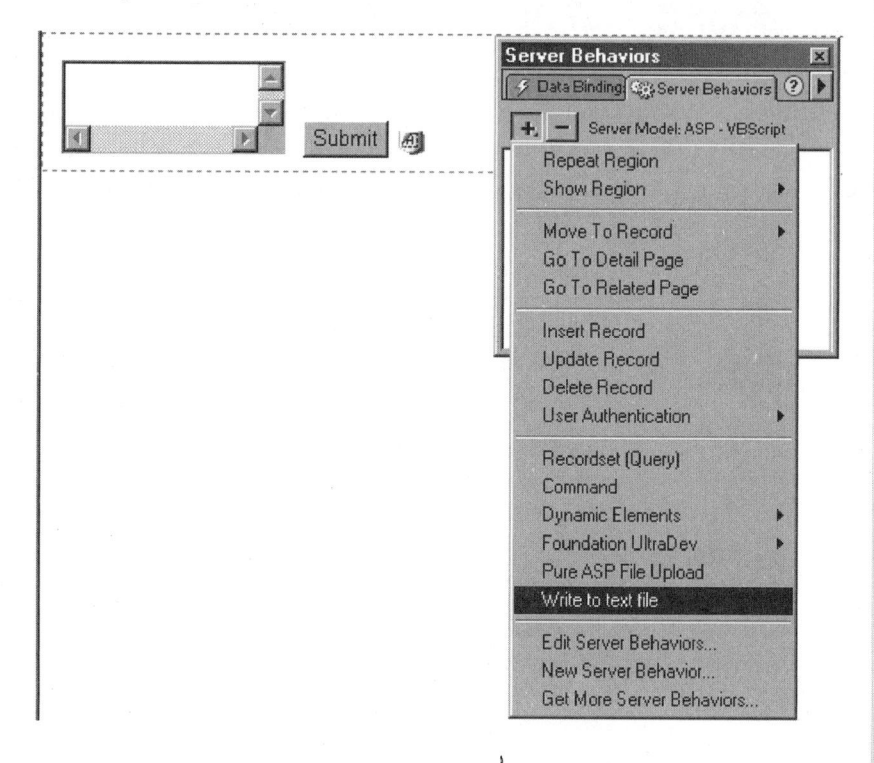

20. Fill the properties that we need into the Write to text file panel.;text_to_write needs to be the name of the multi-line text box on our form (textfield, unless you re-named it), The path is the URL path to the file called `write.txt` in your chapter12 folder (you'll remember assigning this Write *rights* earlier):

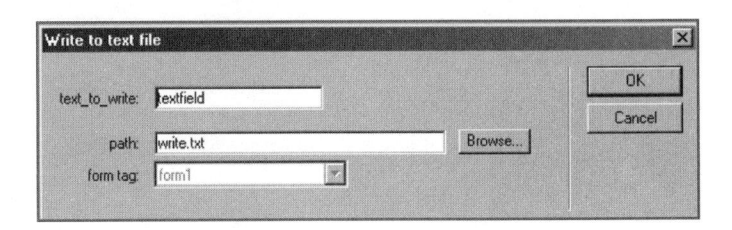

![Write to text file dialog with text_to_write: textfield, path: write.txt, form tag: form1]

21. Click OK and test the page.

    Our user can now enter text in any form and send it to the virtual path. Now we need to create a behavior that will display our text file on any given page.

Reading and Displaying a Text File

1. Create a new page and save it as `Read_Text_Test.asp`. Again, we're going to make sure that the code works before starting work on the server behavior. We don't expect you to understand all the code, but see if you can follow what's going on.

2. Open the Code View and get ready to enter some code. On the first line, we set a variable called `PhysicalPath` to the path of the file we want to read:

    ```
    <%
    PhysicalPath=Server.MapPath("write.txt")
    ```

3. Then we set a variable called `MyFileObject` to a new `FileSystemObject`:

    ```
    Set MyFileObject=Server.CreateObject("Scripting.FileSystem
    ➥ Object")
    ```

Server Behaviors   12

4. Next, we create a final variable `MyTextFile` to the `OpenTextFile` method of our `TextStream` object:

   ```
   Set MyTextFile=MyFileObject.OpenTextFile(PhysicalPath)
   ```

5. We use the `Readline` method of the `TextStream` object to read each line, and wrap everything up in a conditional WHILE/WEND loop until we reach the end of the text file:

   ```
   WHILE NOT MyTextFile.AtEndOfStream
        Response.Write(MyTextFile.ReadLine)
   WEND
   ```

6. Finally, we close the object:

   ```
   MyTextFile.Close
   %>
   ```

7. Test your page and you should see your text page being displayed as HTML. If you get an error, check your path. A slight misspelling in the folder name will make sure that the page doesn't find your text file.

   It's time to change the code into a server behavior that will read any text file. This behavior will be slightly easier than the first one. We're going to follow the steps we used to create the first behavior, but we're only creating one block of code this time.

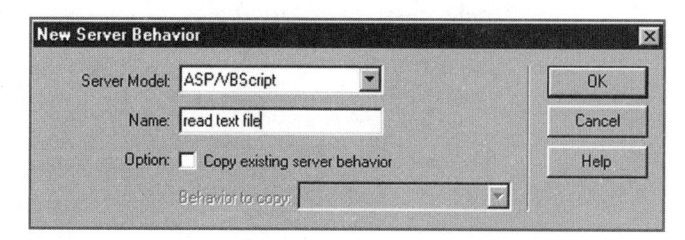

   New Server Behavior
   - Server Model: ASP/VBScript
   - Name: read text file
   - Option: ☐ Copy existing server behavior
   - Behavior to copy:
   - [OK] [Cancel] [Help]

8. Create a new server behavior and enter this code into the first code block:

   ```
   <%
   PhysicalPath=Server.MapPath("@@path@@")
   Set MyFileObject=Server.CreateObject("Scripting.File
   ➥ SystemObject")
   Set MyTextFile=MyFileObject.OpenTextFile(PhysicalPath)
   WHILE NOT MyTextFile.AtEndOfStream
        Response.Write(MyTextFile.ReadLine)
   ```

```
WEND
MyTextFile.Close
%>
```

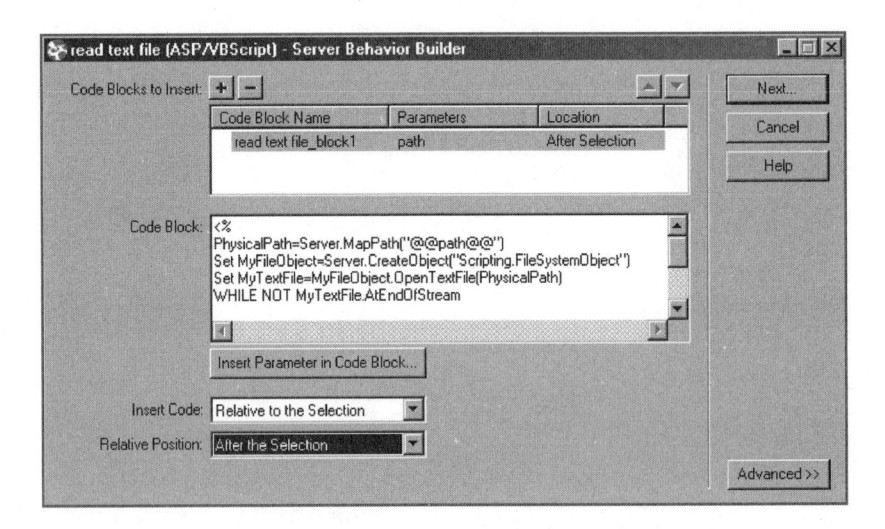

9. Set Insert Code to Relative to the Selection and the Relative Position to After the Selection. The selection is defined as the position of the cursor when you apply the behavior, so this allows the behavior to be applied anywhere on the page.

10. Click Next and the properties input method will be displayed. There's only one this time, for the path to the text field. As before, set the path to Display As a URL Text Field:

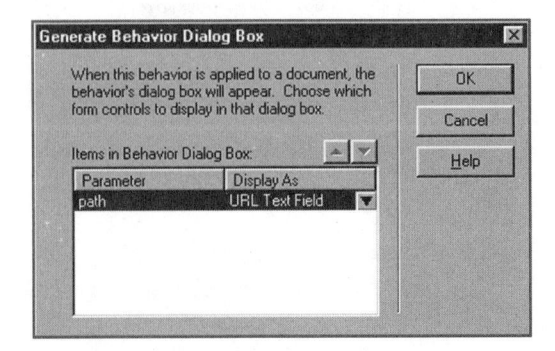

11. Click OK and we've finished with the server behavior. Create another page called Read_Text_File.asp, and drag the server behavior onto

Server Behaviors 12

it. You'll notice that you get a little ASP marker where you place the behavior:

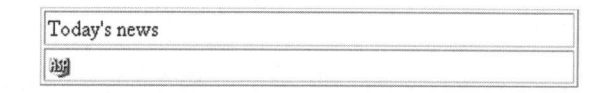

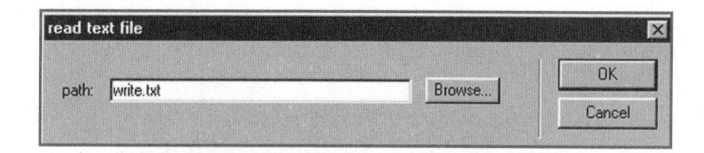

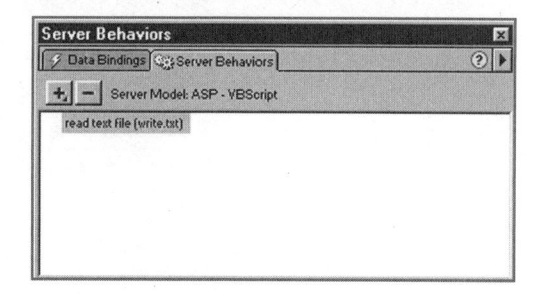

Making it Look Pretty

You're probably thinking that our server behaviors look pretty horrible. As we saw at the beginning of the chapter, the look of our behavior is controlled by an HTML document. Use UltraDev to open the `Write to text file.htm` document from:

//Macromedia/DreamweaverUltraDev
➥ 4/Configuration/ServerBehaviors/ASP/Write to text file.htm

You can now use UltraDev's tools to make the window look better. In the example, we've changed the labels so they are more understandable, changed the font and the colors, made all the edit boxes the same width, and even added a graphic. You can play around and add your own touches.

Packing up Server Behaviors

Once you've created your behavior, if you want to share the file with anyone else, you'll need to pack it up into a single MXI (pronounced 'mixey') file. This used to be a bit of a nightmare, but fortunately some very nice people at www.publicdomain.co.uk have helped everyone out by creating a MXI File Creator program which takes away a lot of the technical knowledge required to make your own server behaviors.

Foundation Dreamweaver UltraDev 4

We have included this file in the chapter12 download but you can also find it at www.publicdomain.co.uk (under Development > Dreamweaver > Available Extensions) and the Macromedia Exchange site at www.macromedia.com/exchange/ultradev (do a search for MXI File Creator Packager).

Once downloaded, the MXI File Creator Packager is installed just like any other server behavior. Unlike most behaviors that we've seen, it appears under the Command menu because it isn't specific to any action or page object like other behaviors. Now that we've written and tested them, let's use this to package up our server behaviors.

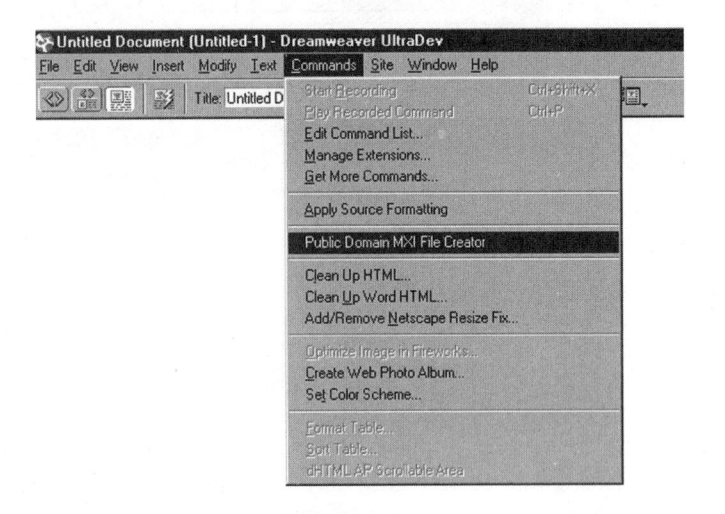

Packing up our Behaviors

1. The first time you open the creator, you'll be asked to enter the defaults for your program. Just type your name in as the author and leave the rest as they are. Should you ever wish to go back to this screen, you can choose Config from the buttons on the right-hand panel of the creator. After selecting your settings, the program will launch.

2. The first thing you will notice is that by default, the Products drop-down box is set to Dreamweaver 3. You can drop down this list to see the entire product list and you'll see that this package creator can create add-ins for a variety of Macromedia products. Set it to Dreamweaver 4, and make sure that you select this as a Primary platform and as Required:

Server Behaviors 12

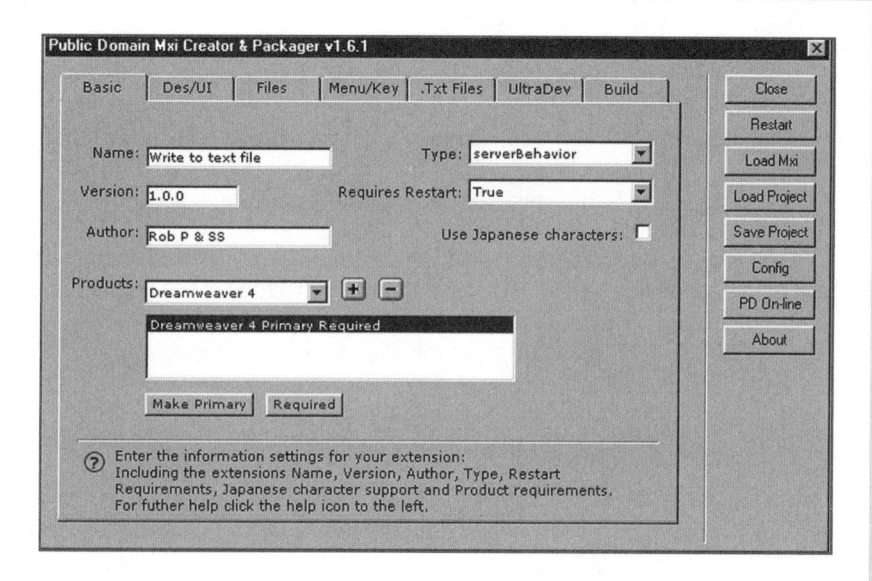

3. If you look at the type, you'll see that it's set to ActionScript (Flash's scripting language) at first, as it's the first in an alphabetical list of add-ins that we can create with the MXI file creator. Set it to serverBehavior instead:

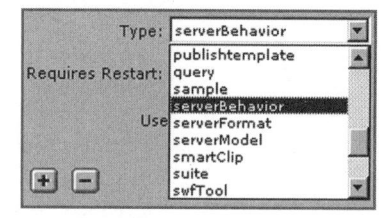

4. Move onto the second tab DES/UI (Description and User Interface). Both of these are instructions that appear when a user installs your behavior. Enter some descriptive text under description. We've gone for the prosaic:

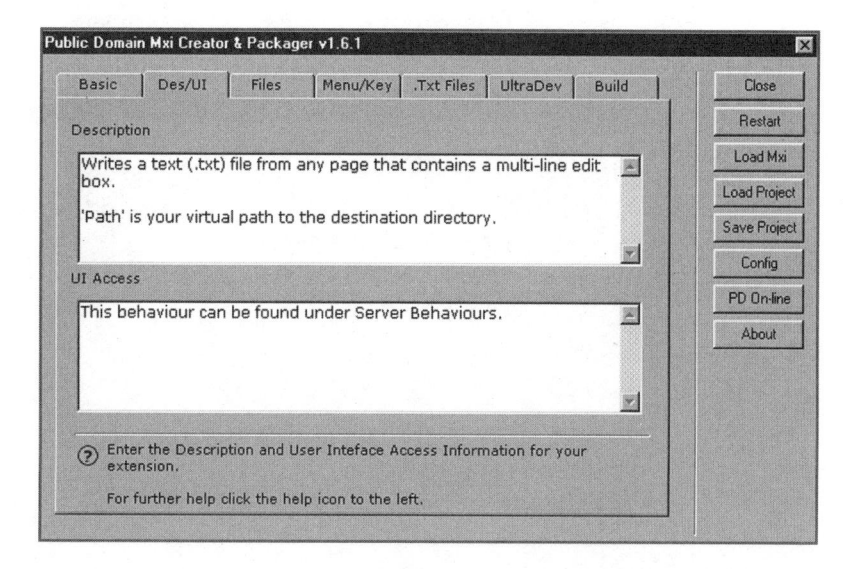

Writes a text (.txt) file from any page that contains a multi-line edit box. 'Path' is your virtual path to the destination directory.

Then describe how your user can access the behavior, in this case:

This behavior can be found under Server Behaviors.

We need to add the all-important files that were created when we built the behavior. During the quick tour at the beginning of this chapter, we saw that there were a number of HTML and XML files generated that make up our individual server behaviors.

5. Click on the Files tab, ignore the File Token section and click the Add File button, which will bring up a separate panel:

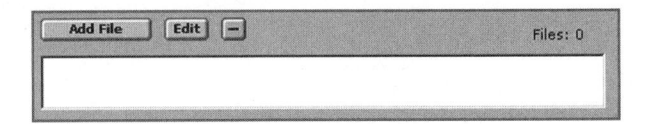

We need to specify the source of each file, and the destination. In our examples, both the source and the destination will be the same path.

6. Find the first file we need, which is the Write to text file.htm in:

    //Macromedia/Dreamweaver UltraDev
    ➥ 4/Configuration/ServerBehaviors/ASP/**Write to text file.htm**

7. For the destination, you need to select the same folder as the file came from:

    //Macromedia/Dreamweaver UltraDev
    ➥ 4/Configuration/ServerBehaviors/ASP/

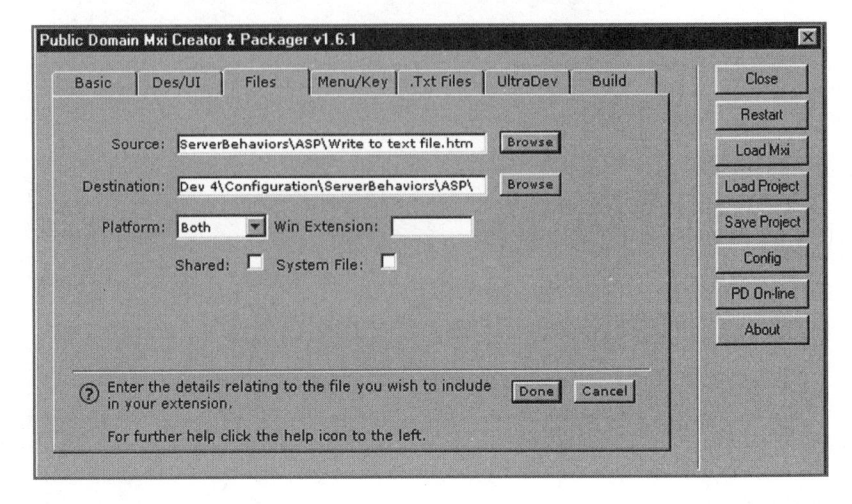

Server Behaviors

8. Once you've completed that, click Done.

9. Repeat this step, and add the following files. You'll need to specify the same destination as before.

   //Macromedia/Dreamweaver UltraDev
   ↪ 4/Configuration/ExtensionData/**Write to text file.xml**

   //Macromedia/Dreamweaver UltraDev
   ↪ 4/Configuration/ExtensionData/**Write to text file_check.xml**

   //Macromedia/Dreamweaver UltraDev
   ↪ 4/Configuration/ExtensionData/**Write to text file_init.xml**

   Once completed, you should have four files.

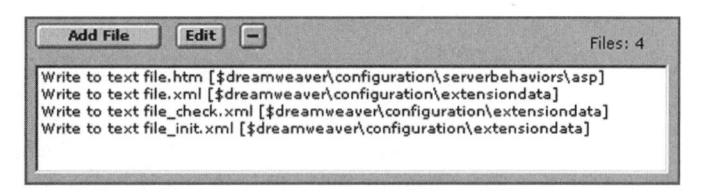

10. We're ready to pack our extension. There are other options we can use but we're going to keep it simple, so move to the Build tab and give your final MXI file a name and an output directory for you to save the finished product to:

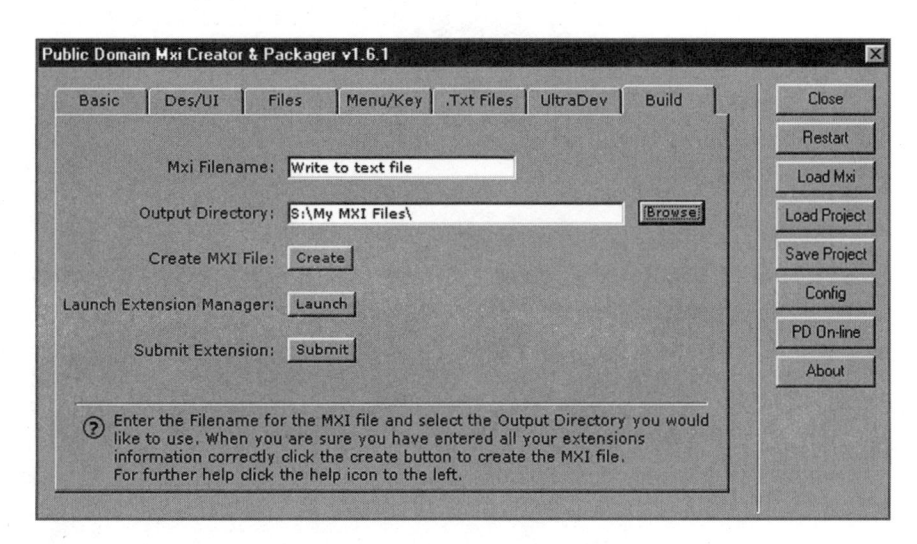

Foundation Dreamweaver UltraDev 4

> You can save your project at any time with the Save Project button on the right-hand side. If you were halfway through creating a complex MXI package, this could be very useful.

11. Click on the Create MXI File button, and you'll be presented with a window that reads something like: Files successfully copied to stage area [your File path] Successfully Created Would you like to launch Packager? We don't want to launch anything at the moment, so click Cancel and then Close the MXI packager. Occasionally this operation will bring up an error, but just ignore it.

12. Exit UltraDev completely, find your MXI folder and open it. You'll see all the individual files listed, as well as a new `Write to text file.mxi` file.

    Now we have all the files and components in one place, we need to launch the final packager, which turns a MXI file into a one-click install MXP file.

13. Double-click your MXI file to launch the packager. The Extension Manager will be launched. Accept the disclaimer, and select the MXI file you wish to package when asked (the program doesn't remember which MXI file you double-clicked in the first place, so you have to specify it all over again):

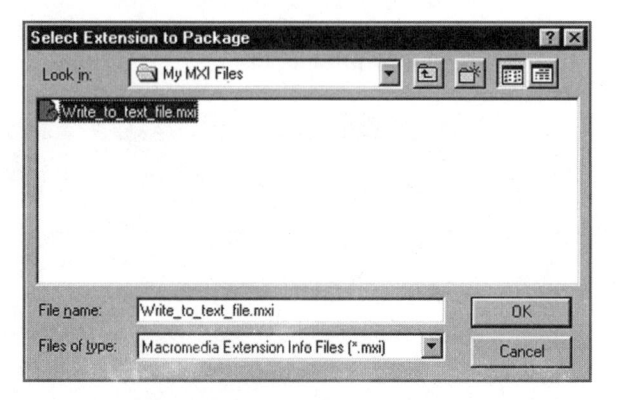

14. Click OK and you'll be asked for a place to save the completed MXP file. Keep the directory the same, click OK again and that's it.

Server Behaviors 12

15. Although the MXP file has been created for you, it's not installed. Close down all your programs again and let's install our new server behavior as if you were a new user.

16. Find your new `Write_to_text_file.mxp` file in Windows Explorer and double-click it. The Extension Manager will launch and install your new file. You'll now be able to see your new server behavior listed in the Extension Manager. You can even see the instructions that we entered earlier showing in the bottom split-screen:

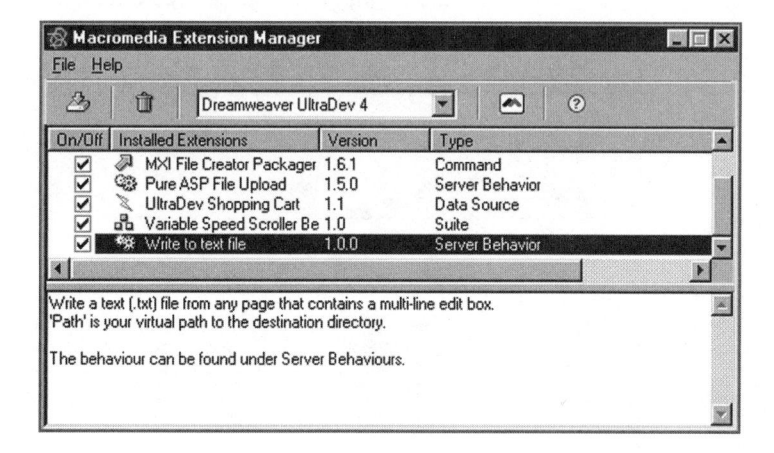

17. Re-open UltraDev and create a new page. Drop a new multi-line box on the page, create a form, and then go to Server Behaviors. Your new behavior should now be fully operational.

Now that we've packed up one behavior, let's do it all again with our second read from text file behavior. This time, we'll add our behavior as a menu item within UltraDev.

Packing and Adding a Menu Item

1. From any page in UltraDev open your MXI Creator again.

2. Call your server behavior read text file, make sure it's a Server Behavior and set the Product setting.

3. Move to the Des/UI tab and enter a description, as we did last time.

4. Move to the Files menu and include the following files, setting the destination to the same folder they came from each time:

//Macromedia/Dreamweaver UltraDev
➥ 4/Configuration/ServerBehaviors/ASP/read text file.htm

//Macromedia/Dreamweaver UltraDev 4/Configuration/ExtensionData/read
➥ text file.xml

//Macromedia/Dreamweaver UltraDev 4/Configuration/ExtensionData/read
➥ text file_block1.xml

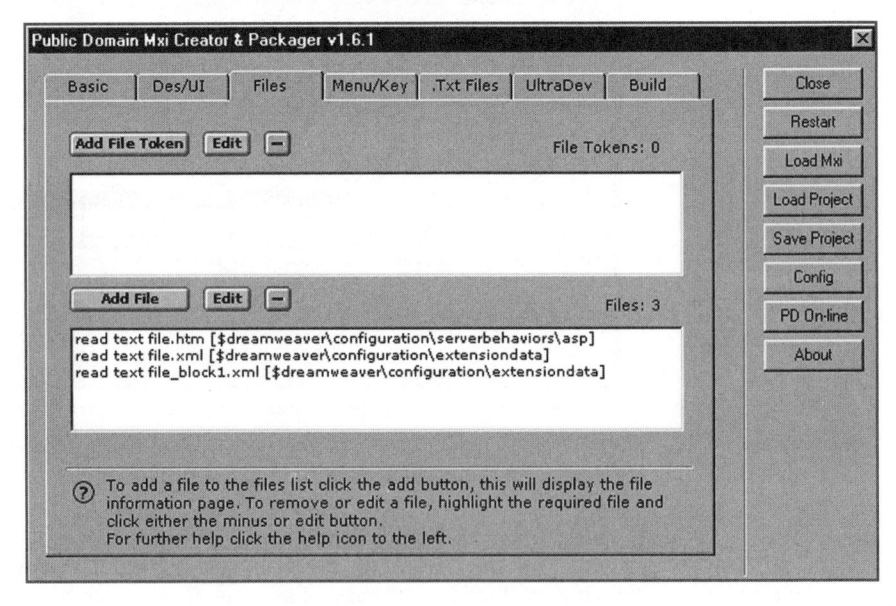

5. Switch to the Menu/Key tab and choose the middle option Add Menu Item. We're going to add a menu option to the Command menu like the one you used to launch the MXI creator:

Server Behaviors   12

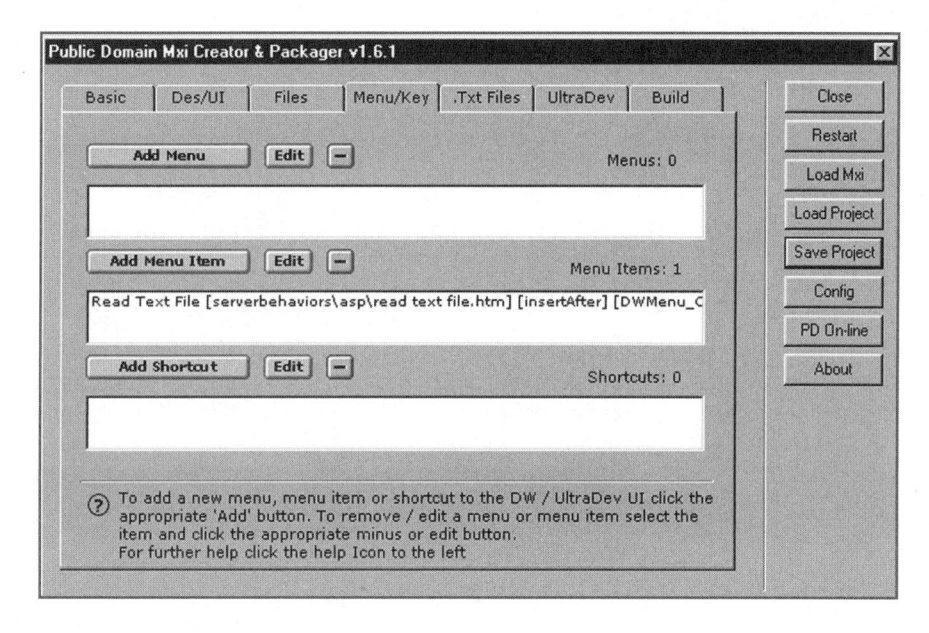

6. Give your menu item the name Read Text File and make sure that you check the Insert Separator before and after check boxes to split the menu item on the Command menu:

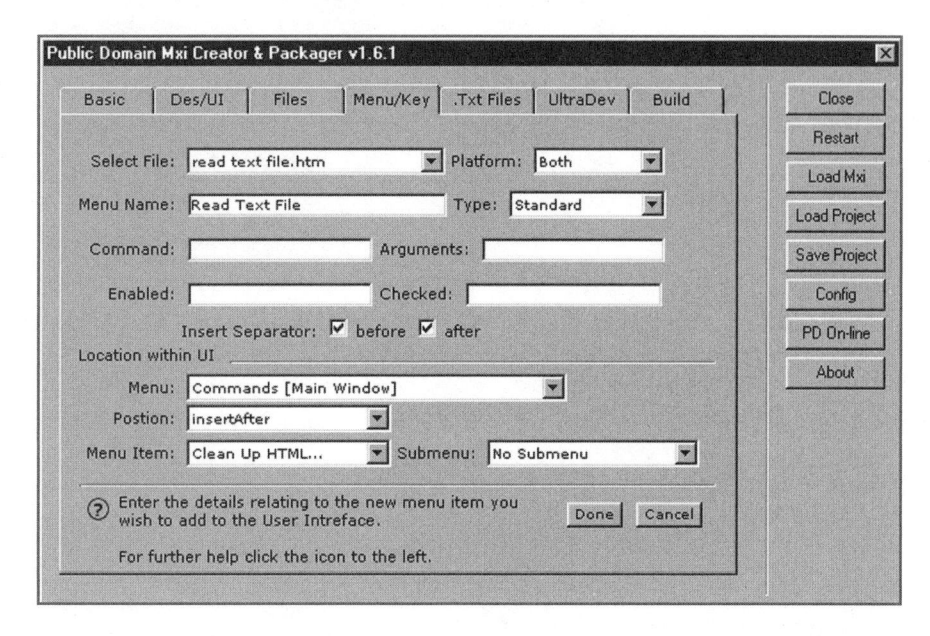

7. The bottom location within UI section tells the creator which menu you want to use and where you want it placed. Select Commands [Main

Window] under Menu:. We've chosen to insertAfter the Clean Up HTML option but you can choose wherever you want.

8. Click Done and go to the End Build option. Save your project and create the MXI file.

9. You should remember the routine from last time. Close down everything, double-click the file, convert it into an MXP file and then install the MXP file.

10. Re-launch UltraDev, open any page and when you look at the Command menu, you'll see the menu item that launches our Read Text File server behavior.

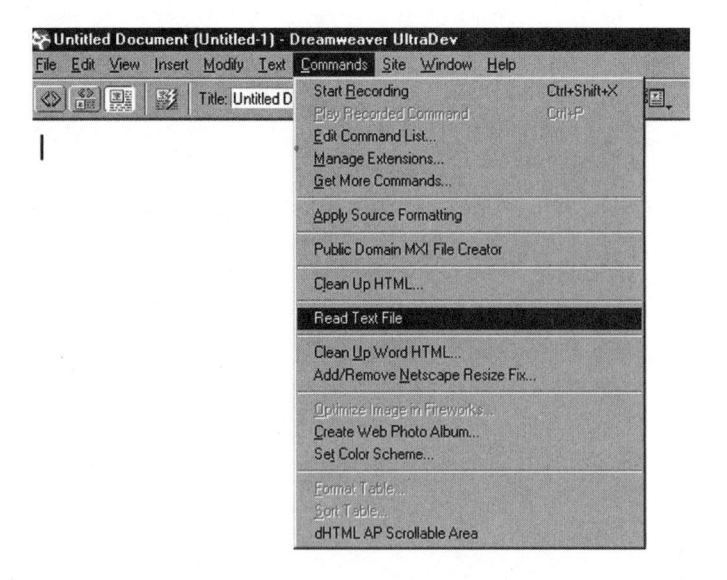

We've looked at creating a simple menu item here, but you can really go to town and add lots of complex embedded menu items. You can even create your own menu to cascade into your custom behaviors.

Server Behaviors

Summary

We're almost at the end of our UltraDev journey. In this chapter we've looked at:

- How to make our own server behaviors

- How to package these server behaviors up so that the whole world can benefit from our genius

- How to include these server behaviors in UltraDev menus for easy access

There's much, much more you can do with the MXI Creator package, but we hope we've got you started. For more information and help on the MXI Package Creator, click the PD Online button on the right-hand side of the Creator.

Building and sharing server behaviors can be fun and there are plenty of news groups out there for novices and experts to share information and behavior.

Many server behaviors are just three or four lines long, but they can be just as valuable and useful as the shopping cart or the ASPupload behaviors.

kool kards

13 Stored Procedures

What we'll cover in this chapter:

- *An introduction to SQL Server and **stored procedures***
- *Creating an **SQL database***
- ***Creating** stored procedures*
- *Using stored procedures to **enhance** your KoolKards application*

As we've seen over the course of this book, building database queries in ASP is easy with UltraDev.

If you did a search on the Internet for articles on enhancing your ASP pages you would find numerous articles telling you not to embed SQL statements in your ASP page. Why? Well the greater the load on the page, the slower it will run.

This is a typical SQL statement within an ASP page:

```
<%
set rsResults = Server.CreateObject("ADODB.Recordset")
rsResults.ActiveConnection = MM_Koolkards_STRING
rsResults.Source = "Select * from products"
rsResults.CursorType = 0
rsResults.CursorLocation = 2
rsResults.LockType = 3
rsResults.Open()
rsResults_numRows = 0

While ((Repeat1__numRows <> 0) AND (NOT rsartists.EOF))
            ' Display the records
Wend

%>
```

Although this is perfectly acceptable, (it's what UltraDev generates for us) if you want to step up the performance of your pages, you can move the processing of the SQL statement from the page to what's known as a **stored procedure** in SQL Server.

Introducing SQL Server

SQL Server is Microsoft's premium, scalable, high-performance database. Although this may sound like sales talk, what we mean by this is that SQL Server can handle *a lot of work*!

Here's an interesting fact that puts it all in perspective. Access has a **single-thread** SQL processor, which means that if five people all run search queries at the same time, customer five will have to wait until all the others have been processed and returned before their search query will begin. When your site traffic goes up this can be devastating to its performance.

SQL Server is capable of handling many multiple transactions and to further improve the performance, you can put your SQL statements into **stored procedures**. Stored procedures are precompiled SQL statements that live in the SQL Server site, ready for action with a simple call.

Stored Procedures 13

An example of a stored procedure would be a 'search' procedure. We know that our users regularly search under Artist and Occasion. With SQL Server we can move this search statement to a stored procedure.

Once written, our stored procedure is compiled, which effectively makes it even faster. SQL Server will then inherently 'know' what to do when you call a search. All it will require are the two parameters. The performance increase can be impressive to say the least.

Unless you have access to a SQL server then you won't be able to complete the examples in this chapter. However you can download a free 120-day evaluation from http://www.microsoft.com/sql/downloads/default.htm and there are educational licences available.

Compared to Access or similar, SQL Server is an expensive product. However, it is a truly scalable product and if you're developing for a company, or looking to target a large audience, this chapter will give you a good overview. It's amazing how many people do need to make the transition over time. Therefore, it's definitely worth spending some time going through this chapter as, even if it's not totally relevant to you now, it will get you ready for the next big thing.

Why Use Stored Procedures?

If you have a series of SQL statements to execute on multiple ASP pages, you can place all the SQL statements in a stored procedure and execute the procedure instead. This reduces the size of your ASP pages and ensures that the same SQL statements are executed on each page.

Having all your SQL statements in a stored procedure is much more efficient than executing them one at a time on your page. By using stored procedures it reduces the number of trips back and forth between your web server and database.

You gain great flexibility from the fact that you can pass values to and from the procedure. When you execute a set of SQL statements from your ASP page, each SQL statement must be passed individually to your database, a stored procedure passes all your SQL statements in one go, thus reducing the amount of traffic on your network.

Permissions on individual tables can be set so that users can only modify a table if they are using a stored procedure. This adds to the security of your database.

Finally it is possible to execute a stored procedure from within another stored procedure. This makes it possible to build very complex stored procedures.

What are Stored Procedures?

There are a couple of ways you can use stored procedures.

Firstly and most simply, a stored procedure can be used to return a basic recordset in exactly the same way you would write a normal SQL query, using a set of parameters or not. As we said before, this can improve performance.

Secondly, as well as accepting parameters, stored procedures return values back to the page. A stored procedure can return a *static* value directly; this is normally used when you want to perform some sort of check that depends on a value returned from your stored procedure. An example of this may be in a login system where a RETURN value of 1 is generated if this is a valid login, where as if 0 was returned then the login would be treated as invalid.

Finally, stored procedures can output dynamic results, that is, rather than return just a recordset they return values too.

Imagine a stored procedure that calculated the total items of current stock left in your warehouse by taking the total number of items and subtracting the total outstanding stock orders. Here our stored procedure could perform some complex math to arrive at a figure, and then only return this figure to your web page. This way the server is performing heavy calculations based on multiple tables and throwing the result back to a page. Which would be hundreds of times faster than returning all the recordsets to the web page and asking the web page to calculate the totals.

Setting up an SQL Database

Before we can begin creating stored procedures we need to set up our database in SQL Server. This will have to be a quick walk through on setting up a database as it really is beyond the scope of this book to cover every aspect of SQL Server.

What we *are* going to do is look at

- Creating a new database
- Importing our KoolKards data from Access into SQL Server (also known as Upsizing)
- Creating and using some stored procedures

This chapter uses SQL Server 7.0. If you have another version, you may find that your screenshots differ slightly.

Stored Procedures 13

Creating a New Database

1. Open Enterprise Manager. Enterprise Manager is the GUI console for managing the server & database objects, a bit like your main Access window but more powerful.

2. Expand the tree until you find the Databases folder. Right-click on the folder and select New Database:

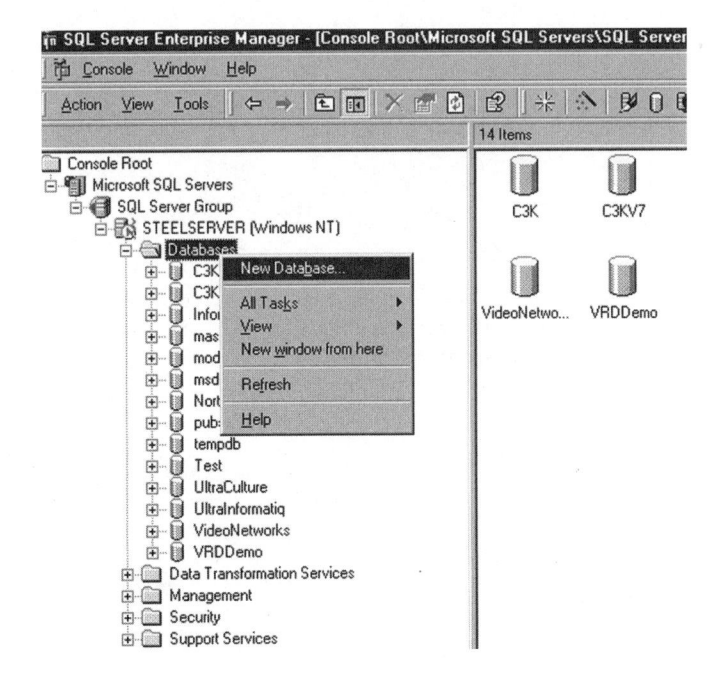

3. Type the name of the database into the window provided. Everything else you just accept.

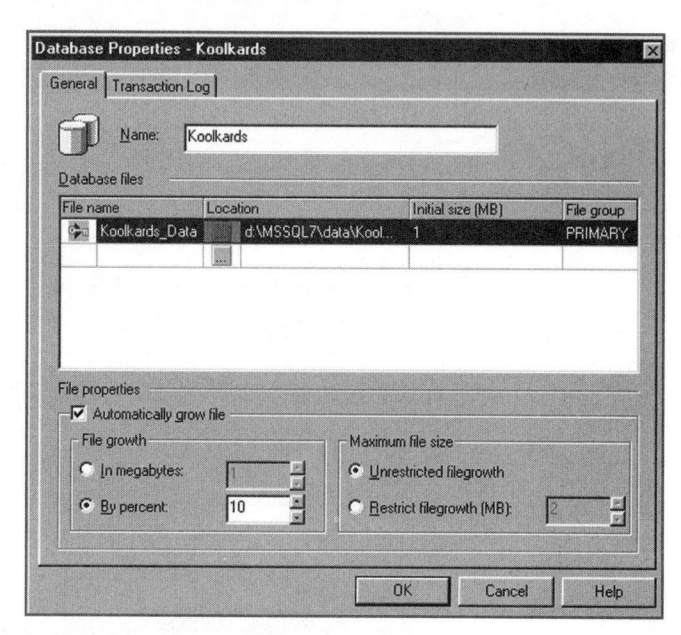

4. You should now see the KoolKards database appear in the left-hand pane. If you click the + symbol you'll be able to see all the administration options for your database.

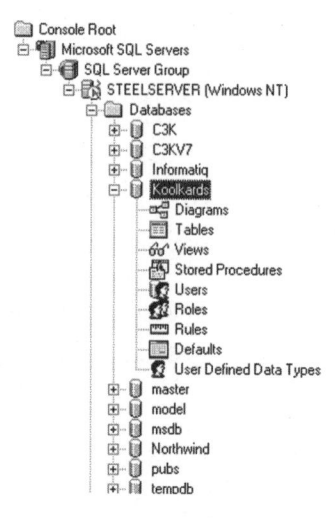

We now need to convert our existing Access database to SQL Server. Fortunately, SQL Server has some wizards to do this type of thing simply.

5. Right-click on the KoolKards database and select All Tasks > Import Data.

Stored Procedures 13

6. This will open up the Database Import Wizard (DTS). Click Next on the introduction page and you should see something like this:

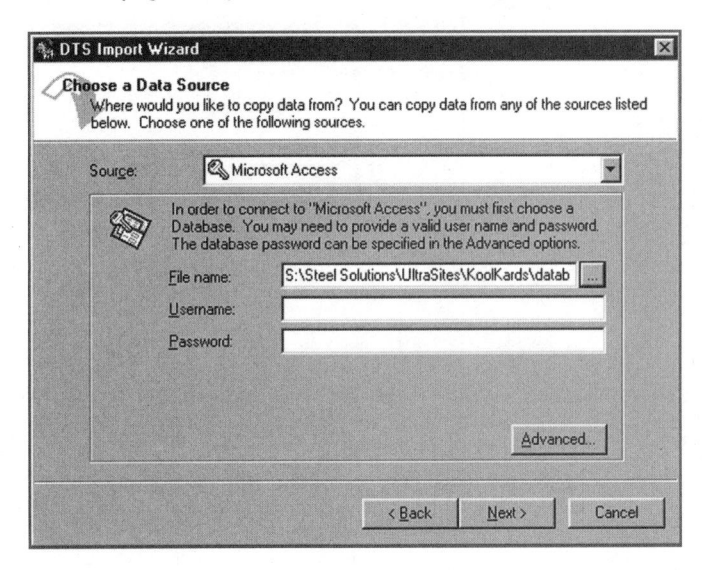

7. Choose Access as your source and locate your database. Click Next.

You now have to choose the destination database you wish to place your access database into. The only thing you may need to change here is to use SQL server authentication not NT. If it is not your own SQL installation you may need to check with your database administrator what the username and password is.

8. Click Next once you've finished.

357

Foundation Dreamweaver UltraDev 4

9. Click Next until you come to the screen below:

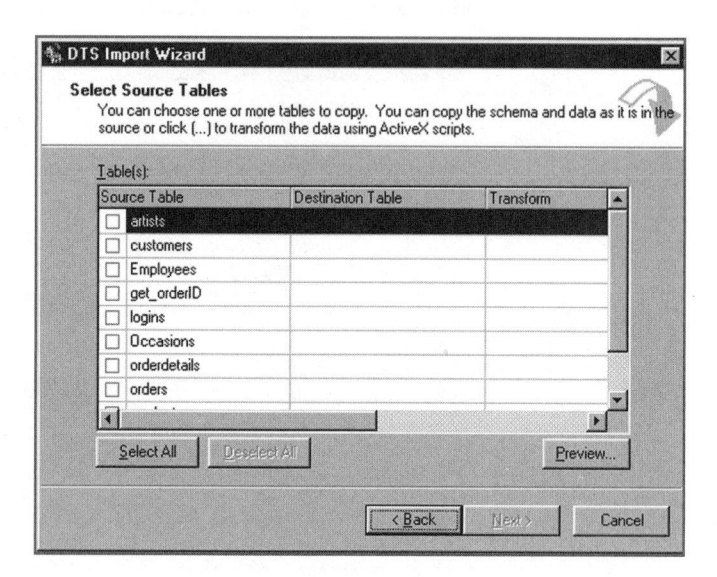

10. You now need to select all the tables from your Access database. Use the Select All button and then confirm by pressing Next.

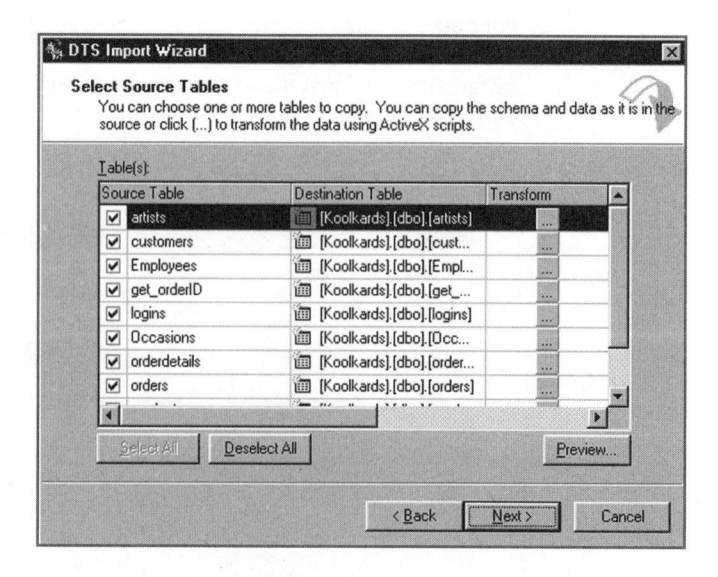

11. Select Run immediately and press Next. You'll be shown a summary page. Press Finish and the copying process will begin.

Stored Procedures 13

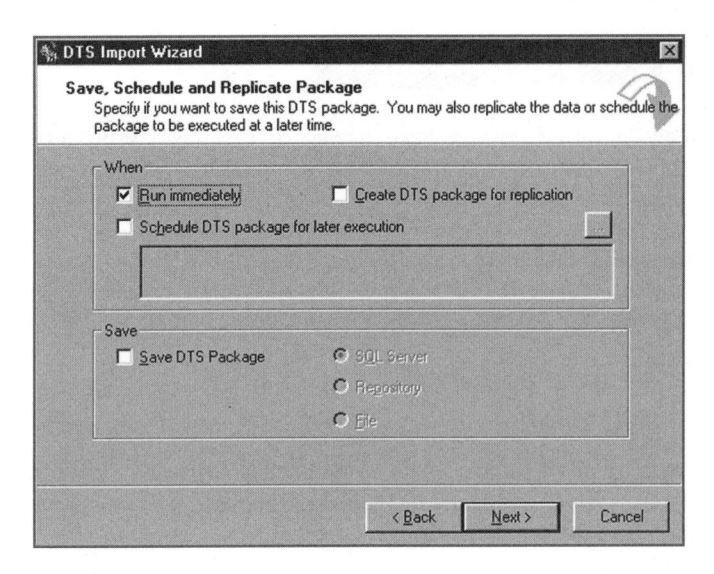

You have now successfully imported your Access database, and you're now ready start using stored procedures.

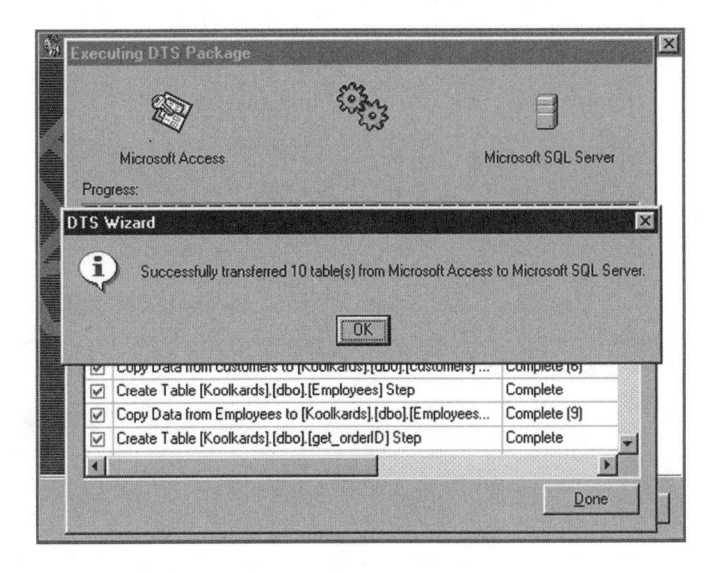

Foundation Dreamweaver UltraDev 4

Creating Stored Procedures

Unfortunately UltraDev doesn't have a way of creating stored procedures within its environment; rest assured it is on our wish list for UltraDev 5. So we're left with three options:

- Microsoft Query Analyzer (I/SQL) – part of SQL Server
- Microsoft SQL Server Enterprise Manager – part of SQL Server
- A web based query analyzer.

For the purposes of this book we'll use Enterprise Manager. Enterprise Manager is the closest thing SQL Server has to the Access table/queries tab. From here you can graphically see your objects in the database. However, SQL Server uses Tables, Views (like queries) and stored procedures.

In the Tree view pane, under your database KoolKards, you'll find a Stored Procedures list. Let's create one now.

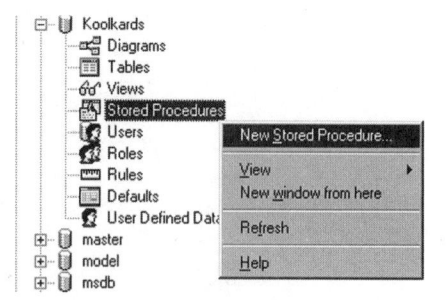

1. Right-click the Stored Procedure container and select New Stored Procedure. You'll be presented with a screen to design your stored procedure in:

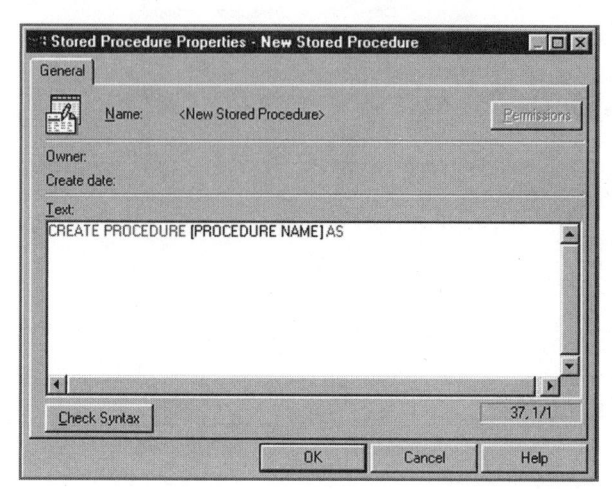

Stored Procedures 13

As we stated earlier in this chapter, an SQL stored procedure can contain a single SQL Transact-SQL statement or hundreds.

> *Transact SQL is Microsoft flavor of SQL. There are certain commands within its version of SQL that are not ANSI standard – but add more power. Most commands are ANSI standard (will work with any SQL ANSI compliant database). It's worth making a mental note of this however, for future reference.*

If we wanted to return all the records from our customers table we would normally say

```
SELECT * FROM Customers
```

2. To make this into a stored procedure, you simply enter this.

```
CREATE PROCEDURE sp_customers AS
SELECT * FROM customers
```

The good thing about doing this with Enterprise Manager is it provides you with a button to check your SQL syntax.

3. After you've entered the code press the Check Syntax button.

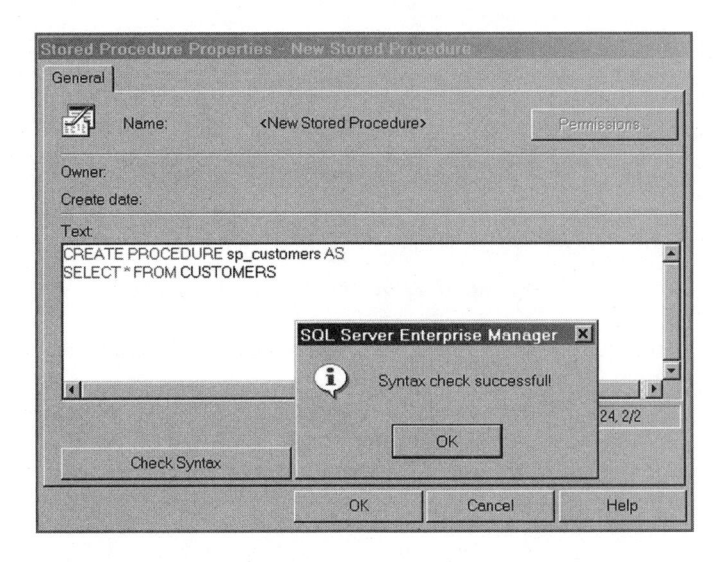

4. Then press OK. You've just created your first (simple) stored procedure!

You could have named your stored procedure anything (the sp_ isn't necessary) but this seems to be a standard used when referencing stored procedures and will help you later on when you are looking at your objects within the database.

The final thing you will have to do is give permission to everyone to be able to use this stored procedure object. This is true of all SQL Server objects (table/views/stored procedures).

5. Open the stored procedure by double-clicking on it in the right-hand pane and click the Permissions button. Make sure you've selected EXEC rights for all users by checking the box shown:

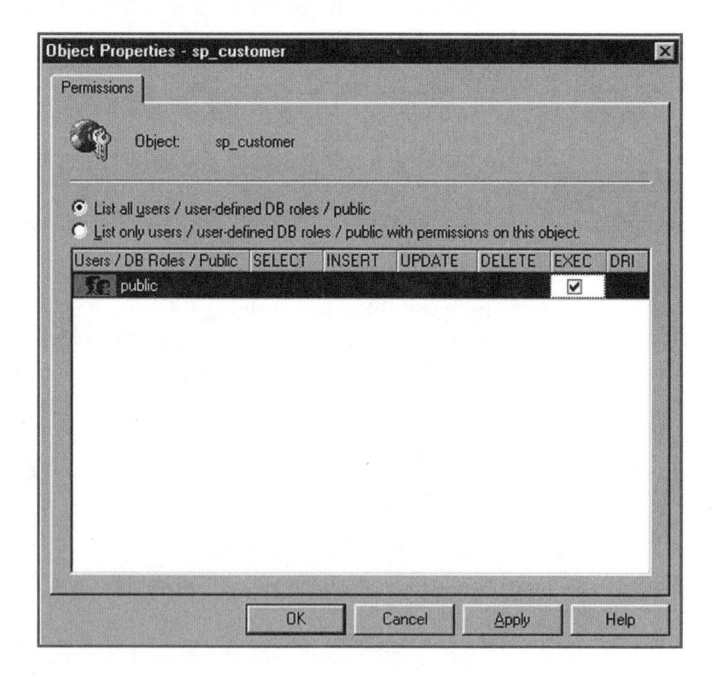

Let's see how we can we use this procedure with UltraDev.

First we need to create a new database connection.

6. Open up UltraDev and click on Modify > Connections to bring up the Connection dialog box that we saw in Chapter 1. Create a new DSN exactly as in Chapter 1, except select the SQL Server database driver.

Stored Procedures 13

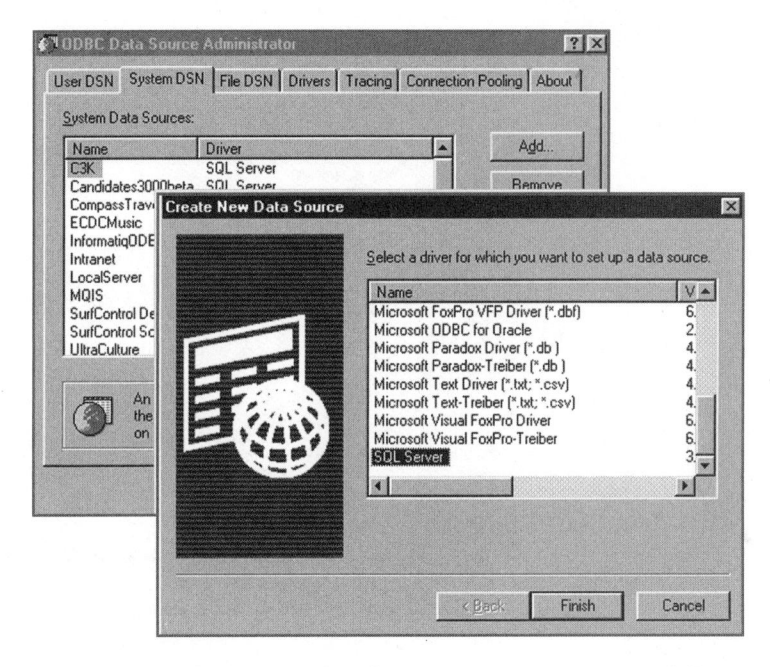

Name your connection KoolKards_SQL. If you run into any difficulties, refer back to Chapter 1.

7. Open up a Recordset (Query) from the Server Behavior panel, choose your KoolKards_SQL connection, and select Stored Procedure from the Database Items (you may have to select the Advanced button to bring up this menu):

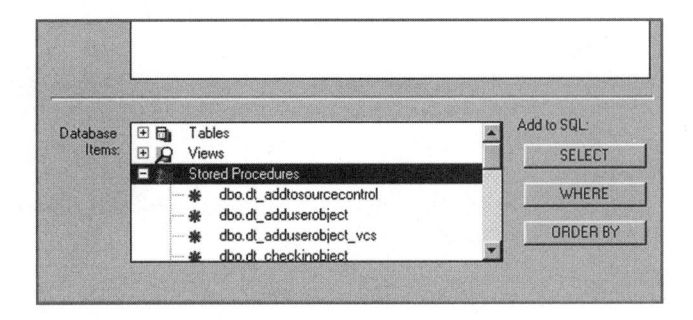

If you highlight the dbo.sp_customers and click the PROCEDURE button it will place the SQL statement needed to call the procedure {Call dbo.sp_customers} in the SQL window.

Foundation Dreamweaver UltraDev 4

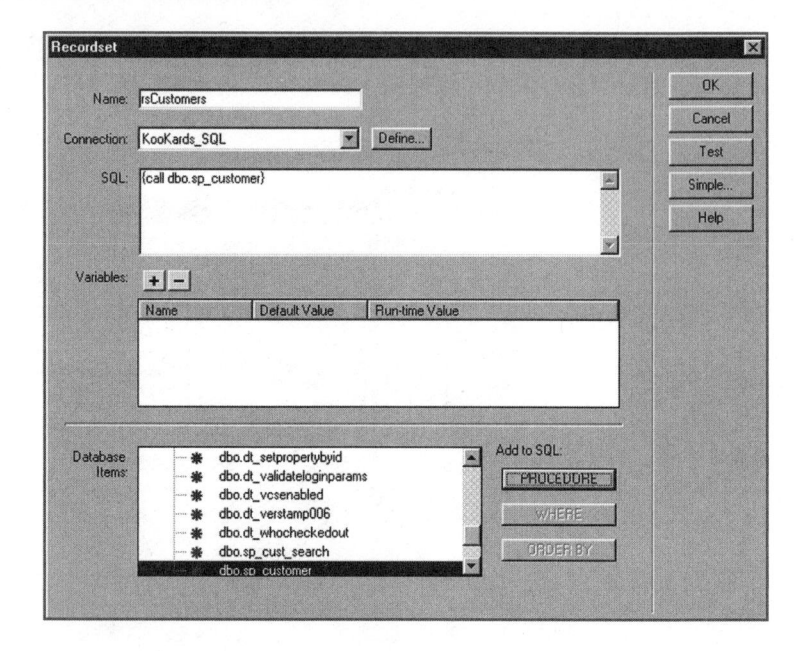

By the way, **DBO** stands for the **DataBase Owner**, which is the person who created the stored procedure. Don't ever change this in SQL Server unless you really know what you're doing. It can result in you not being able to get into your own database or any of its objects.

8. Click the Test button you'll see all the results from your stored procedure.

9. Once finished click OK

If you look under the Data Bindings tab you'll see your recordset with all the fields ,just as you would if you had created a normal recordset query.

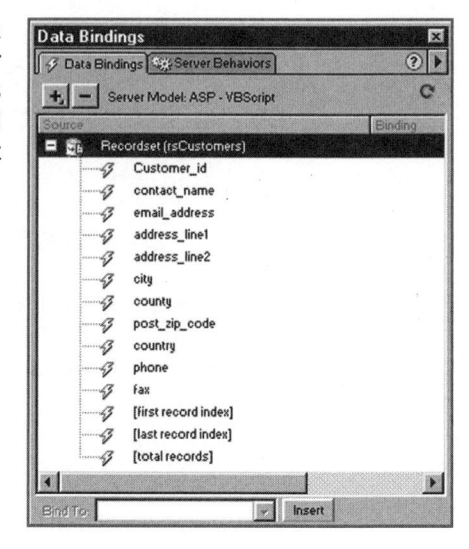

Stored Procedures 13

All the usual recordset behaviors can now be applied (Repeat Regions, Insert, Update etc...)

So what's changed in our code on our ASP page?

```
<%
set rsCustomers = Server.CreateObject("ADODB.Recordset")
rsCustomers.ActiveConnection = MM_KoolKards_SQL_STRING
rsCustomers.Source = "{call dbo.sp_customers}"
rsCustomers.CursorType = 0
rsCustomers.CursorLocation = 2
rsCustomers.LockType = 3
rsCustomers.Open()
rsCustomers_numRows = 0
%>
```

Not a lot.

We have a new connection string. We call the stored procedure with a simple `call` command and the name of the procedure.

Although our stored procedure doesn't actually do much, when you progress into the world of SQL Server stored procedures, you'll discover that you can create stored procedures that are pages in length and very powerful. Let's look at some more examples...

Generating a Random Record

Quite a common question that pops up on many newsgroups is "How do I generate random records?"

Why would people want to do that? Some people want to offer a free prize draw for every subscriber once a month, or maybe a button on their site for a 'random product'. How about a random image to make your site more interesting? There are plenty of examples of times when people want to grab a random row for a table, so let's look at how we can solve this using a stored procedure.

Effectively, we could return the whole recordset to the page and perform a randomize routine in ASP but it's going to be very detrimental to your web site's performance with large tables. This is a perfect example of a stored procedure taking the load on board and returning one solitary record, much, much faster.

Let's take a look at the (surprisingly large) amount of code needed and then we'll explain why.

Foundation Dreamweaver UltraDev 4

You can type this code in, or we've provided it in a text file called sp_RandomRecord.txt in the Chapter13 folder, which you can cut and paste into your stored procedure.

> As a beginner to stored procedures you'll find this code hard to get your head around. Again, don't worry. It's supposed to be complex. We want you to appreciate that complex calculations can be done by the server and returned back to your web pages.

```
CREATE PROCEDURE sp_GetRandomRecord
AS

declare @nRecordCount int
declare @nRandNum int

-- Create a temporary table with the same structure of
-- the table we want to select a random record from
CREATE TABLE #TempTable
(
     [idnum] int identity(1,1),
    [id] int ,
    artist_name varchar(50),
occasion varchar(50),
category varchar(50),
type   varchar(50),
rrp_price money,
cost money,
ref_number varchar(50),
image_path  varchar(50)
)

-- Dump the contents of the table to search into the
-- temp. table
INSERT INTO #TempTable
Select
[id],artist_name,occasion,category,type,rrp_price,cost,
➥ ref_number,image_path
FROM Occasions INNER JOIN (artists INNER JOIN products ON
artists.artist_id = products.artist_id) ON
Occasions.occasion_ID = products.occasion_id
-- Get the number of records in our temp table
Select @nRecordCount = count(*) From #TempTable
```

Stored Procedures 13

```
-- Select a random number between 1 and the number
-- of records in our table
Select @nRandNum = Round(((@nRecordCount - 2) * Rand() + 1), 0)

-- Select the record from the temp table with the
-- ID equal to the random number selected...
Select
   [id],artist_name,occasion,category,type,rrp_price,cost,
➥   ref_number,image_path From #TempTable
   where idNum = @nRandNum
```

If you take some time to read through the code you should be able to understand what's happening, even if you can't write it yet.

The first section is declaring two variables for use later on.

Then we move on to the SQL commands for creating a table. Why are we creating another table? Well, we need to create a temporary table, to add the contents of the table we want to generate a random record from.

Why? Well consider this. In our table we have 20 rows, but someone has deleted 16 and 18. If our random number generator picks 16 or 18 a result will not be found. Therefore, we need to create a temporary table with an incremental UniqueID starting with 1, and copy each row from our target table to this.

So now we can get a random number between 1 and the number of rows in the #TempTable, select the row with that ID and we'll know it exists.

How could we use this in KoolKards?

How about featuring a random card each time the home page loads, with a hotlink to the detail of the card, which the user can click on if the card catches their eye!

To test out the stored procedure create a new page and follow the same steps we used in the first example (without applying a repeat region) and you'll get a single, random record each time you open the page. Neat!

Creating Stored Procedures with Parameters

When we first talked about stored procedures we mentioned that it was possible to pass data back and forth from our ASP pages. Let's take a look at how we can pass parameters to a stored procedure. Then we'll look at how we can send parameters back to a page.

Passing a Parameter to a Stored Procedure

You should now be used to using parameters within your queries. Let's look at how we can achieve the same effect by passing a parameter to a stored procedure.

Before we dive into UltraDev we need to set up the stored procedure to receive the parameter.

Let's look at a familiar example. We'll query the customer table for specific records based on requested information. Let's say we want to find all the customers that are based in the UK.

Our normal SQL statement would be:

```
SELECT * FROM Customers where country ='UK'
```

To make this into a stored procedure we would use the following:

```
CREATE PROCEDURE sp_cust_search
@search varchar(30)
as
Select * from customers where country = @search
```

Notice the `@search varchar(30)`. This is what we use to tell the procedure to expect as input parameter. `varchar` is a SQL Server datatype, a bit like Text in Access. However, SQL Server is a lot more precise than Access because here we're saying, expect a varchar of a maximum 30 characters, but it could be less (variant character). It is possible to pass more than one parameter, although all of them must be declared in this way.

Passing a Parameter using UltraDev

1. Create a new page from the master template. Place a form and a text box called country.

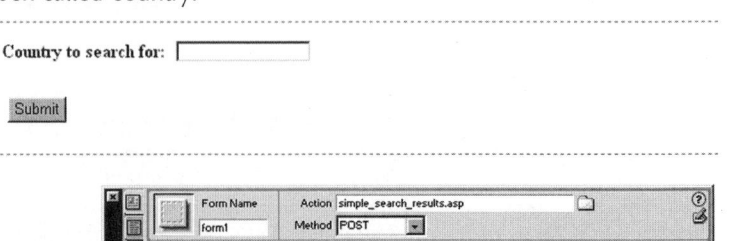

Stored Procedures 13

2. Save the page as simple_search.asp.

   We now need a page to call the stored procedure and display the results.

3. Create a new page from the master template and save it as simple_search_results.asp

   Follow the steps below to create your parameterized stored procedure query recordset.

   - Choose a Name for your recordset: rsResults.

   - Select your Connection. Make sure you choose your SQL connection, not Access.

   - Expand your stored procedures by clicking the + symbol in Database Items. Look for the stored procedure you created earlier: - sp_cust_search. Highlight it and press the PROCEDURE button.

   - Enter a default value

4. The run time value needs to be set to Request("search") which is the name of the text box on the previous page you created.

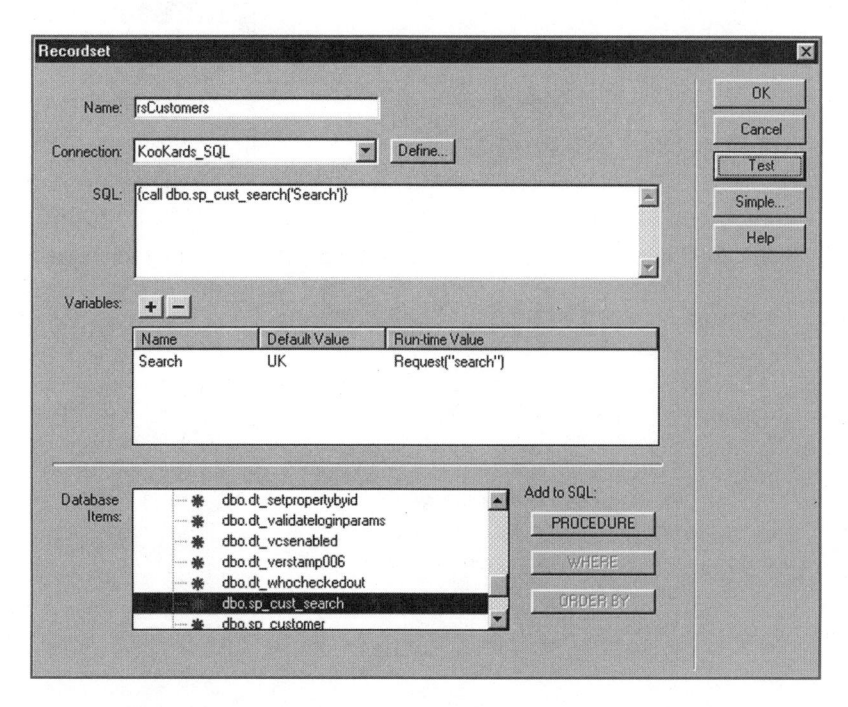

5. Press the Test button and check to see if you get any results back.

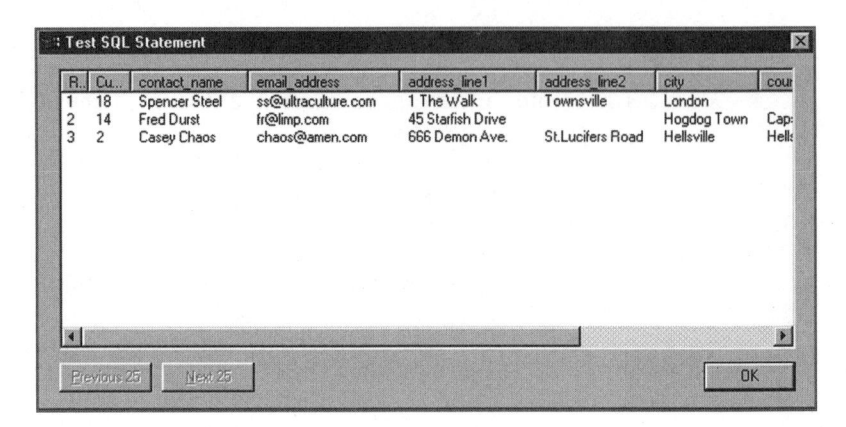

As you can see, it's really is not that much different from setting up standard SQL queries. However, the important thing to remember is that SQL Server does the hard work, not the ASP page.

If you check the Data Bindings box you'll see all your recordset fields available for you to display on your page.

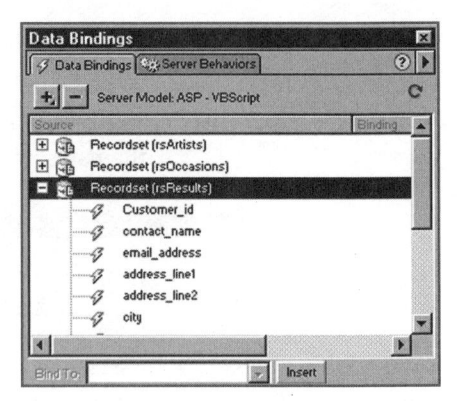

You can now create a simple table with a repeat region on your results page.

Before we move on let's check the code that has been written:

```
<%
set rsResults = Server.CreateObject("ADODB.Recordset")
rsResults.ActiveConnection = MM_KoolKards_SQL_STRING
rsResults.Source = "{call dbo.sp_cust_search('" +
➥ Replace(rsResults__search, "'", "''") + "')}"
rsResults.CursorType = 0
rsResults.CursorLocation = 2
rsResults.LockType = 3
rsResults.Open()
rsResults_numRows = 0
%>
```

Stored Procedures

The highlighted code is the only difference. You should notice all the cursor types, locations, and locks are all the same.

The VB function `Replace` is used to pass the value you entered in the search box on your previous page.

Creating Procedures with Output Parameters

Stored procedures have the ability to return single values, not just recordsets. Let's go back to Chapter 8 where we implemented our login system.

In our login site, a user enters their username and password on which we perform a query to assess if the user is allowed to login with information they typed in.

To achieve this we used the `Log In User` server behavior, which basically uses the code below to connect to the login table and look for a match. Depending on the result it executes the appropriate code.

```
MM_rsUser.ActiveConnection = MM_koolkards_STRING
MM_rsUser.Source = "SELECT username, password"
If MM_fldUserAuthorization <> "" Then MM_rsUser.Source =
MM_rsUser.Source & "," & MM_fldUserAuthorization
MM_rsUser.Source = MM_rsUser.Source & " FROM logins WHERE
username='" & MM_valUsername &"' AND password='" &
CStr(Request.Form("password")) & "'"
MM_rsUser.CursorType = 0
MM_rsUser.CursorLocation = 2
MM_rsUser.LockType = 3
MM_rsUser.Open
If Not MM_rsUser.EOF Or Not MM_rsUser.BOF Then
' username and password match - this is a valid user
………
Else
Response.Redirect(MM_redirectLoginFailed)
```

All this is fine but now let's look at how we may achieve the same thing with a stored procedure.

```
CREATE PROCEDURE sp_Validate_Login
   @UserName    varchar(30),
   @Password    varchar(30)
As
IF EXISTS(SELECT * From login
         WHERE UserName = @UserName
```

```
                                     AND
                            Password = @Password)
              return(1)
         else
              return(0)
```

This procedure takes the username and password as input parameters and performs a query to see if a record exists.

If a record is returned the stored procedure will return a single value of 1, if not the procedure will return 0. No actual recordset is returned, just a success or failure 'bit'.

Before we move to UltraDev to create our page to use this procedure, we'll explain the new SQL statements that we've introduced in this procedure.

```
         IF EXISTS(SELECT * From logins
         WHERE UserName = @UserName AND Password = @Password)
```

EXISTS simply checks for a 'non empty' set. It returns either True or Not True. In other words, if we find a record that matches, it returns True. If no record is found, it returns Not True.

Return [n] is used to exit a stored procedure. [n] is any whole number (positive or negative) to be set as a return status, which can be assigned to a variable when returning to your ASP page.

Enough said on that, let's look at how we execute this type of stored procedure from within UltraDev. In the chapter13 folder you'll find a copy of the login.asp page we used in Chapter 8. We've stripped out the login behavior, so you'll have a fresh page ready to start creating your call for this procedure.

To execute this type of stored procedure we need to use a new feature: the Command object, which can be found under the Data Bindings panel labeled Command (Stored Procedure).

We use the Command object when we're returning values from the stored procedure.

Stored Procedures 13

Creating a Command Object

Let's look at creating a new Command object.

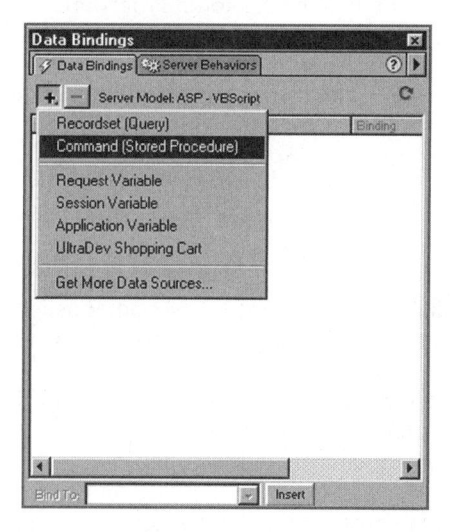

1. Select Command (Stored Procedure) from the Data Bindings panel.

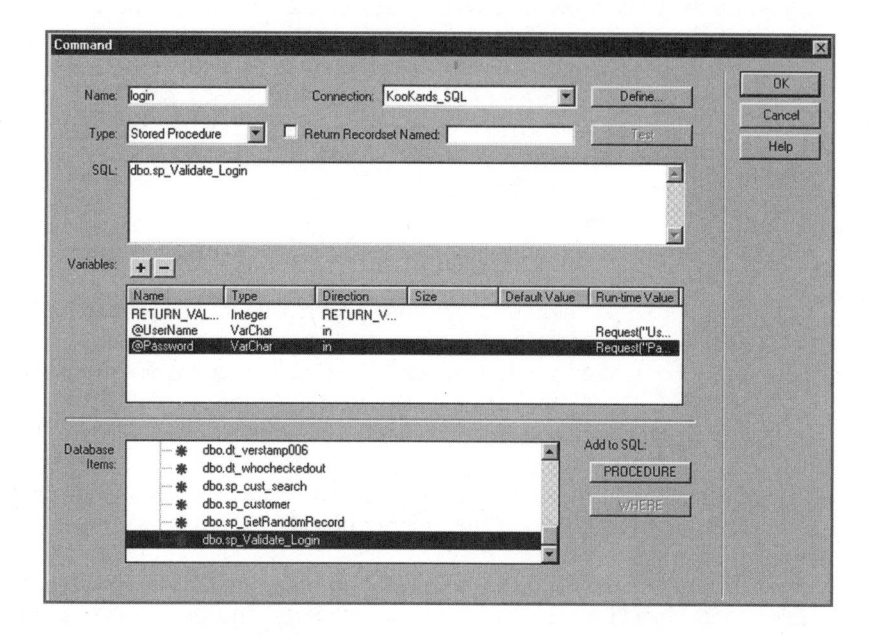

2. Give the command a Name: login.

3. Choose your SQL Connection: KoolKards_SQL

4. For Type enter Stored Procedure.

5. Find your dbo.sp_validate_login stored procedure under Database Items and press the PROCEDURE button. The variable details will be filled in for you. You could of course have done this manually, but it stops you making mistakes. (as if!)

   Unfortunately we need to add the size of the variable for the two VarChars, which in this case is 30

The runtime values need to be set to the names assigned to the username and password text boxes. We use a simple Request to pass the login details to the variables.

RETURN_VALUE is the variable that is returned from all stored procedures by default. We are assigning it the direction of RETURN_VALUE as we wish to use the value in a conditional statement later on in the code.

If everything looks correct, press OK to close the command window

Open up the Code View window and let's take a look at the code:

```
set login = Server.CreateObject("ADODB.Command")
login.ActiveConnection = MM_KoolKards_SQL_STRING
login.CommandText = "dbo.sp_Validate_Login"
login.CommandType = 4
login.CommandTimeout = 0
login.Prepared = true
login.Parameters.Append login.CreateParameter("RETURN_VALUE",
➥ 3, 4)
login.Parameters.Append login.CreateParameter("@UserName",
➥ 200, 1,30,login__UserName)
login.Parameters.Append login.CreateParameter("@Password",
➥ 200, 1,30,login__Password)
login.Execute()
```

The first part is pretty straightforward in that it opens a command object by using the `CreateObject()` method of the `Server` object.

Next the command is associated with an open database connection by using the Command object's `ActiveConnection` property. The `commandText` property provides the name of the stored procedure in the SQL database that will be executed. The

Stored Procedures 13

`commandType` property is used to indicate that the command will be used to execute an SQL stored procedure.

The last part before the `Execute` statement is where the output and input parameters are set up.

Let's take a look at the arguments of the `CreateParameter()` method.

Argument	Use
Name	The name of the parameter
Type	The data type (eg varchar) which is represented by the number 200
Direction	Indicates that the parameter is an input parameter, which is represented by 1
Size	When creating a parameter with a variable length data type, such as a varchar, you must provide the maximum size of the parameter. It's not necessary to provide the size when passing integers

Let's carry on setting up our page.

6. We need to add a hidden field to our login page so we can place a check at the start of the page to see if the page has already been submitted.

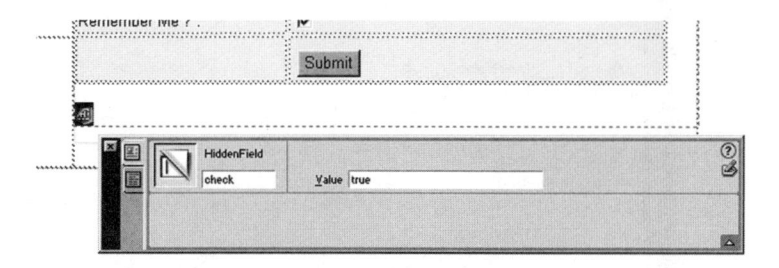

This needs to be placed within the form tags.

7. Set the attributes of the form tag to:

Action = login.asp
Method = POST
Form Name = login

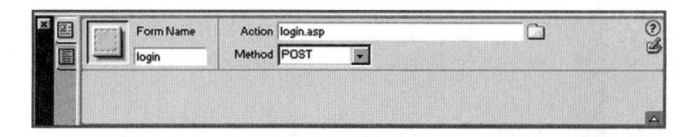

13 Foundation Dreamweaver UltraDev 4

We now need to place some code to set up a variable on success or failure and check if this is the first time the page has been loaded (so don't run the login check code).

Place the highlighted code just under the include file code.

```
<!--#include file="../Connections/
➥ KoolKards_SQL.asp" -->

<% Dim loginsuccess
    loginsuccess = 1 %>

<% If (Request.form("RP_check")="true") then %>
```

Place the highlighted code below just before the HTML Tag. The first time the form loads, this looks at whether the check exists and ignore all the ASP code if it doesn't.

```
<%End If%>

<HTML>
```

```
1  <%@LANGUAGE="VBSCRIPT"%>
2  <!--#include file="../Connections/KoolKards_SQL.asp" -->
3  <% Dim loginsuccess
4      loginsuccess = 1 %>
5  <% If (Request.form("RP_check")="true") then %>
6  <%
7
8  Dim login__UserName
9  login__UserName = ""
10 if(Request("UserName") <> "") then login__UserName = Request("UserName")
11
12 Dim login__Password
13 login__Password = ""
14 if(Request("Password") <> "") then login__Password = Request("Password")
15
16 %>
17 <%
18
19 set login = Server.CreateObject("ADODB.Command")
20 login.ActiveConnection = MM_KoolKards_SQL_STRING
21 login.CommandText = "dbo.sp_Validate_Login"
22 login.Parameters.Append login.CreateParameter("RETURN_VALUE", 3, 4)
23 login.Parameters.Append login.CreateParameter("@UserName", 200, 1,30,login__UserName)
24 login.Parameters.Append login.CreateParameter("@Password", 200, 1,30,login__Password)
25 login.CommandType = 4
26 login.CommandTimeout = 0
27 login.Prepared = true
28 login.Execute()
29
30 %>
31
32 <%End If %>
33 <html>
34 <!-- #BeginTemplate "/Templates/admin.dwt" -->
```

Checking the Parameter Values

To do this we need to access the value of the RETURN_VALUE parameter. If it is set to 1 we can proceed to another page as the login was a success. If not, we need to display a message stating that the login was incorrect.

Place this code after the Command object code block:

```
<% ' Check to see if the user as a valid login
   If (login.Parameters.Item("RETURN_VALUE").Value = 1) then
   Response.Redirect("valid_login.asp")
   Else
   loginsuccess = 0
   End If

%>
```

Here we are saying, if we've received a row from the database, which means there must have been a correct login, then we continue to the valid login page. If not, set the success to 0, which will indicate failure and carry on with the code.

```
25 login.CommandType = 4
26 login.CommandTimeout = 0
27 login.Prepared = true
28 login.Execute()
29
30 %>
31 <% ' Check to see if the user as a valud login
32     If (login.Parameters.Item("RETURN_VALUE").Value = 1) then
33     Response.Redirect("valid_login.asp")
34     Else
35     Return = 0
36     End If
37
38 %>
39 <%End If %>
40 <html>
41 <!-- #BeginTemplate "/Templates/admin.dwt" -->
```

Failure Message

To inform the user that they have entered the incorrect information we need to amend our page so it displays an error code. You can do this easily by clicking on the Gold ASP symbol before the error message and editing the code by bringing up the properties and clicking Edit.

Edit the code so it reads:

```
<% if loginsuccess = 0 then %>
```

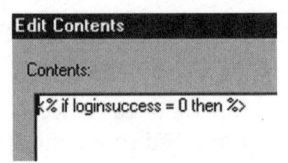

Now end the block of HTML with an `End If` statement. Your whole block will look something like this:

```
<% if loginsuccess = 0 then %>
    <font size="2"> <font face="Arial, Helvetica, sans-serif">
➥ <font color="#000000">
    <font color="#FF0000"> You entered either an incorrect
➥ username or password. Please try again.</font></font>
➥ </font></font>
<% End If %>
```

Here we are saying if the `loginsuccess` variable = 0 then print the error message on the screen. Otherwise just continue with the code.

Now test out your page. If you enter a correct username and password you'll be redirected to another page.

If you enter an incorrect password, you should see the red error message:

Further Discussions

Suppose you want to add in functionality to log all failed logon attempts into another table called FailedLogons. This could be handy to see if you had a potential hacker and if they were getting close to the real logins, or maybe to see how often people are forgetting their passwords.

If we weren't using a stored procedure we would have to make another call to the database from your ASP code. However, in the example using the stored procedure, we don't have to touch the ASP code at all. We simply modify the procedure.

If we add this code to the end of our procedure, we can insert the information into a new table called FailedLogons.

```
CREATE PROCEDURE sp_Validate_Login
   @UserName   varchar(30),
   @Password   varchar(30)
As
IF EXISTS(SELECT * From logins
          WHERE UserName = @UserName
                    AND
                Password = @Password)
   return(1)
else

   begin
      INSERT INTO FailedLogons(UserName, Password)
          values(@UserName, @Password)

   return(0)
end
```

Of course, you could log more information, like the time the failed request happened and even the IP address from the machine. At this point, we'll leave it up to you to think of the possibilities of using SQL Server with your web applications.

Summary

In this chapter we've looked very briefly at how we can combine ASP with the power of SQL Server to take our performance and power to the next level.

SQL Server and stored procedures are huge subjects and are used for a variety of applications, not just web pages. There's therefore a wealth of information available on the Internet and in print.

We hope that we've given you just a small taster of what's available and maybe taken some of the 'fear of the unknown' when you hear people talking and using stored procedures. You'll surprise yourself at how quickly you can get into using them, once you're set up, and you'll amaze yourself at the power of your web sites once you start to move some of those routines to SQL Server.

With SQL Server and ASP, you can truly develop robust, scalable web applications capable of handling thousands of hits an hour.

kool kards

14 A Step Further

What we'll cover in this chapter

- **Alternative** applications that can be built with UltraDev and Macromedia extensions

- Using **Macromedia Flash** with UltraDev to create visually enhanced dynamic sites

- Alternative **Server Models** that UltraDev supports

14 Foundation Dreamweaver UltraDev 4

We'll start this final chapter with an all-important and well-deserved pat on the back. Take a moment and look back at the ground we've covered: fundamental ASP topics like cookies, session variables, interacting with databases, then some more pretty advanced stuff with shopping cart applications, form validation and stored procedures. You've handled all of that, in the process giving yourself the firmest foundation to handle UltraDev like a professional and wow your clients, employers and friends with your UltraDev expertise.

The purpose of *this* chapter is to propel your imagination that little bit further by looking at some alternative methods and applications for UltraDev. We'll be introducing you to the three key ways to take your new skills further: building on the applications you've learned by using UltraDev extensions, integrating UltraDev with Flash 5 and using alternative server models and coding languages. So grab your thinking cap and a strong caffeinated drink and we'll start exploring beyond the foundations.

Taking Web Applications Further

In earlier chapters we looked at some excellent UltraDev functions and showed how they can be effectively utilized in a major web application. Let's look at some variations on that theme and some more alternatives opened up by the power of UltraDev extensions.

Shopping Cart Applications

We've seen the basic shopping cart function in UltraDev but surely now we can use them with a little more imagination? Why use shopping cart applications only for e-commerce related projects? The power of session variables and cookies don't always have to exploit capitalist goals! The actions involved in a user session within a shopping cart application could be put to use in other methods. Instead of using 'add to cart' server behaviors to simply add products to a cart you could use it to select information, articles or leaflets.

For example, think about an application where a company has information brochures available for order from its web site. We could use the shopping cart application to act as the vehicle for the user to order a list of relevant brochures to be sent to them by e-mail. The cart application would involve picking brochures (add to cart) and moving them to a page listing their final selection (checkout), before sending a request for more information (process order section). Using UltraDev means that the user will only be able to select the brochures that are available at that time.

News Updates and Web Diaries

UltraDev allows you the great facility of linking your News or Diary page to a database capable of storing every new and previous article that you've used on your site. This would

A Step Further

allow visitors to search all your previous records, as well as offering you a very simple means of updating your daily or weekly information.

UltraDev Extensions

While we can build some really cool applications with the pre-installed server behaviors that come with UltraDev, there are some great extensions on the Macromedia Exchange that can take the productivity of UltraDev into new and previously uncharted territories.

One 'buzzword' flying around technology and web design at the moment is **WML**. What's that then?

WAP / WML Extensions

WML (Wireless Mark-up Language) is a language which allows devices like WAP (Wireless Application Protocol) phones to browse Internet sites delivered with WML content.

Available from the Exchange are extensions such as the 'Nokia WML Studio' which provide developers with the ability to build WML applications to be run on WAP devices like mobile phones and PDAs (Personal Desktop Assistants). You could then use UltraDev in conjunction with scripting methods such as ASP, JSP or Cold Fusion to create database-driven WML applications – dynamic content in the palm of your hand!

Web Learning Applications

Web Learning is a massive field that will get much bigger in the coming years. Extensions for UltraDev offer the ability to design programs that let users take part in online quizzes and tests. You could create tests in multiple formats and use scripting to allow the test to be placed into a database and stored for reference and reports. This has potential applications way beyond an academic context – you could use it on a commercial site to run a quiz where the winner gets the most recent product that the company has produced.

As we said before, the aim of this chapter is not to be a task-based tutorial like all the rest, but to form a springboard of ideas and inspirations to stretch you beyond the level you're at now. We want to get you thinking about how to move forward with your new skills and add them to the skills you already have with other technologies.

If you've stepped outside your front door just once in the last year or so you won't have missed the noise that's out there about this Flash thing. How many job adverts have you seen with Flash at the top of the list of required competencies?

Just in case you *haven't* heard, Flash is Macromedia's vector-based animation program, allowing designers to create movies that have a real 'wow' factor with stunning visual content. Until now, having a Flash front end interact with a database has involved either a high-end Macromedia product, like Generator, or some pretty complex coding that you wouldn't believe. As we said, until now....

Using UltraDev with Macromedia Flash

You may know that Dreamweaver 4, the base upon which UltraDev 4 is built, includes support for Flash text and button styles. However, in this section we'll use UltraDev to generate code for a form built solely in Flash to interact with a database.

The first step along this exciting road of discovery is to show you a simple example of how we can configure a Flash form for use in the UltraDev design environment. This is subject worth looking into in a little detail so we'll back up the theory with a short exercise. We'll define a site within UltraDev in which we will attach a Flash form to an ASP page, and in that ASP page we'll apply a server behavior that allows the user to delete a record from a database.

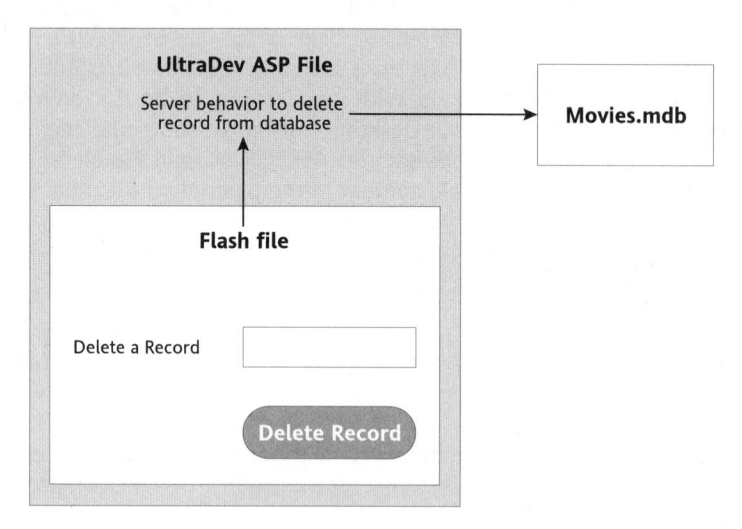

We said that the exercise will be short - with the experience you have now, we'll be able to take you through the Ultradev steps pretty quickly. It's beyond the scope of this chapter to give you a full Flash lesson, so we've kept the form to a very basic level for this exercise. If you don't have Flash, you can download the trial version for free from www.macromedia.com/flash. You'll notice immediately how similar the design interfaces of Flash and UltraDev are, so you should find it relatively easy to find your way around. Once you have Flash 5 installed you can either play around with it and create your own simple form or you can download the form FLA file from our web site.

A Step Further 14

Creating a Flash Form to Delete a Database Record

For this exercise you'll also need the JavaScript Integration Kit extension. You can download this from www.macromedia.com/exchange/ultradev.

1. Define a new ASP site within UltraDev (Site > Define Sites... > New) and create a database with some records in it (you may want to refer to the Access Primer appendix for instructions on creating an Access database). Alternatively, there is an Access database called movies.mdb in the chapter14 folder. As pictured, our database simply consists of a table called Films with two fields: movie and rating.

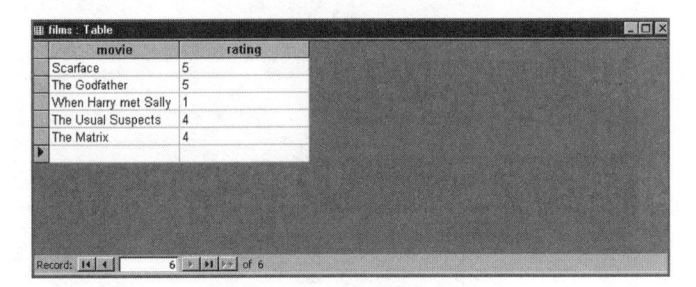

2. Save your database within your site (perhaps in a separate folder called databases, like we did with KoolKards) and create an ODBC connection to it on your system (call it Flash). This is the database from which we'll be deleting our records using the Flash form.

3. To save time use the ready-made form in the flashform.fla file (chapter14 folder). Otherwise, create a Flash file that contains an input text field with a variable name of delete and a standard button underneath it. We'll use the button to allow the user to submit the data to the script that UltraDev will generate through a Delete Record server behavior. There is also some JavaScript code in there to smooth the transport of data into UltraDev.

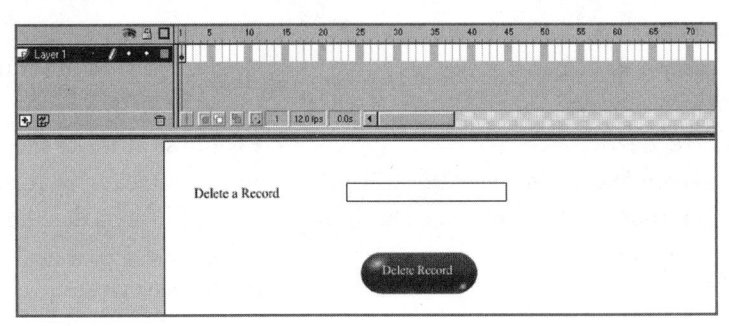

The next step is to nest our Flash form into an UltraDev page.

4. Within Flash, go to File > Export Movie. Once exported, save the movie into our site. The Flash file will now have a `.swf` extension rather than `.fla`.

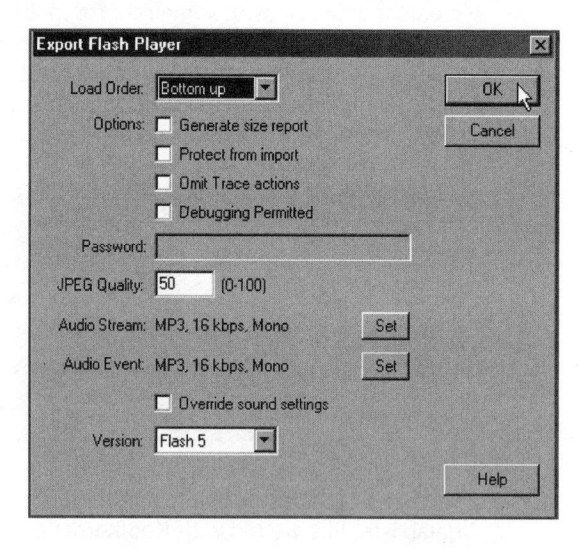

5. Once the file has been successfully exported into our local site folder we're ready to start working with the UltraDev design window. To use Flash content in an UltraDev site environment we need to have a page for it to 'sit' on. Create a new ASP page for this – we've called ours `movie_delete.asp`.

6. In the site window we should now have six items:

Site Element	Description
`FlashForm.fla`	Original Flash form set up for deleting files
`FlashForm.swf`	Exported Flash movie for insert on page
`movie_delete.asp`	Page to sit the SWF file on
Database folder containing `movies.mdb`	Access database for record deletion
Connections folder containing Flash.asp	The tiny include file housing your connection
`after_delete.asp`	A page we've provided for you to jump to after deleting.

A Step Further 14

7. Open up `movie_delete.asp`, which should be a blank page. There are five tasks we now want to achieve before our Flash form is ready to delete records from our database. Firstly, we want to import our SWF file onto the page, and secondly we need to insert a form onto the page. Then we need to insert some JavaScript elements. Finally we want to create a recordset for our application and insert our server behavior onto the page.

8. To import our `flashform.swf` file onto the page go to Insert > Media > Flash and browse to and select `flashform.swf`. You'll now have a gray square on your ASP page design window with the 'Flash' symbol in the middle to let you know that this is Flash content.

9. Open up the Property inspector and select the Flash object on the page. Make sure you change both the title and the ID of the Flash object to delete.

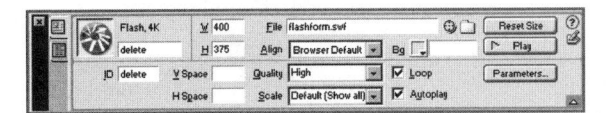

> *If you can't see the bottom half of the panel pictured, click the tiny arrow on the bottom right-hand corner to expand it!*

To put a server behavior like a delete record operation onto a page, we first have to insert a form.

10. Insert a form onto the page beside the Flash content and name it dwform1 in the Property inspector. (This will match with the JavaScript in our FLA file.)

11. Enter a hidden field from the Objects panel's Forms menu and call it dwfield1. When entering the hidden field, make sure that your cursor is located within the form, or else UltraDev will ask you if you want to include a form tag with your hidden field.

12. Now we need to add our JIK validation - don't worry too much about what this does as this stage, but we need it for our Flash form to function. Place your cursor inside the form and open the Behaviors panel (not Server Behaviors) with SHIFT+F3. Click the + button and select Advanced Validate Form - leave the options as default and click OK. Then place your cursor beside the Flash object (so the cursor goes really big) and use the + menu to select Advanced Form Validations > Nonblank Validation. Again accept the default settings.

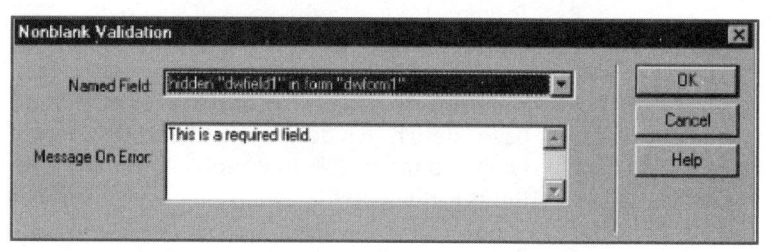

13. Finally on the JavaScript front, go into your Code View and insert the following code about five lines down, after `<script language="JavaScript"><!--`:

```
function FDK_setFormText(form,name,text) {
  textobject = eval('document.'+from+','+name);
  textobject.value = text;
}
```

14. Now we will insert a recordset onto our page that will ensure that we are connected to our database. As you are now pretty experienced in creating recordsets, I'll let you go ahead and create one which uses your connection to the database we created earlier. Call your recordset rsMovies.

15. Finally, we can insert the Delete Record server behavior onto the page, We have set ours up to delete from the movies column on our table, as this is our primary key. After deleting this record we've redirected the application to the after_delete.asp page.

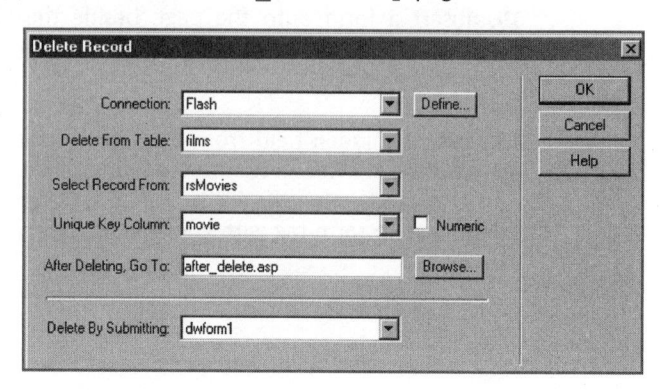

A Step Further 14

16. After we have completed this, our page should look something like this:

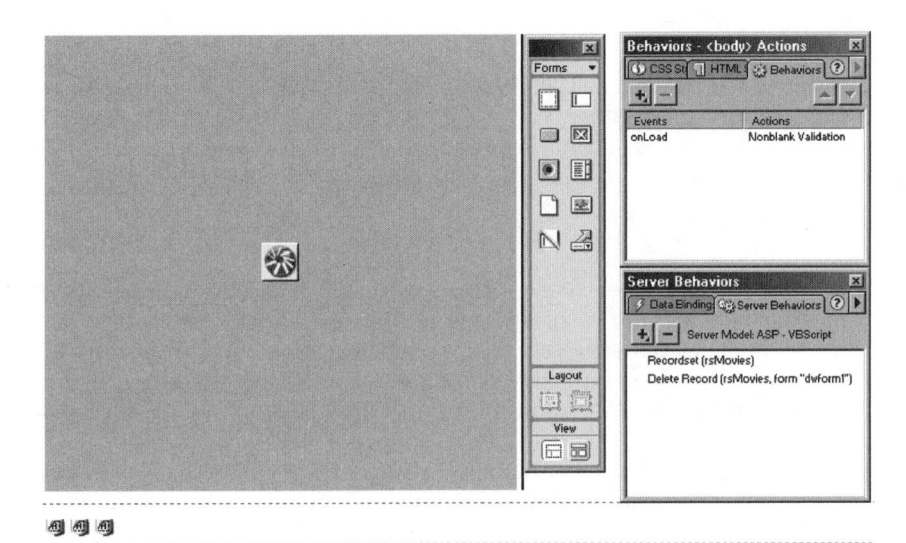

17. Now all that's left for us to do is upload our site to our server and test our work in a browser. Once you have completed your work, check your database and see the entries disappear!

Well done! You have successfully implemented a database driven application using an ActiveX control (Flash) and JavaScript. Could you imagine trying to hand code all of that?

Flash and UltraDev don't always go so well together and there are times you will have to write code to overcome some situations that UltraDev will not work with. However, using Flash with UltraDev Server Behaviors is a valuable time saving way to take Flash applications to the next level.

Just think of the potential of using an animated Flash interface for users to log in using UltraDev to verify the password from your database, or a Flash search page that links into UltraDev to generate the results page. These types of integration may take some work, some hand coding and experimentation but the possibilities of exciting dynamic sites are now more accessible than ever before.

You've still got some learning to do before you can create fully integrated Flash/UltraDev pages but we hope we've given you a glimpse over that horizon.

Okay, so we have looked at some great applications and extensions and we have started the ball rolling on creating a dynamic Flash form through UltraDev so now we are ready to look at the alternative Server Models that are bundled with UltraDev.

Alternative Server Models

So far in this book we have concentrated on one part of the trinity of server models that UltraDev supports, namely ASP 2.0. In this section we are going to look at the potential reasons for using either JSP 1.0 from Sun Microsystems or Allaire Corporation's ColdFusion 4.0 whilst also taking into consideration the possible disadvantages.

Java Server Pages (JSP)

In terms of developer usage and support, JSP and ASP are the 'big boys' of web programming. JSP is a relatively new technology but has the great advantage of being based on the all-powerful Java programming language. JSP can do virtually anything that Java can do, so it is an extremely extensible and well-supported language and is usually the first choice for a non-Microsoft model.

There are several web server models that support JSP, unfortunately too many to detail in this chapter. These are the two main options:

- IBM WebSphere Server is one model suitable for JSP development. There are 3 editions for consideration in development. These editions are Standard, Advanced and Enterprise. Obviously the features and scalability provided by each edition increases as we increase up the scale and cost. WebSphere can run on Windows NT / 2000 and a range of Unix and Linux versions

- Allaire Corporation JRun server, which is available in four editions - Enterprise, Advanced, Professional and Developer. Enterprise is the most senior (and expensive) and Developer is a free version.

You will be happy to know that there are also trial versions of JRun and WebSphere on the UltraDev CD and we have included web site details in our Resources appendix.

JSP Coding

JSP is quite possibly the most difficult to learn out of the three languages available to you. If you have ever looked at a C++ or Java program, then JSP looks similar to them in its 'curly brace' syntax. For anyone from a non-Java background the language can be difficult to both write and debug. This is an ASP script:

```
<%@ Language=VBScript %> <SCRIPT LANGUAGE=vbscript
Dim I
</SCRIPT>
<HTML>
<HEAD>
<%=Date()%>
<% For i = 1 to 10 'Writing from 1 to 10 %>
```

```
        <%=i>
        <%Next%>
        </HTML>
        </HEAD>
```

And this is the same script in JSP:

```
        <%@ page import = "java.sql.*" %>
        <%@ page import = "java.util.Date" %>
        <%
        int i = 0 ; java.util.Date today = new java.util.Date(); %>
        <HTML>
        <HEAD>
        <%=today.toString()%>
        <% (for i = 1; i <= 10; i ++){ //Writing from 1 to 10 %>
        <%=i%>
        <%}%>
        </HTML>
        </HEAD>
```

Even from this brief look at JSP coding, we can see that a higher level of programming experience is needed for JSP. Whilst UltraDev will generate this code for you, it's advisable to learn some of the basics before you start this leg of your journey. As you should already have found out, it's a whole lot easier when you can check the code window and know what is going on in there.

JSP Database Configurations

In between a database and an application is a JDBC (Java Data Base Connection) driver. A JSP application can connect to any database that a JDBC driver can speak to. JSP applications can also use ODBC drivers, if a technology called a JDBC-ODBC *bridge driver* exists for the database. The bridge driver turns your JDBC speaking driver into an ODBC speaking application. Common configurations for JSP/JDBC applications are:

Oracle Java Driver – This driver allows a JSP driver to connect to an oracle database.

DB2 JDBC Driver – This driver allows communication between a JSP application and IBM's DB2 database.

Sun JDBC-ODBC Driver – This driver from Sun allows the JSP application to speak directly to an ODBC compliant database.

JSP is a very powerful server model but you may wish also to consider the third alternative available to you, which is Allaire Corporation's ColdFusion.

ColdFusion

Allaire Corporation's ColdFusion is a *web application* server. In February 2001, Macromedia and Allaire announced plans to merge. Both companies will keep their respective corporate identities, but it's hard to believe that ColdFusion and UltraDev won't move closer together to reflect their shared ownership.

ColdFusion server comes in three varieties. There is ColdFusion Professional Edition, which will quite happily cover tasks such as complex SQL queries, file management, e-mail and e-commerce applications. Above and beyond this is the Enterprise Edition, the proverbial 'big cheese' of the ColdFusion server world. This has all the features of the Professional edition but with advanced security features and support for extremely sophisticated applications running on a truly *enterprise* scale. The last and smallest version is ColdFusion Express, which is free and has extremely limited functionality in comparison to the two other versions.

The Professional edition will run on Windows 95, 98 and 2000. The Enterprise edition is compatible with Windows NT Server 4.0 and 2000 Server/Advanced Server. There is a single user version of ColdFusion Server (Enterprise version) on the UltraDev CD so you can jump in and start coding the ColdFusion way whenever you want to.

ColdFusion application server, be it Express, Professional or Enterprise, runs in tandem with the web server on your machine. For the ColdFusion application server to run successfully, it has to be running concurrently with your web server, which could be Internet Information Server (IIS) or Personal Web Server (PWS).

Once ColdFusion is installed on your machine, the ColdFusion Administrator program runs in a browser window. In this program you can configure and create ODBC Data Sources, security settings and general server settings to name but a few. The Administrator program gives you an extremely easy to use program to manage your web server with.

ColdFusion Mark-up Language (CFML)

CFML is the language that is included in an HTML page to give the page dynamic content when processed by the ColdFusion server. ColdFusion pages (or templates as they are known as in the ColdFusion world) are given the extension `.cfm`. A typical ColdFusion page looks a lot like a HTML page, as ColdFusion is a 'tag-based' language.

The major advantage of working in the ColdFusion environment is that CFML is an easy language to learn. The syntax is different from ASP or JSP and is pretty much like writing HTML. ColdFusion comes with its own tags that the ColdFusion application server recognizes and processes. Tags exist for most functions that web application developers need and extra tags can be downloaded for free or at a premium from the Internet in much the same way as UltraDev extensions.

A Step Further 14

Let's compare how ASP and ColdFusion perform a simple task – we're going to look at the script behind an application that uses the movies database from the Flash exercise to display the movies and their ratings in a web page. As in the Flash exercise the database is called Movies, we have an ODBC data source already setup on our system called Flash and one table in the database called Films. In the Films table I have a two columns called movie and rating. This is the CFML script to display the whole table in a browser:

```
<CFQUERY NAME= "get_movies" DATASOURCE= "Flash">
SELECT * FROM Films
</CFQUERY>
<CFOUTPUT QUERY= "get_movies">#movie# #rating#</CFOUTPUT>
```

The <CFQUERY> tag allows developers to query a database. I gave the query a name of get_movies and we're using our pre-defined datasource Flash. After this, I've nested a simple SQL statement in the query string Select * from Films, where we're selecting the entire Films table. The query is completed with the </CFQUERY> tag and the output of the query to the browser is held within the <CFOUTPUT>. You can see how the start with <TAGNAME> and end with </TAGNAME> is very similar to HTML tags. This is the ASP version of the same code, which you can see is longer, and has more difficult syntax:

```
<% Set OBJdbConnection =
Server.CreateObject("ADODB.Connection")
    OBJdbConnection.Open "Flash"
SQLQuery = "Select * FROM Films"
    Set oRS = OBJdbConnection.Execute(SQLQuery)
    Do Until oRS EOF
Response.Write (oRS("movie") & " " & oRS("rating"))
oRS.MoveNext Loop
%>
```

ColdFusion Database Configurations

ColdFusion applications enjoy their open integration with databases and can talk directly to applications that are ODBC compliant. As ODBC is an *interface* between applications that support ODBC (such as ColdFusion) and databases, ColdFusion does not have to know anything about the database your application is speaking to – only ODBC has to know these details.

14 Foundation Dreamweaver UltraDev 4

Summary

The idea behind this chapter was to open your mind to some of UltraDev's potential. ASP and database driven e-commerce sites are a fantastic example of UltraDev's capabilities, but they're not the only use for the skills you've gained from this book. It's time for you to take all that you've learned and create your own applications, so let your imagination run wild, and enjoy yourself.

The range of extensions available to you at www.macromedia.com/exchange/ultradev is continually growing, and waiting to help you develop incredible interactive web sites. Our exercise using Flash only brushed the surface of the potential for applications using Flash and UltraDev to create eye-catching dynamic sites. If you're not familiar with Flash, then there's a range of tutorials available to you at places such as www.virtual-fx.net as well as a range of Flash specific books from friends of ED.

Get involved by joining the newsgroups. The various groups and sites that are available are what makes UltraDev such an exciting environment to work in – you are never short of the answer, some friends and great discussions.

For now, take what you've learned about UltraDev and build on those foundations to plan, design and implement sites that are truly dynamic and truly great.

This is just the beginning...

A Step Further   14

koolkards

A Preferences

One of the most amazing things about UltraDev is its customizable environment. However, with its wealth of options, UltraDev can be a daunting environment for the novice.

What we would like to do is take you through the Preferences section of UltraDev. There are two main reasons why we consider this to be good practice. Firstly, just about every part of UltraDev is customizable, and therefore it points you to many of its great features. Secondly, it is very tempting to leave the default settings as they are – and never return to them – which is a shame, because you'll be missing out on some handy features.

You can launch the Preferences section from either the Edit menu on any web page...

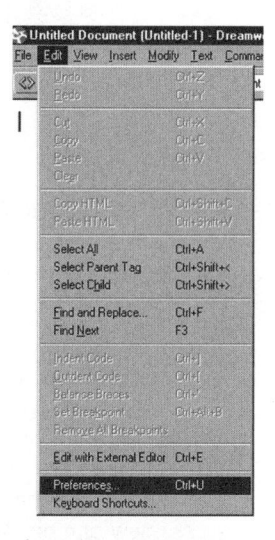

...or from the Edit menu whilst in the Site view (F8).

Foundation Dreamweaver UltraDev 4

Once launched you'll be presented with a daunting array of options. What we would like to do is take you through each of the menu screens, one at a time, to familiarize you with what is on offer. We won't suggest changing too much, as it's really down to personal preference – but we hope it gives you an insight to what you can alter.

General

The General panel deals with some fundamental options.

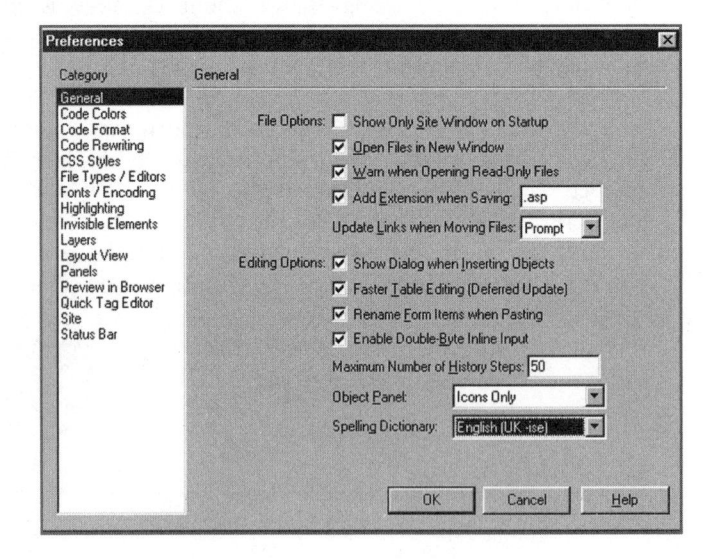

File Options

- Show Only Site Window on Startup – This stops UltraDev launching a new blank web page every time you open the application. We like this to be on, especially when the project is underway.

- Open Files in New Window – If you've ever opened one of your existing pages whilst another is open, you'll notice the previous window does not close and the new one opens in a window of its own. Some people find this messy and it can lead to having multiple copies of the same page open. The benefit, however, is the ability to drag and drop objects from one page to another and view one page as a reference whilst working on another.

- Warn when Opening Read-Only Files – Simply turns on the warning.

- Add Extension when Saving This depends on your server model and is set by UltraDev accordingly. Interestingly, however, you don't need to have an

Preferences   A

.asp extension for .asp code to work. Therefore, you may like to have all your pages as .htm files, even though they contain .asp code.

- **Update Links when Moving Files:** Can be Always/Never/Prompt. When you move a file from one folder to another, any pages that have hyperlinks to that file would need them changed accordingly. For example, if I have a link to http://localhost/chapter7/adminmenu.asp and moved the adminmenu.asp page to the chapter8 folder I would have to change the link. Fortunately, UltraDev is superb at doing this for us and will look at all links throughout the site that would be affected and changes them accordingly. You can have this so it Always does this, or Never, or as in the default Prompts. We recommend leaving it set to Prompts as there are times when you don't want to update your links. Imagine a scenario where you want to move an old page out of the website to an archive folder, but don't want the link updated, because you are going to place a new page in its place.

Editing Options

- **Show Dialog when Inserting Objects** When you drop certain objects onto your web page, like an image or a table, you'll have to set the properties there and then in a pop-up box (if this option is set on) which is pretty ideal, especially for the users. However, you can turn this off, which means you'll have to set the properties in the objects properties panel [CTRL+F3].

- **Faster Table Editing** By default this box is checked. It defers the small adjustments UltraDev makes to a table until you click outside of it. You can force it to apply adjustments to the table by pressing CTRL + SPACE. If this option isn't selected, the finer adjustments will be made on the fly, which will slow down your typing but will more accurately reflect how the finished table will look at any given time.

- **Rename Form Items when Pasting** By default, on. This option renames any form object when you copy it. This is really handy, as problems will arise if you have two form objects with the same name. However, for good coding practice, turn this off as it will force *you* to rename your objects, which will make you give them meaningful names, as opposed to UltraDev's sometimes unhelpful names!

- **Enable Double-Byte Inline Input** The chances are you won't use this one, unless you're using a development or language kit that uses double-byte text, such as Japanese. When this option is deselected, a text input window appears for entering and converting double-byte text. The text appears in the Document window once it has been accepted.

- **Maximum Number of History Steps** This is UltraPowerful! Every time you make a change to your page, what you did is logged, that is until you reach the maximum number of steps, when the oldest step is deleted. This is a really powerful feature that enables you to click undo 50 times! You can change this to an even higher number if you like, but be careful as this will take up more resources.

- Object Panel This can be Icons and Text/Icons Only/Text Only. It defines whats shown in the Object panel (CTRL+F2). It can be very useful to select Icons and Text for the beginner. Try it out!

- Spelling Dictionary This should be self explanatory. You can spell check your web pages by using SHIFT+F7, when the relevant dictionary will be used. Remember to set this if you're from the UK as the US is default.

Code Colors

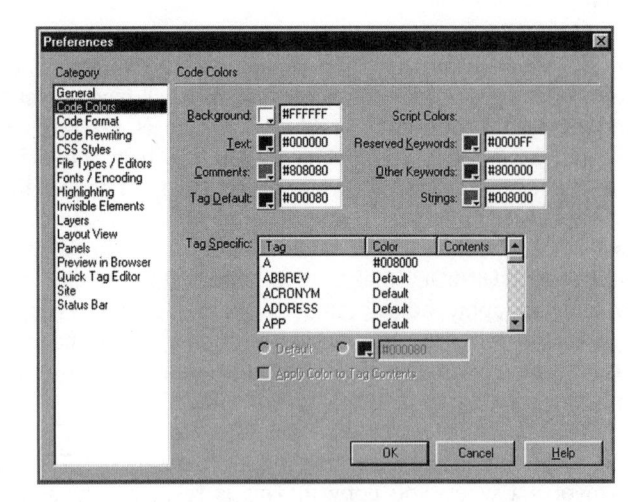

Code Colors is where you can set the colors used onscreen in the Code View. The top half of the screen is where you can use color pickers to set each of the different types of code.

In all fairness, you shouldn't have to change these, unless you have problems seeing certain colors.

The bottom half on the screen is where you can actually change the color of individual tags. We told you that UltraDev was customizable didn't we! You can play with this one in your own time!

Preferences

Code Format

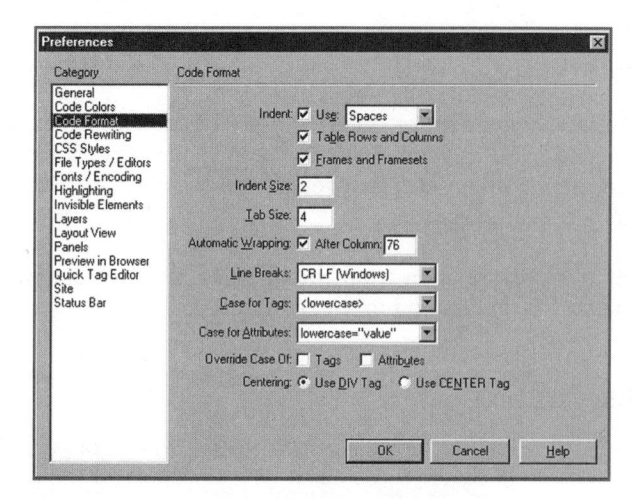

From this panel you can control the code format, such as the length of a line before it wraps, the amount of indentation and the case (uppercase/lowercase) of the tags that are included in your code.

Automatic Wrapping: is where a new line will start in the code view if you continuously type. You may wish to change this depending on your monitor setup.

The thing to note is that making changes here will only affect new HTML pages. If you want to make the changes to an existing page, pull it up and apply the Apply Source Formatting command, which can be found on any page, under the Command menu.

As with changing the code colors, this is really down to preference and as a beginner there is no real reason to change them. Expert coders may have their own style, which they wish to maintain in their UltraDev environment.

Code Rewriting

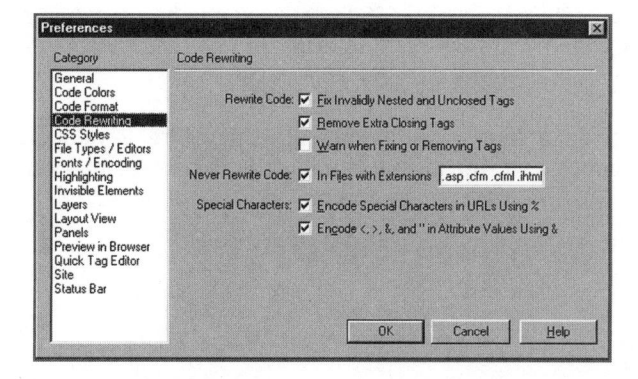

Foundation Dreamweaver UltraDev 4

As a beginner we don't suggest you concern yourself with these options.

However, very briefly, they concern themselves with what HTML rewriting UltraDev does when opening an imported document, for example, an HTML document from Word.

Normally, UltraDev would make changes to the HTML automatically. However, by setting these preferences, you can force UltraDev not to make certain changes, but instead to mark the document where changes would have been made, allowing the developers or designers to address these issues.

You can get more information from the help file, but we suggest that you leave these settings until such a time as you may need them.

CSS Styles

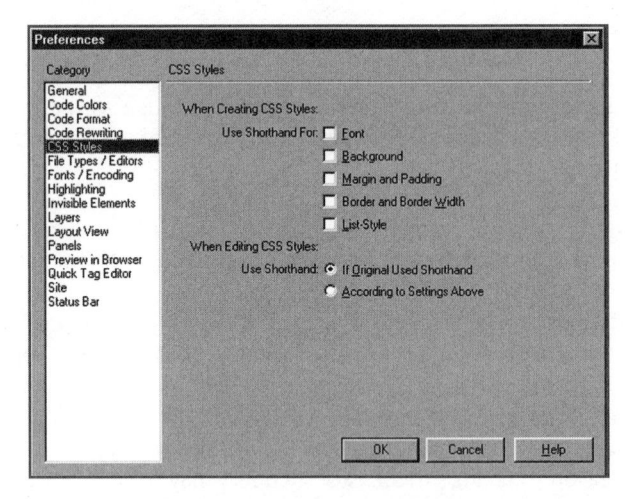

CSS Styles aren't covered in this book as they firmly belong in the Dreamweaver side of things. However, you will probably find yourself using them in your day-to-day web page design.

Here you can determine which CSS Styles parts can be written in shorthand, which some developers prefer. WARNING: not all browsers can read shorthand CSS Styles, so it's best to keep them unselected.

So why include a shorthand option? Well, if you're developing for a platform that definitely supports shorthand, and you like to read shorthand, you can!

Preferences   A

File Types / Editors

A slightly more universally useful panel. It's from here that you can tie UltraDev into other applications that you may have on your system, that you like using. For example, you may find that editing your code in the Code View isn't your preferred method. It's here that you can tell UltraDev to use a third party application.

Let's take a look at each option:

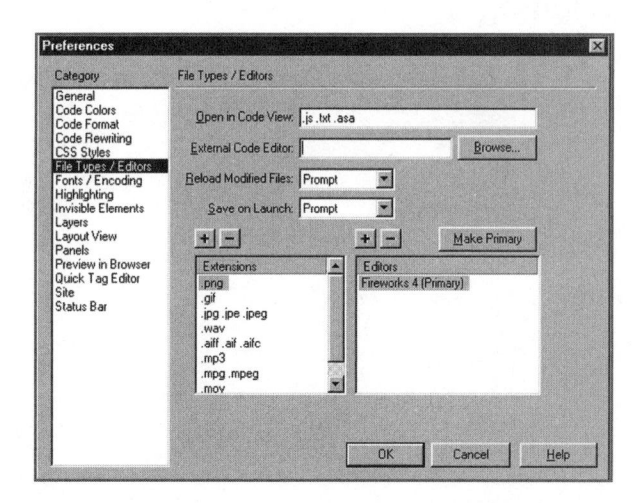

- Open in Code View: This determines the type of files that open with Code View only.

- External Code Editor: It's here that you can browse for your third party code/text editor. We like EditPlus (www.editplus.com) when there is a lot of coding to be done. Then, from any web page you can edit the code by going to the menu Edit > Edit With and the name of the application.

- Reload Modified Files: This determines what UltraDev does when it notices that you've externally modified a file with your third party application.

- Save on Launch: This determines what UltraDev does when you launch your third party application. It's a good idea to save your work before going into another application.

The bottom two windows concern themselves with other file extensions and applications. As you can see from the above screenshot, all image and multimedia types have been linked to Macromedia's Fireworks. This means should we double-click any image file from within UltraDev, the Fireworks application will launch and allow us to edit the image.

If you have another image editing application you can set it to launch here.

You can add other extensions with related text extensions. For example you may create a music site and have a `.wav` editor.

This is a powerful feature once it's been set up.

Fonts / Encoding

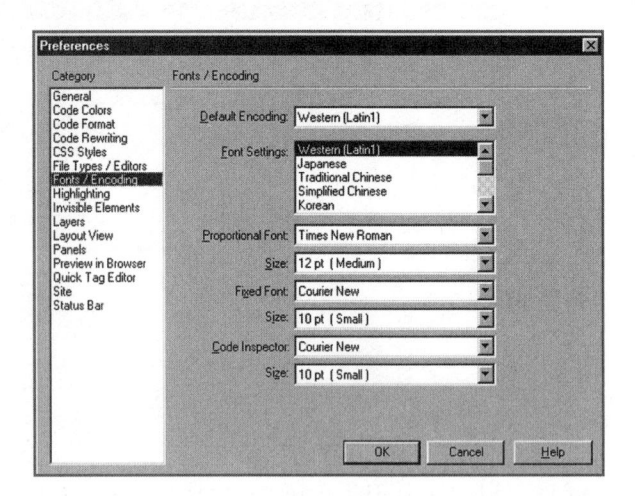

It's here that we can set many different font options for our development environment.

Let's take a look at each option

- Default Encoding: A document encoding determines how your web pages are seen in a browser. For example, setting this to Japanese would enable Japanese characters to be displayed. Normally this is left as being set to Western (Latin1).

- Font Settings: This let's you specify a font for each of the encoding settings, so you can change your default font for your Western settings here too. If you're not a big fan of Times New Roman, select the Western (Latin1) option and change the values below.

- Proportional Font: A proportional font is a font where each letter has a different width. For example, the letter *i* takes up less width than a capital *S*. Most of your day-to-day typing is done in proportional font and here is where you set your preferred choice.

- Size (of proportional font): This sets the size of the above font.

- Fixed Font: This sets the default fixed font. A fixed font is the opposite of a proportional font, where all characters have the same width. It is clearer to read than proportional fonts.

- Size (of fixed font): This sets the size of the above font.

- Code Inspector: This sets the font for your Code View. As a rule, keep this to a fixed width font.

- Size: This sets the size of the above font.

Highlighting

Here you can set many of the visual clues that get displayed on your web pages in design mode:

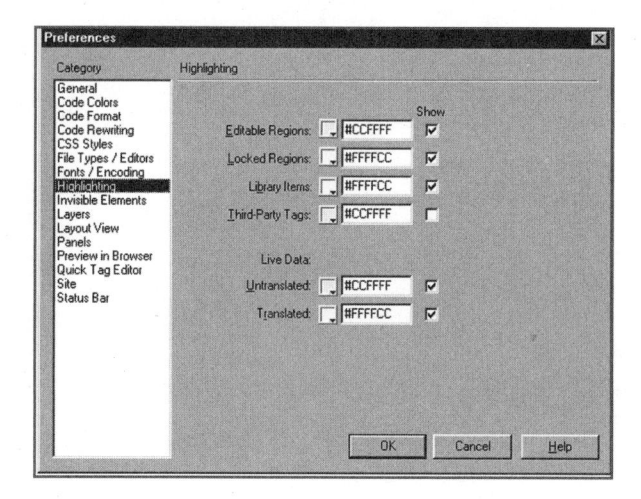

Editable Regions: and Locked Regions: concern themselves with templates. A yellow border will surround a locked region and an editable region will be blue (until you change it!).

Library Items: or Third-Party Tags: will be shown with their respective colors.

The Live Data: part has two color settings to show Untranslated: and Translated: data.

Translated data is data that has been though the server and the visual data tokens have been replaced with actual values from the data source.

Untranslated data is the opposite.

Invisible Elements

Invisible elements are the visual markers on a page in design mode that tell you there is something in the code. From this screen, you can decide which are shown and which are not.

As a beginner, leave them as they are. When you become more of an expert you may wish to turn some off.

However, as an aside, if you're creating a page with a lot of invisible elements and markers showing up which are getting in your way, simply hit CTRL+SHIFT+1 to hide/show all invisibles at once. You can then carry on designing.

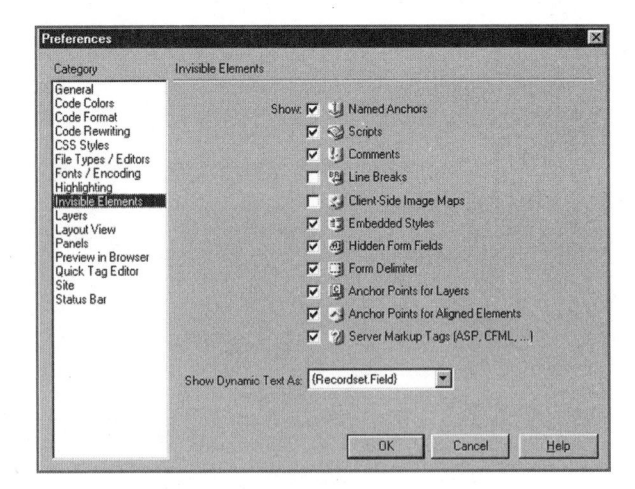

Show Dynamic Text As is an option where you can stop UltraDev from displaying the entire field. This can be very handy if you have long field names that are messing up your table widths. The downside is that you have to be confident the right field is in the right place.

Layers

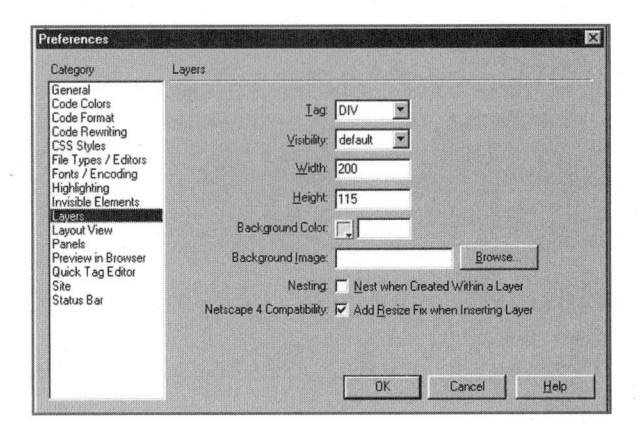

Preferences

Although we don't cover layers during the course of this book (we use tables for the sake of simplicity), layers are a very powerful design tool that you will probably end up using once you start to design more complex web pages.

This is where you can change the settings of the layer functions.

- Tag This sets the default HTML to use when creating layers. Be careful when you're playing with this unless you know what you're doing as the LAYER and ILAYER settings will only work in Netscape 4.x browsers.

- Visibility This determines whether the layer is visible or invisible by default.

- Width and Height This sets the width and height of the new layers when you use the Insert > Menu command.

- Background Color Quite clearly, this sets the background color of the new layer.

- Background Image You can set the default background image to use on all new layers. Click Browse and locate the image you want to use.

- Nesting If turned on, when you create a new layer within an existing layer, this will create a nested layer. You can change this setting as you create a new layer by holding down the ALT key as you draw the layer. You can nest layers manually with the Layers panel (F2).

- Netscape 4 Compatibility Due to a bug in Netscape 4 which causes the page to look wrong if the user resizes the browser window, Macromedia have included this handy fix. This fix will insert code (JavaScript) into the HEAD contents of a page and should the user resize their browser window the whole page will reload and reposition the layers correctly.

Layout View

Here you can set some of the properties that are concerned with designing tables when using the Layout View.

The Layout View is a great way of helping you design complex table based web pages.

Foundation Dreamweaver UltraDev 4

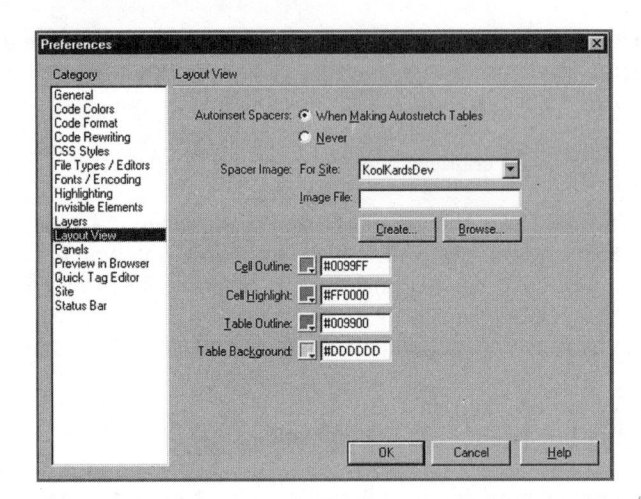

Rather than relying on a traditional row and column table builder, with the Layout View you can draw your cells on the page.

This nifty feature warrants further exploration, although it is not the easiest thing in the world to do first time.

The settings in this section determine the colors by the Layout View as well as the blank image that can be used for 'spacers'.

For more information on the Layout View and how to get the best from it go to the Designing Page Layout > Layout Overview section of the inbuilt Dreamweaver help files.

Panels

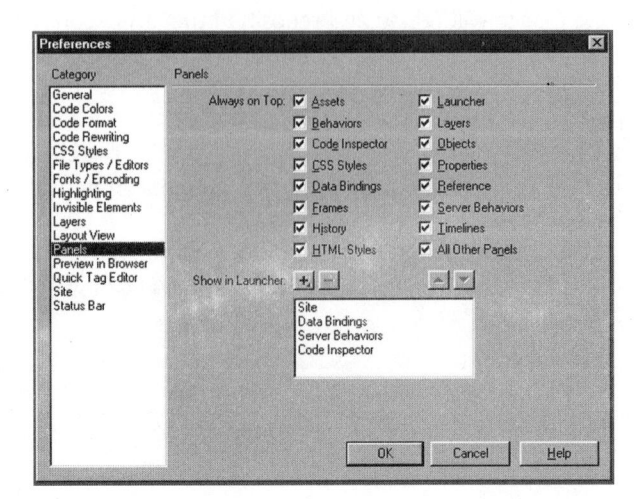

Preferences

Panels are the pop-up boxes that seem to be everywhere, like the Behaviors and the Object panels.

Here you can set which panels appear over others. Note that, by default, they're all set to 'always on top'. We suggest keeping them like this, unless you have a specific reason to change them.

The Show in Launcher option allows you to add panels to the standard launcher.

Preview in Browser

Here you can add a list of the browsers that are currently installed on your machine and they will be assigned hot keys to launch them from within your UltraDev environment.

Preview using Application Server means that you will also browse the remote files rather than your local server. Under most circumstances this will be left on.

Quick Tag Editor

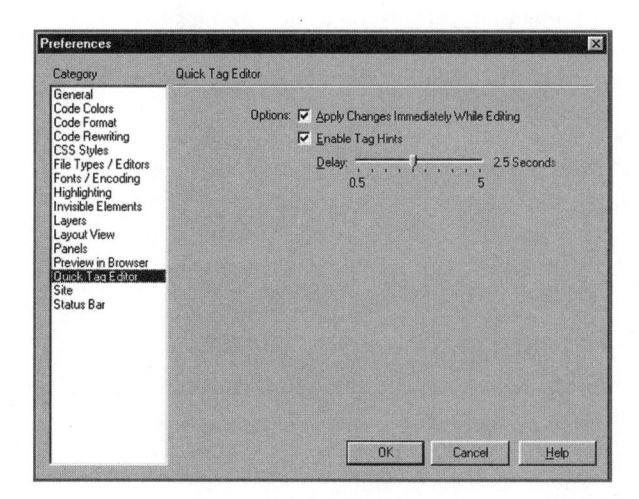

The Quick Tag Editor is a handy way to get the specific tags of an object on your page. To use it select some text, an object, or a tag, then press CTRL+T.

This Preferences section deals with the setup. Normally the defaults are fine for most people.

Foundation Dreamweaver UltraDev 4

Site

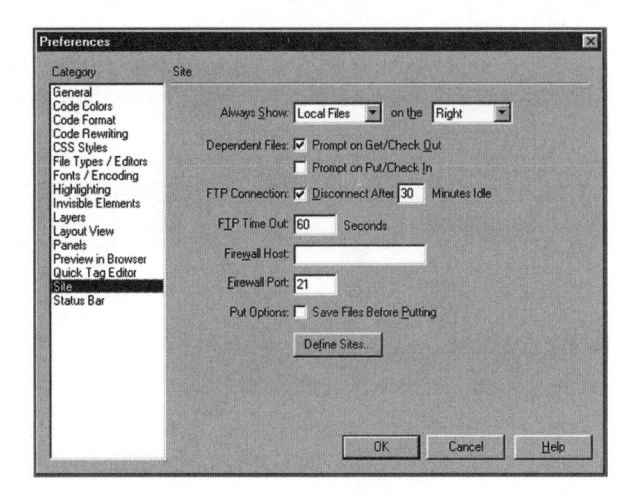

There are some useful settings in here. Let's take a look.

- Always Show Local/Remote Files on the Left/Right: You can change which side your remote and local files are shown in the Site Window panel (F8). The default is logical but some users switch depending on monitor setup, etc.

- Dependent Files: Dependent files are files that are needed by a web page, like images or .wavs. These settings determine whether or not you're going to be prompted to include the dependent file when putting your web pages to your application server.

- FTP Connection: Disconnect after x minutes idle If you're FTPing to your application server, this sets the disconnection time.

- FTP Time Out: This sets the number of seconds allowed to make a connection to the FTP host before it fails.

- Firewall Host: Specifies the address of the proxy server you may have to pass through to get to your application server – leave blank if you don't use this set up.

- Firewall Port: This specifies the port in your firewall that you use to connect to your remote server. Normally FTP is on port 21. If you've been told to use another port, make the setting change here.

- Put Options: Save files Before Putting – This will save any unsaved files before attempting to put them on to an application server. Best left on.

Preferences   A

- Define Sites... This triggers the Define Site box, exactly as you do from the menus. See Chapter 1 for an explanation of its use.

Status Bar

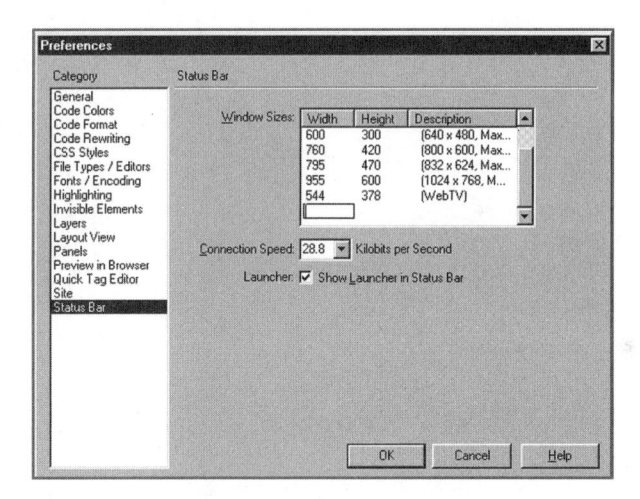

The Status Bar sits at the bottom of any document window. You can set your preferences for it here.

Window Sizes: This is a rather neat feature that lets you define any window size to test your web pages in. There are already a number of predefined, common browser sizes for you, but you may like to add your own. By using this feature you can quickly resize your document window to a number of different sizes to see the restrictions of different resolution window sizes.

Each page has an estimated download time in the status bar, which is really handy if you suspect that your page may take too long to download in real-time. You can change the default modem to something higher than 28.8, but it may be best to leave it low to create a 'worst case scenario' and you'll be pleasantly surprised when most people use a 56k modem.

Show Launcher in Status Bar: This turns the mini-launcher on and off.

kool kards

B Access Primer

If you've recently moved from Dreamweaver to UltraDev, you might not have had any experience with databases. The aim of this section is to provide you with an overview of Microsoft Access (**Access** as it shall now be known), including how to set up a new database, as well as covering tables, queries, and how all these relate to UltraDev.

Access itself is a massive product and a massive topic – there are hundreds of books available on the subject – catering for anyone from beginners to hardened coders. Here, all we need to do is give you a working knowledge, enough to whet your appetite and get you up and running, so you feel comfortable enough to use Access in your day-to-day UltraDev development.

Overview of Relational Databases

Access is what is known as a **relational database** – let's look at what we mean by a relational database.

The first databases implemented during the 1960s and '70s were usually based upon flat data files. Imagine a list of data in a text file and you're getting the idea. These methods of storing data were relatively inflexible due to their rigid structure, and relied on programs to perform even the most routine processing. Basically, it was a nightmare to get anything done quickly. These databases were cumbersome and power intensive.

However – in the late 1970s, the **relational database model** was invented. Designed by an academic research community, the relational database model suggests that pieces of data should be stored with pre-defined **relationships** between them. With the data inter-related, there is a minimum of duplication and maximum speed and efficiency.

In relational databases (such as Access), data is stored in **tables** – like a table of customers – made up of one or more **columns** (Access calls a column a **field**) – like Name, Address or Phone Number.

The data stored in each column/field must be of a single **data type** such as Character, Number or Date. A collection of values from each column of a table is called a **record** or a **row** in the table – that's to say one Customer in a table of Customers is a **row**.

The relationships come in when two tables share the same column. This column and the data in it would be present in just one table and the other tables would be linked (or related) to it.

OK, so that's a lot of new terms – the best way for you to start putting these into place in your head is to start putting them into place in a real database. So let's look at some examples.

Customer table

CustomerID	Name	Address	Town	County	Postcode
Number	Character	Character	Character	Character	Character
1001	Mr. Steel	24 Gladesmere Ct.	Townsville	Hertfordshire	WD1 24D
1002	Mr. Paddock	28 Swan Lane	Villageton	Essex	HP3 79A
1003	Mr. Scott	8 The Fairlawns	Shire	Sussex	SS22 9AD
1004	Mr. & Mrs. Steers	6 Crouchfield	Barnytown	Surrey	HG22 19A

In these tables, the top line is the **column** or **field name**, and the second is **data type** (e.g. number or character). Each row contains a single customer **record**, that is, that customer's name and all their details.

Accounts table

CustomerID	Account Number	Account Type	Date Opened	Balance
Number	Number	Character	Date	Number
1001	9987	Check	10/12/2000	4.27
1001	9980	Savings	10/12/1999	2.69
1002	8811	Savings	01/05/2000	10.00
1003	4422	Check	12/01/2001	6900.00
1003	4433	Savings	12/01/2001	9000.00
1004	3322	Savings	22/08/2000	6500.00
1004	1122	Check	13/11/2000	8400.00

The Customer table has 6 columns (CustomerID, Name, Address, Town, County and Postcode) and 4 rows (or records) of data.

The Accounts table has 5 columns (CustomerID, AccountNumber, AccountType, DateOpened and Balance) with 7 rows of data.

Access Primer

Each of the columns conforms to one of three basic data types: Character, Number or Date. In Access you'll come across other data types – like Memo or Yes/No - but most fall into one of these three categories (exceptions being things like images).

So – where are the relationships? Well, if you look at the two tables, you'll see that they share a CustomerID column. If you compare the two tables, you can see that Mr. Steel has £4.27 in his Check account and £2.69 in his Savings account. This is because writing books is not a very rewarding career choice.

What day did Mr. Scott open his Check account? To what address would we send account details? How much money do the Steers have collectively? It is questions like these – where we need to compare data from two (or more) tables – that our dynamic web applications (using UltraDev) will ask the database.

The beauty of this system is two fold – you don't have to repeat the customer detail for every piece of information about them (you just need one number) – and if, for example, the Steers decide to move house, you only have to update and maintain one record, not dozens.

Each table also must have a special column called the **Primary Key** which is used to uniquely identify rows or records in the table. In the previous tables, you see how CustomerID is the key for the Customer table while AccountNumber is the key for the Accounts table. The only stipulation with these is that they must be unique – no two may be the same.

Our Database Example

In the rest of this section, we will leave the KoolKards database and start to build a new one from scratch. You can then return to the KoolKards database later to investigate how the relationships work.

Here however, we're going to create a small database for a fictitious CD shop called **CD Xtreem** – which will store customer, purchase and CD information.

We'll start by setting up 3 tables:

- Customers – details about our customers
- Purchases – a list of customer purchases
- CDs – a list of CD titles

Let's start Access and begin from scratch...

Foundation Dreamweaver UltraDev 4

Starting MS Access

These examples will work in any version of Access – although the screen shots may look slightly different. The screens you will see are taken from Access 2000 – and there has been a noticeable shift in where the main tabs are kept from the 97 version – but it should be fairly obvious as to where you are looking.

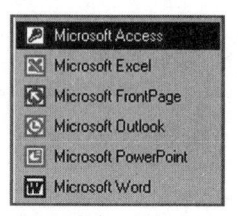

Look for the Access icon on your desktop, or use the Start Menu, and launch the application. You will first be faced with a choice:

- create a new blank database
- create a new database with a wizard or
- open an existing file (default)

Make sure you select Blank Access database and click OK.

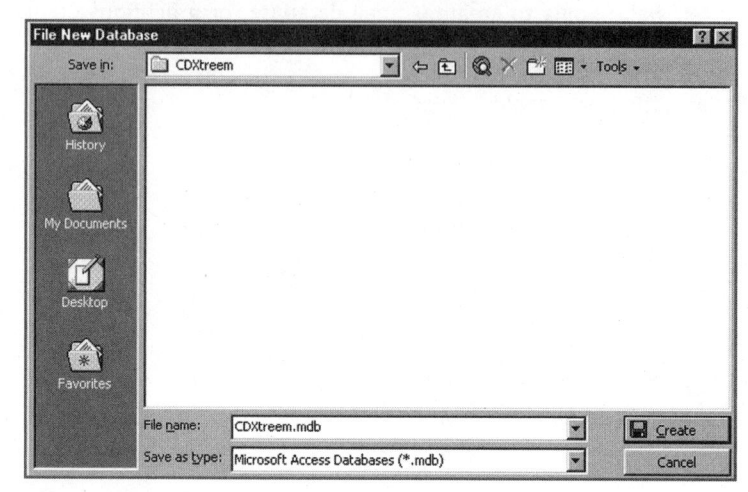

Access Primer

Choose a location for your database file to be created. Create a new folder called CDXtreem (by clicking the little folder icon with the sparkle on it). Open the folder and call your database CDXtreem too.

Click Create.

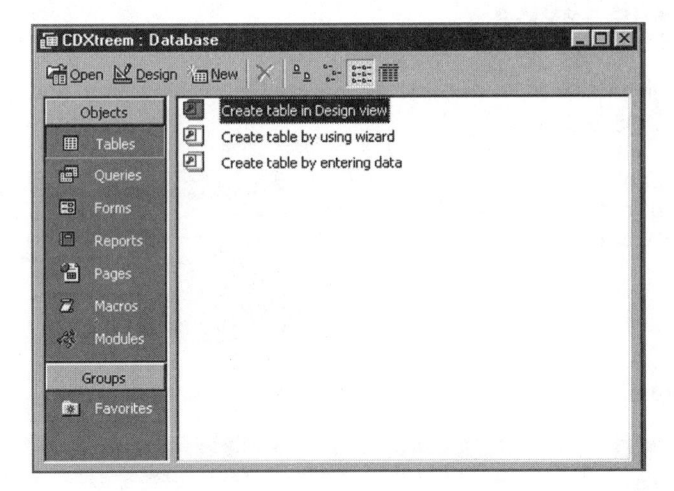

You have now created a new database. Look at the Objects panel on the left (if you are running Access 97, you will see the same options, but running in tabs, from left to right).

You have 6 main Objects:

- Tables – Displays any tables in the database. Tables are where the data is stored.

- Queries – Queries are instructions to retrieve certain pieces of data from the tables; they ask the database to "show us the records associated with Spencer Steel" or "display all the Savings accounts".

- Forms – Forms display data and provide the user interface – although enormously powerful, we won't cover this – as these pretty much do what we use UltraDev web pages for.

- Reports – Reports are normally the product of queries, which can then be outputted or printed to paper.

- Macros – Displays any macros (short programs) stored in the database.

- Modules – Displays any modules (Visual Basic for Applications procedures) we have in the database. Both Modules and Macros are Access developers' tools and beyond our needs for the moment.

As we've seen, we are not going to cover more than we need to – just the critical parts of setting up the **tables** and **relationships**. This is because after you've created your database, you'll want to go back to UltraDev and start building your web pages!

Creating the Tables

Our first table will be the customer table. We'll keep it fairly brief and simple – we don't want you typing all day!

Double-click the Create table in Design view option (you can also click New on the toolbar and choose Design View from the options).

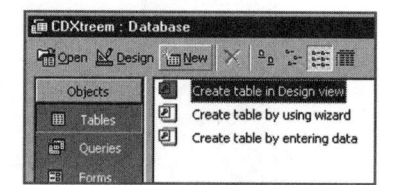

You'll be presented with a new table ready to be designed:

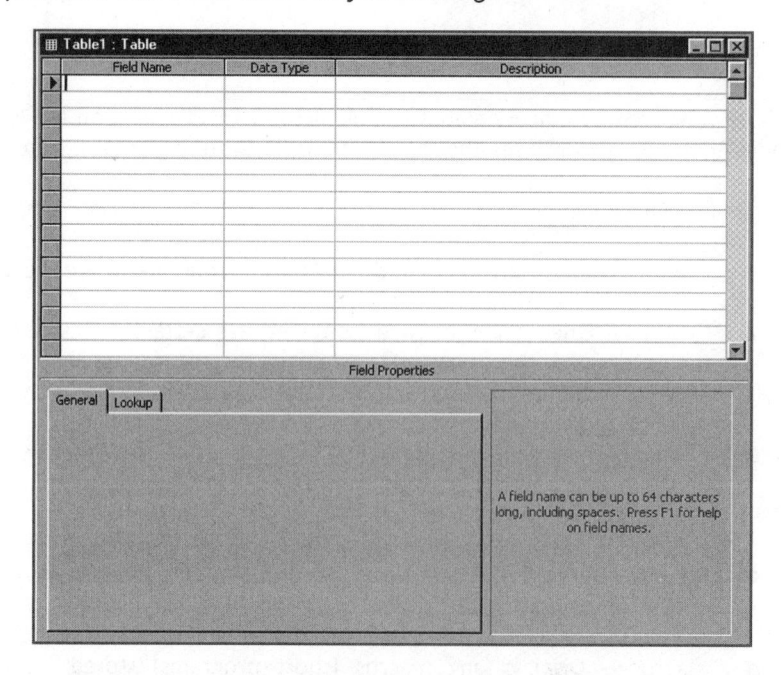

> Note: There are three main columns for each field – the Field Name, the Data Type and an optional Description. Let's fill in some fields and worry about the detail later.

Access Primer

Enter the following information:

- Field Name: CustomerID

- Data Type: AutoNumber (you can use the drop-down box to find AutoNumber or type it in). An AutoNumber is special field type that starts at 1 and increases by 1 each time a new record is entered, thus ensuring all records have a unique number

- Description: Unique identifier for a Customer

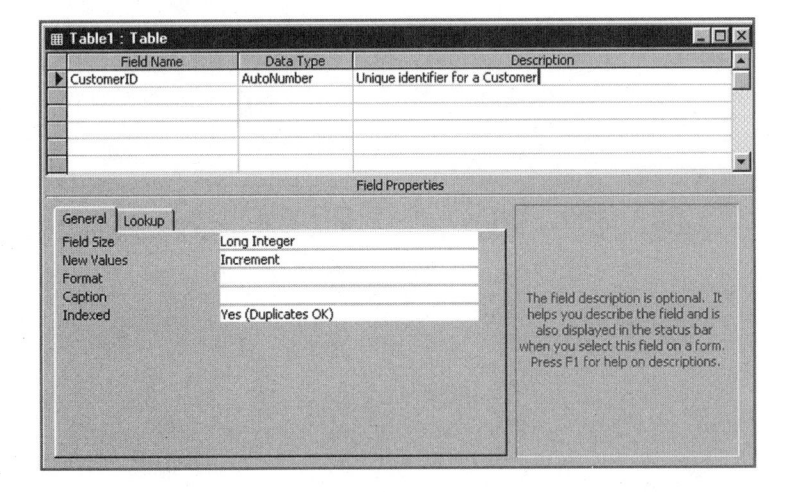

Now enter the following fields to create the rest of the table

Field Name	Data Type	Description
Name	Text	Name of Customer
Address	Text	Address of Customer
PhoneNumber	Text	Phone Number of Customer
Over18	Yes/No	Over 18 years of age? – for research purposes

As we stated before, we've kept it simple. Our real shop may like to have much more information.

> Why is PhoneNumber 'Text'? Well because Access wouldn't accept a space in the field (01923 224481), or you may want to add 'ext. 21' to the end.

Foundation Dreamweaver UltraDev 4

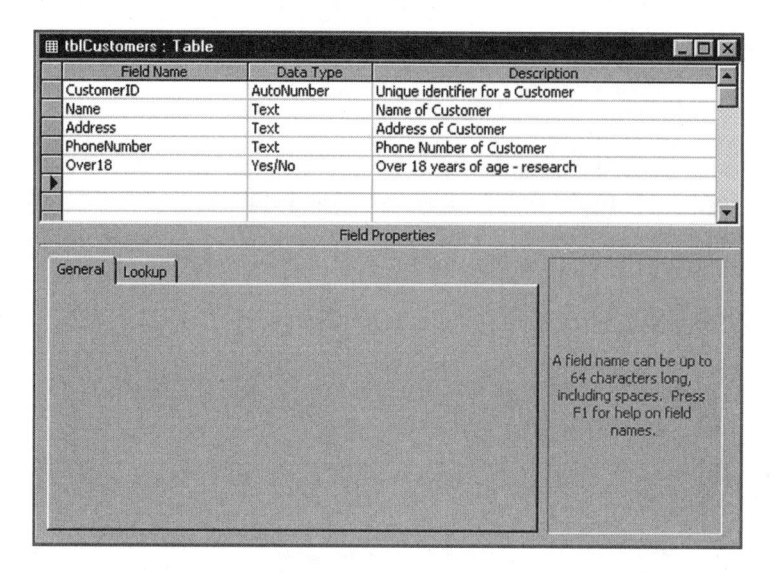

Now we have defined our first table – we need to state what the **Key** is in our table.

> *Look back a few pages to our two sample tables – Customers and Accounts. In the Customer table, there is only one record with each CustomerID – this Key is completely unique, and is known as a Primary Key. In the Accounts table, there are two accounts with the CustomerID 1001 (because a person can have more than one account) – in this table, CustomerID is a Foreign Key.*

We'll be using a **Primary Key** to link to other tables. Just as we used the CustomerID to link to the bank accounts in our earlier example, the Primary Key in our CD Customers tables will also be the CustomerID.

Right-click anywhere in the CustomerID field and select the Primary Key option:

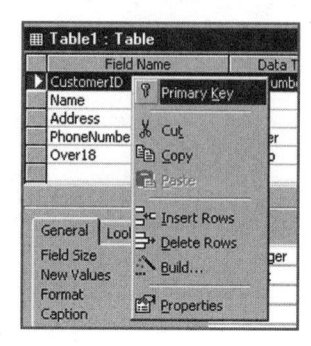

Access Primer

Once successful, you'll see the CustomerID field in marked with a Key icon:

Field Name	Data Type	Desc
🔑 CustomerID	AutoNumber	Unique identifier for a Customer

Now you've created your first table, save it (CTRL+S or File > Save or use the floppy disk icon on the main toolbar). You'll be asked what to save your table as. It's always a good idea to prefix your table names with **tbl**.

Call your table – tblCustomers:

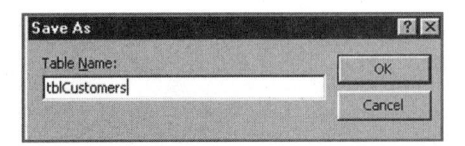

Close the table window. You'll be returned to your Objects panel – and you'll see your new table has been created:

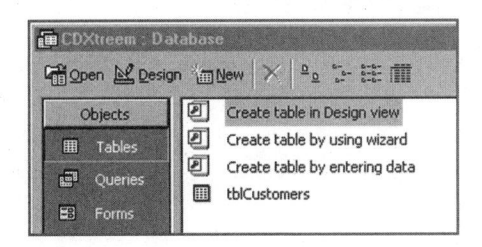

Entering Some Data into your Table

Although you will probably want to build some 'create new customer' web pages with UltraDev, let's first look at how we can quickly get some test data in our table from within Access. Once we've got a few records in, we can build the other tables and look at the relationships.

The easiest way to start entering data into our tblCustomers table is just to double-click the tblCustomers object.

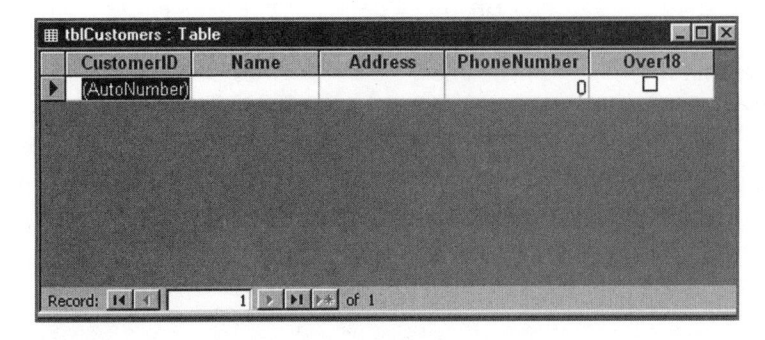

Foundation Dreamweaver UltraDev 4

This is known as the **datasheet** view and it is here you can directly enter data – a bit like a spreadsheet.

Let's put in some data. First of all note that you can't enter any numbers in the CustomerID field because we defined that as an AutoNumber and Access will take care of this itself. As a small exercise, try typing in '10' in the AutoNumber field and watch the very bottom of your screen. See the error?

To move into the Name field use the TAB key. You can use TAB to move forward through the fields and SHIFT+TAB to move back. Try it out now.

Now enter the following information. Note how as soon as you enter the Name, your AutoNumber is assigned.

- Name: Spencer Steel
- Address: 24 Gladesmere Court
- Phone Number: 0778 1233312
- Over 18: Selected. To select a check box like this press the spacebar to toggle on/off

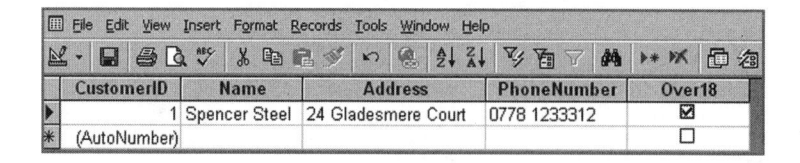

CustomerID	Name	Address	PhoneNumber	Over18
1	Spencer Steel	24 Gladesmere Court	0778 1233312	☑
(AutoNumber)				☐

If you can't see all the Addresses and want to you can stretch the column widths by dragging the column lines along.

Finish off by entering four more records – we'll use these records in some exercises later – although you may add more if you wish.

Name	Address	PhoneNumber	Over18
Spencer Steel	24 Gladesmere Court	0778 123 3312	yes
Rob Paddock	18 Swan Lane	01928 3721	yes
Robert Smith	24 The Priory	01923 2839	no
Susan Clover	142 High Street	01922 2336	no
Michelle Daniels	14 Towerflats	01944 2233	yes

Access Primer

	CustomerID	Name	Address	PhoneNumber	Over18
	1	Spencer Steel	24, Gladesmere Court	0778 1233312	☑
	2	Rob Paddock	18 Swan Lane	01928 3721	☑
	3	Robert Smith	24 The Priory	01923 2839	☐
	4	Susan Clover	142 High Street	01922 2336	☐
⌀	5	Michelle Daniel	14 Towerflats	01944 2233	☑
*	(AutoNumber)				☐

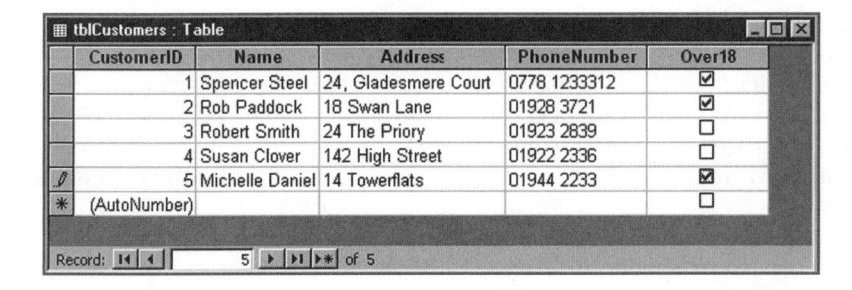

Once the data is in, save and close the datasheet view. You will then be returned to your main Access window.

Creating the Purchase and the Artists tables

We are now going to let you loose on Access – and leave you to create two more tables. We'll give you the fields we want created and some sample data we want entered.

Once both tables have been created and data has been put in we can start to look at the relationships between the tables.

Purchase Table

We want you to create a tblPurchases table so it looks like this.

> *As above we never use spaces in field names. It can cause massive problems later. Just don't do it!*

Field Name	Data Type
🔑 PurchaseID	AutoNumber
CustomerID	Number
ItemID	Number
DatePurchased	Date/Time
PaymentMethod	Text

FieldName	DataType	Comment
PurchaseID	Autonumber + Primary Key	Unique identifier for Purchase
CustomerID	Number	Customer who made purchase
ItemID	Number	Item purchased
Date Purchased	Date/Time	Date item purchased
Payment Method	Text	Payment method of purchase

Once created remember to save your table as tblPurchases.

Items Tables

Here we will create the **tblItems** table – the one which will hold the CD information.

FieldName	DataType	Comment
ItemID	Autonumber + Primary Key	Unique identifier for each item
Artist	Text	Performing Artist on CD
Title	Text	Title of CD
Category	Text	Category of CD
Cost	Currency (see below)	Cost of CD

The special field in this section is Cost. You'll need to make this a *currency* field and change the Field Properties, which you can see in the screenshot below:

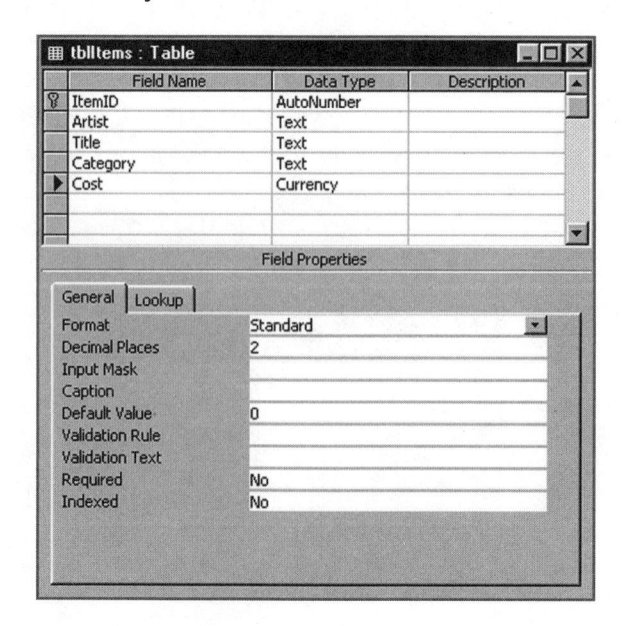

Select the Cost field and make the Format 'Standard' and the Decimal Places '2'. This will ensure the cost of 12.99 will be displayed correctly.

Once done, save and close your table and return to the main Access screen again. You should see all three tables listed.

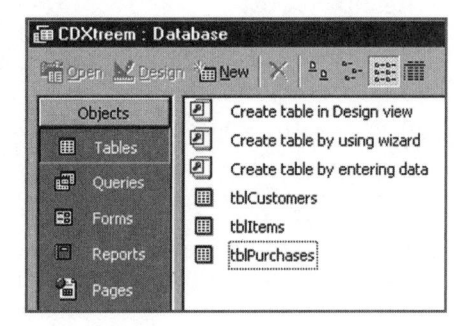

Populate the New Tables with Some Data

Now we have our three tables created, let's put some data in them. Remember, we do this by opening our table in datasheet view, double clicking the relevant table.

Put the data into the two following tables. You can add more if you like. Once done, we'll look at the relationships between the tables.

Enter this information into your tables:

Data for Purchases

PurchaseID	CustomerID	ItemID	DatePurchased	PaymentMethod
1	2	8	04/02/2001	Cash
2	2	9	04/02/2001	Cash
3	3	11	05/02/2001	Cash
4	1	2	05/02/2001	CC
5	1	5	05/02/2001	CC
6	4	10	06/02/2001	Cash
7	3	7	07/02/2001	Cash
8	2	10	07/02/2001	CC

Data for Items

ItemID	Artist	Title	Category	Cost
1	Perfect Circle	Mer de Noms	Rock	12.99
2	Nine Inch Nails	The Fragile	Rock	13.99
3	KLF	Chill Out	Ambient	12.99
4	The Smiths	The Queen is Dead	Indie/Alt	8.99
5	Korn	Issues	Rock	11.99
6	Korn	Follow the Leader	Rock	11.99
7	Prodigy	Fat of the Land	Dance	10.99
8	Britney Spears	Baby One More Time	Pop	10.99
9	Ricky Martin	Sound Loaded	Pop	10.99
10	Dido	No Angel	Pop	0.00
11	Limp Bizkit	Chocolate Starfish	Rock	0.00

Creating a Query

Now we have data in all three tables. Now let's look at the relationships between the three tables and how we can see who is buying what.

The best way to see how everything works is by creating a simple query.

From your main Access window click the Queries tab.

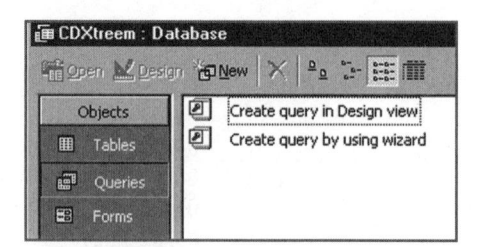

As you can see it looks very similar to the Tables tab.

Double-click the Create query in Design view option.

Access Primer

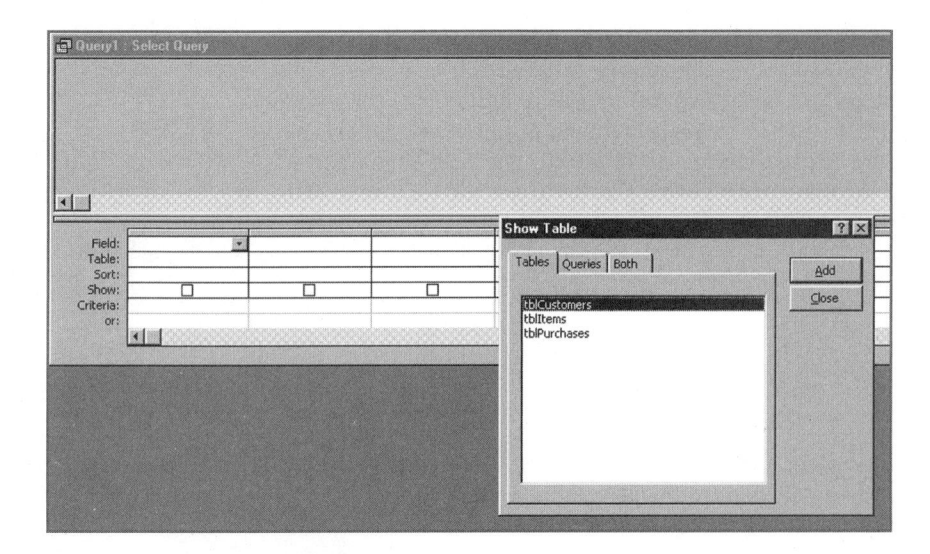

Here we are being asked what table we want in our query. We want them all, so make sure the tblCustomers table is highlighted and click Add, then repeat this for the other two tables.

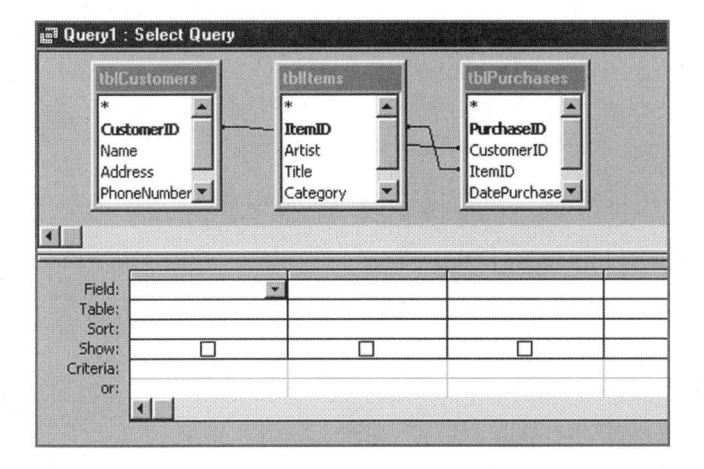

Now all three tables are available for our query. Note how there are lines between the three tables. This is graphically representing the **relationships** between the three tables. Access assumes there is a relationship because the field names from the different tables match exactly. These lines connect our **Keys**.

Using a drag and drop technique take the field Name from the tblCustomers table and drag it into the first empty field slot on the lower pane. If you've done it right, the Name field will appear in the lower pane as in the next screenshot (you can use the drop-down box in the lower pane to select the field manually but be careful to get the right field from the right table if using this method).

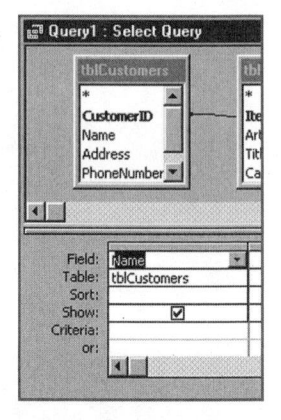

Now repeat the process, but this time move the Artist field from the tblItems table down *next* to the field you've already selected.

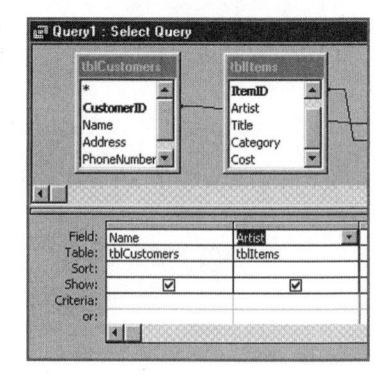

Continue to build the query now, moving down the following fields.

TABLE	FIELD
TblItems	Title
TblItems	Cost
TblPurchase	DatePurchased
TblPurchases	Payment Method

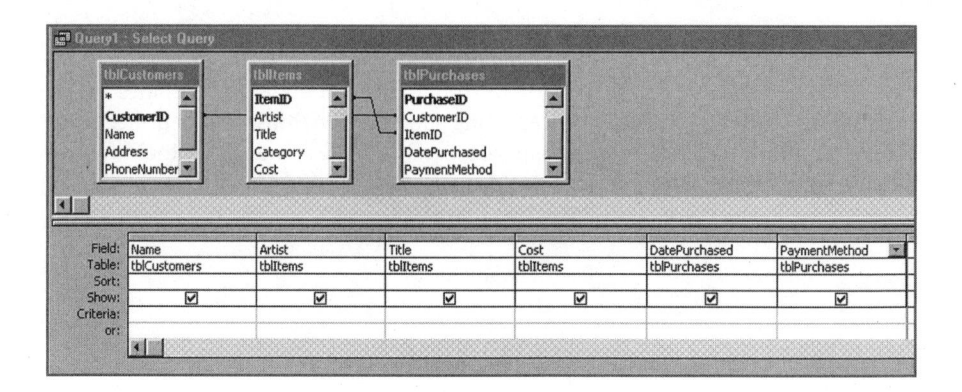

Now click Save and call your query **qrySales**. Don't close it yet though because we want to see it in action!

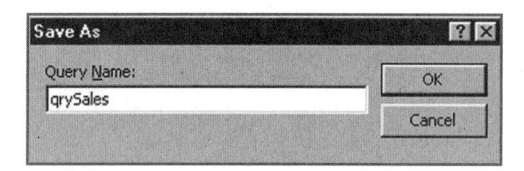

Running your Query

To run a query click the red exclamation mark in the toolbar.

Click it now to see your results.

Name	Artist	Title	Cost	DatePurchase	PaymentMethod
Rob Paddock	Britney Spears	Baby One More Time	10.99	04/02/2001	Cash
Rob Paddock	Ricky Martin	Sound Loaded	10.99	04/02/2001	Cash
Robert Smith	Limp Bizkit	Chocolate Starfish	12.99	05/02/2001	Cash
Spencer Steel	Nine Inch Nails	The Fragile	13.99	05/02/2001	CC
Spencer Steel	Korn	Issues	11.99	05/02/2001	CC
Susan Clover	Dido	No Angel	13.99	06/02/2001	Cash
Robert Smith	Prodigy	Fat of the Land	10.99	07/02/2001	Cash
Rob Paddock	Dido	No Angel	13.99	07/02/2001	CC

As you can see, we've combined information from multiple tables to give us our results. From here we can easily see who's buying what.

Sorting

Another handy tip: click a column, like Name and click one of the two sort icons

Now you can easily group the customers together. Try both sorting icons on different fields.

Structured Query Language

You may be thinking that all of this is a bit far from our UltraDev site.

Well, no, because beginners who stumble into dynamic data-driven web sites generally fail to realise how much of an appreciation of databases they need.

The more experience you get with tables, and especially queries, the better your site building will be.

As you will see throughout this book we use **queries** and **SQL** within the UltraDev environment to get data out of our tables.

And here comes one of most time saving devices that you will gain from learning a little about creating Access queries.

SQL

Make sure your query is open. From the top left icon chose SQL View:

And voila, the SQL code needed to perform that complex query.

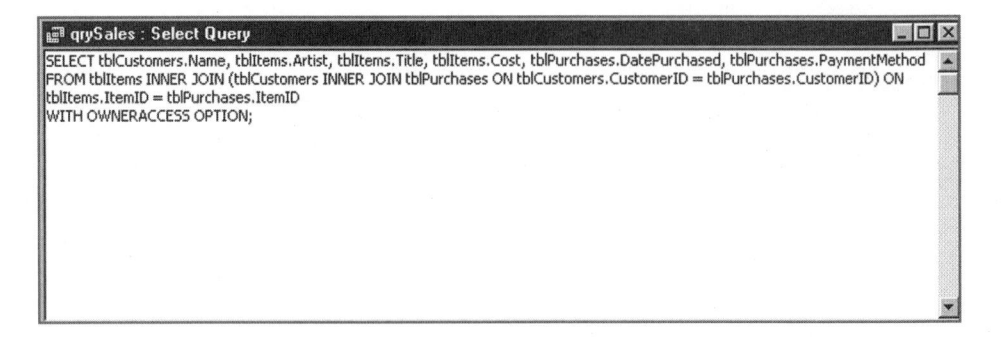

```
SELECT tblCustomers.Name, tblItems.Artist, tblItems.Title, tblItems.Cost, tblPurchases.DatePurchased, tblPurchases.PaymentMethod
FROM tblItems INNER JOIN (tblCustomers INNER JOIN tblPurchases ON tblCustomers.CustomerID = tblPurchases.CustomerID) ON
tblItems.ItemID = tblPurchases.ItemID
WITH OWNERACCESS OPTION;
```

Now you can highlight the code, right-click, copy all the code (except the WITH OWNERACCESS OPTION; which is specific to Access) and then paste it into your UltraDev Query Builder window and it'll work!

This is a fantastic benefit of graphically building SQL statements. We cover SQL in more detail in Chapter 6, but here is a great way of creating SQL statements without worrying too much about all the **syntax**.

Another Query

Great. Now close your query and we'll quickly build one more.

Imagine we want to send a mailshot about a new CD called "The Very Best of Nu-Metal Volume 48".

Let's see if we can get a list of people who buy rock music.

From your main Access window click the Query tab then choose the Create query in Design view option.

Now, we'll need all three tables again, so select them like you did before and then let's add the customer's name and address, the items purchased and their categories.

See if you can match the screenshot below.

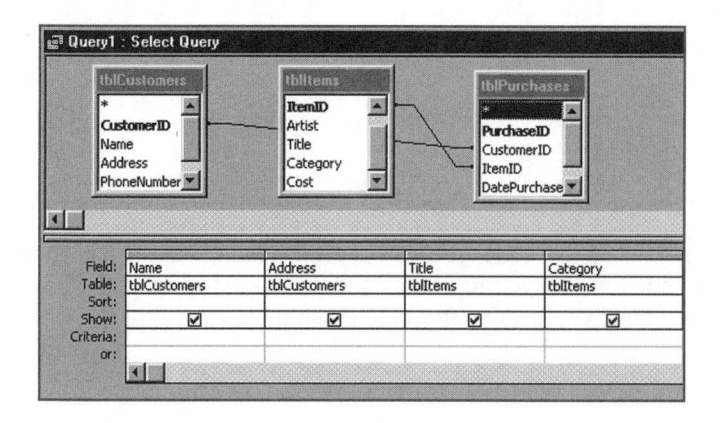

Now before we run this query, we'll need to specify that we are only interested in rock purchases.

In the Category column in the lower panel look for the Criteria row and add the word... Rock

... and press RETURN. Note how the query changes Rock to "Rock" as it 'knows' this is a string and changes it accordingly.

Now, using the red exclamation mark 'run' option, run your query:

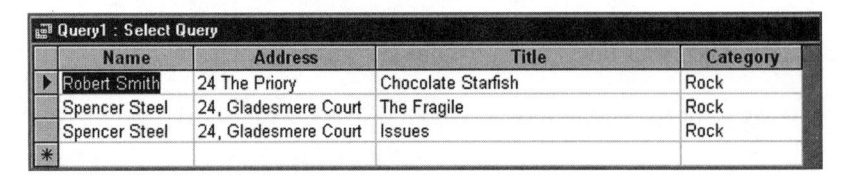

Name	Address	Title	Category
Robert Smith	24 The Priory	Chocolate Starfish	Rock
Spencer Steel	24, Gladesmere Court	The Fragile	Rock
Spencer Steel	24, Gladesmere Court	Issues	Rock

Now we can see only the customers who bought rock albums.

Now go to the SQL View.

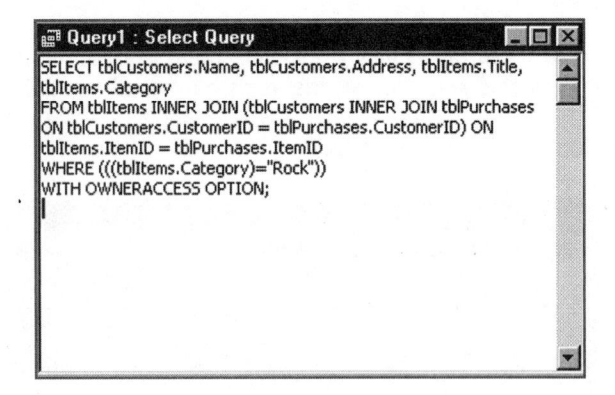

```
SELECT tblCustomers.Name, tblCustomers.Address, tblItems.Title,
tblItems.Category
FROM tblItems INNER JOIN (tblCustomers INNER JOIN tblPurchases
ON tblCustomers.CustomerID = tblPurchases.CustomerID) ON
tblItems.ItemID = tblPurchases.ItemID
WHERE (((tblItems.Category)="Rock"))
WITH OWNERACCESS OPTION;
```

Towards the end of the code, you can see the WHERE clause that adds "Rock" to the criteria. We don't expect you to understand it all – but imagine the power of being able to graphically build you queries and then move them into UltraDev recordsets!

OK, that's enough for now. Close down your query (save it if you like) and exit Access.

Conclusion

That is all we can cover on Access here and we've only just scratched the surface.

However, you have learned some great fundamentals, like creating tables, understanding relationships and creating your first query, gathering data from multiple tables.

When you build your own sites, you'll see how useful it can be to be able to 'get inside' your database. It can make life a lot easier.

The ability to create queries from within Access and copy out the code is an excellent skill you should get used to using. It's especially good for testing. Imagine, getting the exact results you want from within the Access query environment, then simply copying the code, pasting it back into a recordset in UltraDev and your page should return the same correct results first time!

If you're a complete novice to Access, we do recommend spending as much time using the software as possible as it will help you on your web development path much more than you might think.

Only then will you really see the power of the combined programs...

kool kards

C OLE DB Connections

Before we get into creating a connection using OLE DB let me give you a bit of history as to how OLE DB came about.

When databases began it was very difficult to learn all the different ways of connecting to them as everybody had their own database formats, and developers had to code at a very low level for each database they wished to develop for. No drag and drop in those days!

To solve this along came ODBC, which was an early attempt at getting every developer to conform to a set standard.

Unfortunately ODBC still had many shortcomings and it effectively became a hindrance to newer applications being developed.

In response to these shortcomings, Microsoft introduced OLE DB, a COM-based (Component Object Model) data access object that provides access to all types of data.

OLE DB sits between the ODBC layer and the application. With your ASP pages, ADO is the 'application' that sits above OLE DB. Your ADO calls are first sent to OLE DB, which are then sent to the ODBC layer. You can connect directly to the OLE DB layer, though, and if you do so, you'll see an increase in performance in all your database interactions if you use OLEDB. The diagram below should make it easier to understand this concept.

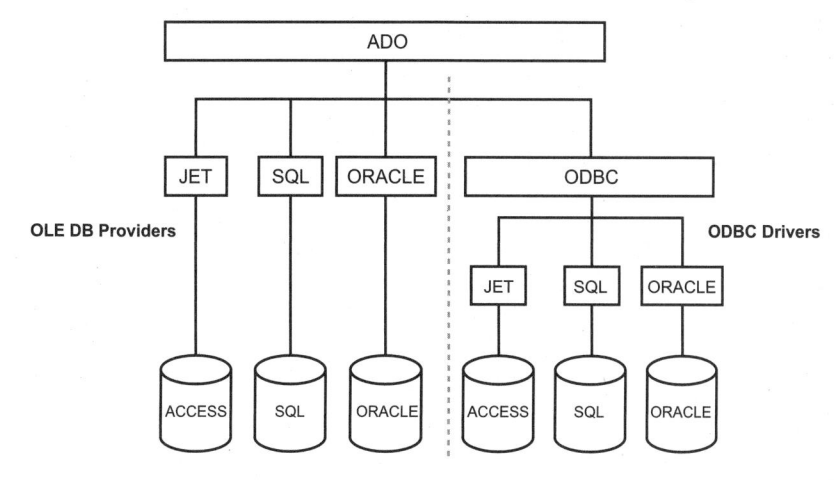

History lesson over – let's learn how to make connections in this way.

Connecting to Access via OLE DB

Firstly we'll show you an easy way to create the connection string you'll use. We are going to create a small file called a Data Link (.UDL – using data link) file – which will automatically create the connection string for you.

1. Open Windows Explorer;

2. Select a folder where you would like to store your UDL file. Probably the best place for at the moment is in your KoolKards directory under the Connections folder;

3. Once you've pointed Windows Explorer to your location, (C:\Inetpub\wwwroot\KoolKards\Connections\), right-click in the right pane, point to New and then click Text Document. This will create us a new .txt file, in which we will create our connection string.

4. Still with Windows Explorer, click the Tools menu, click Folder Options. On the View tab, clear the Hide file extensions for known file types check box, and then click OK. This makes sure we can change the extension of any files – which we will need to do in a moment.

5. Right-click the text file you created in step 3, and then click Rename. Type the name you want to give your file, using the .udl file name extension (for example, mydata.udl). Press ENTER.

6. A warning may appear, explaining that changing file name extensions may cause files to become unusable. On this occasion, we know what we're doing so you can disregard this warning. Click Yes. You may wish to re-hide your file extensions afterwards – personally we always keep them so they are editable!

7. Double-click the .udl file and rather than launching Notepad or Word as you might expect, Windows will open the Data Link Properties dialog box.

OLE DB Connections

On the dialog box that appears, select the Provider tab.

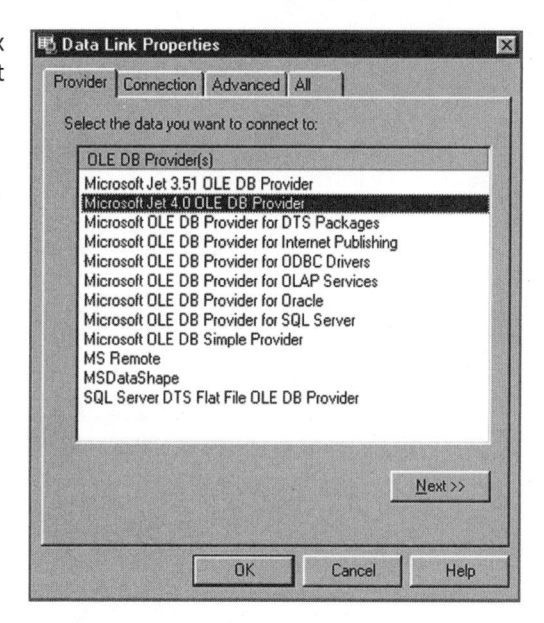

8. As we are using Access select Microsoft Jet 4.0 OLE DB Provider (Access uses Microsoft's 'Jet' engine to work with the data in the database.) - then click Next (if we were developing for MS SQL then you should notice that a Provider is available Microsoft OLE DB Provider for SQL Server).

You should now see the Connection tab.

9. First we need to select the database we are using. Browse your database; you do not need to enter a user name for your database unless you set one. Now click on Test Connection and you should receive the message...

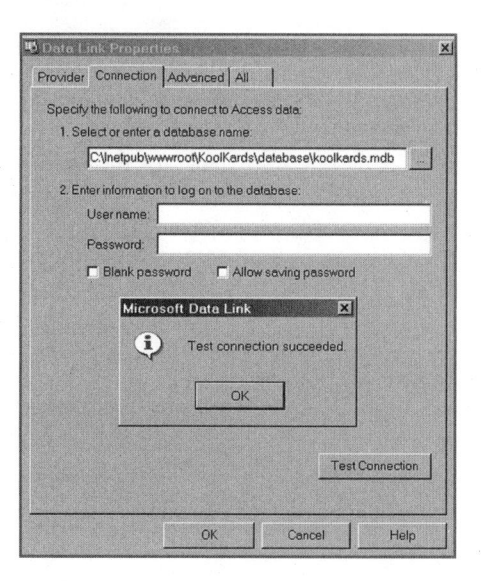

Well done, you have successfully created an OLE DB connection. Now let's look at our connection within UltraDev.

10. Go back to the page `display_customer_records.asp` from Chapter 1 and double click on the recordset under the Data Bindings dialog box.

11. Click Define next to the Connection drop-down box.

12. Make a new connection by clicking on New and selecting Custom Connection String:

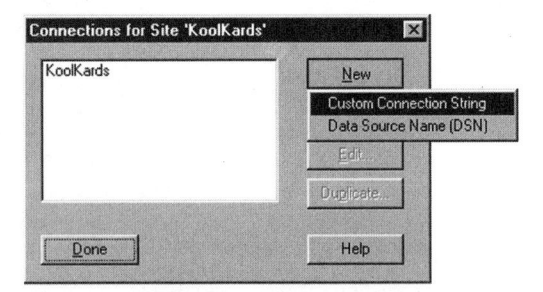

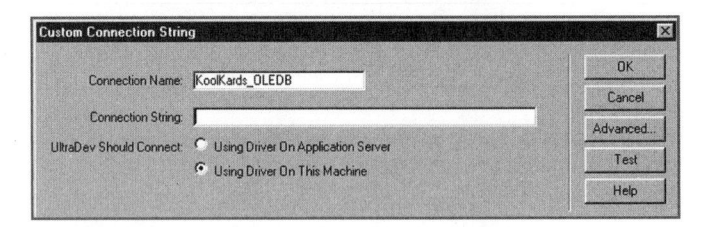

13. Enter a Connection Name – KoolKards_OLEDB.

    Now for the Connection String. This is the `mydata.udl` file we created earlier, it would be nice if we could just point at this file but UltraDev doesn't give us this option so we need to open the file in Notepad or some other text editor.

14. Hopefully you stored it under the KoolKards folder in Connections; open the file in Notepad and you should see something like this:

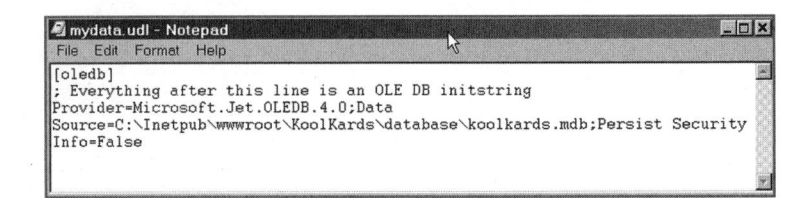

```
[oledb]
; Everything after this line is an OLE DB initstring
Provider=Microsoft.Jet.OLEDB.4.0;Data Source=C:\Inetpub\wwwroot\KoolKards\database\koolkards.mdb;Persist Security Info=False
```

OLE DB Connections

The part we are interested in is this:

```
Provider=Microsoft.Jet.OLEDB.4.0;Data
Source=C:\Inetpub\wwwroot\KoolKards\database\
➥ koolkards.mdb;Persist Security Info=False
```

15. If you copy and paste this into the Connection String (you may need to use the CTRL-V keyboard shortcut to paste) text box and click Test you should see the welcome sight of...

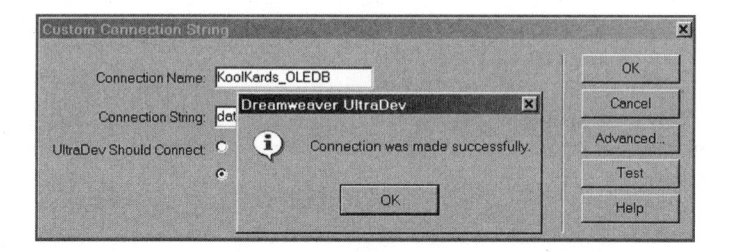

If you have time, take a look at the KoolKards_OLEDB.asp connection page (automatically placed by Windows in the Connections folder). It will now have set the "MM_Koolkards__OLEDB_STRING" to the connection string we just cut and pasted in.

For the purposes of this book we have used the ODBC connection, for the sake of simplicity. However, the OLE DB connection is generally a more efficient way of connecting to a database. Only when an OLE DB provider for the data source you are using is not available should you use ODBC.

There is one more type of connection that I feel is worth mentioning and that is a DSN-*less* connection...

Creating a DSN-less Connection for Microsoft Access

Occasions may arise when you do not have access to set up ODBC or OLE DB connections. If this is the case then a DSN-less connection is the answer.

To set this up you need to create a custom connection string again but this time the string will look like this:

```
"Driver={Microsoft Access Driver
(*.mdb)};DBQ=c:\inetpub\wwwroot\KoolKards\databases\koolkard
➥ .mdb"
```

The `Driver` parameter tells the server which driver to use, which in this case is Access, and the `DBQ` tells the server the path to the database file.

I have seen many questions on the newsgroups of people failing to get this to work. Here are a few of the more common problems:

- Incorrect spelling of the Driver Name
- Database location incorrect
- The connection string must be on one line, both parts are within one set of quotes, separated by a semicolon.

It may be worth looking into DNS-less connections more – but only if the need arises. We imagine 99.9% of you will have access to your data at this time, so you can continue as you are.

OLE DB Connections

kool kards

D Resources

We thought this a good place to share with you some of our favorite places to find information on the Web.

Foundation UltraDev Links

www.friendsofed.com
www.foundationultradev.com

Authors Home Pages

www.webbiz-solutions.net
www.ultraculture.com

Official Links

www.macromedia.com/software/ultradev/
www.macromedia.com/exchange/ultradev/

Top UltraDev Resources

Most of these are run part time by people who just love building stuff with UltraDev.

www.udzone.com
Great new, professional resource – tutorials, downloads and more.

www.magicbeat.com
A must. Offers a really great mailing list. A long established and well recognized resource.

www.powerclimb.com (home of the shopping cart)
Rick Crawford's home page. Basic tutorials and updates here.

www.yaromat.com
More Dreamweaver biased. Nicely designed site with powerful behaviors to download.

www.ultradevextensions.com
As the name suggests, a great resource of extensions.

www.massimocorner.com
Popular site run by excellent extension writer. Get UltraDev, Dreamweaver and Fireworks stuff here.

www.hiran.desilva.com/ultradev/
Great tutorials, including Logins, E-mails and Security.

www.charon.co.uk/Ultradev.htm
Tutorials, extensions and downloads from respected UltraDev developer.

www.basic-ultradev.com
Very professional site. Lots to learn and download.

www.projectseven.com
Some of the best behaviors for Dreamweaver we've ever seen. A must if site design is your thing.

www.dreamweaverfever.com
Great beginners site. Lots of handy tutorials to get you on your way.

www.howtoultradev.com
Cool discussion forum. Got a question? Post it here!

Other Sites

Here are some superb, professional resources on the Web.

www.webmonkey.com
Concerns itself with all things web related. A massive resource and one of the most respected sites going.

www.4guysfromrolla.com
 Superb site. Tons of ASP material. One for the coders of all levels.

www.asptoday.com
A professional technical ASP site brought to you by Wrox Press

www.img2.com
Massive site that concerns itself with a broad range of applications and development technique. Live streamed radio shows! A techie's paradise.

Resources

kool kards

Index

A

Access 416
  options 417
Access database 102, 356, 436
  connecting to via OLE DB 436
  converting to SQL Server 356
  DSN-less connection 439
  Jet engine 437
  koolkards.mdb 102
  making full use of 102
access levels 214
  see also controlling access
  deny the Administrators access to the 'normal' menu 222
  moving the Administrator (level 1) onto their own menu page 222
  push people with different access levels to different pages 222
  SELECT statement 214
ActiveConnection property 374
Add Items pages 258
  Add Item to Cart button 258
  how this cart works 261
  making the Add to Cart Link 259
  testing 262
Add to Cart code
  altering code to return whole recordset 262
  written in JavaScript 261
Add to Cart Via Form option 260
  if you're only displaying one detail of an item 260
  never a good idea to put more than one form element on a page at 260
Add to Cart via Link 260
  identify where the information is coming from 261
  Quantity is a literal value 261
  using the Add to Cart feature with multiple results 260
Admin template 105
  once selected the page is created with overall design in place. 105
administration pages 144
  'hidden' screens can be entered 144
  Administrator can view, add, update or delete 144
  link using AdminMenuscreen 144
AdminMenu screen 144
  series of links 144
Application Server models supported by Ultradev 41
  ASP Servers 41
  ColdFusion Servers 42
  JSP Servers 42
ASP 390
  compared to JSP 390
ASP code
  comment 46
  connection string stored on separate ASP page 45
  display the details of each user in the database 47
  Inside the Code 44
  opening and closing tags 45
  telling the server that we to use VBScript 45
ASP Servers 41
  code pages in VBScript or JavaScript 41
  PWS 41
  run Windows NT or 2000 Servers and IIS 41

B

Behaviors 47

447

Index

Behaviors (continued)
    can be packaged into extensions 49
    example 47
    perform a certain function on your web page 47
    pre-written 47
Birthday cards, find 38
    results pages are effectively the same basic page 38
    server dynamically changes HTML code to show results 38
browser detection 96
    Drag and drop the request variable onto your page 97
    page can tell what browser is running 97
    Request.ServerVariables 96

C

Cart Code 244
    getColumnValue 245
    written in JavaScript 244
Cart e-mail 306
    e-mail the order to the retailer 307
    setting up 306
Cart Page 266
    contents of our cart to the orders table 284
    linking to New Browser Window 266
    linking to our Customer Details page 282
    summary and final payment page 285
CD Xtreem example 415
    CDs table 415
    create a new blank database 416
    Create table in Design view 418
    creating simple query 426
    Customers table 415
    get list of people who buy rock music 431
    lines connect our Keys 427
    Purchases table 415
    put data in new tables 425
    relationships between the three table 427
    select the field for queries 428
    tables wanted in query 427
CDO Form Mailer behavior 300
CDO mail 294
    add code 296
    added functionality but decrease in efficiency 295
    confirmation to the customer 302
    mailing the shopping cart to the retailer 302
    send people reminders 295
    Send property 297
    sending an E-mail using 296
    Simple CDO Message. 297
    test the page out 297
    uses SMTP 295
    will only run on NT Server 295
    won't talk to Unix 295
CDONTS.NewMail 296
    list of properties to apply to mail, 296
Check Box Delete function 264
    apply the Delete Item from Cart behavior 264
    create a basic check box 264
Check Box Remove Code 265
check_if_registered.asp 58
    same directory as your login.asp 62
Christmas cards, search 37
    result pages are effectively the same basic page 38
client-side scripts 39
    JavaScript is the only language supported on the client-side by all browsers 40
    people can easily see your code 40
client/server development 74
client/server techniques 34
    understanding 34
Code Colors panel, Preferences Section 400
Code Format panel, Preferences section 401
Code Rewriting panel, Preferences Section 402
Code View 27, 204, 298
    duplicate usernames 205
    see the code and your graphics on the page 27
    Show Code and Design Views icon 27
    simple CDO code 298
    user authentication 214
    user login 214
Cold Fusion
    CFML 392
    compared to ASP 393
    database configuration 393
    Tags 392
ColdFusion's Mark up Language. See CFML
Collaboration Data Objects. See CDO
columns/fields 413
    Access calls a column a field 413

Index

data must be single data type 414
Command Object 372
  ActiveConnection property 374
  CommandText property 374
  CommandType property 375
  CreateParameter method 374
  creating 373
  Execute method 375
CommandText property 374
CommandType property 374
computing history 34
  Mainframe 34
  networking 35
  smart terminals 35
connection string 46
  found in the Connections folde 46
connection, setting up 21
  between application and the database 21
  Create New Data Source window 23
  Define Connection 22
  first and most important step in creating a dynamic page 26
  select the special Access driver 24
  tell our DSN connection the database location 24
  Test DSN 25
  type in connection name 25
Contact Form 299
  build 299
  get the results in e-mail format 299
  Method set to POST 299
controlling access 222
  Define the level 223
  groups of access 223
  option of what method to use 222
  what levels are allowed in 223
cookies 69
  ASP can create, read and modify on server side 69
  check if there is any cookie on your system 71
  created, read and modified using client-side JavaScript code 69
copying a page 146
  create a file called copy of product_details.asp 146
CreateObject method 374
CreateParameter method 375

arguments 375
CreateTextFile method 330
CSS Styles panel, Preferences section 402
Customer table (CD Xtreem) 418
  Data Type 419
  Description 419
  Field Name 419
  Primary Key to link to other tables 420
Customers Details Order Page 276
  add session variable 281
  form is based on the customers table 277
  Get UniqueID From Table behavior 277
  link from the cart page 281

D

Data Bindings box 78
  Request.Variable box 78
Data Bindings panel 237, 258
  copy and paste cart onto each page 237
  Format drop-down box 238
  see the fields in shopping cart 237
  UltraDev Shopping Cart behavior 258
Data Bindings window 86
  add the name of the session variable 95drag out of the Data Bindings panel into your page 95
  Request.Form 86
  Request.Querystring 89
  Request.Server variables 96
  session is now 'drag and droppable' 95
data driven pages 15
  creating 15
Data Source Name. See DSN
database interactions 435
  DSN-less connection 439
  using OLE DB 435
database searching 164
  creating a SQL statement 165
  creating parameterized queries 169
  dynamic list box, creating 178
  normalisation of database 176
  results page, creating 172, 184
  search page, creating 170
  searching for all on numerical field 191
  SQL 165
  wildcards 169
database security 20
databases 273

Index

databases (continued)
  After Inserting, Go To page 284
  deleting records 385
  JSP configuration 391 insert customer's record 283
  Use the Session value as the CustomerID 283
delete pages 145, 156
  apply Delete Record behavior 157
  change the Submit button label to Delete Record 156
  create 156
  how it works 158
  remove the Update Record behavior 156
  set properties 157
delete_products.asp 156
Destroy statement 303
  disable 303
  turn into reminder or a comment. 304
Detail Pages 128
  create 128
  creating shortcuts to 138
  filtering of records 130
  product_details.asp 128
  view, insert, update and delete pages 128
dictionary cookies 71, 241
  capable of holding several values 71
Dreamweaver's Behaviors 40
Drumbeat 28
  incorporated it into UltraDev 4 as Live Objects 28
DSN 23
  set up 23
DSN-less connection 439
duplicate usernames 204
  creating a user-friendly message 209
  display an error message 209
  send it back to the registration page 204
  server behavior solution 204
dynamic image, create 132
  display all the fields in your recordset 133
  image_path 133
  insert image 133
  link our results page to our details pag 134
  Live Data Preview button 134
  select Data Sources 133
dynamic link, redefining 146
dynamic list box, creating 178
dynamic page 28
  create 28
  Insert Record button 30
  test it in your browser 30
Dynamic Web Application scenario 36
  cannot see the server code from your browser 39
  HTML page could be different each time 37
  server looks up an ASP file 37
dynamic WHERE statement 192

E

e-mailing from within web application 292
  add body of the mail 294
  add the cc (carbon copy), bcc (blind carbon copy) 294
  bulk ordering 292
  mailto feature 292
  receipt for the customer 295
Empty Cart Behavior 250
  code 252
Enterprise Manager 360
  creating stored procedures 360
Execute method 374
extensibility 49
Extension Manager 49, 345
  importing an extension from the Internet 49
  use downloaded extensions 49
Extensions 49
  access your new extension 50
  behaviors can be packaged into 49

F

File Types/Editors panel, Preferences section 403
FileSystemObject object 330
  CreateTextFile method 330
  OpenTextFile method 337
filtering of records 130
  ID number same as that passed from results page 130
  testing 130
  value of the ID passed to SQL statement 131
Fireworks 14
  edit graphics 14
Flash 384
  database, interacting with 385
  using with UltraDev 384

Index

Fonts/Encoding panel, Preferences section 404
Form Mailer 300
   code 301
   creating 300
   email contents of form 300
Form Object Panel 57, 219
   check_if_registered.asp 58
   Insert Button option 59
   Insert Form button 58
   Insert Text Field button 58
   Properties Inspector 58
   Show Code and Design Views button 57
   Submit Form option is checked 59
form uploader 312
   send the file to the server from browser 312
   your computer sends information to the web server 312
FormatCurrency function 240
   standard VBScript function 240
Forms 417
forward-only cursor 118
Foundation UltraDev menu 69
   Write a Cookie option 69

G

General panel, Preferences Section 398
   Editing Options 399
   File Options 398
GET example 88
   data in the URL is obviously not secure 90
   display the information on the page 89
   Drag and drop your QueryString objects onto your page 89
   information displayed on read_form.asp 90
Get UniqueID Behavior 277
GetID code 278
getting started 15
   requirements 15
get_orderID table 276
Go To Detail Live Object 139
Go to Detail Page window 136
   enter the name of your detail page 136
   pass existing parameters 138

H

Hidden Field 75
   invisible Text Field 75

Highlighting panel, Preferences section 405
homemade cookies 68
   written on the client's computer 68
HTML code 37
   code relating to the search 38
   View Source 37
HTML forms 56
   Create 57

I

If Log In Fails 216
   trap failed logins 216
IIS 15
   security 198
   select Using DSN on the Application Server 25
   Windows NT Server ships with 15
image files 317
   uploading 317
Inner Join 186
Insert New Card page 316
Insert Record behavior 283
Insert Record Insertion Form 29
   After Inserting, Go To 29
   Connection 29
   Insert Into Table 29
Insert Record Update Form Wizard 154
   connection setting 154
   deleting records 155
   enter the page to go to after the update has been performed 155
   Insert Record Update 154
   specify recordset to apply the update to 155
   specify the form objects to include on update pages 155
Internet topology 36
Internet Information Server. See IIS
Invisible Elements panel, Preferences section 406
Items table (CD Xtreem) 424
   create 424

J

Java Server Pages. See JSP
Jet engine 437
JSP 390
JSP

Index

JSP (continued)
  coding 390
  compared to ASP 390
  database configuration 391

K

Key 72
  cookie name 72
KoolKards example 14, 199, 292, 312
  ASP 2.0 using Visual Basic Script 20
  connect web site to our database 21
  directory structure 17
  download the web files necessary 16
  generate automatic e-mails 292
  logins table 199
  send file to server to stay 312
  set up your local site 17
  site definition 18
  uploading a New KoolKard 316
  URL Prefix 20
koolkards.mdb 103
  admin template 105
  collect product data and display in web page 104
  creating a new page from a template 104
  master template 105
  New From Template option 104
  not normalized 104
  products table 103
  schema (structure) of our database 103

L

Layers panel, Preferences section 407
Layout View panel, Preferences section 407
linking results to detail pages 135
  Code 138
  launch the Recordset box 135
  parameter called ID used to filter out all but correct details page 137
  select ID and add it to the columns already in the recordset 135
  test the result in your browser 137
Live Data View 113
  can visually resize column widths 114
  site definition must be set with appropriate values 114
Live Objects 28

insert Record Insertion Form 29
  place a record insertion form on our page 28
Live Objects panel 141
  Insert Master-Detail Set 141
LockPessimistic option 279
Log In User panel 211
  Get Level From: access_level 213
  If Log In Fails, Go To 213
  if Log In succeeds, Go To 213
  options 212
  Restrict Access 213
Log Out User 224
login cycle 198
  list of users 198
  login page 198
  secure all the pages in the Administrator's section 198
  send different types of users to different menu pages 198
login page 210
  creating a simple page from our new main Master template 210
  improvements 216
  let user know he entered wrong information 216
  Log In User panel 211
  name text boxes username and password 211
  Remember Me option 218
login screen 198
  building 198
logins table 199
  access_level 199
  Administrator has access_level of 1 199
  data schema 199
  registering with site 200

M

Macromedia Exchange 69
  cookie behaviours 69
Macros 417
mailing the Cart 303
  destroy the cart session 307
  explanation of code 305
  grand total from our cart 305
  Place cart into a string behavior 304
  SaveToDatabase function 303

Index

mailto: system 294
   advantages and disadvantages 294
Master Detail wizard, setting up 140
   Insert Master–Detail Set from Live Objects panel: 141
   MasterTest.asp 140
   select fields to display in results page 141
   select the details page 143
   select the ID field for the Link To Detail Page 142
   Select the ID for Pass Unique Key 142
   test and view your records 143
   wizard can't handle our dynamic image – just a path name 143
Modules 417
moving data between pages 84
   can only use POST method once 88
   information isn't stored anywhere 88
   passing formless data between pages with GET 90
   POST 84
MXI File Creator 339
   Extension Manager 345
   packing and adding menu item 345
   packing up server behaviors 340
   using 340
MyDetails cookie example 69
   create MyDetails cookie 71
   code view 70
   Date of Expiry field 70
   domain property 70
   Write a Cookie box 70

N

navigation bars 121
   build your own 121
News updates 382
Newsletter 308
   add a form called newsletter 310
   code 311
   create an Admin page from where we can send out e-mails 309
   flag any users who request not to receive any e-mails 309
   Method is set to POST 310
   send to all people in database 309
Newsletter behavior 310, 327
   options 311

Newsletter code 311
   While Loop 311
normalisation of database 176
   look-up tables 177
   one-to-many relationship 177
   one-to-one relationship 177
   relationships 177

O

objects 62, 84
   brief look at 62
   collection of pre-defined variables 84
   properties 63
Objects toolbar 56
   form elements located on 56
ODBC 21, 435
   compared to OLE DB connection 439
   shortcomings 435
   simplicity and user friendliness 21
   standard for communicating with different types of databases 21
ODBC Administrator 23
   System DSN tab 23
off-the-shelf shopping carts 229
   advantages 229
OLE DB 21, 435
   benefits of compared to ODBC 21
   compared to ODBC connection 439
   connecting directly to the OLE DB layer 435
   connecting to Access database 436
   flexible and efficient database architecture 21
one-to-many relationship 275
   orders and the orderdetails tables 275
OpenTextFile method 337
Orders table 285
   Insert Record behavior 287
   populate 286
   Save Cart to Table behavior 287
   writing the contents of the Cart to 285

P

Panels panel, Preferences section 409
parameters 367
   checking values 377
   output from stored procedures 371
   passing to stored procedure 368

Index

passing formless data (GET method) 90
  add two parameters called name and telephone 92
  could use it to provide a unique introduction to a page 93
  not best method for moving telephone numbers and names around 93
  page read_form.asp 91
  Property inspector 91
  run it from your browser 92
  till a powerful way of passing information around pages 93
payment options 234
  benefits of real time credit card transaction provider 234
  using service provider 234
Personal Web Server. See PWS
pop-up reminder picture 265
  add the hyperlink tags 267
  create new browser window 266
  linking the Cart Page to 266
  Open Browser Window behavior 268
  properties 268
  set up the Product ID parameter 268
  test your page 269
POST example 85
  add a submit button 85
  confirm to user information entered 86
  create_form.asp. 86
  insert two text boxes into your form 85
  make sure that the whole form is selected 85
  Response.Write statements 87
  Select POST from the drop-down list 85
  test pages in browser 88
posting 84
  GET 84
  POST 84
Preferences section 397
  Code Colors panel 400
  Code Format panel 401
  Code Rewriting panel 402
  CSS Styles panel 402
  File Types/Editors panel 403
  Fonts/Encoding panel 404
  General panel 398
  Highlighting panel 405
  Invisible Elements panel 406
  launching 397
  Layers panel 407
  Layout View panel 407
  Panels panel 409
  Preview in Browser panel 409
  Quick Tag Editor panel 409
  Site panel 410
  Status Bar panel 411
Preview in Browser panel, Preferences section 409
products table 103
  creating recordset 106
  Design button 103
  structure and some sample data 103
product_details.asp 128
  add the all-important recordset for our page 129
  all the fields to be returned here 130
  create a dynamic image 132
  creating a new table 129
  filtering of records 130
  display the details for a specific card 128
  linking results page to detail page 135
  Use the Admin template 128
properties of objects 63
Property Inspector 86, 292
  Link box 92
  mailto 292
  set the Action to read_form.asp 86
Purchase Table (CD Xtreem) 423
  create 423
pure ASP upload 313
  drawback is the amount of code it generates 313
Pure ASP Upload behavior 313
  After Uploading Go To 318
  Allowed Extensions 317
  Conflict Handling to Overwrite 318
  Get files From 318
  modifies the standard update & insert behaviors 316
  Prefix With Full Directory 318
  upload to the images folder 317
PWS 15, 41
  check the Using Local DSN radio button 25
  think of as totally separate computer - the server 41
  Windows 98 comes with 15

Index

Q

queries 106, 165, 417
   copy and paste code into Query Builder window 430
   creating 426
   make tables available for query 427
   run a query 429
   select the fields 428
   sorting 429
   viewing SQL code needed to perform complex query 430
Quick Tag Editor panel, Preferences section 409

R

random records, generating 365
reading from cookies example 72
   create_a_ cookie.asp 72
   Data Bindings box 77
   dragging and dropping cookie data binding 78
   form is created with value of true 77
   get the server to process the additional commands 75
   Hidden Field 75
   move the user on to the final page 75
   OnClick event is client-side operation 74
   Request Variable box 78
   Request.Form object 73
   server must create the cookie 74
   Set Form Value – Cookie 73
   setting Flag to true 76
   Submitting Form to Self 75
Readline method 337
records 123
   keeping track of 123
recordset navigation 119
   controls in detail 121
   inserting a navigation bar 120
recordset row, repeating 114
   Repeat Region, (row in table we want repeated) 115
   speed 116
   SQL statement 118
   using the Tag selector 114
   VB Code written to page after Repeat Region was applied 117

recordset, creating 106
   ASP coders usually start the name with rs 108
   Connection 108
   Data Bindings tab 106
   expand the recordset 110
   Filtering 109
   lays the foundations of your dynamic web pages 107
   Recordset dialog box 107
   select columns 108
   Select table from drop-down list 108
   sort function 109
   Test button 109
recordset, creating table for 111
   do not give recordsets long names 113
   drag field to cell under appropriate heading 112
   Insert > Table option 111
   type headings into table 112
Recordsets 106, 165, 364
   displaying 111
   record counter 122
   returns subset of data 106
   use of query 106
Redirect behavior 66
   example is 'Log In' application 66
   redirects the user to another web page 66
   using 66
Redirect Behavior example 67
   check if user typed name in login.asp. 68
   check_if_registered.asp 67
   create a redirect behaviour 68
   Open login.asp 67
   preview your page in your browser with F12 68
   Request.Form("name") 68
Redirect if Empty server behavior 252
registration page 200
   adding Insert Behaviors 202
   create a form called register 200
   create a table 201
   form validation 206
   improving our Form 207
   insert behaviors 202
   method set to POST 200
   password protection 206
   register.asp 200

Index

registration page (continued)
  testing your page 206
  text fields properties 201
  use the Master template 200
relational database 413
  columns or fields 414
  pre-defined relationships 413
  Key 415
  record or a row 414
  shared ID column 415
  tables 413
relational operators 167
Remember Me option 218
  add a check box to your form 219
  add a row to login table 218
  add routine that makes our Remember Me box actually ticked 221
  cookie to expire after 90 days 219
  if the user then turns off Remember Me – the cookie is killed 220
  name form remember and set its checked value to yes 219
  replace the code for the check box with a custom IF statement 221
  sets two cookies, username and password 219
  used the dictionary properties of a cookie 220
Remote Info 19
  Access 19
  Remote Folder 19
Repeat Cart Region 244
  code written by 244
  written in VBScript 244
Repeat Region behavior 116
REPLACE function 191, 371
Reports 417
Request Object 63
  methods 63
  Form method 84
  Form elements 87
  Querystring 89, 209
  make a user-friendly message for our user 209
  ServerVariables 96
Response Object 63
  methods 64
  Write behavior 65
  code written in VBscript 65
Restrict Access to Page behavior 224
  apply behavior to template 224
results page, creating 172, 184

S

SAFileUp 321
  advanced uploading using 321
  allows file upload from any browser to IIS 321
  basic upload 321
  code that performed file uploading: 323
  needs to be installed on the server itself 321
  Read, Write, and Delete NTFS permissions 322
  server-side control written to handle file sending 321
Sales/Value Added Tax. See tax calculations
search page, creating 170
search_results.asp page 258
  copy the cart to 258
security 198
  Administration pages 198
  number of solutions 198
  provides different sections for different users 198
sending files 312
  from the browser to the server 312
Server Behaviors 48, 64, 114, 136, 326
  create your own navigation systems 122
  creating 328, 329
  Delete Record behavior 157
  examples 48
  FileSystemObject object 330
  Go to Detail Page 136
  hidden element 334
  IIS, using 328
  improving appearance 339
  Insert Record 48
  inserting code 333
  making a cookie example 69
  MXI File Creator 339
  Newsletter behavior 326
  packing and adding menu item 345
  packing up 339, 340
  reading and displaying text file 336
  reading any text file 337
  repeating the recordset row 114

Index

Server Behaviors (continued)
  simple example 64
  testing 335
  TextStream Object 330
  Update Record server behavior 150
  user-interfaces 327
Server Behaviors example 64
  code written in VBscript 65
  preview page from website 65
  select the Response.Write behaviors 64
Server Behaviors panel 48, 51, 115, 202, 236, 259
  Add cart totals to a cookie 241
  check server behavior is registered 51
  copy shopping cart 259
  Insert Record 202
  navigation options 121
  open 48
  Repeat Region behavior 116
  UltraDev Shopping Cart 236
  User Authentication 211
Server Choices 42
  Client Script: Javascript 43
  recap 42
  Server Model: NT/2000 running IIS 43
  Server Script: VBScrip 43
server models 326, 390
  ASP 390
  Cold Fusion 392
  JSP 390
  server behaviors 326
Server object 374
  CreateObject method 374
server-side scripts 39
servers 15
session variable, 93
  create 93
  hold a value for the whole of a session 93
  last for twenty minutes after the user leaves the page by default 96
  store all sorts of information 93
  synonymous with cookies 96
  track the browsing habits of users 93
  used badly and unnecessarily, they can degrade the performance of your web site 96
  won't work unless the client's browser has cookies enabled 93

session variables example 94
  add the following code at the very top of your page 94
  greeting your user by name on several different pages 94
  open create_form.asp 95
  Open the Data Binding window 94
  put our session variable on our read_form.asp 94
shopping cart 228
  add, remove or update item 228
  commercial solutions 228
  job sites 228
  payment options 233
  software or MP3 download sites 228
  temporary way of storing rows of data 228
Shopping Cart applications 382
  alternatives 382
shopping cart example 235, 258, 308
  add an extra column - Occasion 237
  add cart totals to any page we want 242
  add some new tables 273
  add to cart page 246
  Add to Cart via Link 260
  adding items to the cart 258
  adding tax calculations 270
  apply the FormatCurrency technique to the cookie 242
  applying the Redirect Behavior 253
  build the main cart page 235
  creating a Check Box Delete Function 264
  creating a Pop-up Reminder Picture 265
  customers table 273
  Data Bindings panel 238
  define your shopping cart columns 236
  Delete Item from Cart behavior 264
  formatting currency 239
  get_orderID table 273
  inserting the customer into the database 283
  Item and Price totals on each page, downside 240
  make data look presentable 238
  make the Quantity an updateable text box 246
  making Add to Cart link 259
  newsletters 308
  order details table 273
  orders table 273

Index

shopping cart example (continued)
  place a Form element around the shopping cart table 247
  placing the cart columns 242
  relationship between tables 274
  Repeat Cart Region 243
  search_results.asp 258
  select a page to go to now the cart has been emptied 251
  sum[Total] field - drag it to our page 238
  Update Cart page 246
  write total number of items and the Grand Total to a cookie 241
  writing the shopping cart to a database 272
Simple Mail Transfer Protocol. See SMTP
Site panel, Preferences section 410
SQL 165, 352
  AND 167
  BETWEEN 168
  creating a SQL Statement 165
  creating parameterized queries 169
  dynamic WHERE 192
  FROM 166
  IF EXISTS 372
  IN 168
  Inner Join 186
  LIKE 169
  NOT 168
  NOT LIKE 169
  OR 168
  queries 165
  relational operators 167
  SELECT 166
  stored procedures 352
  Transact-SQL 361
  WHERE 167, 188
  wildcards 169
SQL Server 352
  Enterprise Manager 360
  stored procedures 352
  varchar datatype 368
SQL Server database 354
  creating 355
  importing Access database 356
SQL statements. See SQL
static (non-dynamic) HTML pages 36
  how a web server handles a request from your browser to view 36

Status Bar panel, Prerences section 411
stored procedures 352
  checking parameter values 377
  Command Object 372
  creating using Enterprise Manager 360
  examples 365
  further functionality 378
  output parameters 371
  parameters, using with 367
  passing parameters to 368
  permissions 362
  random records, generating 365
  reasons for using 353
  recordsets 364
  syntax 361
  using 354
Structured Query Language. See SQL

T

Tables 417
  create 418
  datasheet view 422
  enter data into 421
  prefix your table names with tbl 421
  state what the Key is 420
tags, CFML 392
tax calculations 270
  add the changes to the HTML 271
  hand code our tax addition on our page 270
Templates 60 105, 183
  changing the template 105
  defining editable region 183
  editable area 183
  maintaining consistency throughout site 105
  Select the master template 61
  use to apply standard KoolKards look 60
  uneditable area 183
test your page 62
TextStream Object 330
  ReadLine method 337
  WriteLine method 330
Transact-SQL 361
tutorial sites 18

U

UltraCart 279
  written with UltraDev 1 279

Index

UltraDev 17, 46, 69, 384, 397
  behaviors 47
  database, interacting with 385
  Define Sites option 17
  extensibility 49
  no Server Behaviour to create cookies 69
  Preferences section 397
  reusable, inbuilt code routines 47
  saves connection string in separate ASP pageof coding 46
  server models 390
  setting up a site 17
  using with Flash 384
UltraDev Downloads file 50
  create 50
UltraDev extensions 383
  Web Learning applications 383
  WML 383
UltraDev interface 12
  Application Server screen 20
  become familiar with UltraDev's keyboard shortcut 13
  Code View 14
  Data Binding window 22
  do not open too many pop up windows at once 12
  edited graphics already updated in site 14
  Local Info 18
  make panel with most used functions on 13
  need clear view of the Objects, Properties and Server Behaviors panels 13
  Remote Info 19
  Setting up a DSN 14
  Site menu 17
  switching from web-building to graphic-editing 14
  ties in with Macromedia's other products, 14
UltraDev security 198
  See also security
  secure the Admin Menu and all subsequent pages 198
  Server Behaviors 198
UltraDev Shopping Cart 230, 259
  ability to empty the cart 245
  ability to redirect from this page 245
  ability to update and delete items from 245
  Add To Cart Via Link behavior 259
  automatically creates a Total field 237
  can use the cart without any knowledge of JavaScript 230
  Cart Name text box 236
  Redirect If Empty behavior 253
  Repeat Cart Region 243
  sum[Total] column 238
  Update Cart behavior 248
  written entirely for the UltraDev environment 230
  written in 90% JavaScript 230
  [numItems] column 238
UltraDev Shopping Carts preview 231
  add items to the cart option 231
  checkout, 233
  information about the total cost 232
  user confirms the order and arranges payment 233
  user is shown the cart's current contents 232
  user searches for items 231
update and delete multifunction page 158
  add an extra button for the delete 158
  switch to Code View and add dode 159
Update Cart page 246
  add a Form Submit button to the page 248
  add the ability to change the quantities of each item 247
  code 250
  creating the Form 247
  form element is text box 249
  make quantity display field into text box 248
  redirect 249
update pages 147
  add a Submit button to the form 149
  add our edit boxes 147
  add Update server behavior 149
  Administrator can edit the data and send it back to the server 145
  boundary of HTML form 147
  change the Unique Key Column to ID 150
  cut and paste our table 147
  Form Elements 151
  Get Values From 151
  give your form a name 147
  rename your text boxes 147
  setting recordset field value148
  Update Record dialog box 150
Update Record behavior 152
  how it works 152

Index

  two hidden fields 152
update_wizard.asp 153
upload code 315
URL parameter - valid 216
  extract and use to trap failed logins 216
URL parameters 131
  pass details around through 131
user rights levels 202
  Level 1 – Administrator 202
  Level 2 – Power Users 202
  Level 3 – Customer Users 202
user-interfaces, server behaviors 327

V

Validate Form behavior 207
  make sure the form is highlighted 207
varchar datatype 368
variables 84
VBScript 191, 371
  REPLACE function 191, 371
View Live Data 20
  see web page within design environment 20

W

WAP 383
web applications 382
  News updates 382
  Shopping Cart applications 382
  Web Diary 382
Web Diary 382
Web Learning applications 383
wildcard character 169
Wireless Application Protocol see WAP
Wireless Mark-up Language see WML
WML 383
WriteLine method 330
Writing Web Pages for Client/Server Models 39
  Client-side Scripting 39
  Server-side Scripting 41

Index

koolkards

friendsof ED

DESIGNER TO DESIGNER™

friends of ED writes books for you. Any suggestions, or ideas about how you want information given in your ideal book will be studied by our team.

Your comments are valued by friends of ED.

Freephone in USA 800 873 9769
Fax 312 893 8001

UK contact: Tel. (0121) 258 8858
Fax. (0121) 258 8868

feedback@friendsofed.com

Foundation Dreamweaver UltraDev 4 - Registration Card

Name _____
Address _____
_____
_____
City _____ State/Region _____
Country _____ Postcode/Zip _____
E-mail _____
Occupation _____

How did you hear about this book?
☐ Book review (publication) _____
☐ Advertisement (name) _____
☐ Recommendation _____
☐ Catalog _____
☐ Other _____

Where did you buy this book?
☐ Bookstore (name) _____
☐ Computer Store (name) _____
☐ Mail Order _____
☐ Other _____

What influenced you in the purchase of this book?
☐ Cover Design   ☐ Content
☐ Other (please specify) _____

How did you rate the overall content of this book?
☐ Excellent   ☐ Good
☐ Average   ☐ Poor

What did you find useful about this book?
_____

What did you find least useful about this book?
_____

Please add any additional comments
_____

What other design areas will you buy a book on soon?
_____

What is the best design related book you have used this year?
_____

Note: This information will only be used to keep you updated about new friends of ED titles and will not be used for any other purposes or passed to any third party.

friendsof ED

DESIGNER TO DESIGNER™

NB. If you post the bounce back card below in the UK, please send it to:

friends of ED Ltd.,
30 Lincoln Road,
Olton,
Birmingham.
B27 6PA

BUSINESS REPLY MAIL
FIRST CLASS   PERMIT #64   CHICAGO, IL

POSTAGE WILL BE PAID BY ADDRESSEE

friends of ED,
29 S. La Salle St.
Suite 520
Chicago Il 60603-USA

NO POSTAGE
NECESSARY
IF MAILED
IN THE
UNITED STATES